AMERICAN ANTHRAX

AMERICAN ANTHRAX

FEAR, CRIME, AND THE INVESTIGATION
OF THE NATION'S DEADLIEST
BIOTERROR ATTACK

JEANNE GUILLEMIN

Times Books
Henry Holt and Company
New York

Times Books
Henry Holt and Company, LLC
Publishers since 1866
175 Fifth Avenue
New York, New York 10010

Henry Holt® is a registered trademark of Henry Holt and Company, LLC.

Library of Congress Cataloging-in-Publication Data

Guillemin, Jeanne, 1943–
    American anthrax : fear, crime, and the investigation of the nation's deadliest
bioterror attack / Jeanne Guillemin.
        p.   cm.
    Includes bibliographical references and index.
    ISBN 978-0-8050-9104-5
    1. Bioterrorism—United States.   2. Anthrax—United States.   3. Postal service—
United States.   4. Victims of terrorism—United States.   I. Title.
    HV6433.35.G85   2011
    364.1—dc22   2011004067

Henry Holt books are available for special promotions and premiums.
For details contact: Director, Special Markets.

First Edition 2011
Designed by Meryl Sussman Levavi

Printed in the United States of America
1   3   5   7   9   10   8   6   4   2

To M.S.M.

CONTENTS

CAST OF CHARACTERS

FIVE FATAL VICTIMS

ROBERT "BOB" STEVENS, photo editor for American Media, Inc., in Boca Raton, Florida, and the first inhalational anthrax fatality

THOMAS MORRIS·JR., government mail sorter at the Brentwood postal facility, Washington, D.C.

JOSEPH CURSEEN JR., mail sorter at the Brentwood postal facility

KATHY T. NGUYEN, stockroom clerk at Manhattan Eye, Ear, and Throat Hospital, New York City

OTTILIE LUNDGREN, retired legal secretary, living in Oxford, Connecticut

SURVIVORS OF INHALATIONAL ANTHRAX

ERNESTO BLANCO, mail handler at American Media, Inc., in Boca Raton, Florida

NORMA WALLACE, mail sorter, Hamilton, New Jersey, postal facility

JYOTSNA PATEL, mail sorter, Hamilton postal facility

QIETH McQUE, express mail office, Brentwood postal facility

LEROY RICHMOND, express mail deliverer, Brentwood postal facility

DAVID HOSE, mail sorter at the State Department mail annex, Winchester, Virginia

JOSEPH PALISCAK, U.S. postal inspector who changed DBCS #17 filters at Brentwood on October 18, 2001 (diagnosis not confirmed by the CDC)

KEY CUTANEOUS CASES

ERIN O'CONNER, assistant to NBC news broadcaster Tom Brokaw, whose diagnosis alerted New York officials

CASEY CHAMBERLAIN, intern at NBC assisting with Brokaw's mail

CLAIRE FLETCHER, assistant to CBS news broadcaster Dan Rather

INFANT SON (unnamed) of ABC news producer, a near fatality

TERESA HELLER, letter carrier in Trenton, New Jersey, whose diagnosis led to the shutdown of the Hamilton postal facility

RICHARD MORGANO, Hamilton postal worker

JOHANNA HUDEN, *New York Post* journalist

FLORIDA

MAUREEN STEVENS, wife of Robert Stevens

LARRY BUSH, M.D., chief of the medical staff and of infectious diseases at the John F. Kennedy Medical Center in Atlantis who correctly diagnosed Bob Stevens' inhalational anthrax

JEAN MALECKI, M.D., director, Palm Beach County Health Department, in charge of local response

JEB BUSH, governor of Florida during the anthrax crisis and brother of President George W. Bush

JOHN OGWUNOBI, M.D., Florida state secretary of Public Health

DAVID J. PECKER, president and CEO, American Media, Inc. (AMI), where Bob Stevens worked

DANIEL ROTSTEIN, senior vice president, Human Resources Department, American Media, Inc.

STEPHANIE DAILEY, mail clerk at AMI who opened the anthrax letter

CENTERS FOR DISEASE CONTROL AND PREVENTION, ATLANTA, GEORGIA (CDC)

JEFF KOPLAN, M.D., CDC director during the anthrax attacks and subsequently director of Emory University's Global Health Institute and the university's vice president for Global Health

BRAD PERKINS, M.D., chief, Meningitis and Special Pathogens Branch, Division of Bacterial Mycotic Diseases, National Center for

Infectious Diseases; led the field investigation in Florida and became chief of the Office of Strategy and Innovation

SHERIF ZAKI, M.D., CDC chief medical examiner and head of the Infectious Diseases Pathology Activity (IDPA), whose test confirmed Erin O'Conner's diagnosis

JULIE GERBERDING, M.D., acting deputy director of the National Center for Infectious Diseases, who coordinated attack responses with the White House and was CDC director from 2002 to 2009

TANJA POPOVIC, M.D., chief of the Epidemiologic Investigations/ Anthrax Laboratory during the anthrax crisis and later CDC deputy associate director for science

STEPHEN OSTROFF, M.D., associate director for Epidemiologic Science, National Center for Infectious Diseases, and special assistant to Mayor Rudolph Giuliani during the New York City crisis

USAMRIID (UNITED STATES ARMY MEDICAL RESEARCH INSTITUTE OF INFECTIOUS DISEASES), FORT DETRICK, FREDERICK, MARYLAND

BRUCE EDWARD IVINS, microbiologist in the Bacteriological Division who specialized in anthrax vaccine development and became the FBI's prime suspect in the Amerithrax investigation

DIANE IVINS, his wife of thirty-three years

ARTHUR FRIEDLANDER, U.S. Army physician and anthrax specialist who retired at rank of colonel and resumed work in the Bacteriology Division as a civilian scientist in 2002

JOHN EZZELL, microbiologist and head of the Special Pathogens Sample Analysis Laboratory, Diagnostic Services Division, who opened the Daschle and Leahy letters and was in charge of the FBI repository at USAMRIID, and later became a senior research scientist

PATRICIA WORSHAM, microbiologist, Bacteriological Division, whose lab was affected by the April 2002 accident, and who researched the morphotypes in B. anthracis from the anthrax letters

TERRY ABSHIRE, microbiologist, Bacteriological Division, who first noticed the morphotypes in the letter material

PETER JAHRLING, senior scientist and virologist who sounded the alert about a possible silica coating on the Daschle letter spores; later director, the National Institute of Allergy and Infectious Diseases (NIAID) Integrated Research Facility, Fort Detrick

Ayaad Assaad, microbiologist, harassed by colleagues in 1991 for his Middle East origins and later employed at the Environmental Protection Agency; in September 2001 was accused of being a bioterrorist in an anonymous letter sent to the FBI

Patricia Fellows, former collaborator of Bruce Ivins on the BioPort project who left in 2002 to work at the Southern Research Institute, Frederick, and was awarded a Decoration of Exceptional Civilian Service at the same time as Ivins in 2003

Mara Linscott, former technician of Bruce Ivins and friend of Fellows who left USAMRIID in 1999 for medical school

Major General John S. Parker, commander, U.S. Army Medical Research and Materiel Command (which oversees USAMRIID) at the time of the anthrax letters

Colonel George W. Korch Jr., institute commander at the time of the FBI's November 2007 search of Ivins' home and office and Ivins' death in 2008

New York

Tom Brokaw, NBC news broadcaster and author, and the first person identified as a target of an anthrax letter

Rudolph Giuliani, mayor of New York during the 9/11 attacks and the anthrax crisis

Marcelle "Marci" Layton, M.D., assistant commissioner, Bureau of Communicable Diseases at the New York City Department of Health and Mental Hygiene

Judith Miller, lead author of the bestseller *Germs*, and recipient of a hoax letter on October 12, 2001

New Jersey

Eddy Bresnitz, M.D., state epidemiologist and deputy commissioner, Department of Health and Senior Services

George T. DiFerdinando Jr., M.D., acting commissioner, Department of Health and Senior Services

Joseph Sautello, manager of the Hamilton facility

Robert "Bob" Unick, mail handler at the Hamilton facility and later shop steward

Steve Bahrle, Hamilton branch president of local 308, National Postal Mail Handlers Union

Washington Federal Government

Tom Daschle, Democratic senator from South Dakota and Senate majority leader; after Tom Brokaw the second known target of an anthrax letter

Patrick Leahy, Democratic senator from Vermont and chair of the Judiciary Committee in 2001, and the third known target of an anthrax letter

Tommy Thompson, secretary of Health and Human Services, 2001–2004

Tom Ridge, former Pennsylvania governor and in September 2001 head of the White House Office of Homeland Security; in November 2002 named the secretary of the new Department of Homeland Security

Lisa Gordon-Hagerty, National Security Council staff member appointed to assist Governor Tom Ridge during the anthrax crisis

George W. Bush, president of the United States, 2001–2008

Dick Cheney, vice president of the United States, 2001–2008

John Ashcroft, U.S. attorney general, 2001–2004

John "Jack" Potter, U.S. postmaster general, 2001–2010

Thomas A. Day Sr., vice president of engineering, U.S. Postal Service, later senior vice president of Government Relations

U.S. Representative Rush Holt Jr. (D-New Jersey) representing the 12th congressional district, including Princeton

Anthony Fauci, NIAID director who promoted research against both infectious disease and bioterrorism

Federal Bureau of Investigation "Amerithrax"

Robert Mueller III, director, Federal Bureau of Investigation, 2001–2011

Thomas Carey, counter-terrorism expert and inspector-in-charge, 2001–2003

Van A. Harp, assistant director-in-charge (ADIC) of the Washington Field Office and chief investigator, 2001–2003

David Lee Wilson, biologist and special agent in charge of Amerithrax 2, concerning its scientific aspects

Mark R. Wilson, a pioneer in DNA forensics and supervisory special agent at the Chemical-Biological Sciences Unit

Douglas Beecher, microbiologist, Hazardous Material Response Unit, Quantico, Virginia

RICHARD LAMBERT, inspector-in-charge of the investigation, 2003–2006, replacing Van Harp

EDWARD MONTOOTH, special agent for the field investigation, 2006–2008

PAUL KEMP, lawyer at Venable LLP in Rockville, Maryland, and legal counsel to Bruce Ivins in 2008 until his death

NANCY HAIGWOOD, who in 2002, when on the faculty of the University of Washington in Seattle, alerted the FBI to Bruce Ivins' obsession with the Kappa Kappa Gamma sorority and other bizarre behavior; later became the director of the Oregon National Primate Research Center and adjunct professor of Molecular Microbiology and Immunology, Oregon Health and Science University

BARBARA HATCH ROSENBERG, professor of microbiology at the State University of New York at Purchase and head of the Federation of American Scientists working group on biological weapons, who in December 2001 raised suspicions of an insider perpetrator of the anthrax letters

FBI SCIENTIFIC CONSULTANTS

PAUL KEIM, microbiologist and anthrax strain expert and professor at Northern Arizona State University, Department of Biological Sciences

JOSEPH MICHAEL, material chemist, Sandia National Laboratory, Albuquerque, New Mexico

RITA COLWELL, microbiologist and director, National Science Foundation, promoted genetic analysis of the anthrax material; later professor of medicine at the University of Maryland and also Johns Hopkins University

CLAIRE FRASER-LIGGETT, president of TIGR (The Institute for Genomic Research), where extensive genetic analysis of the letter material was carried out, and later director of the Institute for Genome Sciences at the University of Maryland School of Medicine

JACQUES RAVEL, microbiologist at TIGR, played a key role in testing for the genomic signature in the FBI repository samples; later research scientist at the Institute for Genome Sciences at the University of Maryland School of Medicine

JAMES BURANS, U.S. Navy captain and FBI consultant, later

associate director of the National Bioforensic Analysis Center at Fort Detrick

MATTHEW MESELSON, molecular biologist, Harvard University, who led the 1992 investigation of the Sverdlovsk outbreak and advised the FBI on the Amerithrax case

U.S. POSTAL SERVICE/BRENTWOOD POSTAL FACILITY

DENA BRISCOE, mail sorter and co-founder of Brentwood Exposed and later president of the local chapter of the American Postal Workers Union in Washington, D.C.

TERRELL WORRELL, mail handler and co-founder of Brentwood Exposed

HELEN LEWIS, government mail sorter and co-founder of Brentwood Exposed

TIM HANEY, senior plant manager during the anthrax crisis and after the building reopened as the Curseen-Morris Mail Processing and Distribution Center; later vice president, Area Operations, Northeast, and in 2010 vice president, Area Operations, Capital Metro (Washington, D.C.)

LARRY KLAYMAN, founder and chairman of Judicial Watch, the legal watchdog organization in Washington that represented the Brentwood employees in their suit against the U.S. Postal Service

TOM FITTON, president of Judicial Watch who took over the organization when Klayman left in the fall of 2003

CHRIS FARRELL, director of investigations and research at Judicial Watch who worked closely with the Brentwood Exposed leadership

BIOTERRORISM POLICY EXPERTS

KEN ALIBEK, M.D., former deputy director of the Soviet Union's Biopreparat division of its biological warfare program and defector to United States from Russia in 1992; became professor at George Mason University

D. A. HENDERSON, M.D., in 1966–1977 leader of World Health Organization campaign to eradicate smallpox and in 1998 the founder of the Johns Hopkins Center for Civilian Biodefense Studies, Baltimore, Md.

TARA O'TOOLE, M.D., associate director of the Johns Hopkins Center; later founder and head of the Biosecurity Center at the University of Pittsburgh Medical Center, and in 2009 appointed under secretary of Science and Technology, Department of Homeland Security

THOMAS INGLESBY, M.D., original staff member at the Johns Hopkins Center and later at the Pittsburgh center where he replaced Dr. O'Toole as director in 2009

RICHARD BUTLER, Australia's ambassador to the United Nations and in 1997–1998 leader of the United Nations Special Commission (UNSCOM) to oversee Saddam Hussein's compliance with the 1991 Gulf War cease-fire agreement

RICHARD SPERTZEL, microbiologist, former employee of the U.S. biological warfare program as well as USAMRIID and, in 1994–1998, leader of the special UNSCOM team searching for biological weapons in Iraq

WILLIAM PATRICK, production engineer employed by both the offensive and defensive U.S. biological weapons programs and during the 1990s a consultant for the CIA and other government agencies

AUTHOR'S NOTE

In October 2001, in the tumultuous wake of the September 11 al Qaeda attacks on the United States, the nation was exposed to a more insidious terrorist threat: a series of five anonymous letters containing a deadly strain of anthrax sent to major media outlets and the U.S. Senate. These letters jeopardized the health of thousands of people in newsrooms, congressional offices, postal facilities, and private homes. They also put bioterrorism front and center as a threat to national security.

Few of those exposed had ever heard of anthrax, an ancient disease of livestock, or knew that its bacterium, *Bacillus anthracis*, was the premier biological weapons agent of the twentieth century. Produced in bulk, the microbe's tough dormant spores, just a micron in diameter, had served as bomb fill in no fewer than five major military arsenals.[1] The intent of weapons scientists was to create lethal aerosols that would infect masses of enemy civilians with inhalational anthrax by pathogen bombs or spray generators. But the impact of anthrax aerosols on targeted victims remained theoretical; states fought their wars by other means or, in the unique instance of Japanese anthrax attacks on China in World War II, the battle chronicles conveniently disappeared.[2]

Unpredictably, the end of the Cold War offered a unique opportunity to estimate the true danger of anthrax as a biological weapon. In June 1992, after the demise of the Soviet Union, a team of academic experts, myself included, traveled to Russia to investigate the 1979 anthrax outbreak that had swept through the city of Sverdlovsk, infecting nearly a hundred people and killing sixty-six of them. Did they die from eating infected meat, as Soviet officials claimed, or, as the CIA contended, had they been exposed to spores accidentally released from a nearby military facility?

Trained as an anthropologist, I went door-to-door to interview the families of the victims, asking them the crucial question: Where was the infected individual physically located in the days and nights before the outbreak started? The result of those interviews was an epidemiological map showing that during the day on April 2, 1979, in a line three miles long and as straight as a pencil, the victims were directly downwind of the military base called Compound 19, where anthrax spores were indeed being secretly produced. Not bad meat, but an accidental release of spores had randomly sickened and killed unsuspecting bystanders in the city. As we charted the deaths of animals in the countryside, we found that the "plume" of aerosolized anthrax extended thirty miles along the same straight line, following the steady southeasterly wind direction of that April day.[3] The accidental spore release in Sverdlovsk demonstrated the frightening reality that an anthrax aerosol could be lethal miles from its source. In the 1990s, as Washington officials became fixated on the threat of mass bioterrorism attacks, that grim fact helped keep anthrax at number one on the list of potential germ weapons.

After investigating the Sverdlovsk outbreak, I became part of a small coterie that studied the disease, which, though it still afflicted unvaccinated livestock worldwide, played a growing role in international security. The 1995 discovery that Saddam Hussein had once developed crude anthrax weapons sparked concern that Iraq (or other small hostile nations or terrorists) would seek a biological weapons advantage. Our anthrax conferences became a mix of U.S. and U.K. defense scientists, various microbiologists, veterinarians, epidemiologists, CIA and MI6 agents, and a new contingent, Russian bacteriologists. Everyone seemed to get along. One conference regular described us as "a small, fun-loving group."[4] The threat of anthrax as a viable weapon sometimes seemed remote.

In 2001, the 9/11 attacks made almost any menace seem possible. Anthrax was quickly identified as the most likely "second blow" that al Qaeda would launch against Americans. My phone began ringing with requests from reporters and news stations to outline the basics about the disease. On October 4, when the diagnosis of the first anthrax letters case was announced in Florida, I was in the CBS newsroom, having come to New York, my hometown, to brief reporters. For the next several weeks, as the anthrax crisis skipped from Florida to New York and then to Washington, D.C., I averaged thirty phone calls a day from the media and spoke on dozens of television and radio shows. My consistent message was, "Stay calm." But the belated diagnoses of anthrax cases and the accumulation of five deaths generated new episodes of chaos that government missteps and media coverage only amplified.

By early 2002, the furor over the letter attacks abated. Washington's attention shifted to funding biodefense research on anthrax, smallpox, and other pathogens. On a quiet morning in early February, my telephone rang and a soft voice hesitantly offered a greeting: "Hello, Mrs. Guillemin." Then there was silence. Having already experienced my share of odd phone calls about anthrax, I was about to hang up when the voice resumed: "Please excuse me. I have never spoken to an author before."

The caller was Terrell Worrell, one of the founders of Brentwood Exposed, the organization of Washington postal workers who had lost two colleagues to inhalational anthrax the previous October. Worrell had found my book on the Sverdlovsk outbreak in his local library and wanted to know if I would speak at a meeting of this new group. I flew to Washington the next week and gave a talk to about forty Brentwood employees. They, like nearly 2,000 others, had been exposed to aerosolized spores at the capital's largest postal facility. With Dena Briscoe, Helen Lewis, and Terrell Worrell leading them, Brentwood Exposed members were just then taking their first steps toward healing from the trauma and embarking on a unique legal quest for justice.

As goals, healing and justice were intertwined, not just for the Brentwood community but for everyone affected by the letters—those who had lost a loved one, became sick from anthrax, were evacuated from their workplace, stood on line for antibiotics, or wondered with good reason how close they and co-workers, friends, and family had come to lethal exposure. The path to healing was often obscure or difficult—when before had Americans ever been vulnerable to the intentional use of anthrax?

The path to justice seemed equally problematic. The first question about the anthrax letters was: "Who sent them?" The early expectation was that the criminal would be caught and justice would be served. As months and then years passed, with no suspect apprehended, the question became: "Will the FBI ever find the perpetrator?" In late July 2008, after six years of developing the new science of microbial forensics, the Bureau finally had a prime suspect, Bruce Ivins, a civilian microbiologist at the U.S. Army's medical institute at Fort Detrick, Maryland, and one of the small, happy group of anthrax experts. In July 2008, when Ivins committed suicide, the question became: "Was he really the murderer?" His incredulous friends and colleagues believed the FBI had blundered, and dozens of critics faulted the Bureau's long and sometimes meandering investigation. The Internet became an active forum for civilian sleuths to ponder the mystery of the anthrax letters and make their own conjectures.

The whodunit question, which may never be answered, remains a distraction from a larger problem: the failure in national security that set the stage for the anthrax letter attacks. By the time of Ivins' suicide, the FBI had solid scientific proof that the spores in the anthrax letters matched those in a flask, labeled RMR (Reference Material Receipt)-1029, that was in Ivins' keeping at the Army's medical institute at Detrick. Even if the bioterrorist was not Ivins, some criminal had secretly gained access to those highly dangerous spores—technically categorized as weapons of mass destruction—and used them against the American public with lethal consequences.

In June 2002, I was invited to give a talk about Sverdlovsk at Fort Detrick. On a giant screen, to an audience of about 300 defense scientists, including retirees, I showed my map of the April 2, 1979, spore release, with its red dots locating each of the victims in the path of the deadly aerosol from Compound 19. To give the tragedy a human face, I presented a half-dozen photographs of the victims who had died. Bruce Ivins was in the audience, along with several other longtime anthrax experts who had conducted research using spores from RMR-1029.

As I ended that presentation in 2002, I questioned why the Soviet military had never taken responsibility for the outbreak and the fear and suffering it caused. It was unthinkable then that, in 2008, a similar question would be asked of the U.S. Army. Yet the anthrax pathogen in the letters was pure American, from Texas soil, and assigned to the U.S. Army for safekeeping—and suddenly some criminal hand had secretly dispersed it. For all its amazing complexity, the story of the anthrax letters always circles back to this fatal biosecurity breakdown— and whether another like it might again jeopardize public safety.

Writing this book gave me an opportunity to review in depth my files on the 2001 letter attacks, to converse again with friends and colleagues who figured in the story, and to interview key actors who had earlier recounted their experiences.[5] Although the FBI officially closed the anthrax letters case after Ivins died, the controversy about the crime's implications continues and will for years, if propelled only by conspiracy theories. (As one FBI analyst put it to me, "It's the grassy knoll in Dallas again.") In *American Anthrax*, I aim to move future discussions to questions of how best to protect the public against bioterrorism and to guarantee justice if those protections should again fail.

AMERICAN ANTHRAX

THE BIOTERRORISM THREAT

July 27, 2008, Frederick, Maryland. It was 1:15 a.m. and in a car parked on a quiet street adjacent to the guarded expanse of the U.S. Army's Fort Detrick, two FBI agents kept watch on a small frame house, number 622 Military Road. Suddenly, a town ambulance, siren blaring and lights flashing, careened around the corner and jammed to a stop in front of the house. A pair of paramedics jumped out and rushed up the front walk carrying emergency equipment and a portable stretcher. A middle-aged woman in glasses opened the door for them and ten minutes later the unconscious Bruce Edward Ivins was carried out and sped to Frederick Memorial Hospital. He died there two days later, an apparent suicide at age sixty-two.

To the surprise of many who heard the news of Ivins' death, he was the FBI's prime suspect in the 2001 anthrax letter attacks, on the brink of a federal indictment. A microbiologist respected for his research on anthrax, he had worked for twenty-seven years at Detrick's U.S. Army Medical Research Institute for Infectious Diseases (USAMRIID). Loyal, dependable, and a family man, he was probably the last person anyone would think of as a terrorist. In the months before his suicide, his colleagues at the institute had witnessed the FBI legally close in on Ivins, who seemed to mentally disintegrate under the strain.

In those months, the pressure on the institute—colloquially referred to as USAMRIID, pronounced "u-sam-rid"—had been extreme. FBI agents were conducting interviews with its staff and Ivins' closest colleagues were giving grand jury testimony. It was unthinkable to many that anyone from within this respected defense research establishment could intentionally use a "select agent" pathogen to kill people. Created in January 1969, USAMRIID's mission was to defend American troops against dangerous infectious diseases. At the time, the U.S. Army had an active biological warfare program, centered at Detrick, to make strategic weapons out of anthrax, tularemia, plague, hemorrhagic fevers, and dozens of other diseases and toxins. Then, in November 1969, with the stroke of a pen, President Richard Nixon ended the entire biological weapons program rather than pioneer an unpredictable and relatively inexpensive kind of WMD. Quite purposefully, he kept USAMRIID as a symbol of America's commitment to purely defensive, open research involving vaccines, antibiotics, antiviral drugs, and other protections. The rest of Fort Detrick—its weapons laboratories, its eight-story anthrax production plant, its million-liter Horton Sphere, the world's largest aerobiology chamber for testing germ weapons—was shut down and disinfected, and stockpiles of munitions and pathogens (including 220 pounds of dried anthrax spores) were destroyed.

In 1972, the institute moved into a new $17.8 million center with state-of-the-art high containment laboratories, offices, a conference hall, a library, and two clinics. Former weapons scientists who revised their project descriptions for defensive purposes helped fill the staff slots. That same year, the United States and the Soviet Union agreed to the 1972 Biological and Toxin Weapons Convention, the international treaty that bans the production, stockpiling, and development of biological agents, except for peaceful purposes. In 1975, after a fifty-year delay, the United States ratified the 1925 Geneva Protocol that forbids states to use chemical or biological weapons in war. It looked as if the history of biological weapons had ended. As the Cold War continued, though, speculation that the Soviet Union was secretly violating the 1972 treaty fueled USAMRIID's defensive mission.

In 1980, USAMRIID had a position open in its Bacteriology Division and Bruce Ivins interviewed for it. At age thirty-four, he came with solid but not stellar academic credentials—undergraduate and graduate degrees in biology from the University of Cincinnati and postdoctoral training at the University of North Carolina and the Uniformed Services University of the Health Sciences in Maryland. The son and grandson of pharmacists in the small town of Lebanon, Ohio, he had been a gawky teenager with horn-rimmed glasses—a high school science nerd shunned by the popular kids and unhappy at home. His father, who had graduated from Princeton in the Roaring Twenties and then returned to run the family drugstore in Lebanon, was an alcoholic; his mother suffered from depression and fits of violence. The youngest of three sons, Ivins sometimes worked in the family store. Then, in 1966, he escaped to university and found his vocation. For fourteen years—the turbulent years of the civil rights movement and antiwar protests—he centered his life on laboratory research. An idealist, Ivins identified with the hero of the Sinclair Lewis novel *Arrowsmith*, a biologist uncompromisingly "passionate on behalf of mankind."[1] That idealism fit well with USAMRIID's mission, plus the institute needed civilian scientists, even those who, like Ivins, sported long sideburns and bell-bottom trousers, rode a unicycle, and loved '70s pop music.

Another microbiologist turned out to be the hiring committee's first choice; Ivins came in a close second.[2] As fate had it, the top-ranked candidate rejected USAMRIID's job offer, which then went to Ivins. He accepted, joined the Bacteriology Division in late 1980, and, with secret clearance, became a member of a respected, large defense establishment; even after the Nixon decision, Detrick remained a significant research enclave, Frederick County's largest employer.[3]

To all appearances, Bruce Ivins and his wife, Diane (who was ten years his junior and from Cincinnati), became upstanding members of the Frederick community. They adopted twin toddlers, Andrew and Amanda, and bought a small house near the base; later they purchased the Cape Cod cottage at 622 Military Road, a short walk from USAMRIID. Ivins taught juggling, one of his hobbies, and started a local jugglers club. An amateur pop musician, he performed at town events and marched in parades. Raised a Presbyterian, in graduate school Ivins had converted to Catholicism, his wife's religion. In Frederick, they joined the parish of St. John the Evangelist in the town's historic downtown. On Sundays, Ivins played hymns on the keyboard for the overflow crowd at what he called the "hippies' mass." Diane Ivins became active in her children's school activities, eventually started a home-based daycare center, and became a leader in the Frederick County Right-to-Life organization.

Like his family life, Ivins' work life prospered. In 1980, the United States confronted the Soviet Union about rumors of a large anthrax outbreak in Sverdlovsk, a closed city near the Ural Mountains with a large military base. The 1979 incident, dismissed by the Soviets as a natural event caused by infected meat, had direct repercussions at USAMRIID. The CIA and the Defense Department saw the outbreak as a signal the Soviet military might be developing anthrax weapons and the institute began ramping up its defensive research on *Bacillus anthracis*. The path of Ivins' life for the next twenty-seven years was set: he would focus exclusively on this dangerous, still mysterious microbe.

The timing for Ivins could hardly have been better. The 1980s developed into "a golden age" of anthrax science.[4] During that decade, he worked closely and productively with his USAMRIID colleagues, usually in the Biosafety Level 3 suite in Building 1425 or, when conducting aerosol tests on animals, in Building 1412 next door. Two men in particular were his close contemporaries: the strapping, outgoing John Ezzell, who was also a civilian, and the professorial, Harvard-educated Arthur Friedlander, an Army physician. Of the three, the gangly Ivins was in style the odd man out. He kept wearing bell-bottoms and packed a health food lunch—it might still be the 1970s—and he enjoyed playing practical jokes, like rigging a piece of laboratory equipment in the hallway to randomly emit an "elephant fart." Yet he made key scientific contributions, particularly in understanding the role that plasmids play in the virulence of anthrax strains, that is, their ability to evade host defenses and cause disease. His research also clarified the role of one of the microbe's proteins, protective antigen (PA), in conferring protection from the disease and moved vaccine research forward by developing recombinant PA and exploring new additives to improve vaccine formulas. In the eyes of his colleagues he was one of the world's anthrax experts.[5] He and a half-dozen others in the Bacteriology Division regularly published journal articles and reports that explored the *B. anthracis* toxins, its two plasmids, and the capsules on the bacteria that affect virulence.

If there was a kind of Holy Grail for these defense researchers, it was the development of a better vaccine than Anthrax Vaccine Adsorbed (AVA), the one the United States relied on to protect military lab employees and veterinarians who worked with livestock. AVA was cumbersome to administer, requiring six shots over the course of 18 months, plus a yearly booster. How well it would protect troops exposed to large doses was nearly impossible to gauge. Anthrax was too dangerous to allow human subject research (its inhalational form was known to have a 90 percent mortality rate). This left Ivins and his colleagues to develop intriguing theories to test on rabbits, guinea pigs, mice, and monkeys. Over the years, no one made any particular inquiry about AVA's adverse side effects; it could cause some soreness at the inoculation site and provoke flulike symptoms, but these seemed to be minor, short-term discomforts well worth the protection against potential infection from sick animals or defense research.

Suddenly, in August 1990, Iraq invaded Kuwait. The history of their boundary dispute dated back fifty years, but, ominously, in 1986 and 1988, Saddam Hussein had acquired deadly *B. anthracis* from the American Type Culture Collection. Saddam had aggressively used chemical weapons during the Iran-Iraq War, from 1980 to 1988, and had killed hundreds of Iraqi Kurds with nerve gas. Who knew what he would dare do against the international coalition gathering to force him out of Kuwait? Faced with the probability of battlefield anthrax, USAMRIID was forced to advise the use of AVA for mass vaccination. There were 200,000 U.S. troops being mobilized for deployment to the Middle East who had to be protected—and quickly. The campaign was so rushed that doses were sent by courier on commercial flights and records of troop inoculations were at times incomplete or lost.[6]

To determine the best post-exposure intervention (whether vaccination or antibiotics or some combination of the two), the institute's anthrax experts conducted quick rounds of experiments with dozens of rhesus monkeys.[7] As a result, USAMRIID approved the distribution of the broad-spectrum Ciprofloxacin (produced by the German pharmaceutical giant Bayer) for post-exposure treatment. Penicillin was effective against most anthrax strains, but the idea was that Cipro (or as an alternative doxycycline) was too new for Saddam's scientists to have concocted a strain of *B. anthracis* that could resist it.

Started on January 17, 1991, Gulf War hostilities ended just weeks later, on February 27, after Iraqi troops exited Kuwait. Saddam's quick agreement to the United Nations cease-fire stipulations ended the state of hyper-emergency at USAMRIID, but only temporarily. The Gulf

War ushered in a decade of major disruptions for the institute, each caused by changing perceptions of threats to U.S. national security. Iraq's quick transformation from an occasional ally to an enemy with WMD ambitions radically changed the future of the institute.

On a broader scale, the end of the Cold War forced USAMRIID to reinvent its project priorities and accommodate to "peace dividend" budget cutbacks, which it did only with difficulty. In 1992, the disorganization and demoralization at the institute seemed so out of control that the U.S. Army sent an investigator.[8] Pathogens, including anthrax bacteria and Ebola virus, went missing from laboratory inventories and were never found. In the context of the Gulf War, flagrant harassment of Ayaad Assaad, a scientist of Middle Eastern origin, by colleagues—they formed a ritual "Camel Club" to taunt him with insults—led to reprimands of the scientific staff. Later came age discrimination lawsuits from Assaad and two other scientists who lost their jobs due to the need for RIF (Reduction In Force).[9] The cases lost on appeal for lack of evidence that institute authorities had acted with any prejudice in determining the institute's research needs. Other researchers whose projects were canceled refused to stop their experiments; with the aid of an accomplice, at least one military microbiologist, let go in an earlier RIF, penetrated security barriers and reentered his old lab.

Despite a staff reduction of over 30 percent, Ivins, Ezzell, and Friedlander survived the purge and along with others developed a sense of "lifeboat" solidarity. As the USAMRIID commander at the time put it, "I've never known a group so tight, so together."[10] At the same time, though, the institute's scientists had to get used to an increased number of contract workers, whose sense of mission was less than theirs. Simultaneously, the institute's reputation came under serious attack as veterans suffering from Gulf War syndrome began blaming the AVA inoculations for their ailments. In 1999, Ivins was personally targeted when journalist Gary Matsumoto described two of his vaccine innovations as contributing to AVA's special toxicity.[11]

The broader threat to the institute was much more daunting: it was losing its twenty-year monopoly on select agent research. With the Soviet Union defunct, Washington national security analysts began theorizing about a new existential threat to the United States: intractable, belligerent small states or terrorists armed with weapons of mass destruction and capable of "asymmetrical warfare."[12] Within this new framework, American civilians were at high risk of mass attacks. In the aftermath of the initial, 1993 al Qaeda attack on New York's World Trade Center, the 1995 Oklahoma City bombing, and that same year the poison gas attacks by the Aum Shinrikyo sect on the Tokyo subway, the idea of civil defense against mass attacks made sense. In 1995 President Bill Clinton issued a presidential directive (PDD-39) that for the first time involved the Department of Health and Human Services in an interagency collaboration—eventually called the Counter-Terrorism Security Group—centered in the White House, to defend the nation against terrorists armed with unconventional weapons.[13] Soon Clinton's new counter-terrorism czar Richard A. Clarke had the main responsibility for creating a network among individuals from the departments of State, Defense, Justice, the CIA, and the FBI.[14] But a network was far from sufficient to ensure emergency cooperation among federal bureaucracies. By Clinton's directive, the Public Health Service and, within it, the Centers for Disease Control and Prevention in Atlanta were expected to be prepared to respond to a large-scale terrorist attack. Yet it was widely acknowledged that state and local responses to large-scale terrorism might fail to coordinate with federal agencies.[15]

To foster a crusade for "domestic preparedness," the Department of Defense began allocating millions of dollars to 120 of the nation's most populous cities to fund emergency response equipment and stage training scenarios of hypothetical attacks with radiological "dirty" bombs or chemical and biological weapons.[16] Like federal programs that fostered air raid drills and underground shelters in the 1950s—"Operation Alert" of 1956 was the most vigorously publicized—the domestic preparedness program presumed American communities were total war targets.[17] Since biological weapons were part of the threat, civil defense soon developed a new branch: civilian biodefense.

Different from nuclear or chemical weapons, germ weapons have a slow, insidious impact that could be forestalled by exactly the medical defenses—primarily vaccines and antibiotics—that USAMRIID had been researching for troop protection. That civilians now needed these interventions seemed beyond debate. In 1995, United Nations inspectors in Iraq found documentation that Saddam had developed and tested crude anthrax weapons.[18] At the same time, revelations about the Soviet violation of the 1972 Biological Weapons Convention—its vast production of anthrax and perhaps smallpox agents and munitions, plus its basic science experiments to increase virulence—raised suspicions that other hostile nations were seeking the same covert advantage. The epidemiological map of the 1979 Sverdlovsk anthrax outbreak, showing the release of a lethal plume, became a model for what American civilians might have to fear from foreign bioterrorists. The funding for defensive research on anthrax, plague, tularemia, smallpox, Ebola, and other diseases, once the sole province of USAMRIID, began flowing to other government agencies and to universities and commercial laboratories. The Department of Health and Human Services saw the most radical budget increase, from $16 million to $265 million in just one year, but the wealth was spread, from the Department of Agriculture to the Justice Department and the Department of State.[19] USAMRIID, its mission limited to troop defense, was sidelined by the new science-based competition for "civilian biodefense" funding that took on the aspects of a gold rush.

As part of the institute's reinvention, in 1996 John Ezzell left the Bacteriology Division and took charge of the Special Pathogens Sample Test Laboratory in the institute's new Diagnostic Services Division. It had a service to offer: any potential use of anthrax (battlefield or anti-civilian) could be evaluated in the high-containment laboratory there. Ezzell's new workplace was still in Building 1425, right next to the office of Bruce Ivins and the high-containment suite where he worked. With the institute in flux, Art Friedlander became a senior research scientist, a top-level advisory role. Seemingly without ambition, Ivins continued his laboratory research on defenses against *B. anthracis* while the world of anthrax research grew larger and more complex and his place within it more precarious. From an organizational perspective, his career was blocked and his power over resources was diminishing.[20] At times he had to argue over travel reimbursement and technician funding and off-site meeting plans. He should have been unhappy— there were, in fact, signs that he was—yet Ivins was altruistically committed to his research—"selfless in giving service," as he was frequently described.

◆

As the framework shifted toward bioterrorist threats, USAMRIID scientists were called on to share their expertise. Just prior to the Gulf War, Bruce Ivins had accepted an apprentice from the Navy, Jim Burans, and taught him how to culture anthrax, as part of a Navy initiative to create an effective battlefield detector for *B. anthracis,* in direct competition with USAMRIID. After the cease-fire, Ivins traveled to Canada's Defense Research Establishment Suffield (DRES) in Alberta to help scientists there design a Biosafety Level 3 (BSL-3) laboratory for anthrax research and he subsequently shared with them Ames strain anthrax from the USAMRIID collection. John Ezzell made trips to the CDC, where a new anthrax analysis laboratory was being built and protocols for *B. anthracis* identification written. The CDC, which housed one of the world's two remaining repositories of smallpox strains (the other being in Russia, at the Vector Institute in Novosibirsk), also played host to USAMRIID's Peter Jahrling, who was conducting animal research on the disease, which, though globally eradicated in 1980, had reemerged as a bioterrorism threat.

USAMRIID maintained its post-1969 openness. In contrast, in the late 1990s the CIA and the Defense Intelligence Agency took on a series of top-secret anthrax experiments—for example, on spore production in bulk, the replication of a Soviet anthrax bomb, and the creation of a vaccine-resistant strain—that blurred the line between defensive and offensive research.[21] Some projects required the resources of top security commercial contractors like the Battelle Memorial Institute in Ohio or involved the Dugway Proving Ground in Utah, a site for large-area testing. Some projects created new careers, as when tissue samples preserved from the Sverdlovsk outbreak were, with CIA support, analyzed at the Biology Division at Los Alamos National Laboratory.[22] That research started Paul Keim, a young plant biologist at Northern Arizona University, on his career as an expert on the genetic identification of anthrax strains, a promising new field.

※

In addition, the bioterrorism threat revived the careers of some biomedical scientists who during the Cold War as "bioweaponeers" had developed germ weapons and now stepped forward as experts on the horrors of mass attack. The best known among them was Ken Alibek (originally Kanatzhan Alibekov), a former deputy head of the Soviet Biopreparat program, who in 1992 defected to the United States. Alibek was the CIA's primary source of information about his division of the Soviet enterprise.[23] To debrief Alibek, the CIA turned to William Patrick III, once in charge of anthrax production at Fort Detrick. With a master's degree in microbiology, Patrick had been a specialist in aircraft attacks in the 1960s, when the United States was experimenting with pathogen dispersal in the Pacific. Richard Spertzel, another veteran of the Detrick offensive program, was charged in 1994 with leading the United Nations search for Saddam's biological weapons. Moving easily between the intelligence community and media appearances, Alibek, Patrick, and Spertzel separately and, at times, together, insisted on the imminence of foreign bioterrorism attacks on America. Although their model of threat perception looked backward toward the Cold War, they were much sought after as authorities.

A fourth man, Dr. D. A. Henderson, knew less of the "dark arts" of biological weapons and yet, in the late 1990s, he became highly effective in warning about bioterrorism as a national security threat. Of the generation of Patrick and Spertzel, Henderson started his career at the Centers for Disease Control in Atlanta in 1955, where he led the Epidemic Intelligence Service.[24] The elite service (EIS) was invented to track Soviet germ attacks on America, during the time of the U.S. biological warfare program, which meant that Henderson was no stranger to Cold War "looking-glass" military strategies.[25] When no Soviet attacks occurred, trained EIS officers instead tracked strange diseases and their adventures became the source of many popular medical detective stories.[26] Henderson became best known for his leadership, from 1967 to 1977, of the World Health Organization (WHO) campaign to eradicate smallpox, after which he became the dean of the prestigious Johns Hopkins School of Public Health. In 1998, increasingly compelled by the bioterrorism threat, he came out of retirement to found a think tank, the Johns Hopkins Center for Civilian Biodefense Studies in Baltimore. Maryland Democratic Senator Barbara Mikulski arranged federal seed money for the new enterprise, as did the Alfred P. Sloane Foundation in New York.

At Henderson's center, strategies to counter mass bioterrorism, especially using anthrax and smallpox, flourished. The new crusade became the protection of the nation against a new apocalypse: foreign terrorist attacks against unprotected Americans with invisible, lethal germ weapons. Members of Congress and high government officials came to the center's conferences. Past and present USAMRIID commanders and scientists (among the latter, Art Friedlander and Peter Jahrling) and public health experts (including New York City's Marcelle Layton) participated in the consensus groups that the center organized to write a series of seminal articles on biological weapons— both as "select agent" pathogens doctors should learn more about and as threats of mass casualties. With a boost from Nobel Laureate Joshua Lederberg, who for decades had predicted the twin threats of germ weapons and emerging infectious diseases, the first two articles, on anthrax and smallpox, appeared in 1999 in the prestigious *Journal of the American Medical Association*.[27]

✦

As perception of the bioterrorism threat acquired legitimacy, its impact on USAMRIID became increasingly troublesome. In 1997, Clinton's defense secretary, William Cohen, began to argue for an increase in his department's domestic preparedness budget; its unregulated distribution of funds was widely criticized, but remained a favorite in Congress.[28] Cohen also wanted Congress to approve another defensive initiative. With the approval of the Joint Chiefs of Staff, he had decided to start the mandatory AVIP (Anthrax Vaccine Inoculation Program) for all 2.3 million military personnel, to replace the policy of selectively vaccinating only troops likely to be sent to conflict areas. A believer in military outsourcing, Cohen wanted a new private company, BioPort, to take over the supplies of AVA, produced at the time in the state of Michigan. BioPort would then sell the vaccine to the Pentagon for the new AVIP initiative and develop its own production capability. Congress was being asked to allocate a million dollars or more to help the company upgrade the Michigan facility in East Lansing.

In November, Cohen went on national television to make his case. A clean-cut former Republican senator, he hardly looked the menacing type. Yet, to illustrate the threat of an anthrax attack, he held up a five-pound bag of sugar and warned the nation that the same amount of spores sprayed by airplane over Washington would kill two-thirds of its population. Bill Patrick, who had given Secretary Cohen this spore calculation, understood that it was guesswork—but the public got the message. And Patrick was pleased that Cohen had publicized the bio-terrorism threat.[29]

Persuaded, Congress added more millions to the domestic prepared-ness budget and also approved Cohen's AVIP plan. (It helped that Admiral William J. Crowe Jr., former chairman of the Joint Chiefs of Staff, was on the BioPort board and testified on its behalf.) But the Michigan AVA stocks varied greatly in quality and BioPort employees at the East Lansing facility lacked the skills to institute quality control. Displeased with BioPort's failure to meet product standards, in November 1999 the Food and Drug Administration refused certification. The U.S. Army then instructed USAMRIID and its anthrax experts, including John Ezzell and Bruce Ivins, to help evaluate the potency of BioPort's stocks so that the company could regain FDA approval.

They all pitched in, but at the time of this instruction, in February 2000, Bruce Ivins fell into a serious depression. AVIP and the BioPort project raked up the continuing controversy linking AVA and the Gulf War syndrome which, circulating on the Internet, had a growing audi-ence among soldiers and their families.[30] Ultimately, over 400 enlisted men and women, fearful of negative side effects, refused to be vacci-nated and were dishonorably discharged.[31] When National Guard pilots with the same trepidations began resigning, Congress started to hold hearings. Dignified, with a neatly clipped moustache, Colonel Art Friedlander became the USAMRIID spokesman who defended AVIP as necessary against Iraq's known threat.[32]

An unexpected consequence of Cohen's sugar-bag speech was a national surge in anonymous anthrax hoax letters and white powder sightings. The alarms they caused threw emergency responders into high gear and consumed the very domestic preparedness funds Con-gress had approved in the name of counter-bioterrorism. The FBI, with both a WMD division and a Hazardous Materials Response Unit in Quantico, Virginia, on the vast Marine Corps base that also houses the FBI Academy, was charged with evaluating the incidents that rose above the level of pranks. From 1998 through 2000, Bureau agents, assisted by U.S. Postal Service inspectors, evaluated several hundred possible threats—and found none that were real. Along the way, they pursued rabid anti-Semites and anti-abortion protesters and discovered among the perpetrators a handful of errant schoolboys.[33] Still, most of those who sent letters were never caught. In time, the hoax incidents became like an alarm that went off too often while federal policy remained focused on mass bioterror attacks.

In retrospect, the most important repercussion of the late 1990s anthrax hoaxes was that the FBI turned to John Ezzell and his Special Pathogen unit, with its high-containment lab, to help with analyses. In one notorious instance in February 1998, the FBI arrested Larry Wayne Harris, a microbiologist who was fervently publicizing the Iraqi threat, for possession of a sample of *Bacillus anthracis*. Consulted, Ezzell was able to prove it was only a harmless vaccine strain.[34] The highly publicized arrest of Harris provoked another rise in powder hoax incidents. With the FBI as a client, Ezzell gained experience with standards for trial-worthy evidence. He was also asked to lecture FBI recruits about responses to potential anthrax attacks.[35] Ezzell's work had integrity; he was trusted and so, by extension, was USAMRIID and its other anthrax experts.

✦

President Clinton admitted to having nightmares about mass bioterrorism: a single living cell on a petri dish could in a day generate a colony of "living weapons."[36] To promote the integration of Health and Human Services into biodefense planning, he gave that department (rather than Defense) control over domestic preparedness programs. This move led to two other innovations: the National Strategic Stockpile, to ensure the availability of antibiotics and vaccines in the event of a mass attack, and the Laboratory Response Network, a plan to equip public health laboratories nationwide with the resources to identify select agents. In case of emergency, the CDC would oversee both— verify the detection of select pathogens like anthrax and transport medicines and extra medical personnel to the attack sites. Clinton also designated the FBI as the lead federal agency in the event of an actual bioterrorist incident.

After Clinton left Washington, the bioterrorism threat seemed to lose its importance; the new administration and Congress were less enthusiastic about biodefense. By the end of August 2001, USAMRIID was considering a full retreat from anthrax vaccine research, an area fraught with legal liabilities and competition from commercial companies. Bruce Ivins, unaware of the possible change, had just received an anthrax booster shot and was eager for work. Instead, he was in for a jolt. When the head of the Bacteriology Division asked if he would mind switching to research on glanders (also known as stable boy's disease), a deadly but hardly a developed weapons agent, Ivins was flummoxed. According to co-workers, he replied, "I am an anthrax researcher. This is what I do!"[37]

＊

Less than two weeks later, on the morning of September 11, one jet plane and then a second crashed into the Twin Towers at the World Trade Center in New York City, killing all aboard along with nearly 3,000 people trapped in the buildings.[38] The filmed collapse of both towers was transmitted around the world. A half hour later, a third plane dove into the Pentagon's E Ring, killing 184.[39] A half hour after that, a fourth plane, diverted off course by passengers who defied the hijackers, crashed in a field in rural Pennsylvania, with no survivors.

The millions of Americans who witnessed the 9/11 attacks on television were at first unsure what had happened or who was in charge. President Bush, visiting Florida, was at first whisked away on Air Force One; Vice President Cheney took refuge in a bunker. At the Pentagon, Secretary Rumsfeld disappeared for an hour and then reappeared as a stretcher-bearer helping victims. Senate majority leader Tom Daschle and other members of Congress were escorted by police to disparate safe havens, while thousands of government employees who worked on the Hill fled in panic to the Metro or their cars or, as happened in New York City, simply ran away as fast and far as they could. At the FBI, its new director, Robert Mueller III—who was sworn in on September 4—mobilized 6,000 agents in an all-out effort to find out what had caused arguably the worst national security failure in U.S. history.

In New York City, Mayor Rudolph Giuliani, emerging as a dynamic force, urged his stunned constituents to concentrate on "getting the city through this, surviving and being stronger for it."[40] Another New Yorker, NBC star newscaster Tom Brokaw, rushed downtown to the crash scene and began a 12-hour vigil of nonstop reporting. "This is war," he declared to viewers after he saw the carnage. "This is a declaration and an execution of an attack on the United States." Then, and in the following days of on-site broadcasts, he never lost his professional demeanor.

On 9/11, John Ezzell was visiting the CDC, which was evacuated for fear it might become a terrorist target. As a result, he missed the first transport of containers of air from the Pentagon site to Detrick, sent for analysis at his Special Pathogens lab. The mordant fear among government officials was that the terrorists had used the plane crashes to launch an anthrax attack. The hourly deliveries of air samples went on for a week, bringing physical reminders of the site where young first responders, overwhelmed by the stench of burning flesh, had to be replaced by experienced soldiers and FBI agents. At his office, Ivins heard the dispatchers as they arrived at the Diagnostics Division next door—every new package potentially brought proof that al Qaeda was in possession of *Bacillus anthracis*. At night, two minutes from Detrick's main gate, he and his wife and two teenage children could hear the sirens of the squad cars as they approached.

No anthrax pathogens were found in the Pentagon air samples or in similar samples taken at Ground Zero in New York. Still, the 9/11 attacks made it seem anything was possible; fear persisted at the highest levels in Washington that al Qaeda's next attack on America would be bioterrorism.

In group therapy for depression at the time, Ivins could barely control his anger against the 9/11 terrorists. At night he sought refuge alone in his laboratory, where stored flasks of virulent anthrax spores were in his charge. But this phase passed. When in September the local Red Cross offered courses on disaster response—how to search for victims in rubble, how to bandage their wounds and secure them to stretchers—Ivins signed up and then joined as a regular volunteer, citing his anthrax expertise. He felt he had something to offer, especially, he told the organizers, if there were a biological weapons attack.[41]

CHAPTER 1

THE DIAGNOSIS

Anthrax is a disease of animals, particularly sheep and cattle, and to a lesser extent man, caused by infection with *Bacillus anthracis*.

—C. A. MIMMS,
The Pathogenesis of Infectious Disease, 1987

Wednesday, September 26, 2001. Bob Stevens, a fifty-six-year-old senior photo editor for the national supermarket tabloid *The Sun*, was in his third-floor cubicle, hunched over his computer. The modern glass and concrete building where he worked, set in a landscaped office park in Boca Raton, Florida, was owned by *The Sun*'s parent company, American Media, Inc. (AMI), whose headquarters were in Manhattan and whose business was big-circulation, celebrity journalism. *The Sun* and the *National Enquirer* were its weekly flagship moneymakers.

Stevens was rushing to meet his deadlines before taking a long weekend off. He and his wife, Maureen, were driving to North Carolina to visit their daughter Casey, a student at the state university at Charlotte. Bob was a Brit, gregarious and cheerful. Maureen, equally good-humored but more shy, had been born in Ireland. They had arrived in America in the early 1970s, when they were still in their twenties, and started a new life together. They became American citizens and settled in Florida, happily so. Both had been married before and were already parents, with three children between them, and then they had Casey, the last to leave the nest.

Bob had planned a packed agenda. He wanted to set out for Charlotte at the crack of dawn, go hiking with Casey on the Appalachian slopes near Chimney Rock, take a side trip to Durham to meet her boyfriend who was in school there, and then on Monday he and Maureen would drive back to their home in Lantana, about ten miles south of Palm Beach.

While Stevens edited photos on his computer, another AMI employee, Ernesto Blanco, was working in the first-floor mail room. A Cuban émigré, the wiry Blanco was seventy-two but had a thick head of hair and the stamina of a much younger man. Every morning he drove the company van to the local post office to pick up 10,000 to 15,000 pieces of pre-bundled mail, which he brought back, sorted, and, using a wheeled cart, delivered to the building's three floors of offices. Stephanie Dailey, a young woman with a desk near the mail room, often helped him when she wasn't busy opening mail for the *National Enquirer*. Ernesto never minded doing the work himself. Every morning he took the train from North Miami to Boca, eager to start his work day, sorry when it was done. All his life he'd been like that—full of energy, never missing a day of work. Six years before, thinking it was time for retirement, he'd sold his small upholstery business in Miami—and almost immediately grew bored. "AMI saved my life," he often said. "Hanging around the house, doing nothing, that was driving me crazy."[1]

The year before, Bob Stevens had also tried retirement. After nearly thirty years of rushing to meet deadlines, he thought he'd like a life of biking, fishing, and gardening. He and Maureen, a retired secretary, could finally travel. But like Blanco, he missed work, and he missed his friends at AMI, a company that prided itself on a family-like atmosphere. In six months, he was back at his desk, editing photos of celebrity newsmakers.

As planned, early on Thursday, September 27, Bob and Maureen Stevens left for North Carolina. Robert (as his wife preferred to call him) loved driving and was in a great mood. Maureen, who was recovering from a sinus infection and taking the antibiotic Ciprofloxacin (Cipro), counted on his enthusiasm. They both missed having Casey at home. As they traveled north, they talked and laughed and made plans to celebrate their twenty-seventh wedding anniversary, which was coming up on October 18.[2]

The next day, Friday, after Ernesto Blanco finished sorting the mail at AMI, he felt weak and feverish and was shivering like never before in his life. Concerned, Daniel Rotstein, the personnel director, arranged for a company driver to take the older man home to North Miami. On Saturday Blanco felt better but bewildered and a bit embarrassed. He'd always prided himself on his iron constitution, and now his wife, along with his stepdaughter and her husband, were hovering over him. On Sunday, the feeling of weakness returned, this time with chest pains.

Up in North Carolina, on the Sunday drive from Chapel Hill to Durham, flulike symptoms of weakness, fever, and chills hit Bob Stevens like a blow. He crawled into the backseat, letting Maureen take the wheel. On the highway, they kept passing exit signs for local hospitals; Bob adamantly refused to stop for help. After a few hours of rest at Casey's boyfriend's apartment, he felt much better. On Monday morning, he and his wife set off on the return trip to Florida. Bob, although quieter than usual, drove the whole way. They made it home at around 5 p.m., and tired, went to bed at eight.

That same Monday, Ernesto Blanco was admitted to Cedars Hospital in North Miami. His physician there, Carlos Omenaca, was baffled by his condition, which at first seemed like a heart attack. Blanco had some sort of infection, but what was it? Omenaca tried different combinations of intravenous antibiotics, but the weakness and chest pains persisted. Prostrate, Blanco listened to the bedside discussion of his mystery illness. "My father thinks it's from an animal," Dr. Omenaca remarked. "He used to be a farmer." Those were the last words that Blanco remembered hearing before he slipped into a coma.

At 1 a.m. on Tuesday, Maureen Stevens woke to the sound of her husband retching in the bathroom. He was fully dressed and this time, dizzy and weak, he made no objection when Maureen insisted on driving him to the John F. Kennedy Medical Center (JFK) in nearby Atlantis, just five minutes away. Bob had been a patient there before for minor heart problems, and his daughter Heidi had a job in the hospital's administration. Once checked in, Stevens was given a bed to lie down on and, to calm his nausea, a sedative. Then he fell unconscious and, with his vital signs failing, was transferred to intensive care.

A physical examination and routine tests shed no light on Stevens' sudden collapse—it wasn't a heart attack or stroke or pneumonia or trauma from a fall. Maureen took the attitude that no news was good news. Around 5 a.m. she went home to sleep and returned promptly at eight for Robert's scheduled spinal tap. She and Heidi watched in anguish as, still unconscious, he struggled against the painful procedure.

Larry Bush, the hospital's chief of infectious diseases, knew that otherwise healthy adults don't suddenly collapse without cause. A transplant from the urban Northeast, he focused on the clouds, letting others search for silver linings. In his field, his pessimism had yet to let him down. Attuned to the bioterrorism threat, he had in his office a well-read copy of a 1999 article on anthrax as a biological weapon, co-authored by USAMRIID's Art Friedlander and a group put together by the Johns Hopkins Center for Civilian Biodefense Studies. When Bush examined Stevens' spinal fluid under a microscope, he found in it a proliferation of rod-shaped bacteria, like jumbled chains of bamboo, certainly a type of bacillus. Bush ran a simple test and discovered that the bacteria were "gram positive," one of the characteristics of *Bacillus anthracis*. To be sure, Bush needed more sophisticated tests, the kind that, according to protocol, should be done at the Florida Department of Health laboratory in Jacksonville, which was part of the Laboratory Response Network created under the Clinton administration. For this he needed an assist from a public health official.

Bush telephoned someone he knew on a first-name basis: Dr. Jean Malecki, head of the Palm Beach County Public Health Department. Nearly twenty years before, Malecki had been his colleague at JFK, when both were newly minted infectious disease specialists, he from the University of Pennsylvania, she from New York University.

The dynamic Malecki, six feet tall with long red hair, was already a local legend. In the public eye for nearly twenty years, starting with the early 1980s AIDS fatalities linked to a Florida dentist, and through dozens of high-profile incidents since then, she was in charge of the health of two million county residents and she counted them all as her people. With Florida on alert after 9/11, she had convened a meeting of 200 first responders to assess the potential bioterrorism threat.[3] At 2:15 p.m., when Bush's call was forwarded to her, a panel of experts had just finished discussing whether terrorists could effectively use a crop duster to spray anthrax spores. In Florida, the front-page news, based on FBI reports, was that before 9/11 al Qaeda operatives had circulated under cover in Palm Beach, Delray, Venice, Hollywood, and Jacksonville and that, while taking flying lessons, they had inquired about crop dusters.

Advising Malecki to sit down, Bush explained that he had a patient who might have inhalation anthrax and asked her how soon she could come to the hospital to give her evaluation. The patient had presented as a meningitis case, with signs of general acute infection, but Malecki trusted Bush's judgment. Tied up with her meeting on domestic preparedness, she told him that the best she could do was seven that evening. The patient's history of possible exposure would be vital, but with Stevens in a coma Malecki would have to get the details from his wife. "I'll have my staff bring an anthrax questionnaire," she told Bush.

Public health professionals work in essentially two modalities. One is routine preventive management—making sure schoolchildren have their vaccinations, pregnant women their vitamins, and old people their flu shots, and that chronic and infectious disease incidents are monitored. The other is emergency mode, the team mobilization to contain disasters that is the equivalent of marshaling troops for war. A seasoned administrator, Malecki handled the former every day, but she was no stranger to real-life emergencies or mass attack models. In the late 1990s Malecki had participated in two exercises for responding to mass anthrax attacks that pushed the emergency response model beyond the envelope—which was exactly where Bush's patient, if this were the index case of a larger outbreak, might be heading. The exercises were designed to teach local authorities—herself, hospital officials, police, firefighters, and the WMD experts from FBI field offices—in fact, the very people at her meeting—to make rational decisions that would, if the threat were real, trigger state and federal government rescue responses. The effect should be like a computer game in which communication channels light up, the troops arrive with medical supplies, and hundreds if not thousands of lives are saved from deadly anthrax.

Throughout the response, public health officials had to stay calm and keep the affected community informed, cooperative, and free from panic, or the rescue effort could fall apart. Since 9/11, though, the public was primed for panic, and anthrax and other disease attacks were being touted widely in the media as the next worst terrorism.

Bush's phone call left Malecki with some troubling uncertainties. The minute she asked Jacksonville to test for anthrax, alarms would ring in government offices from Florida to Washington. If the results were positive, louder alarms would ring and the media would be all over the story, no matter how the man at JFK had been exposed. Malecki had spent years cultivating good relations with the press. Did she have enough capital with them to keep communication focused on education and not scare-mongering headlines?

Unfortunately, fear of anthrax was hardly irrational. Its ferocious natural cycle uses the host mammal as a live incubator that must die for *B. anthracis* to multiply and survive. Within the host's body, the proliferating bacteria rapidly cause massive internal hemorrhage so that, bursting from every orifice in waves of blood and fluid, this new generation of microbes can assume their sturdy spore form and await a new host to infect. As the disease evolved over many centuries, a grazing animal feeding in a spore-contaminated field was usually the next victim. By learning to live successfully off livestock, human beings became potential hosts. When twentieth-century armies developed *B. anthracis* as a weapon, the potential for the human host population expanded to mass targets, not what nature intended.

Another uncertainty was how federal agencies would react, even to a single confirmed anthrax case. State health officials in Tallahassee would have to invite the CDC (Centers for Disease Control and Prevention in Atlanta) to investigate: anthrax was not endemic in Florida and the last U.S. case of inhalational anthrax dated back thirty years. If evidence pointed to an intentional cause—an act of malice against a single individual, or worse, a mass attack—the FBI would step in as the lead agency to conduct a criminal investigation. If more cases of illness emerged, beyond what Malecki's department, the state, and the CDC could handle, Washington would send the Federal Emergency Management Agency to coordinate a disaster response. Malecki hoped that Bush was sounding a false alarm. Whatever had happened or would happen, she had to stay calm.

When Malecki arrived at the hospital that evening, Bush led her to his patient's room. "I've put him in isolation," he explained, "and he's on broad-spectrum antibiotics." They put on masks and gloves before they entered.

Stevens lay on the narrow bed in a coma, attached to a respirator and an array of drip bags and monitors. He was a big man, husky but muscular. His wife, Maureen, also masked and gloved, sat next to him holding his hand. When Maureen Stevens stood, the look she gave Dr. Malecki was more inquisitive than worried. No one had mentioned the possibility of anthrax in order not to upset her unnecessarily. Instead, Dr. Bush had told her that her husband had a general infection, meningitis, that was affecting his brain and that more tests had to be done. While Maureen waited, she wanted to stay at her husband's side in case he should wake, but she understood that the county health department had some questions for her and that its director, Dr. Malecki, was here to help.

Three of Malecki's assistants then met with Maureen in a small conference room. They had written the questionnaire themselves, on the fly, after finding nothing available from the CDC. In her soft, precise Irish accent, Maureen gave them a detailed account of the trip to North Carolina and described her husband's everyday routine and his hobbies. She answered every question, even the odd ones. Yes, she kept a clean house and frequently laundered their clothes, sometimes daily. No, they had not been at any country fairs or crowded events. Yes, he liked genuine leather shoes. No, as far as she knew, he didn't handle mail at work.

She had no idea how these questions could help her husband's diagnosis, but realizing these officials were nearly as puzzled as she was, Maureen summoned new energy and told them everything she could remember, including how on their hike Robert had stopped to drink from a mountain stream, which he (unlike Maureen and Casey) trusted was unpolluted.

After going over Stevens' case records and viewing the bacilli from his spinal fluid, Malecki reached the same startling conclusion as Bush: the patient was likely infected with anthrax. By 10 p.m., a sample of the bacteria from the spinal tap was on its way by express mail to the Jacksonville laboratory. Phil Lee, one of the lab's microbiologists and its biological defense coordinator, had recently returned from a course on anthrax analysis at the CDC, given by Tanja Popovic, head of the CDC's Anthrax Laboratory, with an unrivaled reputation for *B. anthracis* identification. In 1989, Popovic had come to the CDC as a Fulbright scholar from Croatia and found her niche in the lab science of domestic preparedness. By October 2001, she had trained sixty public health employees like Lee to recognize anthrax in their own laboratories, all part of the nation's Laboratory Response Network.

As Malecki expected, her Tuesday night request to Jacksonville rang alarm bells. When her office opened the next morning, two FBI agents were waiting for a transcript of Maureen Stevens' interview, which Malecki's staff, having worked through the night, had ready by 10 a.m. The interview, with Malecki joining in, had lasted until nearly eleven the night before. Maureen Stevens would have stayed even later, if asked. As one interviewer reflected, her narrative, with all its careful detail, was "a love story" told by a wife who wanted her husband brought back to health, to her.[4] In addition, Malecki alerted Steve Wiersma, the state epidemiologist, and John Ogwunobi, the young pediatrician who had just assumed the post of Florida's secretary of health.

At the Jacksonville lab, Phil Lee proceeded with the first and then the second of the tests he'd learned at the CDC. Both involved growing and staining the bacteria to elicit an important identifying trait: dangerous anthrax bacilli are distinguished by a capsule, a casing essential for virulence. The third and most conclusive test, which had been developed at USAMRIID, involved exposing the bacilli to a virus called gamma phage that would invade and destroy them if they were truly *B. anthracis.* By late afternoon, the first two tests had registered positive—the distinguishing capsule was present. Larry Bush called for the results, but Lee was reluctant to draw a definitive conclusion. The third test had just been started and could take twelve hours or more. Lee, to make sure he was doing everything right, contacted Tanja Popovic at the CDC, who calmed his apprehensions. As far as she could tell, Lee was being meticulous and should reach a valid diagnosis.[5]

In Palm Beach, awaiting Lee's results, Malecki began planning a three-team public health investigation to determine the source of Stevens' infection—strictly by the book. One team would search the Stevens house and garden, another would track possible exposure sources outside the home, and a third would investigate his workplace, the AMI building. Stevens' recent trip to North Carolina meant that public health officials there might have to check with hospitals for any suspicious meningitis cases and with veterinarians for any unusual livestock or other animal deaths. A visit to Casey Stevens' apartment and that of her boyfriend—where Bob had taken a nap—would also be necessary. As a precaution, Malecki telephoned AMI in Boca Raton with the message that if any other employees had an unusual illness or skin infection, they should call her department right away.

Lee left his laboratory at 10 p.m., with no result yet from the gamma phage test. When Bush called the next morning around eight, the result was in, but Lee, knowing the fallout was going to be calamitous, hesitated to tell Bush about it. Irate, Bush reminded him that it was *his* patient whose life was at stake. Lee then revealed that the gamma phage had destroyed the bacilli: Bob Stevens had anthrax.

The news went immediately to Tallahassee and John Ogwunobi, who brought the news to Governor Jeb Bush. Once he was updated, the governor had one question: "Is the disease contagious?"[6] His foremost interest was in keeping the public panic level down. Since 9/11, he had been focused on protecting potential terrorist targets in Florida—Cape Canaveral and Disney World were two of them—while at the same time worrying about the precipitous drop in tourism to the state. People were afraid to fly, which could spell disaster for Florida's winter economy. Tourists would be even more likely to stay away if Florida were hit by a contagious disease outbreak, especially if it were intentionally spread. To the governor's relief, there was no cause to worry about contagion—and the single case in Lantana might have been naturally caused.

At the JFK Medical Center, Larry Bush consulted with hospital administrators and his staff about what steps to take next. Not only the governor's office, but the White House, cabinet secretaries, the National Security Council, and a network of federal counter-terrorism officials were being alerted to the diagnosis, which could signal the start of a mass attack—or nothing more than an isolated infection. In reaction to rumors, media inquiries had already started. The decision was to hold a press conference that afternoon, at the hospital, to make an official announcement.

◆

In all the excitement, no one had told Maureen Stevens about her husband's diagnosis. At noon, she left his bedside to pick up photographs from their North Carolina trip, as reminders to talk about with Robert. She and Heidi acted on the presumption that, although unconscious, he could still hear their voices and that they needed to stay connected with him. After picking up the photos Maureen made a brief stop at home. As the news of Bob's hospitalization spread, the answering machine became full of get-well messages from friends and co-workers and, despite the heat, a kind neighbor had volunteered to mow the lawn. Maureen was in the kitchen when Dr. Malecki telephoned.

"I have some difficult news for you," she said. Malecki then explained that Bob had contracted a disease called inhalational anthrax. She cautioned that his chances of survival were not good. The infection had been treated late, after it had spread.

"Is there no hope?" Maureen asked. She remembered the hospital exit signs between Charlotte and Durham—and Robert's refusal to stop.

"There's always hope," Malecki assured her, sparing Maureen the facts about the ferocity of the disease. Then she added that word of the diagnosis had necessarily spread and would soon become public. "There's a press conference scheduled for two o'clock at the hospital."

As soon as she hung up the phone, Maureen began contacting the children. She called Casey in North Carolina, who immediately made arrangements to take the next plane home. Maureen reached Heidi at JFK, just minutes before a senior administrator took her aside to tell her about her father's diagnosis. Bob's son Neil was already driving down from Tallahassee, where he lived, and Maureen's daughter Tania was arriving the next evening from Scotland. Still in her kitchen, Maureen telephoned the news to Daniel Rotstein, the AMI personnel director who had been in close touch with her since Bob had fallen ill. He was shocked and then he suddenly apologized. "Maureen, I'll call you back. There's something important I have to do right away."

That something important was to find out what had happened to Ernesto Blanco, who had yet to return to work. When Rotstein learned he was at Cedars Hospital, he tried to reach his physician there but couldn't get through. Might Blanco have the same disease as Bob Stevens? The implications for the company and other employees in Boca could be terrible.

Just before the press conference at JFK, Larry Bush met with Maureen Stevens to explain the anthrax diagnosis and that this particular disease was not contagious. Maureen didn't recognize most of the other people gathered around them, except for some hospital staff.

Events were moving faster than she could comprehend. She had just one question for Dr. Bush: "Is my husband going to die?"

Bush repeated what Malecki had said, that when treated late in its course inhalation anthrax is nearly always fatal. But, like Malecki, he told her there was always hope. Just the idea of hope gave her strength and calmed her.

But then, abruptly, Maureen was forced to confront the possibility that her husband had been deliberately attacked. She signed one form permitting the FBI to search the Stevens home and property the next day. She signed another form given her by officials from the Atlanta office of the Postal Inspection Service, the plainclothes criminal investigation division of the U.S. Postal Service. That signed form gave the postal inspectors the right to appropriate and examine the family's mail. Perhaps, they explained, someone had personally targeted her husband by sending an envelope or package with anthrax powder in it. Another postal attack might be coming—a frightening thought. A Miami FBI agent was detailed to watch over her. It was dawning on Maureen that the news about her husband's diagnosis had been passed along to strangers—to hospital officials, the FBI, postal investigators, even to the governor of Florida and the president of the United States—without her knowing anything.

Thinking only of her husband, she hurried to the new room where he was sequestered under guard, surrounded by even more medical equipment and nurses. With no threat of contagion, the masks and gloves were no longer necessary. Afraid of losing him, she stroked his forehead, and whispered words of comfort.

The press conference was held on the first floor of the hospital, off the lobby in the conference room usually used for medical lectures, and at least fifty news representatives from local and national print, radio, and television outlets jockeyed to get near the speakers. State epidemiologist Steve Wiersma had arrived from Tallahassee. Jean Malecki was by far most familiar to the Florida press, but the star of the event was Larry Bush, who had flagged a case that other physicians might have misdiagnosed or dismissed as a medical mystery.

Privately, Bush believed the maxim expressed in the 1999 Johns Hopkins article on anthrax, that any new anthrax case should be presumed intentional until proven otherwise. But he, Malecki, and hospital officials agreed beforehand to make no speculations about how

Stevens had contracted anthrax and certainly not to promote the idea that the case had anything to do with a bioterror attack. Instead, they announced that an unnamed hospital patient had contracted inhalational anthrax, a diagnosis confirmed by the Florida Department of Health Bureau of Laboratories, and they described how medical tests supported this diagnosis. By way of instruction, they presented a recent x-ray showing unusual mediastinal widening—an enlargement in the midchest area often characteristic of this form of the disease. About his patient, Dr. Bush commented dispassionately, "He is critically ill, but hopefully he'll respond to treatment."[7]

✦

The sensational news of the Florida diagnosis went out immediately on the wire services, sparking national attention. In Washington, Tommy Thompson, secretary of Health and Human Services, interrupted a White House press conference to announce the news, but he too insisted, "This incident has nothing to do with terrorism."

Behind the scenes, President Bush was worried that the Florida case was the first sign of a mass attack.[8] Since 9/11, the president had been taking Cipro, on the advice of a federal consultant on bioterrorism threats. President Clinton's dread of an apocalyptic outbreak intentionally inflicted on Americans was based on nightmarish conjectures. For Bush, the Stevens diagnosis and its implications crossed the line to the fact of an anthrax infection and a possible "second blow" struck against the nation. As the United States moved closer to attacking the Taliban in Afghanistan—the first missile assault was only days away—there were fears in the administration that al Qaeda would retaliate with bioterrorism. Vice President Cheney, officially in seclusion as tension mounted, was anxious about both germ and chemical terrorism. After 9/11, he kept a gas mask and protective clothing within easy reach and he was nearly always accompanied by a physician.[9]

From Florida's capital, the call for assistance went to the CDC, which was at some disadvantage. The 9/11 attacks had diverted some one hundred of its field officers to New York City and exhausted them with the extraordinary public health demands of a traumatized city. The CDC's usual mission was the statistical documentation and prevention of the nation's everyday health care problems, which ran to chronic diseases like heart and kidney ailments and cancers common in industrialized nations with older populations. It was only late in the Clinton administration that the centers were put in charge of the nationwide domestic preparedness program and of organizing the national Laboratory Response Network and the stockpile of emergency antibiotics and vaccines. At the CDC's National Center for Infectious Diseases, its director, Jim Hughes, had a global perspective on disease prevention, and its acting deputy director, Julie Gerberding, came from a background in hospital and health care safety. Given the rarity of anthrax cases—only eighteen in the United States in the previous hundred years—there was no expert with field experience who understood dose response and the random risk of even a single inhaled spore. A retired CDC officer, Phil Brachman, had conducted studies of inhalational anthrax cases among American textile and tannery workers in the 1950s and 1960s.[10] But Brachman's research, done with U.S. Army cooperation, had been neglected by the younger generation of epidemiologists focused on contemporary plagues: AIDS, malaria, cholera, drug-resistant tuberculosis, and other dangerous diseases. Not even the 1994 publication of the Sverdlovsk investigation results and their implications for dose response were well known among CDC infectious disease experts. By far the person in the strongest position was Tanja Popovic, the head of the Anthrax Laboratory, with a staff of forty-three and expertise to spare. But at the time not even she understood the enormous difference between preparing for bioterrorism and the emergence of an actual case of deliberately caused anthrax.

The Stevens diagnosis also rang alarms at the FBI, which had intensely combed Florida, including Lantana, for the pre-9/11 presence of al Qaeda operatives. At its Quantico, Virginia, campus, the Bureau's WMD division had spent years tracking international and homegrown terrorists. There chemist Benjamin Garrett had long studied biological and chemical weapons history, as well as handled the strange cases—like the 1984 poisoning of salad bars with salmonella by the Rajneesh cult in Oregon—that came with the chem-bio watch. After 9/11, Garrett's division was on high alert for another al Qaeda attack, as was the Bureau's Hazardous Material Response Unit (HMRU), also at Quantico, where microbiologist Doug Beecher, experienced in pathogen detection, worked. These and other experts, a veritable brain trust, would prove key in responding to the Florida and subsequent crises. But on October 4, the Bureau, concentrating fully on its 9/11 investigation and unsure if a crime had actually been committed, delayed coordinating a top-down response.

Still, the FBI had the flexibility of a large, decentralized organization whose field agents could be locally deployed. Two of them quickly drove from Jacksonville to Atlanta to deliver a sample of Stevens' bacteria to Tanja Popovic so that she could verify Lee's results at the CDC's Anthrax Laboratory. Carefully growing the bacilli in culture medium (which could take another day or more) was essential to accurate identification at the CDC's gold standard level.

The missing clue was strain identification: Which of the forty or so known virulent anthrax strains had infected this patient in Florida? The Quantico brain trust turned immediately to Paul Keim, the Northern Arizona University scientist who had developed advanced methods for genetic strain identification and maintained a considerable archive of strains. Doug Beecher telephoned Keim to give him a heads-up. Beecher, experienced in hazardous material response, had previously visited Keim's lab and understood the science of *B. anthracis*. The message from Beecher to Keim was that a share of the CDC sample was being flown by a chartered plane to Flagstaff, where Keim himself should collect it for analysis.

Until 9/11, when his university put his lab under strict protective security, Keim's work life had been placidly academic, with a mix of intriguing microbial projects, not just ones on anthrax. Lanky and sandy-haired, Keim looked more like a graduate student than a professor. Late in the afternoon on October 4, though, Keim was about to enter the world of crime scene investigation.[11] He drove out onto the tarmac at the Flagstaff airport to meet the chartered plane, from which descended an attractive blond woman who handed him the box containing the bacteria from Stevens' spinal fluid. Speeding back to his laboratory, Keim organized his assistants to begin the process of matching its genetic markers against those in his archive of anthrax strains from around the world.

◆

At the U.S. Army Medical Institute for Infectious Diseases (USAMRIID) at Fort Detrick in Frederick, Maryland, the news of the Florida diagnosis sparked interest but caused no shock waves. The case, after all, was a civilian matter, unlike the analyses of air samples from the

Pentagon that USAMRIID's Special Pathogen lab, run by John Ezzell, had just finished.

Bruce Ivins, angry and withdrawn after the 9/11 attacks, seemed energized by the October 4 news of the Florida diagnosis. That afternoon and into the next morning, he fired off emails to colleagues to offer his ideas about the source of the exposure, which he theorized was natural, somehow from the environment. Although unaware of Beecher's recruitment of Paul Keim, he knew about the Anthrax Laboratory at the CDC. (His friend Ezzell had actually been there on 9/11, and was evacuated with everyone else from the CDC's main campus.) Ivins posted an email to the centers, to ask a perceptive question: Had its experts identified the strain and did they know if it was native to Florida? In fact, Tanja Popovic at the CDC was trying to identify the strain at the same time as Paul Keim.

But no return message was sent to Ivins. Even if the CDC hadn't been deluged with emails, Ivins' inquiry would have gone unanswered. Popovic understood that the Stevens diagnosis could embroil her and her bosses in a major bioterrorism incident—and that national security necessarily narrowed channels of communication.

＊

That evening, Bob Stevens' wife, his son, and his two daughters surrounded him with affection, taking turns holding his hands and keeping up a conversation about good times past and good times to come. Heidi went home early to her family. Later, near midnight, the rest of the Stevens family—Maureen, Neil, and Casey—wished Bob good night. As they reached the lobby, what seemed like a SWAT team burst through the main doors, backlit by klieg lights from the camera crews still waiting outside. It was a mixed group of county public health officers and FBI agents with a hurried request for blood samples from Maureen and Casey. The two were tired but consented. When the procedures were done, they dashed past the press lingering in the parking lot.

Arriving home, they found that a media blitz was waiting for them. Vans with satellite dishes were parked on both sides of the narrow street. In the glare of spotlights, reporters crowded the newly mowed front lawn. With microphones in hand, news anchors talked nonstop to cameras about their on-site coverage of the Stevens case. A swarm of reporters and photographers, avid for news about the victim, attempted to interview the family members as they ran for cover. The brightly lit, noisy broadcasts continued for hours. Finally, to block the lights, the Stevens family hung blankets and sheets over the windows.

✦

While the Stevens family tried to sleep, Paul Keim and his team worked through the night to identify the Florida anthrax bacteria. In the early morning, they finally matched them to the highly virulent Ames strain. The name, as they found out later, was a misnomer. The strain, from a Beefmaster heifer that died in Texas in 1981, had been shipped to USAMRIID with an envelope that bore the return address of Ames, Iowa. Iowa had nothing to do with the strain's origin, but the mistaken attribution stuck.

From his lab, Keim telephoned the news to the FBI and the Department of Energy (his two main funders) and then to the CDC.[12] That same day, Friday, October 5, at the CDC, Tanja Popovic corroborated Keim's discovery.

For Doug Beecher and others at the FBI in Quantico, the strain identification was a game changer: the Florida inquiry stopped being a public health inquiry and became a criminal investigation, one with heavy national security implications.[13] The Ames strain, found once in nature and never again, was currently used in defense research laboratories for testing vaccines and antibiotics and other protective interventions. The defense laboratories that possessed the Ames strain—whether government labs or private contractors, whether in the United States or in allied countries—would have to be determined. Since the intelligence community was engaged in anthrax research projects, the Bureau might hit what policy analysts called "the wall"—the separation between criminal investigation and intelligence activity that divided the internal organization of the FBI and blocked communication between the Bureau and the CIA.[14]

There was another, worse problem. According to Keim—and this was well known among anthrax researchers—the Ames strain, like other strains of anthrax, was so genetically conservative that it would be unlikely to vary in successive generations or from one laboratory sample to another. That is, it was fundamentally generic. The anthrax weapon was identified, but it no more had a distinct signature than a bottle of Tylenol pills. When a weapon was that generic, the criminal might never be found.[15]

By interagency agreement, the news of the Ames strain identification—which practically canceled out a natural source—was withheld from the press. From Florida to Washington, authorities were denying that the diagnosis had any connection to terrorism. To anyone listening to the news—the perpetrator included—no bioterrorist attack had taken place, or at least none had been launched that any terrorist group was claiming.

CHAPTER 2

THE CRIME

Terror is meant to strike us dumb.

—SUSAN NEIMAN, *Evil in Modern Thought*, 2002

Friday, October 5, 2001. Dressed for hot weather in a regulation short-sleeved white shirt with epaulettes and black trousers, Dr. Brad Perkins, a meningitis expert from the CDC's Special Pathogens branch, arrived in Florida with two junior assistants and a single objective: to determine the dimensions of the anthrax crisis. The key question was what population was at risk. If just a few people, the CDC might stand down and let local authorities do their job. If a larger population was in danger of infection, the CDC would assist in protecting those people. The operative word was *assist.* CDC officials gave advice, not orders; they never overrode state authorities.

Perkins was an officer in the CDC's elite Epidemic Intelligence Service (EIS), created in 1952 as a Cold War invention to track potential Soviet germ attacks on America. Its founder, Alexander Langmuir, had top-secret clearance and kept in close contact with Fort Detrick as the offensive program expanded. When the Soviet attacks failed to occur, the EIS became famous for its medical detective adventures—scientifically based discoveries of why indigent men in New York City turned blue, what new disease troubled Lyme, Connecticut, what went fatally wrong with a batch of polio vaccine, and many more—that were popularized by Berton Roueché in *The New Yorker*. At the CDC and beyond, those trained by EIS became an elite corps—Jeff Koplan, the CDC's director, was an EIS officer—who knew its microbial science and statistical epidemiology and how to take on tough field inquiries.

Perkins was stalwartly handsome and, with a disarming smile and a soft Alabama accent, adept at managing crises. At the time of the Florida diagnosis, the CDC could ill afford any adverse publicity or wrangling at the federal level. The transition from the Clinton to the Bush administration had put it under pressure to narrow its traditional public health mandate. Department of Health and Human Services Secretary Tommy Thompson, a former Republican Governor of Wisconsin, wanted Koplan to pull back from programs that aggravated one or another Bush constituency, namely, anti-smoking campaigns, workplace safety initiatives, and women's reproductive health education. Koplan, whose considerable public health career included participation in the World Health Organization smallpox eradication campaign and lending assistance to India after the horrendous Bhopal chemical explosion, balked. Thompson, although he lacked a medical background, designated himself the lead federal spokesman on the Florida case. The best strategy in Florida, Perkins' superiors in Atlanta believed, was to keep a low profile—not easy to do when anthrax was on the news day and night, increasing alarms about bioterrorism.

Perkins had no intention of adding to the disruption. If necessary, rather than put forth scare scenarios, he would advise the public about "medically insignificant" levels of anthrax contamination.[1] For example, trace amounts on surfaces were unlikely to cause harm, except perhaps a cutaneous infection, but that could be cured by taking antibiotics. About anthrax aerosols, the conventional wisdom at the CDC was that anthrax infection commenced only with the inhalation of 8,000 spores, a misinterpretation of old U.S. Army research.

After arriving in West Palm Beach, Perkins proceeded directly to the JFK Medical Center, where he consulted with Larry Bush, reviewed Bob Stevens' medical records, and examined the still-unconscious patient. Somewhat to his surprise, he found Stevens' wife and the three children optimistic that Bob would recover. From what Perkins could tell, Stevens was seriously ill, but he said nothing to discourage them— sometimes even the sickest patients made surprising comebacks.

Perkins next conferred with Jean Malecki and Steve Wiersma, the state epidemiologist who had come down from Tallahassee, about the direction the public health inquiry should take. A North Carolina investigation and surveillance for other cases had started but produced no leads.[2] FBI agents, aided by Malecki's staff, were at the Stevens home, taking environmental samples from the house—from clothes, shoes, hair brushes, the kitchen shelves, the refrigerator—and outside, from the potting shed and garden soil. Others were searching for clues at the feed and hardware and food stores that Stevens frequented. The third environment that needed testing was the American Media, Inc., office building down the highway in Boca Raton, where any trace of *B. anthracis* would tilt the investigation toward a deliberate terrorist attack. Perkins, with a mixed team from Malecki's department and the FBI's Miami office, would go there directly.

Perkins would also visit Ernesto Blanco, whose physician had reported his case; Blanco, who remained seriously ill at the North Miami hospital, could be another arrow pointing to the AMI building as a source. The announcement of the Stevens diagnosis had put area hospitals and physicians on alert for other recent cases of unexplained toxic shock. Any suspicious cases that emerged would have to be tested by the CDC Anthrax Laboratory or by Phil Lee and others at the Florida public health laboratory in Jacksonville.

As the public health authority in charge, Jean Malecki listened carefully to everything Perkins said. His judgments determined how quickly and to what extent her department could tap the crucial resources controlled by the CDC: antibiotics from the Strategic National Stockpile, test kits for individual exposure, environmental test equipment, backup CDC personnel, and the Anthrax Lab for bona fide sample analyses.

That afternoon, when Perkins and his team arrived at the AMI building, the media vans and reporters were already there in full force, on the hunt for the Stevens story. Perkins ordered the hazmat crew to sprint to the back entrance and garb up inside the building—not the usual procedure for investigating contamination, but the presumption was that just two places, Stevens' cubicle and the mail room, would reveal anthrax spores—not the whole building.

Inside, the AMI building looked like any other fairly new office setting; the company had relocated from Lantana the year before. It had fresh wall-to-wall carpeting, an open first floor with a library, cafeteria, and mail room, and above, two floors of cubicles and offices plus a parking garage with storage for news files. The crew of four took the elevator to the third floor and found the cubicle Bob Stevens used, which had been cordoned off the day before.

Following the protocol that Tanja Popovic had provided, the team used cotton swabs to carefully wipe the surfaces of Stevens' desk, his computer, its monitor and keyboard, the wastepaper basket (inside and out), and the nearby floor, walls, and air vents. As they worked, they placed each sample in a plastic bag marked with the precise location. Next they went to the first floor and took surface samples from Stevens' slot in the mail room.

Perkins wanted the swabs done well but quickly, without upsetting AMI employees. The workers, many of whom counted themselves Stevens' friends, were on edge. "Your worst day at work," he commented later, "must be when the CDC arrives in hazmat suits and you're unprotected."[3]

Perkins and his team interviewed AMI management and employees to get a sense of whether Bob Stevens had any enemies or if someone bore him a grudge. About three hundred people worked at this AMI office. Personnel director Daniel Rotstein and Stevens' co-workers described him as well liked, always congenial. Stevens' playful manipulation of photographs had caused a few lawsuits (one involving the movie star Raquel Welch), but those had been resolved and the company and Bob faced no complaints at present.

Nonetheless, some of Stevens' co-workers suggested that the tabloids were a magnet for nutty anonymous messages. They remembered gathering around Bob's cubicle on September 19 for a good laugh about a wacky letter that, in addition to proposing marriage to Jennifer Lopez, contained some powdered material and a Star of David medal. Being nearsighted, Bob had held it close to his face to read. But that letter or package (accounts differed) had been hauled away in the trash to be incinerated.

In the early afternoon, while Perkins and his team were at AMI, Maureen and the Stevens children decided to leave the hospital and go home for a short break. Bob seemed comfortable, he was surrounded by attendants, and the door to his room was guarded. A reporter dressed like a doctor had been found looking for Bob; now no one could enter the room without signing in. To protect the family, AMI had hired bodyguards from a local agency with the chivalrous name Paladin. Two of them were ready to drive the family home, but Casey, who had gone ahead, telephoned that the street was blocked by the media and FBI vehicles. Instead, with the bodyguards, the family went to the home of friends in Delray, about twenty minutes south of JFK. The hospital staff had given Maureen a pager to alert her if anything went wrong. The pager sounded just as she put her head down for a nap. The Stevens family rushed back to JFK, but as Dr. Bush told them when they arrived, they were ten minutes too late. Bob had died at 3:55 p.m., without regaining consciousness. After all the medical equipment—the respirator, tubes, and wires—was disconnected and removed, in grief and shock, they surrounded him.

Later the family's two bodyguards escorted them home. The media circus on their street had intensified, with more lights and cameras and commotion. Photographers had paid for perches on the neighbors' roofs to get the best shots of the grieving family. That evening Maureen's daughter Tania arrived but was too late to see her stepfather alive; FBI agents drove her home from the airport to a street ablaze with television lights and noisy with broadcasters.

Bob Stevens' death was the lead story on the Friday news, but how he'd contracted anthrax was open to speculation. Earlier that day, on national television, Secretary Thompson confused the issue by suggesting that drinking polluted spring water had caused Stevens' illness, not likely in a case of inhalational anthrax.

Brad Perkins was sitting in an AMI office talking with employees when a phone call brought the news of Stevens' death. A pall settled over the room, and then, as word traveled, it spread throughout the building. The company allowed all the employees to go home early. As they left—upset for the Stevens family, unsure of their own risks— some cried and hugged each other.

Meanwhile, Perkins hurried to Cedars Medical Center, where he reviewed Blanco's medical records and interviewed his physician, Dr. Omenaca. Admitted on Monday, October 1, Blanco definitely suffered from toxic shock, just like Stevens, but his x-ray showed no marked widening in the midchest area and his blood tests and spinal tap were negative. The various combinations of antibiotics he had received might have affected his test results—killing the rampaging bacteria—or he could be suffering from another mysterious disease. Still unconscious, Blanco was unable to say anything about suspicious mail; later he remembered feeling the pain of that spinal tap.

Despite Blanco's condition, a nasal swab—the insertion of a long Q-tip deep into the nasal passages—was performed to test for any residue of spores he may have inhaled. Along with the AMI samples, the swab was packaged and flown express to the CDC, for testing at the Anthrax Lab. As a precaution, Blanco was put on intravenous Cipro.

❖

At USAMRIID, as Stevens' death dominated the news, Bruce Ivins complained to colleagues about how little information was available about the case.[4] All the media speculation was so frustrating—how was the nation supposed to mobilize against the threat? His co-workers were used to his tendency to raise alarms. On 9/11, after the attack on the Pentagon, he'd raced through the corridors of Building 1425 yelling for everyone to evacuate. As his colleague John Ezzell commented later, the reaction was rational—given Detrick's proximity to Washington, it was officially evacuated—but it was the wrong way to convey the message.[5]

Ivins' family was equally used to his retreating to his lab when he was stressed. That Friday, October 5, as he had done the night before and several weeks earlier, Ivins left home after dinner and went to his laboratory, where he stayed alone until almost 1 a.m.

❖

Early the next morning, with a team to help him, the CDC's chief medical examiner Sherif Zaki arrived from Atlanta at the office of his Palm Beach counterpart, pathologist Lisa Flannagan, to prepare for the autopsy of Bob Stevens' body. It was a bloody procedure with some risks of cutaneous exposure; everyone involved had to gown up and wear masks, face shields, three layers of gloves, hair coverings, and rubber boots.[6] Flannagan was cooperating—she would make the initial incisions and cut back the ribs to expose the chest cavity—because the case was important and the soft-spoken Zaki promised that the premises would afterward be thoroughly disinfected.

Egyptian by birth and a longtime CDC official, Zaki had his own pathology laboratory there, where he was experimenting with how to discover anthrax bacteria in tissue samples. Despite the rarity of the disease, he knew enough about anthrax autopsies—forty-one of the Sverdlovsk ones had been well described in the literature and he even had tissue samples from that outbreak in his collection at the CDC—to expect massive internal hemorrhaging and disintegrated organs. Nonetheless, he was surprised when he saw first-hand how the bacteria had devastated their host: the lymph nodes in Stevens' chest were swollen to five times their normal size and the chest cavity was filled with blood and fluid.

At noon, when the autopsy was done, the decontamination crew began its work. Flannagan's staff, uneasy, wanted Bob Stevens' eviscerated body, now repacked in a double body bag, quickly taken away. Her office telephoned Maureen Stevens to insist it be removed, informing her it would not, as originally agreed, be held at the morgue pending funeral arrangements. Further, since Stevens' body was considered a public health hazard, it had to be cremated. After making a few frantic phone calls, the Stevens family found a local funeral home willing to send a hearse to pick up the body at the morgue and do the cremation, which Bob, in any case, had always said he preferred. Maureen and Neil Stevens rushed over with a check to seal the contract. Then they waited on a bench across the street for the hearse to arrive. Nothing had prepared them for this calamity, but waiting seemed the right thing to do. The hearse soon appeared, with an escort from the sheriff's office. Maureen and Neil left only after they were sure Bob's body had been securely delivered.

◆

That Saturday evening, Tanja Popovic's Anthrax Lab at the CDC reported two test results that ruled out any natural source for Stevens' death. One was that his AMI keyboard was contaminated with Ames strain anthrax, an indication he had somehow been intentionally infected at work. The second discovery, from Ernesto Blanco's nasal swab, was that he, too, had been exposed to an anthrax aerosol, also the Ames strain. Environmental samples from the AMI mail room where Blanco worked also proved positive for the Ames anthrax bacteria. Somehow, a letter or package containing the spores had arrived inside the building. More environmental tests had to be done at AMI to check for a trail of spores or multiple hot spots. A round-the-clock police guard was stationed outside Blanco's hospital room while technicians began taking blood, tissue, and pleural fluid samples to better understand this historic case.[7] His wife and close family members were limited to two brief visits a day. No word to the press was allowed.[8]

For Malecki, the test results from AMI meant she had to quickly mobilize to protect the company's employees. Ten days had passed since Blanco first fell ill, eight since the start of Stevens' symptoms. These two clinical cases could mark the end of the anthrax outbreak or be warnings of more to come. By contacting county officials, Malecki found a convenient venue to treat those at risk, the Delray Health Clinic, where her staff and extra helpers could distribute antibiotics, take blood samples, and perform nasal swabs. Thanks to Perkins, the CDC was flying in supplies of Cipro and test kits and dispatching two dozen more officers. The team headquarters was the Emergency Operation Center in Boca Raton, a two-story bunker built as a hurricane shelter in 1997 (and later the site of the 2000 Bush-Gore ballot recount) that had room to spare if the outbreak grew.

Brad Perkins planned another round of environmental sampling at AMI, starting the next day, Sunday. The sampling process was admittedly tedious, the laboratory analyses slow. Still, the patterns of spore residue in the building could reveal the risks of exposure—how dangerously dense the aerosol release had been, if there had been more than one, and where. Perkins could hardly believe what was happening. As an infectious disease physician, he understood the natural transmission of disease, but now the enemy was a skilled bioterrorist who had caused death.

For the FBI's Doug Beecher, who was rushing to Florida from Quantico, the AMI building was a storehouse of evidence and he had to protect its chain of custody. The Miami FBI office had already been alerted to shut the place down early the next morning and bring trained teams in hazmat suits to start the search inside. Coordination with the CDC wasn't in the game plan. Nor was Perkins or the CDC prepared to cooperate in a criminal investigation.

Early Sunday morning, October 7, AMI President David Pecker, down from the firm's Manhattan headquarters, was in his office at the Boca Raton building.[9] The college-educated son of a Bronx bricklayer, at age 50 Pecker had become a media mogul by promoting celebrity journalism and moving into the fitness magazine market. After acquiring American Media, Inc., in 1999, he enjoyed being photographed with stars, but he was no snob. He treated his AMI employees as if they were his large extended family and, after 9/11, he was deeply worried about terrorism. He was convinced that terrorists had attacked his company because it had the word *American* in the title.

The phone on Pecker's desk rang. It was an FBI agent telling him that he and the handful of employees who had shown up for weekend work had to evacuate the building because it was a crime scene.

Thinking the disruption might last two weeks at the most, Pecker decided to treat it like a hurricane emergency. His employees could easily be contacted by the company's automated phone list. Stories on reserve that weren't time-sensitive could be used as filler for the next two issues of *The Sun* and the *National Enquirer*. Out of respect for the Stevens family, there would be no articles on Bob's death, not right away.

Pecker gathered up a few things from his desk and went to round up his employees. Once outside, they found the FBI was already winding yellow plastic tape around the building and unfamiliar black vans blocked the circle drive. A short distance away, several dozen news cameras were filming the shutdown.

Shortly after the building was evacuated, Brad Perkins and his crew drove past the media vans, pulled up near the circle drive, and began unpacking their gear. But FBI agents approached and told him the area was closed.

Perkins knew better than to argue, especially in sight of news cameras. He retreated and then telephoned Atlanta, where he had been maintaining direct phone contact with Jeff Koplan, CDC's director. His message was urgent: people's lives were at stake and, without CDC cooperation inside the building, the FBI was delaying the estimates of public health risks. As a short-term solution, Perkins and his team gave technical instructions to the Bureau to pass on to its hazmat team inside the building.

That same Sunday morning, Neil and Maureen Stevens returned to the funeral home. Maureen rode home with her husband's ashes in a cardboard box on her lap. AMI had arranged for a memorial service the next Wednesday, at the Unity of Delray Beach church, near Boca. Kind messages and bouquets of flowers piled up on the Stevens' doorstep.

Friends and strangers alike were telephoning to offer condolences. One stranger called to tell Maureen that Satan had caused Bob's death.

Maureen Stevens left her husband's voice on the answering machine. It seemed as if he should appear at any moment, that she would look through the window and see him in the garden or that he would come in the kitchen door and call her name.

✦

Working all day Sunday, October 7, and through the night to Monday morning, Malecki and her team prepared for the Delray clinic. Their first goal was outreach. Using AMI's automated phone lists, they gave the employees directions to Delray and explained that the clinic would run all day Monday and Tuesday. Through company records, they contacted recent former employees and visitors who had spent more than an hour in the building in the sixty days before Bob Stevens fell ill on September 30. They contacted employees of the several companies that leased office space in the AMI building. They enlisted local television and radio stations to alert anyone who might have been exposed to anthrax at AMI.

Their second goal was public education. They put together press releases and, for distribution at the clinic, an informational flyer with two main messages. The first was that anthrax is not contagious person-to-person. The second was that the spores are capable of "time-release" infections: symptoms could erupt weeks or more after exposure. Anyone potentially exposed should start a course of antibiotics and stick with it. To help, the county department of health would make Cipro refills available. Finally, those who came to the clinic should be prepared for nasal swabs and blood tests, to check for community patterns of exposure.

Malecki and her staff estimated that as many as six hundred people might respond. The CDC and six local physicians were ready. AMI had hired a team of private nurses to help with the blood tests. Red Cross volunteers were set to handle registration. Federal marshals, the local police, and FBI agents would be patrolling, just in case any law enforcement was needed.

On Monday at 8 a.m. hundreds of people lined up in the Delray clinic parking lot—the outreach effort was successful. But the day got off to a bumpy start. Because of the Columbus Day holiday, the clinic building (under Palm Beach County jurisdiction, not the county health department's) was locked shut. Using her cell phone, Malecki tracked down the custodian and, in an hour, the clinic was accepting patients.

But there were more bumps. First, the turnout proved to be nearly twice what had been expected. AMI employees, worried that they had inadvertently carried home spores on their clothes or in their cars, brought their spouses and children to be tested and receive antibiotics. Second, the nasal swabs and blood tests took more time than antici-pated. Third, the psychological stress among employees was more than the public health officers were prepared for. The random, invisible way in which Stevens had been killed added to the traumatic reactions to his murder. "It could have been me," was a frequent comment. One AMI executive broke down sobbing because, in late September, he had brought his seven-year-old daughter to work. "I don't care what hap-pens to me," he wept, "but I've put her at risk."

The lines moved slowly. Obviously anxious, people waited for hours in broiling heat and intermittent rain. The national and international press that was parked at curbside—another media blitz—chronicled what looked like a public health meltdown.

Malecki, when she wasn't reassuring the press otherwise, stayed on trouble-shooting patrol. When a white powder in the clinic hallway alarmed a marshal on duty—it turned out to be plaster dust from the boots of construction workers—she swept it into a trash bin and put yellow tape around it. In another incident, a man arrived in the park-ing lot and wildly claimed that his neighbors had poisoned their cows and him with anthrax. The police restrained him until Malecki and one of her physicians calmed the man down and arranged for him to be driven home. The news media filmed the incident and that night it was featured on national and international news to illustrate "panic in Florida," while the clinic's accomplishments were ignored. In three days, 1,076 people were tested and given antibiotics. To speed germina-tion, the nasal swabs were each immediately applied to a culture medium plate prepared with agar and then rushed to the Florida health laboratory for analysis. As for blood tests, 436 were submitted to check for antibodies.[10] Simultaneously, case surveillance was being aggres-sively pursued in the county and state, with emergency rooms and intensive care units already reporting suspect illnesses.

On Wednesday, October 10, withheld from the press, tests from the Anthrax Lab revealed that Ames strain spores had contaminated

Ernesto Blanco's van and the North Military Trail post office in Boca where he picked up AMI's mail. The CDC was inclined to identify him as the second Florida inhalational anthrax case, but his ambiguous clinical history delayed the official confirmation.

That same Wednesday, October 10, an anonymous law enforcement source in Florida told CNN that "the anthrax found in Florida seems to be the Ames strain."[11] The next day, a story in New York's *Newsday* reported an interview on strain analysis with veterinarian Martin Hugh-Jones, a longtime anthrax expert at Louisiana State University, who mentioned Paul Keim.[12] Soon after, a news helicopter was buzzing over the campus of Northern Arizona State University and reporters arrived by the dozen looking for Keim—a media unknown who passed through the crowd unrecognized. When he finally introduced himself, Keim kept his responses to press inquiries as brief as possible. Like the CDC's Popovic, he recognized a calamity when he saw one, and in this instance, whether the public was informed or not, the calamity was a WMD murder case.

Also at midweek, early results of tests from the Delray clinic yielded news that was made public: a nasal swab showed that another AMI employee, Stephanie Dailey, the young woman who helped Ernesto Blanco with mail sorting, had definitely been exposed to an anthrax aerosol. Interviewed by the FBI, Dailey remembered a letter containing powder she had opened at her desk, probably on Tuesday, September 25, after she returned from a two-week vacation. When the powder spilled on her skirt, she threw the letter into her wastepaper basket and went to the women's room to clean her hands and clothes. Now taking Cipro, Dailey, age 36, had been in good health for two weeks. The anthrax letter, though, was lost. In reaction to Popovic's two findings and Dailey's account, the FBI deployed sixty field agents to interview AMI employees, their relatives and friends, and recent visitors to the company.

The victim of key interest remained Ernesto Blanco, the AMI mail handler, who was still hospitalized but had regained consciousness. At the Boca Raton operations center, FBI agents and CDC officers had a shouting match about how to interview him—whether for criminal evidence or epidemiological information. The FBI wanted a single statement that would stand up in a trial; the CDC wanted more data about possible exposure. A directive to cooperate straight from FBI

Director Robert Mueller quickly ended this disagreement as well as the standoff at the America Media building. Perkins' complaints to the CDC had gone to the very top, to Secretary Thompson, and then to Justice and down the organizational stovepipe to Mueller, who brooked no nonsense. Henceforth, a CDC officer had to be included on every Bureau team. Reciprocally, an FBI agent would join each of the public health teams.

The trade-off was a gain for the FBI, which drew on CDC expertise, but something of a loss for public health officials, whose ability to communicate with the public and with each other became restricted. No information that CDC officers acquired through joint teamwork with the Bureau could be shared, not even with other officers. Several of them reported to Atlanta that they were learning about the Florida outbreak on the local news. That source, though, dried up as well with top-down pressure from Tallahassee.

For Florida Governor Jeb Bush, Stevens' death and the designation of AMI as a crime scene raised the stakes of the anthrax crisis to the national security level. He personally consulted about guarantees for his state's protection with Condoleezza Rice, the president's national security advisor, and with FBI Director Mueller. Most of all, he wanted to be kept thoroughly informed of any information about terrorist threats. If Florida had been targeted, he needed to be the first to know. In response, Mueller quickly assigned the Bureau's number three Washington official, Reuben Garcia Jr., to its Miami office to act as a direct liaison with the governor, giving him constant updates on the anthrax investigation.

In addition, the governor wanted all information about the public health response to come from Tallahassee, not Boca Raton. Instead of being contained in an orderly way, the Florida anthrax incident had been publicized around the world as a frightening calamity—enough to endanger tourism and commerce. Governor Bush designated John Ogwunobi, his state health secretary, as his sole spokesman, and sidelined Steve Wiersma, the state epidemiologist.

Jean Malecki felt the repercussions of the decision immediately. On Tuesday, as the testing at the Delray clinic was winding down, she was informed by the governor's office that she could no longer speak to the media. She had been holding daily press conferences filling in the gaps left by the CDC, which was struggling to organize its media response.

For Wednesday, she had planned to talk about the Stevens autopsy report (which Dr. Zaki had completed), but that press conference was canceled. From the governor's perspective, more information only caused undue excitation—the public needed to calm down. The balance between educating and calming the public, difficult during natural outbreaks, was even more difficult when an intentional disease attack was combined, as it had to be, with a federal criminal investigation. What followed in Florida was an informational shutdown, without official press updates. Local media complained—the FBI wasn't talking and neither was the governor's office, and the CDC wasn't returning calls from journalists. The impact of terror was silence.

◆

In a bizarre reversal of their usual roles, AMI co-workers became featured in local news stories. Gathering at Bob Stevens' favorite pub, the Blue Anchor in Delray Beach, they discussed the oddity of their situation with the local press. They were skilled at digging dirt on celebrities and creating "facts" about alien abductions, but now their pictures were on the front page and Stephanie Dailey was being flown to New York for appearances on NBC's *Today* show and ABC's *Good Morning America*. The pub's owner, a former tabloid editor, summed it up: "It's really weird for them to be the story and it can only happen in the tabs. It's the nature of the beast and it can come back to bite you."[13] Some paranoid readers of *The Sun* were fretting that the bacteria might be in the paper or ink, a fear the company took pains to allay by pointing out that the paper was printed in another state.

That week, throughout Palm Beach County, public anxiety rose. Cipro and other prescribed antibiotics, along with latex gloves and face masks, disappeared from pharmacy shelves. Physicians and hospitals were besieged by people worried about chest coughs and skin sores, and just plain worried—especially in the aftermath of 9/11—as reports of anthrax scares filled the daily headlines.[14] A low-flying mosquito-control airplane, reported as a crop duster spreading anthrax, caused an area-wide traffic jam. Teams of first responders raced from one false alarm to another—spilled powders, imagined chemical smells, a man in a face mask cleaning his pool.

In reaction to the news from Florida, across the nation the number of hoax anthrax letters and sightings spiked upward, putting police, postal inspectors, and the FBI on alert, and diverting public health laboratories from actual disease outbreaks.

◆

After the CDC reported contamination at the North Military Trail post office in Boca, Jean Malecki asked Brad Perkins if the facility should be closed. In Atlanta, Perkins' superiors were debating the same question. The answer communicated to Perkins was no. The U.S. Postal Service was a federal behemoth, with 900,000 employees and 14,000 postal facilities across the nation, and zero tolerance for disrupted services. Its Florida spokesman had just denied that the Stevens diagnosis had any proven connection to the mail system.[15] Besides, the level of contamination seemed minimal and confined to the storage cubicle where AMI mail was stored. Malecki directed disinfection of the surface contamination with bleach and moved immediately, on October 12, to conduct nasal swabs of thirty potentially exposed postal workers at the Boca facility. But she wanted to do more. Although time had passed with no apparent signs of anthrax among postal employees, she asked postal officials for direct access to workers who might have handled mail sent to AMI. She had in mind a campaign to offer the options of nasal swabs and antibiotics, plus an educational presentation about the risks of anthrax, essentially what had been provided at the Delray clinic, only this time at each affected workplace. The U.S. Postal Service had no history of cooperating with local public health authorities, yet, because circumstances were unusual, permission was granted for Malecki and her staff to meet with the three worker shifts in the three facilities "upstream" from AMI—a campaign conducted over the next week under the media radar and largely ignored by the CDC.

On Friday, October 12, at a carefully orchestrated press conference in Boca Raton, FBI agents, CDC officers, and U.S. postal inspectors together updated their progress in containing the anthrax crisis. They all agreed that except for Ernesto Blanco and Stephanie Dailey, no other AMI employees showed evidence of exposure, and that the anthrax spores were confined to the AMI building, mainly the mail room.

Still, the head of the FBI's Miami field office, Hector Pesquera, had to admit an uncomfortable fact. Without using the word *contamination*, he noted that three local postal facilities were being "looked at very carefully" as "a very precautionary measure." He put the responsibility for this inspection on the CDC:

> CDC will make the determination and the individuals will be swabbed, not swabbed, or whatever the course of action. Trust them. They are good at that, and we rely on them.[16]

Henry Gutierrez, the U.S. Postal Service inspector at the press conference, gruffly rejected questions about anthrax risks to postal employees. Instead, he emphasized that to protect customers the postal service had alerted every one of its facility managers to be on the watch for suspicious mail.

Representing the CDC, Brad Perkins gave a brief, careful response, also avoiding any use of the word *contamination*. "We are applying methods," he said, "that are quite common in public health, and this is the identification of concentric circles of possible risk for exposure. And we are identifying and suggesting that a very small number of postal mail sorters involved with the delivery of mail to the AMI building be tested with nasal swabs. Again, this is a step of extraordinary precaution, to ensure the public's safety."

In reply to a reporter's question, Perkins said that some postal workers had been tested for exposure that morning, but pressed to say how many, he admitted he didn't know. Perkins looked wilted, and he had reason. He had been on a conference call at three that morning with CDC director Koplan about a newly diagnosed case of anthrax in New York City, a cutaneous infection almost certainly connected to an anthrax-laden letter.[17] The crisis, far from being contained, seemed to be lurching out of control.

CHAPTER 3

NEW YORK

I suspect that many of us have the same surreal feeling,
that we are watching a movie—and we're in it.

—Tom Brokaw,
NBC News, October 15, 2001

Sunday, October 7, 2001. After Erin O'Conner, a thirty-eight-year-old
editorial assistant to NBC newscaster Tom Brokaw, saw the televised
footage of the FBI shutdown of the AMI building, she began searching
the Internet for information about anthrax, especially the cutaneous
form. Ten days earlier O'Conner had developed a nasty sore on her chest,
near her left shoulder, plus a fever and swollen glands in her neck. She
went to an internist who gave her a Cipro prescription and suggested
she might have been bitten by a spider, although she mentioned a letter
containing white powder sent to Brokaw that she had recently opened—it
warned of a looming "unthinkable" attack. After O'Conner left his
office, the internist reported her case to the city health department,
which set in play a chain reaction: an alert to the FBI WMD coordinator in Manhattan, who contacted NBC security, which retrieved the
suspect letter, postmarked September 25, St. Petersburg, Florida, and
brought it to the city's public health lab for analysis. The result: no anthrax
spores whatsoever. It was a hoax. According to the health department's

protocol for suspicious powders, no follow-up of O'Conner's case was required.[1]

Compared to the constant reverberations from the 9/11 attacks on the World Trade Center, O'Conner found it easy to dismiss a hoax anthrax letter. Her husband, a city policeman, had lost twenty-three of his NYPD brothers in the disaster. Her NBC job put her in the middle of a flood of breaking news about the terrorist attacks: revelations about al Qaeda operatives and the plane hijacking plot, the identification of perpetrators and victims, and the search for the missing. At the center of New York coverage was Mayor Rudolph Giuliani, who from the first had taken a stand at Ground Zero.

O'Conner's boss had also risen to the occasion on 9/11, betraying no fear as he reported from the site. In his 1997 bestseller *The Greatest Generation*, Brokaw wrote about the valor of ordinary Americans during the Second World War; television viewers appreciated his valor in the face of terrorism. After 9/11, when national news consumption was at an all-time high, practically obsessive, Brokaw's ratings edged out those of his two rivals, anchors Dan Rather at CBS and Peter Jennings at ABC.

Although 9/11 news coverage dominated the media, the looming possibility of a biological or chemical attack—al Qaeda's second blow— was the other big story. Even before the Stevens diagnosis, the major media were promoting potential bioterrorism. From September 12 to October 3, the *New York Times* ran 76 stories about chemical and biological weapons (CBW), with 27 of them making special mention of anthrax. The *Washington Post* was close behind, publishing 55 stories on potential CBW terrorism, with 25 highlighting the anthrax threat.[2] The major networks kept up a steady stream of interviews with experts on the bioterrorism threats, who rarely hesitated to revive the apocalyptic mass attack scenarios concocted in the late 1990s. After 9/11, with the nation's vulnerability to a large-scale terrorist assault a clear-cut reality, more and worse enemy attacks seemed all too possible.

The media concentration on the bioterrorism threat had its impact on the public. A September 23 *Newsweek* poll indicated that eight out of ten Americans thought that a biological attack was at least "somewhat likely."[3] Then, on September 25, CIA director George Tenet, Defense Secretary Donald Rumsfeld, National Security Advisor Condoleezza Rice, and other Bush administration officials told the press that they had reliable intelligence that Iraq had trained al Qaeda terrorists to use chemical and biological weapons.[4] Once Bob Stevens' case became a criminal investigation, Erin O'Conner couldn't ignore the implications: if an anthrax letter was sent to a Florida media office, why not a New York one? On October 8, encouraged by Brokaw, O'Conner called the FBI office in New York. "I've found pictures of skin anthrax on the Internet that look exactly like what I've got," she explained, making it clear who her boss was.

The FBI put O'Conner in direct contact with Marcelle "Marci" Layton, the director of Communicable Diseases at the city's Department of Health. Layton, a pioneer in disease surveillance, worked out of one of the cramped offices in the department's historic building at 125 Worth Street. Layton's division served the city's eight million residents, plus two million visitors, whose infectious disease calamities never stopped.

An authority on domestic preparedness, Layton also contributed to the city's enormous terrorism response capacity that Mayor Giuliani had developed.[5] After the 1993 bombing of the World Trade Center, he aggressively lobbied for federal funding for emergency WMD response, including for biological attacks. His successful argument, worth millions in funding, was that New York City, vital to the national economy, was a known terrorist target. By 2000, different teams of first responders—police, fire, public health, and hospital officials—had participated in five major bioterrorist attack exercises with federal agencies. The CDC and the FBI, which both maintained permanent offices in Manhattan, were participants. The FBI's Joint Terrorism Task Force in New York, one of dozens that served major cities, drew on a network of human resources (including 30,000 police officers) that would have done credit to a small country.

On 9/11, the Department of Health building, not far from Ground Zero, lost electrical power and then was temporarily evacuated. Nonetheless, Layton was able to direct emergency surveillance of the medical response to the disaster, in addition to planning surveillance of hospitals and laboratories for any signs of a biological attack. After the October 4 Florida diagnosis, Layton mobilized her staff to screen every hospital and infectious disease laboratory in the city for inhalational anthrax cases—in case a mass aerosol attack had been launched.[6] None had surfaced, but O'Conner's potential infection raised a red flag, especially after the two AMI cases.

Layton arranged for O'Conner to have a skin biopsy; the experienced dermatologist who performed it reported that he was sure she had cutaneous anthrax. Layton wanted the CDC in Atlanta to handle the biopsy tissue test. But the Anthrax Lab was overwhelmed by clinical and environmental samples from Florida. Sherif Zaki, the medical examiner who performed the Stevens autopsy, himself had carried back two hundred of them that needed immediate analysis. Despite its connection to the media, Layton's request was rejected, with the suggestion that she ask the New York State lab in Albany.

Perhaps no other city in the nation or even the world had invested as much as New York in counter-terrorism—and Layton herself was a known disease surveillance expert. Yet when she needed help, the response system was jammed. It was no one's fault. Everyone was on a steep learning curve, making some decisions correctly, others not so well.

Meanwhile, Casey Chamberlain, a twenty-three-year-old NBC intern, reminded O'Conner of another powder-laden letter that had arrived in the office around September 18, earlier than the St. Petersburg letter. A desk assistant who often opened Brokaw's fan mail, Chamberlain remembered that a grainy brown powder—like sand or brown sugar—had spilled out of the envelope. She also recalled that the letter inside, written in what looked like a child's hand, threatened death to Israel and also misspelled the word *penicillin*.[7] After shaking the powder into a wastebasket, Chamberlain put the letter in a pile with others to be passed on to O'Conner.

The weekend starting September 28, Chamberlain began experiencing neck swelling and fever, just like O'Conner, but she never connected the symptoms to the sore that had erupted on her leg. That Monday, instead of going to work, she paid a visit to her doctor, who suggested she was allergic to an anti-acne drug she had been taking. He prescribed antibiotics and advised bed rest. Chamberlain stayed home from work for most of that week until she felt better. By then, O'Conner was also on the mend and neither of the women thought their illnesses were related.

Frustrated by what he saw as FBI bureaucratic incompetence, Brokaw intervened in O'Conner's case. With a few phone calls, he was able to arrange for her biopsy to be analyzed at Fort Detrick in USAMRIID's Special Pathogen lab. On October 10, a biopsy from O'Conner's

lesion was packaged and flown express to Washington, where a motor-
cycle courier picked it up and delivered it to the institute.

Instead of sending O'Conner's biopsy material to Albany, Layton
called Dr. Stephen Ostroff at the CDC's National Center for Infectious
Diseases. Layton had worked with him during the 1999 mosquito-borne
West Nile virus outbreak in New York City, the first in the Western
Hemisphere, when Ostroff was the CDC's officer in charge. Upbeat, with
a sporty black mustache, Ostroff proved he knew how to communicate effectively with the press and a public made nervous by the random deaths of seven elderly people.

Layton tracked Ostroff to Washington, where he was set to give
Congressional testimony on food safety regulations, and he gladly
agreed to intervene for her in Atlanta. On October 10, O'Conner's
biopsy material was packaged and express-mailed to the Anthrax Lab,
where it arrived the next day. Once there, the initial tests of O'Conner's
biopsy—the same process for capsule identification used in Florida—
proved negative. At Fort Detrick, Ezzell's attempt to grow *B. anthracis*
from the tissue sample also failed. It could be that O'Conner's sore had
healed, eliminating all traces of the pathogen, or that some other infection was to blame.

Medical examiner Sherif Zaki, though, who ran the CDC's Infectious Diseases Pathology Activity (IDPA), an investigative unit within
the Division of Viral and Rickettsial Diseases, wanted to try another
test. He had recently developed a new way to identify anthrax in
human tissue, which he had successfully tested on material from the
Stevens autopsy. The process was simple. Antibodies were created in
mice that bonded to the cell wall and capsule of virulent *B. anthracis*
and, through a series of chemical reactions, produced a magenta-
colored dye. If the distinctive rod-shaped bacilli were present in human
tissue, the antibodies should have the effect of staining them magenta.[8]

It took Zaki and his assistants until 3 a.m. on Friday, October 12,
to find the magenta bacilli in O'Conner's biopsy.[9] Jeff Koplan himself
checked the results. Just before dawn, Koplan called Layton at home
and gave her the news. Switching into emergency mode, she used a
phone tree to mobilize her staff. There were hundreds of people at NBC
who would need antibiotics and nasal swabs. Some members of the Joint
Terrorism Task Force would show up, she knew, although its ranks had
been decimated on 9/11.

Neal Cohen, New York City's commissioner of health, broke the news about O'Conner's diagnosis to Mayor Giuliani, who then insisted on speaking directly to Koplan. As Koplan was explaining that Zaki's diagnostic test had a high probability of accuracy, Giuliani impatiently interrupted.

"Does she have it?" he asked.

"Yes, she has it," Koplan replied.[10]

Later that morning, Mayor Giuliani stormed into a meeting of NBC executives on the 52nd floor of 30 Rockefeller Center. Tom Brokaw, the target of the anthrax attack, was there and Jeff Koplan was virtually present on speakerphone. From Brokaw's perspective, it seemed that no one had a plan. In that, he underestimated Giuliani. Years before, in 1994, the mayor had engaged one of the best tutors, Joshua Lederberg, the Nobel Prize–winning microbiologist and former president of Rockefeller University. Lederberg taught him about the infective power of anthrax and its danger as a bioterrorism weapon.[11]

As he absorbed the implications of O'Conner's diagnosis, Giuliani stayed focused on his main goal, the protection of his already wounded city from any more trauma.[12] The day before had marked the one-month anniversary of the attacks on the World Trade Center, where thick yellow smoke was still billowing from the crater. Every day the mayor went to yet another funeral service for al Qaeda victims; his desk at the Emergency Operations Center at Pier 92 was covered with black-bordered memorial cards. Economically, New York was losing millions of dollars a day from empty hotels, theaters, and restaurants. Headlines about an anthrax threat would only scare tourists and add to the downturn. And Giuliani refused to have already nervous New Yorkers feel they had to wear "moon suits" to move around the city safely.

Even one anthrax case could be disastrous, but Giuliani saw a silver lining: it was the only case. Two weeks after the presumed exposure, the only known impact in New York City was a single, cured skin infection. Not one inhalational case like those in Florida had occurred.

Koplan was ready to assist the mayor. He offered thirty-five CDC officers and all the necessary test kits and antibiotics for the 1,200-plus NBC employees. He dispatched Stephen Ostroff to act as Giuliani's aide-de-camp and, in the unlikely event the mayor needed one, a spokesman to the press.

In these negotiations, the FBI took a bit of a back seat. As with the

AMI building, it counted on being able to shut down NBC's 30 Rocke-feller Center as a crime scene and begin a search for evidence—so far the September 18 letter had not been found. Mayor Giuliani flatly refused. From his perspective, closing the seventy-story Art Deco trea-sure, a major tourist attraction, would dominate the news, frighten the public, and further depress the city's economy. Koplan agreed. The decision was made to evacuate just the building's third floor, where Bro-kaw and O'Conner had their offices, and to test that area and the mail room for contamination.

To capture the headlines, Giuliani staged a 12:30 p.m. press confer-ence at Rockefeller Center.[13] Against the backdrop of a giant American flag, he allowed health commissioner Cohen to announce the diagno-sis, and then he took the podium to assure everyone that there was, in effect, no cause for anxiety. The CDC would be testing just one floor at NBC and perhaps one or two other places, where, he emphasized, con-tamination was "a possibility, not a certainty." The CDC and the New York Department of Health would also test any employees who might have been exposed and give them Cipro. Giuliani repeatedly stressed that all these efforts were being made "out of an excess of caution." And consigning the threat of the letter to the past, Giuliani assured the public that "if anyone else was going to be infected, it would have hap-pened by now."

One reporter, given his chance, asked the elephant-in-the-room question: "Has this case anything to do with the attacks on the World Trade Center?"

Giuliani passed the question to FBI Special Agent Barry Mawn, who was with him on the podium. Mawn, head of the Bureau's New York field office, had shepherded the city through 9/11. "We see no connection whatsoever to 9/11," Mawn replied tersely. With this state-ment, he remained in sync with the FBI's refusal to go even one step beyond the evidence it had in hand. The day before, one of its spokes-men had testified to Congress that despite "media suggestions to the contrary—there is no evidence that the presence of anthrax in the American Media building is a terrorist act."[14]

To calm his constituency, Mayor Giuliani concluded with a practi-cal message: the best response to a suspicious letter was to "immedi-ately contact the police or the FBI, leave the envelope where it is, leave the room, and don't move the envelope, just leave it there."

While Giuliani reassured the public, city reporters were concerned that the media (which included them) had become the target of a broader bioterrorist attack. Just prior to the press conference, the police and public health officials had converged on the *New York Times* building on 43rd Street and Broadway where journalist Judith Miller, the lead author of a newly published book on bioterrorism, had received a powder-laden threat letter.[15] The *Times* building was in a lockdown; outside, crowds of distraught employees and the arrival of a hazmat team in full gear were being filmed by national and international news crews. The arrival of a similar team at 30 Rockefeller Center and its third-floor evacuation were also being filmed for the news. The targeted media, feeding on their own fright, had become the subject of their own news coverage. As Tom Brokaw put it, "I suspect that many of us have the same surreal feeling, that we are watching a movie—and we're in it."[16] New York had experienced its "second blow" after 9/11 and the world was watching.

Late on Friday, October 12, at the NBC building, NYPD officers found the anthrax letter that had infected O'Conner and Chamberlain. Postmarked September 18, in Trenton, New Jersey, it probably reached Brokaw's office a short time later, after which Chamberlain likely opened it and gave it to O'Conner. O'Conner then put it in a gray envelope with other suspicious mail and, after some days, a security guard picked the envelope up and put it in a plastic shopping bag, which was then left on the 16th floor. From there it was brought to the NBC mail room, where two policemen took custody of it.

The text of the momentous letter, dated September 11, 2001, pointed to a militant Islamic source with enmity for the United States and Israel:

THIS IS NEXT

TAKE PENACILIN NOW

DEATH TO AMERICA

DEATH TO ISRAEL

ALLAH IS GREAT

◆

Even before 9/11, the FBI had a protocol for evaluating bioterrorism threats. Its Strategic Information and Operations Center would review the facts by telephone with its WMD Operations Unit and the Hazardous Materials Response Unit in Quantico to decide what was a "credible threat." With O'Conner's diagnosis confirmed, this September 18 letter met the criteria.

Whoever sent it had used a pharmaceutical fold (creasing the squared-off page horizontally in even thirds and then vertically on each side) to make a pocket for the powder. But by the time the New York police photocopied the letter and took it to the New York public health laboratory on First Avenue near East 26th Street, little spore powder remained for analysis. Chamberlain had dumped some of it, more spilled at the building and in the mail room as the police handled the letter, and still more was dispersed in the squad car and at the laboratory. Yet by putting just a trace amount under the microscope, a lab microbiologist saw her first *B. anthracis*, which she described as "many large, oval structures lying on top of each other, packed like sardines."[17] Within hours, tests confirmed that the oval structures had capsules and were virulent *B. anthracis* spores.

The letter was transported to the Anthrax Lab in Atlanta for more analysis, after which it was quickly sent to John Ezzell at USAMRIID. A sample of the Brokaw spore material was also delivered express to Paul Keim in Arizona for strain identification.

That Friday, millions of viewers nationwide watched Tom Brokaw's *Nightly News* for the moment when, toward the end of the show, he cast off his detached newscaster demeanor and exposed his anger and vulnerability. His eyes flashing and his voice hoarse, he described the letter attack as "so unfair and so outrageous and so maddening, it's beyond my ability to express it in socially acceptable terms."

The mayor's pronouncement that any other infections would have already happened was true, but it didn't mean they had been correctly diagnosed or reported. After the announcement about O'Conner's case, other media cases in New York began to emerge. Claire Fletcher, a personal assistant to Dan Rather at CBS news, reported a lesion that had erupted on her face on October 1 and was attributed to a spider bite. Even before her case was confirmed by a blood test, the city's Joint Terrorism Team rushed to CBS, where traces of anthrax spores were discovered in the news area, some on a desk used by Dan Rather. But no letter could be found. Following Rather's example, the CBS staff declined the offered antibiotics. A few nights later, Rather broke down in tears about the incident on the *Late Show with David Letterman*.

Journalist Judith Miller, targeted by a hoax letter on October 12, was interviewed at length on Saturday, October 13, on CNN's *Larry King Live*.

Another possible cutaneous case surfaced over the weekend: at New York University Medical Center a seven-month-old infant was recovering from a near-fatal skin infection. The child's mother was a producer at ABC news who assisted newscaster Peter Jennings. On September 28, the baby had been at her office and the next day the sore appeared. The city's Joint Terrorism Task Force went to ABC to test for employee exposure and office contamination, and to interview possible witnesses. Again, as at CBS, the contamination levels in the offices were low and no letter was found. A biopsy from the infant went to the CDC for analysis and tested positive, indicating the danger of trace amounts of spores. As a precaution, the mail rooms of other media centers around the city were quarantined and tested for anthrax spores, with no positive results.

The most perplexing case emerged early, but was confirmed and understood late. Johanna Huden, a journalist at the *New York Post*, reported a sore on her finger that had erupted on September 22. It too had been diagnosed as a spider bite and was now largely cured with the help of antibiotics. Although Huden said she hadn't opened any envelope containing powder, the search for a letter resembling Brokaw's began. *Post* employees were encouraged to riffle through their piles of past mail—not a health-conscious suggestion—and toss anything suspicious in a common bin. Huden's biopsy tested negative for anthrax and she was given a blood test to detect anthrax antibodies. Its analysis, stalled in the backlog at the CDC Anthrax Lab, left Huden's infection and its source in limbo and deflected attention from the possibility of sealed envelopes leaking powder.

Meanwhile, public fear, stoked by media reporting, kept rising. In a reprise of his appearances at Ground Zero after 9/11, Mayor Giuliani, accompanied by Stephen Ostroff, set a stoic example by staging press conferences at the contaminated CBS and ABC newsrooms. At the same time, taking Giuliani's advice, every day hundreds of anxious New Yorkers were calling the FBI or dialing 911 to report suspicious powder sightings. Concerned citizens delivered anything they thought was contaminated—boxes, bottles, clothes, and furniture—to the public health laboratory. But the lab had its own problems: because of spores spilled from the Brokaw letter, it was shut down for decontamination. The scientist who did the analysis, her lab director, and the two policemen who had handled the letter had all had positive nasal swabs and were taking Cipro.

＊

On principle, the CDC promoted the free flow of information during disease outbreaks to inform the public and receive feedback from medical providers. After October 4, though, hundreds of emails about anthrax—inquiries about the disease, reports of incidents, demands from a concerned public—overwhelmed its capacity to respond.

One email lost in the chaos was a message from the small group of Canadian military researchers in Medicine Hat, Alberta, at the Defence Research Establishment Suffield (DRES), the same group that Bruce Ivins had assisted in creating its BSL-3 laboratory. They were trying to send a report they had written on what might happen if a real anthrax letter were opened in an office setting. In late 2000, high officials in the Ottawa government had been targeted by several threatening hoax letters and it fell to these DRES scientists to scientifically demonstrate the damage an actual anthrax letter attack could do.

The researchers pondered their alternatives—no published office model existed—and decided to stage a dramatic set piece, to be repeated six times. A man in protective Tyvek coveralls, a canister filter over his nose and mouth, enters an office (actually an 8- by 10-foot aerosol chamber). He flips a switch that activates air samplers, sits down at a table, and begins randomly opening a series of ten business envelopes, each containing a folded sheet of copier paper. One of the envelopes also contains a gram of *Bacillus globigii* spores (the substitute for anthrax once used in U.S. weapons testing) inside the folded paper. From each envelope, the man removes the single sheet of paper. When he unfolds the one containing the spore powder, he pushes back his chair, stands up, and steps back from the table. While the air samplers and room filters record the spore dispersal, he waits for precisely ten minutes and then leaves the "office."

The received wisdom at the time was that an anthrax letter was relatively harmless. Bill Patrick, the former Detrick production engineer, argued the conclusion openly and promoted it in intelligence circles. In 1999, for example, Patrick wrote a report on anthrax aerosols for the major defense contractor SAIC (Science Applications International Corporation). In it, he emphasized the dangers of a mass anthrax attack and referred dismissively to the "futility of the envelope-powder scenario."[18] Although he hypothesized that simply opening a letter containing a quality gram of spores—in particle sizes between one and five microns—would generate a dangerous, highly infective aerosol, he reasoned that only the person opening the envelope would likely be at risk. He estimated that others in a mail room or office would be "at risk" provided approximately 10,000 spores or more were inhaled.[19] Otherwise, he said, they were not in danger of anthrax infection. This assertion was incorrect but suited his threat perception.

Patrick's reference to a 10,000-spore threshold was military shorthand harking back to the 1960s, when many studies were done on monkeys to estimate the human dose responses of enemy civilians attacked by anthrax bombs. In one study, researchers concluded that around 4,000 to 5,000 inhaled spores constituted a lethal dose for 50 percent of the monkeys exposed (the LD50).[20] To calculate the LD50 for human targets, the numbers were simply doubled to a range of 8,000 to 10,000 spores. In highly purified anthrax material—the kind that was once made at Fort Detrick—there can be a trillion spores in a gram. Depending on the size of the target area, weapons engineers would calculate the required amount of spores to disperse for an effective mass assault. At the same time, while thousands of inhaled spores do increase the odds of killing individual victims, even a single spore, successfully germinating in the body, could cause anthrax. In fact, numerous careful studies done in the last century support what is called the "single organism hypothesis," whereby a single organism, rather than cooperating with others of like kind, acts alone and is capable of infecting a host.[21] Frightening as it is, a single inhaled anthrax spore has its own chance, perhaps small, of overcoming the immune system. The key question is whether an individual has been exposed to spores that are airborne.

The results of the Canadian DRES experiments upended Patrick's risk estimate: with the opening of the envelope, a significant number of the released spores rose in a dense aerosol and overloaded the air samplers throughout the room. The primary aerosol stayed in the air for the full ten minutes; anyone who walked through during that time without a mask would be in grave danger if the spores were B. anthracis.

Anyone in the vicinity could be exposed to as much as 3,000 times the estimated LD50—the 8,000–10,000-spore range.[22]

The Canadian researchers, excited by their results, soon found that no one else was. In the spring of 2001, they made a total of five presentations, at international meetings of U.S., U.K., and Canadian military officials—whose minds were on battlefield threats—and to representatives of the FBI and the Federal Emergency Management Agency, whose main concern was mass terrorism. In March, two members of the Canadian group visited the CDC to discuss possibly linking with the Laboratory Response Network.[23] While there, they presented the results of their letter experiments, but their findings made little impression.[24]

In preparing for their letter experiments, the Canadian researchers found that, before the envelopes were opened, the spores leaked. If an envelope was not thoroughly sealed, the report suggested, it could also pose "a threat to individuals in the mail handling system." The final Canadian report, dated September 20, 2001, warned of trouble ahead. It concluded: "It is only a matter of time until a real 'anthrax letter' arrives in some mail room."[25]

Months before Bob Stevens' diagnosis and the discovery of the Brokaw letter, the Canadians distributed their report to scores of U.S. officials and to the eight authors of the 1999 Johns Hopkins article on anthrax, including Art Friedlander at USAMRIID.[26] None, if they read about the experiments, grasped their significance: opening an anthrax letter could endanger an entire area and perhaps the mail system. Moreover, few were willing to bring up the potential risks of small doses or the single organism hypothesis. Those who had read the old Army studies knew that some monkeys died of small doses, much less than the LD50. For animals or humans, even small doses of virulent *B. anthracis* could be infective. Individual vulnerability plays a part. The victims of the 1979 Sverdlovsk outbreak, for example, were generally middle-aged or older, suggesting age as a factor. The challenge was to predict who might be exposed to anthrax aerosols, under what conditions.

Reacting to known exposures that, except for Bob Stevens' death, seemed medically insignificant, CDC officials and others began informing the public about an 8,000- to 10,000-spore threshold below which no infection could occur.[27] The calculation of a threshold for radiation or chemical exposures, a common way of positing tolerable risks for entire populations, had been applied by the CDC to anthrax before

2001.[28] Now it became a way to reassure frightened Americans, very few of whom were at any risk at all. On CDC authority, the press began asserting that "studies suggest that at least 8,000 spores of the bacteria [sic] *Bacillus anthracis* must be inhaled so that enough small particles can reach the lungs, where they activate and overwhelm the body's defenses."[29]

The Canadian researchers showed that opening an envelope containing less than a gram of spores could generate a dangerous aerosol, enough to badly contaminate an office ventilation system. The obvious next question would have been to ask about the mechanical sorting of the same type of letter, before it was delivered to an office. In New York City, the question of how aerosols might be generated by postal processing remained unasked, although evidence from Florida—known to the CDC and postal inspectors—showed that an anthrax letter could release spores at post offices, "upstream" from its arrival in an office mail room. The spores in Ernesto Blanco's van and in the three postal facilities revealed a trail of spores dispersed by the missing letter—taped shut or not. The signs could hardly have been clearer. But no one seemed to notice.

In New York City, the Brokaw letter confronted the postal inspectors with the unavoidable fact that virulent anthrax spores had been transported through the mail. The letter's postmark showed that it had been processed on September 18 at the Hamilton postal facility in Trenton, New Jersey, then delivered to the city's Morgan Station distribution and processing facility, at Ninth Avenue and 29th Street.

From Morgan Station, it was sent to Rockefeller Center via the Radio City Station at 52nd Street. Since the letter had been sealed with tape, it might have released no spores in transit—spores perhaps escaped only when the letter was opened at NBC, the target. It was possible to hold on to that assumption by avoiding any environmental tests that might challenge it. The U.S. Postal Service did not clamor for anthrax spore tests at the Morgan Station or the Radio City post office, nor did the CDC advise them. Instead, the main focus of environmental testing was on targets—the known NBC target at Rockefeller Center, the suspected targets at CBS and ABC and other media offices and mail rooms—and later on the homes of Erin O'Conner and Casey Chamberlain, which both proved significantly contaminated.

Without tests "upstream" in the mail processing system, there was no postal facility contamination, and all the disruptive consequences—the testing and treatment of workers, possible facility closures, the decontamination of complex machinery, and adverse publicity about germs in the mail system—could be avoided. Presuming that low levels of exposure to anthrax spores posed no health risk, it was possible to dismiss the leaks in Florida and characterize Jean Malecki's unusual public health intervention on behalf of postal workers as "undue precaution." To make the point that postal workers had nothing to fear, Steve Ostroff went to the Morgan Station facility, rolled up his sleeves, and joined in sorting the mail.[30]

◆

On Sunday, October 14, the FBI delivered the Brokaw letter for safe-keeping to John Ezzell at USAMRIID's Diagnostic Division. That same Sunday, out in Arizona, Paul Keim confirmed to the FBI that the spores in the Brokaw letter were Ames strain—the same bacteria that had killed Bob Stevens and nearly killed Ernesto Blanco. To the press, the Bureau had been denying any connection between the two incidents. The previous Friday, speaking in Florida, the FBI's Doug Beecher had correctly cautioned that even if the AMI and Brokaw strains were the same, it would not prove they came from the same lab or a single source. Anthrax was genetically conservative: Ames strain samples all looked alike—that was the conventional understanding.

Government spokesmen—Mayor Giuliani, FBI, CDC, and postal officials, Secretary Thompson and Attorney General Ashcroft—had all avoided connecting the dots between the Florida and New York cases, whatever they speculated privately. Even so, Keim's strain identification forged an undeniable link to the U.S. defense establishment. By associating two disparate incidents with the Ames strain, his discovery pointed directly to a perpetrator with exceptional insider access and the scientific capacity to launch more attacks. A major security violation had occurred—but how?

CHAPTER 4

"WE HAVE THIS ANTHRAX"

The FBI is quite effective in the black-and-white world of domestic law enforcement, but national security consists mainly of shades of gray.

—RICHARD A. FALKENRATH, ROBERT D. NEWMAN, and BRADLEY A. THAYER, *America's Achilles' Heel*, 1998

Attorney General John Ashcroft and Secretary of Health and Human Services Tommy Thompson were ideological compatriots (both were members of the Christian conservative Council for National Policy), but until Mayor Giuliani's news-grabbing October 12 press conference, they had had little reason to face the public together. That afternoon, Ashcroft hurriedly joined Thompson at his HHS office on Independence Avenue and together they reiterated the gist of Giuliani's message to the nation: the government was in control and citizens should not panic. They then repeated the mayor's advice that anyone with a suspicious article or event to report should call the FBI or 911.[1]

Across the country, thousands of Americans did panic—Cipro and other antibiotic sales soared—and hundreds called the FBI and 911 to report suspicious powders. The Brokaw letter also unleashed a new wave of hoax letters, some more than mere pranks. In a repeat of a 1999 hoax barrage, ninety family-planning clinics in thirteen states received anonymous hate mail containing a suspicious white powder.[2] In cooperation with postal inspectors, FBI headquarters increased its "credible threat" evaluations and channeled the most suspect powder material to Ezzell's Special Pathogen lab at USAMRIID.

In Washington, the Brokaw incident triggered fears that al Qaeda terrorists, having attacked the New York media, had set their sights on the nation's capital—in a reprise of the double targeting on 9/11. The Bush administration and Congress already had some technical defenses in place. For example, the protection of key government building ventilation systems from exterior germ attacks had been implemented during the Clinton administration. After 9/11, sensors were installed to monitor the air in offices where top officials, especially the president and vice president, held meetings. After October 12, mail items for high administration officials, especially at the White House, were even more scrupulously screened than before.

Curiously, among the dozens of experts who knew about the Canadian DRES estimates of spore dispersal from anthrax letters, none stepped forward to warn about the generalized risks. Instead, in congressional offices, which received thousands of letters a week from constituents, administrators took time that Friday to give staff the most rudimentary instructions for handling a suspicious piece of mail: put it down, step back, and call the Capitol Hill police.

◆

Few terrorist analysts in New York or Washington thought about New Jersey as a bioterrorism target. If they thought about the Garden State at all, it was as a threat source: al Qaeda operatives had circulated undercover in the Newark area before 9/11 and Trenton had a growing Muslim population. But the impact of the Brokaw letter, like all successful terrorist attacks, diffused fear beyond the target to the broader population. On October 13, when Mayor Giuliani announced that the Brokaw letter had been processed in Trenton, at a large facility in Hamilton Township, hundreds of New Jersey residents, feeling acutely vulnerable, inundated police and FBI offices with reports of worrisome white powders and medical ailments. To respond, the police established an Emergency Operation Center in Ewing, near Trenton, and asked officials from the New Jersey Department of Health and Senior Services to assist.

Eddy Bresnitz, New Jersey's deputy commissioner of health and state epidemiologist, answered the call. The pragmatic, highly qualified Bresnitz (he had degrees in infectious disease, epidemiology, and internal medicine) would otherwise have been addressing the public health needs of the state's 8.4 million ethnically diverse residents, who had enough public health problems to keep his department in permanent overtime. When Bresnitz first heard about Bob Stevens' diagnosis—it was on October 4, at a medical conference, from a physician who had trained Larry Bush—he had quite reasonably dismissed its relevance to New Jersey.[3] With the discovery of the Brokaw letter, he began fielding a steady stream of white powder alarms, any one of which could have been real.

Among the many reports flooding the Emergency Operations Center, Bresnitz received one about a skin lesion that he thought might be significant. A dermatologist had recently treated a letter carrier, Teresa Heller, for a sore on her hand that had developed a black scab like Erin O'Conner's. He had done a biopsy but had not sent it out for analysis. Although Heller's mail route was in Ewing, fifteen miles away from the Hamilton facility, Bresnitz had two FBI agents pick up the biopsy from the dermatologist's office and deliver it to the state laboratory in Trenton. To guarantee the procedure was carefully documented, he asked the state medical examiner to make the preliminary assessment. (By coincidence, the medical examiner had actually seen a cutaneous anthrax case years before, in India, where he was from.) Then Bresnitz rang the CDC to give it a heads-up on a possible new case.

That weekend, Bresnitz received another unusual call, this one from Joe Sautello, the manager of the Hamilton postal facility. In the excitement generated by the Brokaw letter, no one at the CDC or elsewhere in government thought of postal facilities as vulnerable. To the contrary, postal employees were being urged to protect targets by identifying suspicious mail. On October 10, in reaction to the Florida cases, the U.S. Postal Service had sent an "Emergency Action Plan" to facilities nationwide, a reinforcement of previous alerts to report any unusual letters or packages.[4] The discovery of a suspicious article of mail required the employee to inform a supervisor who would, in turn, alert the FBI.

In the long years of the Unabomber threat, which started in 1978 and lasted for seventeen years, postal employees were on the alert for rattling packages with no return addresses. Spotting a possible anthrax letter, especially in an age of mechanized processing, was much more difficult. Unlike bomb scares, which would evacuate a building, the appropriate response to a suspected anthrax letter was not always clear. If sealed, the suspect letter or package might pose only a minimal risk, with no need for work stoppage or medical intervention.[5] For protection, postal workers had the option of wearing blue gauze face masks and latex gloves—the same items that were flying off the shelves around the country.

Joe Sautello, understanding that the discovery of the Brokaw letter troubled many of his 1,200 employees, invited Eddy Bresnitz to give them a lecture on anthrax. Just as was the case in Florida, cooperation between postal management and public health officials was far from typical. For a postal manager to actually reach out to a state public health department was extraordinary—but Sautello understood the times were extraordinary, too. A New Jersey native, gregarious and yet a no-nonsense administrator, he cared about keeping the numbers up, as the postal expression goes, but he also cared about his employees' morale. Bresnitz agreed to come early Monday morning, October 15.

※

Helen Lewis, who sorted government mail on the night shift at the Washington, D.C., Mail Processing and Distribution Center, was alerted to the October 10 Emergency Action Plan. The facility, located at 900 Brentwood Avenue, three miles northeast of the National Mall, was the major clearinghouse for mail to U.S. government offices. Government mail, separated into zip-coded bins, still needed personal oversight. The Brentwood facility was ten times the size of the Hamilton facility, with twenty digital bar code sorters processing mail electronically around the clock. If a letter lacked postage or a zip code or a legible address, the machines were likely to reject it, which meant that a worker like Lewis would retrieve it from a reject bin and correct its course. At the far end of the building, near the loading dock, sacks of mail were opened and workers there transferred them into the mechanical sorters. A longtime postal employee like Lewis, Leroy Richmond worked in that area, but only for about two hours a day; he was in charge of picking up express mail from the Baltimore airport and was never involved in sorting the ordinary flow of letters to Brentwood—he never touched an envelope, although he was occasionally asked to sweep up debris that accumulated around the sorting machines.

On October 13, with the Brokaw letter in the news, Lewis went to work as usual. Around 2:30 a.m., she noticed a letter with a scrawled address and a zip code for Washington, not for Congress or any of the federal agencies. As she was putting the letter into the city bin, it spilled powder on her apron. She immediately carried the letter to her supervisor, who called the FBI to pick it up. Although she was unnerved, Lewis finished her shift at 8:30 a.m. and went to a local hospital, where she was refused help—she had no symptoms and no proof of exposure. The next evening, the 14th, she again reported for work and this time her supervisor and she agreed that they both should seek medical help. Early on the morning of October 15, the two women went together to the hospital's emergency room, where by coincidence they came upon Dena Briscoe and two other Brentwood women in the waiting room anxiously awaiting attention. Mail sorters, they had felt sickened by a strange smell coming from the government mail and had heard about the powdery letter that Lewis had discovered. Lewis and her supervisor both had their noses swabbed and received Cipro prescriptions.

Once at home, having been given a phone number for the CDC, Helen placed a call and reported what happened. The officer who answered asked her if she had breathed in any of the powder. "Yes," Helen answered, "I was holding the letter and, yes, I was breathing." The officer then reassured Helen that she was in no danger because she probably had inhaled less than 8,000 spores.[6] Helen decided to take Cipro and stay away from work until she felt it was safe. The shy, diminutive Dena Briscoe and her two co-workers left the hospital after waiting two hours for attention that never came.

Dena Briscoe had been having anxiety attacks for weeks. The atmosphere at Brentwood had darkened after 9/11, the day Washington became a ghost town; even Brentwood, which almost never closed, had shut down for twelve hours. Briscoe, a postal worker for more than twenty years and the daughter of postal workers, had started at the National Capitol Post Office near Union Station and then, in 1986, moved with hundreds of others to the new building at Brentwood. Although dispersed throughout its vast space, the workers kept up old ties and made new ones. On breaks, they played cards or checkers or studied the Bible. One mail sorter, Joseph Curseen, who like Briscoe worked the night shift, regularly led scripture readings, which Leroy Richmond attended. On weekends and holidays Brentwood workers organized picnics, potluck suppers, and musical "cafes" and went bowling together. But the post–September 11 tension at the facility had destroyed that sense of conviviality. At work, when Briscoe felt anxious and short of breath, her supervisor, reassuring her that the plant was safe, urged her to pull herself together.

✦

That same Monday morning, October 15, Eddy Bresnitz arrived at the Hamilton facility in New Jersey to give his talk. Manager Joe Sautello greeted him with a handshake and led him to the cafeteria, where around three hundred workers were waiting. Bresnitz told them about anthrax and especially about its cutaneous and inhalational forms, but he saw no need to emphasize their risks of infection. The known epidemiological facts were reassuring, as Mayor Giuliani had emphasized. Since September 18, only one cutaneous case had been confirmed—that of Brokaw's assistant—and that of the infant son of the ABC producer was suspected. Furthermore, the letter to Brokaw had been taped shut. The presumption was that it had posed a hazard when it was opened, not before, and not to postal employees. It was also presumed that no other anthrax letters were sent after Brokaw's, that the attacks were over and done.

Bresnitz left Hamilton without seeing the plant floor, where workers were feeding envelopes into high-technology electronic sorting machines, including the digital bar code sorter (DBCS) that subjected envelopes to 70 pounds of pressure and twisted each around a spindle. He knew nothing about the contamination in the three Florida post offices or of the nasal swabs and antibiotics Jean Malecki had offered to workers there. Had he known, he would have at least had the Hamilton facility tested.[7] But the risks to Florida postal workers were being downplayed. After Bresnitz left, maintenance crews as usual cleaned the digital bar code sorters using air pressure hoses set at 70 pounds per square inch. The fact of spores escaping from letters within the postal system, known in Florida, went unnoticed in the northeast. In New York, emerging suspect cases at the CBS and ABC news offices were attributed to other real anthrax letters that had been opened and tossed out weeks before—not to cross-contamination from leaking, sealed envelopes. As Bresnitz reflected later, "We were playing by the seat of our pants."[8]

At the emergency center in New Jersey, Eddy Bresnitz received word from the state medical examiner that the preliminary result for Teresa Heller's skin biopsy was positive. Bresnitz contacted the CDC in Atlanta and the biopsy was express mailed to the Anthrax Laboratory for further testing. The CDC—Brad Perkins had become their point man on state response—made it clear that no team would be sent from Atlanta unless Heller's biopsy was confirmed as positive. The contamination of the Florida post offices was a known fact, but it raised no flags at the CDC to test Hamilton.

Meanwhile, the reassurance that anthrax need not worry them was repeated to Hamilton postal workers on subsequent shifts that Monday.[9] On one of those shifts was Norma Wallace, age 55, who had spent the previous day in bed, racked by what she thought was the flu. By Monday, Wallace, who was black and lived alone in a nearby suburb, had rebounded and was back sorting mail. Another Hamilton employee at work that day was mail sorter Jyostna Patel, age 44. She and her husband were émigrés from India who had settled in south Jersey. As the day progressed, she began feeling chest pains.

One Hamilton postal worker, Bob Unick, who unloaded truck mail, was skeptical of reassurances that the facility was safe. Originally from Brooklyn, he had formerly worked in Manhattan at the Church Street facility near the World Trade Center. On 9/11, the manager successfully evacuated the building before debris from the falling towers destroyed it. Unick, with friends who had narrowly missed being killed by terrorists, instantly became risk averse. Over the October 12 weekend, while he was recovering from a bad cold, his buddies from the crew of the loading dock—all of them physically fit, if not brawny like Unick—telephoned him to talk about the Brokaw letter. Afterward, Unick immersed himself in the news coverage, which he found alarming.

✦

On October 15, while Eddy Bresnitz calmed the fears of Hamilton employees, an intern for Senate majority leader Tom Daschle, Grant Leslie, began sorting mail on the sixth floor of the Hart Senate Office Building in Washington. Ten other staff members were busy in the same area, the top floor of the senator's two-story suite.[10] Around 9:45 a.m. Leslie slit open a letter that released a puff of white powder. Leslie followed instructions: she put the envelope down, stepped back, and called for help. Leslie and others near her dusted with powder stayed put while one staff member telephoned the Capitol Hill police and the office manager blocked the open stairwell to the fifth-floor suite.

For weeks, the Hill's police force had been averaging at least one "anthrax" or "suspicious material" incident a day. The alarm from Daschle's office was their third that morning and, to their credit, three officers responded within a few minutes. Unaware of any persistent aerosol, they herded the ten bystanders into one room and isolated Leslie in another, giving her a chance to wash off the powder residue and change her clothes. The area cleared, two of the policemen put on hazmat suits and, using a rapid antibody assay, they tested the dispersed powder to see if it was really anthrax. The assay, developed by the Navy's Jim Burans for battlefield detection, was superior to those available to community first responders, and the Capitol Hill police were trained to use it. When the test showed a positive result, the three policemen, used to hoaxes, were surprised. They repeated the assay, and again it was positive. They then immediately called for a team from the Capitol's Office of the Attending Physician to rush over with Cipro and nasal swab kits.

The police then counseled Leslie to brace herself for a positive exposure result and gave her the option of being hospitalized, which she refused. The ten other staffers, once they had also washed their hands and faces, were ushered to a ninth-floor conference room to have their clothes swabbed for spores. Staffers from the adjacent sixth-floor suite of Wisconsin Democratic Senator Russ Feingold joined them. Meanwhile, Daschle's twenty-five staffers on the fifth floor were held in quarantine, their exposure uncertain.[11]

Senator Daschle was at his Capitol Building office, oblivious to this tumult. The pressures of Senate leadership after the trauma of 9/11 were literally giving him terrible headaches—that morning he had had an MRI at Bethesda Naval Hospital, on the advice of the Capitol's chief attending physician. Daschle's legislative headache was the USA PATRIOT Act (the acronym for the Uniting and Strengthening America by Providing Appropriate Tools Required to Intercept and Obstruct Terrorism Act), which was intended to increase federal latitude for domestic surveillance of potential terrorists, including access to private telephone and financial records. Two Democrats, Vermont Senator Patrick Leahy, head of the Senate Judiciary Committee, and Senator Feingold, were both arguing that the legislation might violate American civil liberties, while Attorney General Ashcroft protested that any delay in passing the act threatened national survival.

At 10:30 a.m. Senator Daschle was about to telephone his fellow South Dakotan Tom Brokaw—he had yet to talk with him about the anthrax letter—when one of his assistants interrupted him. "The staff over at the Hart office," he said, "just opened a letter that appears to have a toxic substance in it. We don't know what it is, but it may be anthrax."[12]

Advised to remain at his Capitol office, the shaken Daschle next took a phone call from President Bush. Bush was calling Daschle about Senate support for a range of anti-terrorism legislation and for his proposed tax cuts, meant to stimulate the economy. Daschle apologized for being distracted and explained the reason. With barely time to absorb the alarming details, President Bush hurried to a scheduled noontime press conference, a welcome for Italian Prime Minister Silvio Berlusconi. After Bush thanked his guest for his help in fighting terrorism, he announced, in response to a reporter's question about bioterrorism, the anthrax attack on Daschle.

"I just talked to Leader Daschle," the president said. "His office received a letter, and it had anthrax in it. The letter was field tested. The staffers that have been exposed are being treated. The powder that had been field tested is now, obviously, going to the CDC."

Looking stricken—President Bush had his own fears of being targeted—he then repeated the alertness advice the public had been hearing for three days. "The key thing," he said, "is for the American people to be cautious about letters that come from someone you may not know, unmarked letters, letters that have got—that look suspicious."

If the White House and its Office of Homeland Security expected Daschle to coordinate a crisis response with them, they were disappointed. Daschle turned instead to the Senate sergeant-at-arms, retired Army General Alfonso Lenhardt.[13] Lenhardt ordered the Capitol Hill police to contact the FBI, which assumed jurisdiction over the case and sent a team from its Hazardous Materials Response Unit in Quantico to take physical charge of the letter. Meanwhile, Lenhardt talked with Pentagon officials who put him in touch with USAMRIID, where the advice was to send the letter and its contents to John Ezzell at the Special Pathogen Sample Test lab for definitive analysis. Lenhardt also ordered the collection of all unopened Senate mail and the indefinite suspension of mail delivery.

Van Harp, assistant director-in-charge (ADIC) at the Washington FBI field office, followed established procedure for anthrax alerts on the Hill—there had been a number in Washington, including, in 1999, a hoax letter to Tennessee's Republican Senator Bill Frist. At first alert, Harp's office notified the FBI's Strategic Information and Operations Center, and a conference call was convened with the WMD brain trust at Quantico. All agreed that the letter should be categorized as a "Credible Threat" based on its message, which was a close rephrasing of the Brokaw letter, and the two assay results.

Around 1:15 p.m., not to be upstaged by the president, a consternated Senator Daschle held his own press conference on the Capitol lawn. He offered the familiar post-9/11 exhortation: Americans must not give in to terrorism. But Daschle was the highest U.S. government official personally targeted post-9/11 by a terrorist and the first ever victimized by an actual bioterrorist. The incident, even more serious than the attack on Tom Brokaw, showed that high American government officials were in personal jeopardy from terrorists.

A crowd of reporters had already gathered at the Hart Building, taking advantage of its atrium balconies and glass-walled offices to film an EPA team in hazmat suits vacuuming Daschle's suite for spores. The office blinds were eventually drawn, but the Daschle letter discovery was soon major broadcast news. Since every Hart office had televisions, its employees, including Daschle and his staff, watched with the surreal feeling that they, like Brokaw, were in a bioterror attack movie.[14]

In a protective move, the Office of the Attending Physician, assisted by the CDC, offered packets of a three-day supply of Cipro to any Hart employees who had been in the Daschle office that morning or anywhere in the vicinity—to err on the side of caution, as it was explained. With little or no information for gauging their risks, staffers guessed and gambled. Some rushed for their antibiotics; others, young enough to feel invincible, ignored the offer; still others, having heard that Cipro could have negative side effects, decided the risks of the drug outweighed the risks of infection.

While most Senate employees in the Hart Building stayed at their desks, the areas of contamination seemed to expand, with more offices around Daschle's being closed for testing and not reopened. The ventilation system for that quadrant had been left running, which raised EPA concern about spore dispersal, but not enough for a general building alert.

At the same time, FBI agents began interviewing Daschle's staff to learn more about hate mail and any other signs of hostility against the senator. The Capitol Hill police kept records of any threats against Daschle, who, as a liberal Democrat who was Catholic but also pro-choice, was a magnet for right-wing fanatics and right-to-life advocates. Every lead, including email correspondence, had to be tracked.

✦

The fastest way to deliver the Daschle letter to Fort Detrick was for FBI agents to drive north through Maryland with all the bagged material: the letter and envelope, several other letters gathered from the office, and the police assays that had been put in separate metal containers. After being cleared at the gate, they drove to the rear of Building 1425, where John Ezzell, who knew the drill, was waiting to fill out the required chain-of-custody forms that basically put him in charge of the evidence. But from the start, the packaging and handling of this material was problematic. Ziplock bags, tin foil, metal containers—all went through a Biosafety Level 2 (BSL-2) lab and then were passed to the next level laboratory suite, Biosafety Level 3 (BSL-3), which was standard for anthrax research and did not require the full suit and mask protection of the BSL-4 labs. The physical characteristics of the suspect powder and its virulence were unknown, which made staging the test environment a problem. The only certitude was that the Diagnostic Services Division and Ezzell had never taken on an assignment that affected such a high-ranking government official and, consequently, national security.

Since the discovery of the Brokaw letter and its delivery to the Special Pathogens lab (after a detour to the CDC), the excitement level in Building 1425 had risen. Bruce Ivins in particular was noticeably agitated, as might be expected of a longtime anthrax expert and one with a quirky personality. As top Army brass and FBI agents filled the halls, one of his colleagues emailed a former assistant, "Bruce has been an absolute manic basket case the last few days."[15]

Having worked before for the FBI, Ezzell had a grip on the general procedures he had to follow. Based on the assumption the assays were accurate, he would gear up in a protective suit, mask, and gloves and open the Daschle letter in a high-containment laboratory, at the Biosafety-3 level. This lab, like the others at USAMRIID, was also high security—with no entrance without a personal card and code number.

But in physically handling the letter, Ezzell ran into two unforeseen problems. In order to meet the FBI request for a photo of the envelope, he propped it up in a biosafety cabinet, a sealed transport container with built-in protective gloves. He had decontaminated the bottom of the box with chlorine bleach and then lined it with paper towels to soak up extra moisture. The towels were wet, and while Ezzell and the FBI negotiated the photo shoot, the letter's bottom edge wicked up the chlorine, blurring the address and some of the tracking codes.

Then the spore material itself proved unpredictable. To extract the letter from the envelope, Ezzell chose a container with a laminar flow hood to reduce air turbulence and prevent any cross-contamination. Using tweezers to gently pull the letter out, he found that, like the Brokaw letter, it had been folded into a pharmaceutical pocket to hold the powder. Unlike the grainy Brokaw powder, this powdery substance was uniformly pale white with a fine texture. As he unfolded the paper, the regulated air flow drew much of the material into the hood. As Ezzell used a spatula to extract more powder from the envelope, it too rose and dispersed. Ezzell still had enough powder material, though, to attempt to culture whatever bacteria it contained, which he estimated would take overnight.

✤

In Denver, the new Postmaster General of the United States, Jack Potter, right after giving the keynote address to a national meeting of mail vendors, was taken aside by a postal inspector and told the news of the Daschle letter.[16]

The Bronx-born son and grandson of postal workers, with a business degree from MIT's Sloan School, Potter had only that year been promoted. As head of the $70 billion corporate empire known as the U.S. Postal Service, he ruled what had been since the Nixon era a hybrid government-commercial entity with serious fiscal woes. With its monopoly on mail delivery eroding—FedEx and UPS were heavy competitors in package mail—USPS leaders kept investing in technologies that sped mail processing, improved tracking, and cut costs. These technologies (like the digital bar code sorters) also reduced employee numbers—nothing new in the history of industrialization. Yet, because of the strength of the postal unions, the workforce was shrinking mainly through retirement, which meant it was aging and expensive although overall highly efficient. Unfortunately, every economic downturn, like the one after 9/11, hurt postal revenues, which depended heavily on commercial bulk mailing.

The Daschle letter made it impossible to deny that the postal system might be the route for more attacks. Potter took the next plane back to Washington and at the USPS L'Enfant Plaza headquarters convened a task force of both postal and union officials. That afternoon he announced to the press that his group would meet daily until the anthrax problem—the rapid detection of what Potter now thought of as letter "missiles"—was resolved.[17]

Tim Haney, the general manager of the Brentwood facility, was at the Denver convention and had heard Potter's speech, which was upbeat about the future of printed mail. Haney, though, was at the front lines, working constantly to keep his nearly 2,000 workers performing like clockwork, against the counter-pressure of formal grievances and absenteeism.[18] In addition, the mammoth Brentwood facility, comprising 632,000 square feet, had chronic infrastructure problems—the roof had leaked since the building went up in 1986; the dilapidated workers' restrooms were defaced by graffiti; mice and cockroaches were common on the plant floor; and sparrows hovered at the drinking fountains.

Back at Brentwood, Haney invited union officials and CDC officers to give a special afternoon floor meeting to reassure workers that they were in no danger. Terrell Worrell, who drove a forklift to deliver small bundles around the entire plant, was impressed by how confidently local union leaders stood side-by-side with the short, stocky Haney, a demanding manager. With them were several CDC officers; their clean, neatly pressed uniforms also impressed Worrell, whose daily work was strictly blue collar. Worrell asked a question about the dustiness of the plant—in his daily rounds he had to continually wipe his eyeglasses. One of the CDC officers assured him that anthrax spores settled quickly on surfaces and tended to stick (which is true for individual spores in static environments) and posed no airborne risk.[19] Nonetheless, the tensions among workers were rising. During a regularly scheduled floor meeting, a DBCS technician requested a briefing on anthrax and proper safety procedures. His supervisor refused, a dispute about regulations broke out, and the technician was threatened with a seven-day suspension—a warning to other workers thinking about bucking authority. In an unusual reaction, a Brentwood supervisor refused to read out to workers a bulletin from the USPS asserting they were safe from anthrax; he himself did not believe it. Rumors about these and other incidents increased the anxious atmosphere at Brentwood.

That Monday night, Dena Briscoe was at work as usual. No one had briefed her shift about the Daschle letter. Instead, workers were whispering among themselves, on the plant floor and in the break rooms that opened directly onto it.[20] Her breathing short, with tears spontaneously pouring from her eyes, Briscoe barely finished her shift.

Early Tuesday morning, tests from Bethesda Naval Hospital showed that twenty of Daschle's staff tested positive for significant anthrax exposure, along with two of Feingold's staff, and six first responders, among them the three Capitol Hill policemen who had responded to the call—which fit the unheeded Canadian report estimates. In reaction, hundreds of government employees on the Hill joined the line to the dispensary that had been set up in a hearing room at the Hart Building. Still, while investigators in hazmat suits continued with environmental testing, the building remained open and many staffers stayed at their desks.

✦

That same Tuesday morning, at USAMRIID, Ezzell reported to his institute superiors that the Daschle letter powder was made up of *B. anthracis* spores. At 8:30 a.m., with the letter evidence secure in his division's BSL-3 lab, Ezzell discussed his findings in an hourlong conference call with the FBI WMD division. In that call, he described the Daschle spores as "weaponized." He'd been impressed that the spore material was unusually pure, lacking much of the vegetative debris that accumulates as anthrax bacteria revert to their spore form. Ezzell's description also seemed to imply that USAMRIID was in the clear as a suspect source, that its *B. anthracis* spores, used only for defensive research, lacked this level of refined purity, whereas insiders knew its aerosol experiments required debris-free preparations.

Ezzell's term "weaponized" was passed up to the White House and shared with the intelligence community, which had become part of ongoing interagency conference calls about anthrax organized by one of the National Security Council staff. The characterization was soon leaked to the press, where former Detrick scientist Dick Spertzel, then a consultant for ABC News, and others advocating regime change in Iraq seized on spore "weaponization" as proof positive that Saddam Hussein, with his known anthrax capability, was colluding with al Qaeda.

For USAMRIID to become a party to national security speculation was beyond its mission. Major General John Parker, director of the institute's governing authority, the Army's Medical Research and Materiel Command at Detrick, was tasked with pulling back from the weaponization term, starting with a Tuesday briefing for Senate leaders. A surgeon with over thirty-five years of Army service, Parker knew little about anthrax, but through no fault of his own. The Army had long routinely rotated officers with medical or general biology degrees through the positions that governed USAMRIID, leaving defense researchers free to pursue their scientific goals without military meddling. To the senators, Parker used other words, like *potent* and *virulent*, to describe the Daschle letter material.

Immediately after Parker's briefing, Daschle faced the press. Visibly upset, he struggled with verbal nuance: "We were told it was a very strong form of anthrax, a very potent form of anthrax which clearly was produced by someone who knew what he or she was doing." Whether "very potent" or "weaponized," it made no difference; speculation associating Iraq and the Daschle letter took off. That night, Arizona Republican Senator John McCain, a guest on the *Late Show with David Letterman*, confided to the nation that "some of this anthrax may—and I emphasize may—have come from Iraq." If that were the case, McCain asserted, "some tough decisions are gonna have to be made."

In public, President Bush and his top officials were reluctant to speculate about the source of the anthrax letters, although the phrasing of the Daschle letter pointed to al Qaeda. Dated September 11, 2001, like the Brokaw letter, its text differed in its specific mention of anthrax, as if the perpetrator wanted no more mistakes made:

YOU CAN NOT STOP US.
WE HAVE THIS ANTHRAX.
YOU DIE NOW.
ARE YOU AFRAID?
DEATH TO AMERICA.
DEATH TO ISRAEL.
ALLAH IS GREAT.

About the Brokaw letter, Vice President Cheney expressed no doubt that al Qaeda was responsible. In an interview for Public Broadcasting that aired on October 12, he embellished on fragmentary intelligence to argue his point:

> We know that [Osama bin Laden] has over the years tried to acquire weapons of mass destruction, both biological and chemical weapons. We know that he's trained people in his camps in Afghanistan—we have copies of the manuals that they've actually used to train people with respect to how to deploy and use these kinds of substances.[21]

Yet immediately after the Daschle letter discovery, Cheney kept quiet about his convictions.[22] The government response to media inquiries about anthrax had turned into a cacophony of sound bites from too many officials.[23] The White House wanted a single government spokesman on anthrax who could calm public fear, not incite it. The obvious choice was former Pennsylvania governor Tom Ridge, who had been sworn in on October 8 as head of the White House Office of Homeland Security, established the same day.

Tom Ridge, who as Pennsylvania governor had rushed to mourn the victims at the site of the Flight 93 crash, arrived in Washington with his mind on border security.[24] Less than two weeks later, he was the administration's spokesman on the anthrax crisis. On Tuesday night, October 16, Ridge appeared on Tom Brokaw's *Nightly News* to reclaim the podium for the White House. Although he referred to the virulence of the spores, he emphasized that, for the Bush administration, countering the bioterrorism threat to Americans was "the number one priority this week and for the weeks ahead." Behind the scenes, Ridge was being educated by the interagency anthrax crisis group, which included the

CDC's Jeff Koplan and Julie Gerberding, along with Art Friedlander from USAMRIID, plus U.S. Air Force physician Bob Kadlec, who was on the Homeland Security Council. A quick study, Ridge planned his debut press conference for Thursday morning, to calm public anxiety about the anthrax threat.

✛

At his home in New Jersey, Hamilton postal worker Bob Unick watched Governor Ridge's interview with Brokaw and, more apprehensive than ever, went to work the night shift.[25] Although the Daschle letter (its photograph already posted on the FBI Web site) had a return address of nearby Franklin Park, New Jersey, Hamilton supervisors had no new information or plans to close the facility. "Don't panic," they told employees, "we are in touch with the CDC." When Unick asked about the "weaponization" of the Daschle spores, his supervisor replied, "Don't worry. Just do your job."

Yet Hamilton supervisors and workers knew that the possibility of harmful spore exposure was on the USPS agenda. That day, its engineering division in Washington had ordered all postal facilities nationally to use vacuums to clean dust from sorting machines, with only selective use of reduced air pressure (at 30 pounds per square inch instead of 70) for hard-to-reach places and absolutely no use of air pressure for general surface cleaning. In Florida, noticing the aerosols the air hoses caused, Jean Malecki had already advised postal managers to switch to vacuums. At Hamilton, Steve Bahrle, the branch president of local 308 of the National Postal Mail Handler's Union, along with others, noticed that air hoses were still being used full force. As Bahrle saw it, the fact of the Brokaw and Daschle letters both having been processed via Hamilton meant that harmful exposure had taken place and the plant ought to have been closed the day before, on Monday.[25]

Postal worker Jyotsna Patel of Hamilton was absent from work that Tuesday. Her physician diagnosed her chest pains and her trouble breathing as bronchitis, prescribed the antibiotic Levaquin, and advised bed rest. That evening, Norma Wallace felt the return of flu symptoms that on Sunday had kept her in bed all day.

✛

At 10:30 a.m. on Wednesday, to Senator Daschle's surprise and dismay, Republican Majority Leader Dennis Hastert announced that he was adjourning the House out of concern for the members' safety.

Searching for anthrax spores, the EPA crews kept finding them: in the hallway that joined the Hart Building to the adjacent Dirksen Senate Office Building (which was then boarded off with plywood), and then, backtracking, in the Dirksen mail room, which served the Hart Building, and then on the House side, in the Ford Annex mail room. On Wednesday afternoon, the decision was made to shut down the Hart Building, which was proving widely contaminated.[26] Fifty senators and their staffs, plus thirteen committee staffs had to be immediately relocated, taking only essentials, in a bizarre reenactment of the 9/11 evacuation of Congress. At the end of the day, Daschle reluctantly adjourned the Senate, which stopped debate on the PATRIOT Act. After the attack on the Pentagon on 9/11, a terrorist attack had again succeeded in obstructing the U.S. government.

In the midst of this havoc, the DRES scientists who authored the Canadian anthrax letter report arrived in Washington mostly unnoticed, gave a presentation on spore dispersal on Tuesday at a joint military meeting hosted by the U.S. Army, and went back to Medicine Hat on Wednesday. Similarly unnoticed was the implication of the contamination in the Dirksen hallway and the two congressional mail rooms: the Daschle letter, sealed with tape like Brokaw's, had leaked spores *before* it was opened.

THE POSTAL VICTIMS

The contingency we have not considered seriously looks
strange; what looks strange is thought improbable;
what is improbable need not be taken seriously.

—NOBEL LAUREATE THOMAS SCHELLING, 1962

Early Thursday morning, October 18, Eddy Bresnitz in New Jersey
received a call from the CDC that the skin biopsy for Teresa Heller, the
mail carrier, was positive for anthrax. A small investigative CDC team
was on the way. "They knew the letter had gone through Trenton,"
Bresnitz commented. "New Jersey was now on the map."[1]

Bresnitz drove to the emergency operations center in Ewing, where
he shared the news with acting health commissioner George DiFerdinando, a physician with a master's in public health whose area of
expertise was worker safety—providentially, as it turned out, for Hamilton employees. DiFerdinando then called the governor's office, while
Bresnitz called Joe Sautello at Hamilton to tell him about Heller's test
results. In response to a message from Sautello, postal inspectors and
New Jersey FBI agents arrived quickly at the facility and the decision
was made to immediately shut it down as a crime scene and to test it
for contamination.

The day before, Wednesday, October 17, Steve Bahrle, the local Hamilton union leader, submitted a formal complaint citing the "anxiety, pain, and suffering" of the workers in an environment that, after the discovery of the NBC and Daschle letters, was obviously unsafe.[2] On his night shift, Bob Unick, in reaction to the news about contamination at the Hart Building, filled out a leave form, handed it to his supervisor, and made his exit.

Around 1 p.m., Thursday, when Bresnitz arrived at the Hamilton facility, Sautello's office was closed, the workers had been evacuated, and the kitchen crew was closing the cafeteria. Bresnitz found Sautello and asked for a tour of the Hamilton processing area, the "factory floor" of the large building. For the first time he saw the digital bar code sorters (DBCS), now silenced, and began to realize the problem of turbulent air and spore dispersion. The CDC team arrived that day from Atlanta. As planned, the FBI delivered environmental samples from Hamilton to the state laboratory in Trenton for analysis.

That night, in a Princeton hotel conference room, Bresnitz and DiFerdinando met with CDC, FBI, and postal officials to discuss the next step.[3] Postal officials proposed that if the environmental samples revealed contamination, they would hire a local company to do a quick cleanup and reopen the facility the next day. They understood almost nothing about anthrax contamination and thought first of protecting the routine of mail processing. Cautious, the CDC team agreed with them. DiFerdinando, although he had no authority over the decision, argued that it would be prudent to wait until the environmental test results came back. Bresnitz seconded this approach. In addition to Heller, Richard Morgano, a Hamilton mail sorter, had a suspect sore on his hand; his test results were pending.

Debate continued until, near midnight, DiFerdinando declared that he wouldn't be on the podium with postal officials if they announced a quick reopening of Hamilton. As he said later, "I would not stand with them and would not vouchsafe for the safety of the work site to the workers and managers involved."[4] Realizing that this vote of no confidence from the New Jersey Department of Health would be embarrassing, the postal officials agreed to wait until Saturday, October 20, for the contamination test results. Compared to Florida and New York, DiFerdinando and Bresnitz had a distinct advantage in making public health decisions about Hamilton. There was no Governor Bush or Mayor Giuliani putting pressure on them. New Jersey Governor Christine Todd

Whitman had been recruited by the Bush administration to head the Environmental Protection Agency. The acting governor, Donald DiFrancesco, trusted DiFerdinando to run his department as he saw fit—under the political radar.

The shock for both DiFerdinando and Bresnitz was that, despite the confirmation of the Heller case, the CDC team they had been sent refused to recommend more personnel or the delivery of antibiotics or nasal swabs for Hamilton workers. On their own initiative, DiFerdinando and Bresnitz requisitioned antibiotics from supplies around the state and went ahead with preparations for an emergency clinic at the Robert Wood Johnson Hospital in Hamilton.[5]

In the scramble to provide basic medical protection and without CDC assistance, public health surveillance for potential anthrax cases among Hamilton workers faltered.[6] On Thursday afternoon, after a chest x-ray showed signs of what looked like pneumonia, mail sorter Jyotsna Patel was admitted to Robert Wood Johnson Hospital, the same hospital that was hurriedly preparing for the Hamilton clinic. But Hamilton postal supervisors, the CDC, and state public health officials had lost track of Patel and another patient, Norma Wallace, who was overwhelmed by flulike symptoms.

Earlier that same Thursday, Governor Ridge began his debut press conference on the anthrax threat, with Postmaster General Potter at his side. The two men, who had never met before this week, got along famously. They shared working-class roots as well as exceptional administrative skills. In addition to Potter, Ridge was flanked by a full retinue of carefully chosen and scripted federal officials, most notably Attorney General John Ashcroft, FBI Director Robert Mueller, Surgeon General David Satcher, and Major General John Parker from Fort Detrick. Ridge's main message was to assure the public that "on a daily basis, on an hourly basis, every single day, there is communication and collaboration between all agencies of government."

Ridge, like all high federal officials, relied on what his underlings told him. He had an assistant, counter-terrorism expert Lisa Gordon-Hagerty, who in response to the anthrax crisis had drawn on her interagency network and united it with CDC officials in Atlanta for what became nearly hourly conference calls, some, by necessity, at midnight or later. But the CDC, its resources stretched to the limit, was the weak link. The Heller diagnosis from New Jersey was relayed to Governor

Ridge, but he didn't understand its import. The CDC conveyed the information to Jack Potter, yet neither Potter nor Mueller seemed aware that the Hamilton plant could be a hazard. Federal interagency communication was active, but collaboration with local officials had failed.

The first order of business at Ridge's press conference was the surge in anthrax hoaxes, which was disruptive and costly. Powder in an envelope from Malaysia, sent to a Microsoft office in Reno, Nevada, was identified as anthrax, but the test turned out to be a false positive. Similar threat letters were sent to a suburban Denver hospital, a television studio in Burbank, California, and the State Department's Foreign Services Institute in Virginia. On cue, the outraged Ashcroft and then the gimlet-eyed Mueller, formerly a tough Department of Justice lawyer, warned that perpetrators of anthrax hoaxes were subject to state and federal prosecution.

Then Mueller made a surprise announcement. Vowing to bring whoever had sent the anthrax letters to justice, he said that the FBI and the U.S. Postal Service together were offering "a reward of up to $1 million for information leading to the arrest and conviction of those responsible for the terrorist acts of mailing anthrax." In truth, the FBI, still concentrating on 9/11, had yet to organize a comprehensive response to the anthrax letter attacks.[7]

Postmaster General Jack Potter promised that every household in America would receive a postcard describing the criteria for how to identify and report potentially dangerous mail.

It fell to Surgeon General Satcher, a grandfatherly African American appointed by President Clinton, to calm those worried about the disease threat. Satcher was the kind of traditional public health officer who urged people to wash their hands and cough in their sleeves, and he, too, believed his subordinates. They might have mentioned that Jeff Koplan was struggling with chaos in Atlanta or that the CDC Web site had crashed, leaving the public to seek information from alternative sources. For example, the Johns Hopkins Center for Civilian Biodefense Studies' and Senator Bill Frist's Web sites were both up and running and promoting the concerns about mass attack threats.

In keeping with the White House agenda to calm the public, Satcher emphasized that Senate and other Capitol Hill employees had been protected, which became his message to America:

We are delivering the appropriate medications to those
who need it, and we are erring on the side of caution in
making health care available to those who may have been
exposed to anthrax spores.

As Governor Ridge reassured the public, Brentwood manager Tim
Haney received two disturbing messages. One was his nightmare—
Postmaster General Potter would arrive at noon for an impromptu
press conference, on the plant floor. Haney hastily instructed a cleanup
crew to start hauling away the accumulated debris from packaging and
sweep the floor.

Then Haney learned that environmental tests performed the day
before by the Fairfax County, Virginia, Fire Department showed
anthrax contamination at the facility. The tests could be wrong, but
after a meeting that morning he approached one of the USPS's vice
presidents, Deborah Willhite, "to let her know the mail was leaking
and we were affected."[8] Rather than turning to the CDC or the EPA—by
no means customary partners of the postal service—Willhite arranged
for a well-known private company, URS Greiner Woodward Clyde
Engineering Consultants (URS), to conduct more environmental tests
(at a cost of $500,000), that very afternoon, after Potter's press confer-
ence was over.

Leroy Richmond, having finished his express mail delivery—he
reported to Qieth McQue, who worked near him—was recruited to help
clean up for the press conference. He had pitched in like this before; the
dust and debris around the bar code sorters were a chronic hindrance,
and on this day unacceptably unsightly. Richmond felt sick, but he finished the cleanup. As he left for home, he glimpsed the event's celebrity guest: John Walsh of the Fox television show *America's Most
Wanted*, which had an impressive record of over 600 criminal apprehensions in twelve years. Since 9/11, Walsh had been working with the
White House communications staff to broadcast information about
President Bush's list of twenty-two "most wanted" foreign terrorists.
Without a comprehensive game plan to investigate the anthrax letters,
the FBI promoted this same strategy: engage the public to spot the culprit.

At noon, Postmaster General Potter arrived at Brentwood and
found everything in order for his press conference. Twenty television
cameras were lined up to face him; the busy Brentwood floor made an

impressive background, proof of Potter's resolve to keep the nation's mail moving. With FBI Deputy Director Tom Pickard and John Walsh alongside him, Potter again announced the million-dollar reward for any information leading to the arrest of the anthrax terrorist. After the press conference ended, Potter toured the plant floor, shaking hands with workers, few of whom had clocked out to watch the event. In his career up the ranks, Potter had been on both sides of the bargaining table, representing employees and management, and he kept the common touch. He had no inkling at the time that he or the Brentwood workers were in harm's way.[9] Potter then left for yet another media appearance, on the Postal Service cable network.

At 2:20 p.m., a URS crew in hazmat suits arrived at Brentwood and began by testing the government mail section—where Helen Lewis and her co-worker Thomas Morris worked. At the other end of the vast floor, the crew also swabbed the digital bar code sorters near the loading dock. During the day, as the testing went on, manager Haney conducted floor meetings around the enormous plant to assure workers that there was no anthrax threat in the building, that no one was going to die from it, and that they should continue working.

Among postal workers on the floor, big factory-like facilities were sometimes jokingly referred to as "plantations," where management oversaw the "slaves." Terrell Worrell, the forklift driver, never found the joke funny. Like overseers, white managers at Brentwood had offices on the second floor with windows that overlooked the hundreds of black workers on the plant floor. The college-educated Worrell, in his midthirties, married to a schoolteacher, was the father of two young children. His Brentwood job gave him security and some spare time to write and compose pop-gospel keyboard music. He was soft-spoken but when he sang at church his tenor voice soared. When Worrell arrived for the night shift on Thursday, he found the URS crew in hazmat gear was still taking environmental samples and they had been joined by another hazmat team from Fairfax, Virginia. As Brad Perkins might have predicted, this was Worrell's worst day at work, and others at Brentwood were just as upset by the men in moon suits. Then, to make matters worse, the news of Hamilton's closing began to circulate.

Manager Haney sensed that tensions were again rising. But he expected his employees to keep working, to soldier on. The Postal

Service motto was, after all, about keeping to its appointed rounds, and there would be no mail delivery if processing stopped.

At a scheduled floor meeting, Terrell Worrell summoned his courage and asked the question that was on everyone's mind: With men in hazmat suits testing for contamination, wasn't it time to evacuate the building? Haney responded that the postal service could not afford to have employees "sitting at home" during the URS testing, that it could cost up to $500,000 a day to shut Brentwood down, and that uncooperative workers could lose their jobs.

By the end of the day on Thursday, the CDC declared the crisis in Washington over. No new cases of anthrax exposure had been found on Capitol Hill, after 3,000 individual tests. For four intense days, Koplan and his infectious disease experts, along with Tanja Popovic's Anthrax Lab, had worked overtime to coordinate the field and laboratory effort that made this unprecedented emergency response possible, while still responding to the Florida and New York crises. There had been neither the time nor the resources to explore possible risks within the USPS system, even though the signs of danger were emerging.

Despite tests that showed Florida postal workers had been exposed to anthrax and despite Teresa Heller's confirmed cutaneous case in New Jersey, neither the CDC nor the D.C. Department of Health had time to ponder the vulnerability of Brentwood employees. And in New Jersey, the CDC team was still refusing to recommend intervention. With Brentwood still open, public health officials had the option to initiate surveillance of anthrax symptoms. The regimentation of postal work—every on-the-job employee could be electronically located in space and time—made top-down communication easy. Just a simple health alert transmitted at floor meetings or posted in break rooms would have revealed that, starting Monday, four Brentwood men were feeling the first symptoms of inhalational anthrax. But that alert was never sounded.

On Thursday, Thomas Morris, age 54, who sorted government mail, finally sought treatment at his HMO, a Kaiser Permanente affiliate in southern Maryland. For several days he had been suffering from flu-like symptoms. The nurse practitioner who examined him concluded Morris probably had the flu and sent him home with Tylenol. Qieth McQue, age 53, and Leroy Richmond, age 57, who worked in federal express mail near the loading dock, were each feeling sick but "soldiered on" through the week, as did Joseph Curseen, who sorted mail at DBCS #17, also near the loading dock. Age 47 and usually in good health, Curseen thought he was suffering from a bout of food poisoning.

The URS team continued environmental testing at Brentwood until 2:30 a.m. Friday. At this point, according to Haney's office diary, the team reported to him that at least two areas of Brentwood had "tested hot" for anthrax—government mail and the last rows of the bar code sorters near the loading dock. A postal inspector had told Haney on Thursday that the Daschle letter's ID tag code, which would have revealed the exact DBCS and time of processing, was unavailable; the letter was being carefully decontaminated at Fort Detrick. After contacting Hamilton management, on Friday morning Haney figured out that DBCS #17 had processed the Daschle letter. The machine was shut down, but, on a later shift, a supervisor compensating for the breakdown of another sorter ordered #17 cleaned with compressed air—against the new rules—and restarted.

Just after the URS team left early that Friday morning, Leroy Richmond arrived for his usual 3 a.m.-to-noon shift. In his more than thirty years of postal service, he had never taken a sick day. As noon approached, though, he felt exceptionally weak and sought a medical referral. The nurse at Brentwood who examined him could find no fever and concluded nothing was really wrong. Failing to get the attention of a supervisor, who was instructing a group of workers about suspicious mail that might contain anthrax, Richmond filled out his own medical release form and brought it to another supervisor, who signed it. He then drove to his Virginia HMO, where his wife, Susan, who worked the evening shift at Brentwood, joined him.

That afternoon, CDC officials arrived for a meeting upstairs at Brentwood, where Haney told them about contamination at DBCS #17 and the mail bins used for the Senate. According to Haney's notes, the CDC team responded methodically that it would help with further environmental testing, notify the D.C. Department of Health, and use this information to identify potentially exposed employees.

The CDC did not communicate any great urgency about disease risks to either Haney or other USPS officials—nor was the New Jersey CDC team changing its risk assessment. Like Stephen Ostroff in New York, the CDC's lead officer in Washington, Rima Khabbaz, promoted the fictitious threshold of 8,000 anthrax spores, which was the received wisdom in Atlanta.[10] "Spores might have been leaking from envelopes," Khabbaz later told the *Washington Post*, "but it was unlikely that the totals reached 8,000. That is the number that decades-old studies with monkeys had suggested was the threshold for inhalation anthrax." Those old Detrick studies, often cited and seldom read, contained no evidence whatsoever for the existence of a threshold for inhalational anthrax. Nor were they designed to set safety standards, but rather the opposite: to calculate munitions requirements for Air Force attacks on targeted enemy cities.[11]

The possibility that anthrax aerosols could be created by the powerful sorting machines, which "pinched" each letter with sudden, extreme force, went unrecognized, although CDC officials had walked the noisy Brentwood floor where the digital bar code sorters ran constantly and were routinely cleaned with blasts from air hoses. The early URS positive results might have justified closing the facility, just as the discovery of contamination at the Hart Building helped justify its shutdown and the suspicion of contamination at Hamilton had, after some argument, kept it closed. Even without closing Brentwood, public health officials in charge in Washington had the twofold option Dr. Jean Malecki chose in Florida: first, advise postal workers about the risks of contamination and then offer antibiotics and nasal swabs. On Friday, the USPS reportedly requested that the D.C. Department of Health distribute antibiotics to the Brentwood employees. But Ivan Walks, the health department head, relied on the CDC for advice, and CDC officials, overburdened, hesitated.

At his HMO in Virginia, where Leroy Richmond went after leaving work, the examining doctor suggested he had the flu. But Richmond pleaded that his illness was something worse. His HMO's policy was to refer ambiguous cases to a central provider, in this instance the Fairfax Inova Hospital, also in Virginia, not far from where the Richmond family lived. There, the first physician who examined him also attributed Richmond's symptoms to the flu. When a second physician on duty, Cecele Murphy, agreed and was about to leave him, the ailing Richmond asked her not to go. "I have never felt so awful in my life," he insisted. "I know my body."

Alone among the health care professionals Richmond saw that day, Murphy paused to ask about Richmond's place of employment and made the connection between his symptoms and the passage of the

Daschle letter through Brentwood. Richmond himself had missed this connection. Responding to a request from his supervisor, a few days before he had read to other workers the precautions about powder spills and suspicious envelopes, but he himself was not a mail sorter and had seen nothing unusual. After Richmond's chest x-ray showed mediastinal widening, Murphy called Ivan Walks' office, which alerted the CDC, the mayor's office, postal inspectors, and the Senate Crisis Center, which was coordinating information.

Leroy's wife, Susan Richmond, called Tim Haney at Brentwood to warn him that her husband might have anthrax. Getting no response, she left a recorded message. Haney received another call about Richmond's illness that night, from the Mayor's Office of Emergency Response. Haney was to report to a 6 a.m. meeting the next day, Saturday.

That Friday in New Jersey, postal sorter Norma Wallace was hospitalized at Virtua Memorial Hospital near Trenton. The doctor there, suspicious she had anthrax, put her on an intensive regimen of antibiotics and began the painful process of draining liquid from her lungs. He also contacted New Jersey public health officials to arrange a blood sample analysis, but an error at the hospital delayed the transport of the sample for two days. That small mistake consequently delayed any alarm the case might have raised at Brentwood.

That same Friday, in New York, the FBI finally found the anthrax letter sent to the *New York Post*. After a delay at the Anthrax Lab, *Post* worker Johanna Huden's sore had finally been confirmed as cutaneous anthrax, but the *Post* letter, taped shut, had never been opened. Here was more evidence that intact anthrax letters in transit could spill spores. Like the other evidence of leakage, it was overlooked.

On Saturday morning Tim Haney joined other postal officials and staff from the CDC and the D.C. Department of Health at the mayor's emergency response office. All seemed loath to take responsibility for decisive action about Brentwood. Leroy Richmond's clinical record showed the classic signs of inhalational anthrax. He had routinely worked near DBCS #17. But the Anthrax Lab had yet to finish his blood analysis, and the full URS report, which would pinpoint contamination at DBCS #17, had not yet been submitted. The meeting ended with the decision that no action should be taken. Brentwood would remain open until there was complete proof of dangerous anthrax exposure. No one from the Washington FBI office acted to shut the facility down as a crime scene—and there was no one like George DiFerdinando in New Jersey, who spoke in the name of workplace safety.

✦

While postal, CDC, and Washington health officials delayed their response, the higher levels of government reacted to Richmond's illness as if it were a national security alert—the possible index case in a major outbreak. Senator Bill Frist, Congressional spokesman on the crisis, telephoned Tom Ridge that Saturday morning to argue that the case "could explode as a national security issue and a national public health emergency."[12] In a follow-up conference call with Secretary Thompson and officials from CDC and FEMA, he argued for a "surge capacity" in medical response should more cases arise. Urging everyone on the line to "make a list," Thompson gave assurances all would be provided.[13] Frist's list would be very long. Appearing on CBS's *Face the Nation* on October 15, he had already revived the 1997 "sugar-bag" scenario: "If an airplane flew over and exposed hundreds of thousands of people, you couldn't handle it in our public health infrastructure."

That same Saturday, Brentwood worker Qieth McQue, in a state of collapse, was admitted to Fairfax Inova Hospital and put in the same intensive care unit as Leroy Richmond. His physician there, Susan Matcha, had him put immediately on Cipro and then told McQue about his likely diagnosis, which terrified him. His first reaction was flight. "I come from the West Indies," he said later, "where a hospital is just for two things: birth and death."[14] Like Richmond's, his chest cavity was full of pleural effusions—the anthrax bacteria had overcome his immune system and he would be lucky to live.

Brentwood worker Joseph Curseen fell unconscious that Saturday afternoon, during mass at his parish church in Maryland, but then he revived and worked his regular night shift.

CDC surveillance efforts to identify Brentwood workers at risk finally began Saturday night, when Rima Khabbaz, assisted by manager Haney, attempted to reach absentee employees who might be ill and tried to identify those who had routinely worked near Richmond in order to give them priority in receiving antibiotics. Late that night, Khabbaz and her team telephoned local hospitals and clinics to check for Brentwood patients and called individual employees, but no suspicious cases surfaced. The Kaiser HMO that Thomas Morris had visited on Thursday was not on the list. On the floor below, on the night shift, Joseph Curseen was sorting mail.

That same night, rumors circulated among floor workers that the building would be closed and the employees put on medications and relocated to other facilities, but Brentwood remained open and running as usual.[15] At an 11 p.m. floor meeting, as Dena Briscoe recalled, Haney was upbeat about Richmond's condition. "We have an employee," he announced, "who is not being identified, in the hospital. He has not been diagnosed as having anthrax but is being looked at very carefully. In fact, he is doing good and looking forward to watching the football game tomorrow. [The Washington Redskins were to play the Carolina Panthers.] I wanted you all to know the building is safe, the mail is safe, and you are safe. We want to keep the mail moving and keep our numbers up."

Joseph Curseen was at the meeting, looking, as Briscoe noticed, exhausted and barely able to stand as the talk continued.[16]

At Fairfax Inova, Richmond was in toxic shock and on intravenous antibiotics. Anthrax bacteria had flooded his system and liters of fluid were being drained from his lungs. Dr. Murphy told him and his family that his odds of survival at this late stage were low. Richmond obstinately turned his face to the wall, refusing to accept a death sentence.[17]

At 4:39 a.m. Sunday, Thomas Morris telephoned 911 from his home to summon medical help. In the tragic call, which was later widely broadcast, the failing but still articulate Morris identified himself, where he lived, and explained that he thought he had been exposed to anthrax where he worked, at the Brentwood post office. (He was thinking of the letter Helen Lewis had discovered.) "I feel dizzy," he said, "I'm vomiting." An ambulance was quickly dispatched and brought him to Greater Southeast Hospital in Washington.

Around 2:30 a.m. that same Sunday, having finished his shift, Joseph Curseen went to the emergency room at Southern Maryland Hospital Center. He had been vomiting and sweating heavily. His chest x-ray, which showed mediastinal widening, was misread as normal. He was discharged with a diagnosis of stomach flu and sent home after receiving intravenous hydration.

At 7:30 a.m. the same morning, the CDC informed D.C. health commissioner Ivan Walks of Richmond's positive test results. Not yet alerted, at 8 a.m., Haney and his staff nonetheless arrived at work to discuss "evacuation and contingency plans" and how to maintain "mail flow." According to Haney, the CDC notified him only at 11 a.m. In a meeting shortly after that in the facility's cafeteria, he told a group of employees that a Brentwood postal worker was hospitalized with a confirmed diagnosis of anthrax and that as a "precautionary measure" the facility would be "immediately evacuated" and closed. He would need their help for an orderly shutdown. Word of the closure was broadcast on local television to alert workers on subsequent shifts that they should assemble in the parking lot for their new assignments and other information.

As the plant was evacuated, Haney and his supervisors canvassed the crowd with lists of names, arranging reassignments to six other area facilities. Many workers, still in their smocks and aprons, planned to show up at their new workplaces the next day, with no leave time, and they also anticipated the plant closure would be brief, a few weeks at most.

In the parking lot, CDC and District health officials distributed fliers offering basic information about the emergency closure. The first question on the handout read: "Why am I here today?" The answer was: "A worker in your facility has been diagnosed with anthrax. The investigation of where this employee became exposed is ongoing. However, as a precaution, workers who worked in the same area of this employee have been contacted to come and have an evaluation as well as start a course of medication." There was a warning that the medication would have to be taken for a long time because of a "prolonged incubation period," a phrase left unexplained.

The phrase puzzled Terrell Worrell, who arrived at Brentwood around 3 p.m. To him the atmosphere in the parking lot seemed almost festive.[18] Pizza and soft drinks were available. One tent had been erected to shelter employees from the sun and another to divert incoming mail. A sense of urgency about distributing antibiotics seemed missing. Traffic congestion from an afternoon rock concert blocked access to Washington General Hospital, where an emergency clinic would otherwise have been set up. The District government offered a temporary distribution center at One Judicial Square, where employees were instructed they could go right away—or they could wait until the next day when the Washington General clinic would open.

Unlike Hamilton (which was evacuated, as one employee later put it, in twenty minutes flat), Brentwood remained open until 7 p.m., while a team of ten workers without protective gear organized the mail inside into trays and hampers and loaded it into postal service trucks—where much of it remained for the next five months, awaiting decontamination.

Dena Briscoe heard about the Brentwood closure on television and drove there in a daze. Without getting out of her car—she stayed as far from the building as she could—she managed to get the necessary flyers and, still in a blur, drove to Judiciary Square. Once she'd registered, had a nasal swab, and received her packet of antibiotics, she started to leave, but a nurse asked her to stop for a blood test. Briscoe agreed but was unsure why she had been singled out or what the test was for. As she was again about to leave, a man it took her a minute to recognize stopped her and asked if she needed help. The nephew of one of her co-workers, he was a Washington social worker who was treating people traumatized by 9/11. She hadn't realized how disoriented she looked.

"Take my card," he said, "and call if you need to."

Briscoe slipped his business card in her pocket without looking at it. As she drove toward home, she went into a fugue state and lost her way, ending up in the Washington neighborhood of her childhood. Her throat was sore and she was short of breath. More than anything, she felt afraid.

At home, frustrated and fearful, Helen Lewis from Brentwood government mail felt she had sounded the alarm on October 11 with the suspicious letter she turned in to her supervisor, even though the FBI had been unconcerned about it. On October 15, she had paid out of her own pocket to fill her Cipro prescription. As she thought about it later, it might have been the best eighty dollars she had ever spent. But why hadn't everyone been protected earlier? Why hadn't Brentwood employees been tested for anthrax exposure when the men in hazmat suits arrived that Thursday, October 18?

As Sunday drew to a close, three Brentwood workers—Richmond, McQue, and Morris—were hospitalized, but only Richmond had been officially confirmed as a case of inhalational anthrax. As Cipro was pumped into his body and more liquid was drained from his lungs, he struggled for life. In moments of stress, he always carried rosary beads. He kept a string of them in his hands during this ordeal.

Thomas Morris, age 55, died at 8:45 that evening at Greater Southeast Hospital, with his wife and family around him—shocked and grieving just as the Stevens family had been sixteen days before.

Early Monday morning, Celestine Curseen found her husband, Joseph, unconscious on the bathroom floor. She called 911 and then drove him to Southern Maryland Hospital. He died there six hours later, also surrounded by a family that could hardly believe its loss. No official would say for sure whether it was anthrax that had killed him and Morris. The diagnoses had to wait for CDC confirmation.

That Monday afternoon, October 22, Tom Ridge held a press conference, along with Jack Potter and the CDC's Mitch Cohen, a senior scientist from its Center for Infectious Diseases who had been seconded to the FBI's Washington office. Asked if the Brentwood facility should have been closed earlier, Ridge relayed what he had been told, that after the Daschle letter was tracked to Brentwood, the CDC and USPS had "immediately put everybody, the hospitals and everybody else, on alert to see if anybody presented themselves with symptoms."

In full uniform and obviously distraught, Postmaster Jack Potter praised Morris and Curseen as public servants who had died serving their country. His voice cracking, he continued:

> It's clear to us, like other symbols of American freedom and power, the mail and our employees have become the target of terrorists. It is equally clear that we must take extraordinary steps to protect them both.

Vowing that nothing would stop U.S. mail delivery, Potter avoided the burning question: Why had the response at Brentwood been fatally delayed? Inexperience was certainly one explanation. The CDC's Brad Perkins, who had experienced the crisis starting in Florida and through the deaths in Washington, described it as "like trying to build an airplane while you are flying it over a football stadium full of news reporters."[19] Appearing after the press conference on the PBS *NewsHour*, Mitch Cohen explained that the CDC simply had lacked information. "At first, we had no evidence that any of the mail handlers were at risk," Cohen explained. "This phenomenon of first having skin disease in New Jersey and now having inhalational disease [in Washington] is an evolution," he added, discounting the two Florida cases.[20]

The same day, Bush press secretary Ari Fleischer announced that a mail slitter at an off-site facility that served the White House had tested positive for anthrax spores. Had the president been targeted? According to one administration insider, the anthrax crisis intensified the president's feeling about terrorism: "It was a hard stare into the abyss."[21] In a spontaneous televised appearance, President Bush assured the nation, "I don't have anthrax," and, he added, "it's hard for Americans to imagine how evil the people are who are doing this."

CHAPTER 6

THREAT PERCEPTIONS

From the mistreatment of individuals to the total break-down of social interactions, disease outbreaks have distorted society.

—William H. Foege, CDC director, 1977–1983

After a three-day anthrax shutdown that began on October 17, Congress reconvened and quickly passed the USA PATRIOT Act. Along with other counter-terrorism provisions, it required submitting the name of anyone with access to select agents, that is, those that could be used for biological weapons, to be cleared by the Attorney General's office and the Department of Health and Human Services, not only to prevent terrorist access but to weed out felons or those with a history of mental disturbance. On October 26, when President Bush signed the bill into law, he praised Thomas Morris and Joseph Curseen as "postal workers who died in the line of duty"—putting their deaths squarely in the framework of the "war on terror." The president, assuring the nation that over two hundred postal facilities in the Northeast Corridor were being tested for anthrax contamination, promised that "we will move quickly to treat and protect workers where positive exposures are found."

The test results showing postal contamination were already accumulating. Pulling no punches, Postmaster General Jack Potter went on national television to warn the nation that "there are no guarantees the mail is safe" and to urge Americans to "wash their hands thoroughly after contact, and to be aware of any symptoms that they might have on their bodies."[1] Nationally, the sales of protective gloves, masks, and antibiotics again soared. Potter himself was on Cipro; his Thursday press conference at Brentwood, especially the time he had spent shaking hands on the plant floor, had put him at risk.

In the coming weeks, Tom Ridge continually updated the public on the anthrax crisis and top federal officials were in close communication. An unexpected newcomer, Jack Potter now attended urgent national security meetings, taking a seat next to CIA Director George Tenet. Through the interagency network that Lisa Gordon-Hagerty at the White House had put together, the CDC was in constant contact with Ridge as the big-league federal bureaucracies—Health and Human Services, Justice, the Pentagon, the Department of Energy, the State Department, and the CIA—staked out their policy positions. Meanwhile, local officials and the CDC, snapped to attention by the two postal deaths, reorganized for renewed emergency response—with strategies that varied as widely as their first responses.

In Florida, surveillance in Palm Beach County and surrounding areas had been ongoing since the Stevens diagnosis, with medical examiners and hospitals reporting suspect cases. There were none; nor was exposure indicated among the 31 postal workers who asked for nasal swabs. Except for Ernesto Blanco and Stephanie Dailey, no AMI results were positive. After October 21, cases of illness among the 3,263 employees in the Palm Beach County postal facilities revealed no signs of anthrax infection.

In New York City, the Department of Health officials and the CDC finally tested Morgan Station on Ninth Avenue for anthrax spores. Positive results from the third-floor mechanical sorters led to an immediate distribution of antibiotics to its 5,000 employees, plus 2,000 others employed in the city's mail system. Outraged, the American Postal Workers Union sued to have the entire facility shut down, a move rejected by the courts three weeks later because the decontamination appeared effective; later environmental tests revealed that spores still remained, leading to another furor.[2]

Thanks to Marci Layton's team, surveillance for clinical cases in New York City continued; no inhalational anthrax cases emerged, although two *New York Post* reporters came down with cutaneous anthrax, due to mail contamination at the newsroom. Mayor Giuliani was less visible during this phase of the anthrax crisis management which, more than the Brokaw letter discovery, heightened anxiety about routine mail delivery.

In New Jersey, four days after the Hamilton facility closed, the CDC finally pitched in to help George DiFerdinando and Eddy Bresnitz hold clinics for the exposed postal workers. Environmental tests inside the Hamilton facility revealed that nearly every surface of the processing area was positive for anthrax spores; the risks to its employees were serious and undeniable. Some employees, like Bob Unick (who had left the facility the day before it was shut down) had already obtained Cipro from their own physicians who had no way to assess the threat; Unick's doctor, for example, advised him against taking antibiotics.

In response, New Jersey public health officials and social workers threw their energy into multiple workshops to persuade Hamilton employees to comply with the precautionary two-month regimen of antibiotics, despite uncomfortable side effects.[3] The cases of Norma Wallace and Jyotsna Patel, who both nearly died of inhalational anthrax, were belatedly discovered and confirmed, along with two more cutaneous cases, one involving a mail sorter at another New Jersey plant and the other a bookkeeper residing in Hamilton who was apparently infected by postal cross-contamination. Subsequently, the New Jersey Department of Health, in cooperation with the CDC, launched an intensive tristate regional surveillance campaign to discover other anthrax victims.[4] None were found, but what was striking was that the effort was not replicated in the other major crisis area, Washington, D.C.

The heavily contaminated Hamilton facility would be closed indefinitely—a setback that its employees had not expected. DiFerdinando and Bresnitz continued working with Joe Sautello, Hamilton's manager, who arranged for them to meet with postal officials, union leaders, and employees to discuss long-term prospects. The options were to make the infected building safe or tear it down. By scale alone, every large building affected by the anthrax letters—starting with the AMI building in Boca Raton, followed by the Hart Senate Office Building—posed a significant decontamination problem: How much chlorine dioxide gas would it take to eliminate every spore from every surface? No one had done the calculations. AMI and Hart were simply office buildings; the enormous Hamilton and Brentwood facilities, full of complex machinery, were cleanup nightmares orders of magnitude beyond what the Postal Service or the EPA had ever imagined. And anthrax spores were not just pollutants; they were lethal infectious disease agents.

Hamilton workers, shifted to other facilities, working as backup crews in tents or trailers or in a nearby warehouse the Postal Service was able to lease, wanted their building reopened quickly. But the chances of that were slim; an effective cleanup process depended on the right mix of disinfectants, how they were applied, at what temperature, and whether the EPA safety regulations could accommodate a first in industrial history: grand-scale anthrax decontamination.

Jack Potter appointed Tom Day, the vice president of engineering at the Postal Service, as his point man on postal decontamination.[5] Like Potter, Day came from a two-generation postal family in New York City. Unlike Potter, who had risen through the ranks, Day had entered the Postal Service at the managerial level, after having graduated with an engineering degree from West Point and serving as an officer for five years. Day understood every new advance in postal machinery down to the circuit board, plus he was a gifted communicator with seventeen years of management experience. But the anthrax contamination problem was colossal—and not just because two dozen facilities in the Northeast Corridor eventually tested positive. The mail itself, as Potter made clear, could be coated with spores, especially if it had mixed with mail in Washington, where the small particles from the Daschle letter had done the most damage.

Destroying contaminated mail was not an option; before delivery, it had to be irradiated with electron beams or x-rays to destroy any spore residue. For safety's sake, 39 trailers of government mail taken from Brentwood (4 intended for the U.S. Senate, 20 for the House of Representatives, and 15 for the Library of Congress) were held until the Postal Service finally selected a contractor in Ohio to begin bulk irradiation, which would take months.[6] In the meantime, current federal mail was irradiated—the fumes sickened some postal workers who had to handle it—and circumvented to off-site stations where staffers (some of them also nauseated by the smell) picked up the "fried" letters and parcels. Ninety million pieces of Hamilton mail were also slated for irradiation.

Postmaster Potter considered Tom Day an expert on biological weapons, but from Day's perspective, he was more like the one-eyed in the land of the blind. In his days as an Army captain, he had taken a course on WMD, but that was in the 1980s when the emphasis was on the Soviet nuclear threat.[7] Before his promotion to USPS vice president in 2000, Day became familiar with emergency postal drills, which were held to test responses to intentional threats, including bombs, dangerous chemicals, and employee violence. The anthrax threat was nominally addressed; the protocol—reaffirmed on October 10—was to isolate the mail item and notify authorities. As for closing a facility, that wasn't necessarily required. "The view then," Day later recalled, "was that you had a fairly crude form of anthrax, which was dangerous if inhaled or touched or ingested, but its being weaponized or [causing] contamination was not on the radar screen."

Earlier in his career, Day had been the manager of the Hamilton facility. In late October 2001, he returned to New Jersey for what became a protracted series of meetings to shore up worker morale. Tearing down the facility, it was soon clear, meant job losses that New Jersey political forces and postal employees strongly resisted. Agreeing, Day assured Hamilton employees that he would give them back their work space, and that it would be stripped down, refurbished, and reopened better than before—no matter how long it took. As for cost, the U.S. Congress was promising special appropriations, in the tens of millions of dollars.[8]

In Washington, the decontamination of the Brentwood facility presented a radically different set of problems. It was twice the size of Hamilton, set in a densely populated minority neighborhood, and it was notoriously the place where two postal workers had been fatally infected. After touring the closed Brentwood facility in a hazmat suit, Tom Day became concerned about how its neighbors would react to the cleanup process, which would require enclosing the plant in a huge plastic bubble and generating chlorine dioxide gas on site. Necessarily experimental, the process could take months. In the short term, Day ordered the extermination of the rats he noticed gorging on rotting cafeteria food before they invaded the local community. For the long term, he began thinking about biosensors positioned at sorting machines and improved air quality—using high pressure air blowers to clean sorters had been stopped—as ways of preventing repeat contamination.

While the Postal Service pursued technical solutions, the Brentwood rank-and-file displaced to other facilities on October 21 received almost no attention regarding either their compliance with taking the prescribed antibiotics or other health issues, including psychologically adjusting to the deaths of their two colleagues. In a grand ceremony, Postmaster Potter presented each of the widows of Morris and Curseen with a specially struck "Medal of Freedom" commemorating their husbands' valor—and reinforcing the need for stoic resolve among postal workers in an age of terrorism. Manager Tim Haney visited the facilities in the District of Columbia, Virginia, and Maryland to which the Brentwood employees had been reassigned, but it was his job to see they were keeping up the mail numbers, which had taken a beating from the anthrax letter attacks—not to monitor their health.

The Postal Service, though, did keep a list of Brentwood employees who sought medical care immediately after the facility was shut down. Eleven, including Dena Briscoe, were admitted to area hospitals. The CDC and postal inspectors reviewed the cases, none of which seemed to be inhalational anthrax, although given the rarity of the disease, the diagnostic criteria—blood tests and even x-rays—could not be perfectly reliable. Briscoe, diagnosed with bronchitis, was treated at the same Maryland hospital where Thomas Morris had died; after a week she was discharged, still bothered by a persistent throat ailment and the same disorientation that had afflicted her the day the Brentwood facility was shut down.

After the Morris and Curseen deaths, the Postal Service, the CDC, and local authorities were fundamentally engaged in "mop-up" operations. For the FBI, the anthrax alarms kept ringing as reports of anthrax incidents poured in from its field offices. In the first weeks after the Brentwood deaths, Ben Garrett and others at the WMD brain trust at Quantico fielded one anthrax incident report about every twenty minutes, worse by far than the dozens generated by Secretary Cohen's 1997 "sugar-bag" speech. U.S. postal inspectors also confronted an unprecedented upsurge in alleged anthrax letters and sightings. From mid-October 2001 to December 2002, its Inspection Service responded to over 17,000 anthrax reports, all of them hoaxes or innocuous incidents.[9] But at the height of the crisis, the FBI and postal inspectors could not afford to ignore the possibility of more lethal letters or the advent of a mass attack.

While the alarms kept sounding, the FBI was faced with the problem of three actual anthrax letters from which all apparent distinctive marks—certainly any human DNA or fingerprints—were missing. The envelopes were the 34-cent, pre-stamped blue federal eagle variety, mass produced by the hundreds of thousands and for sale at post offices around the country. Each letter had been sealed by ordinary clear cellophane tape. To avoid leaving identifying ink or signs of a particular pen tip, the perpetrator had photocopied both the letters and the envelope addresses. The Brokaw and *Post* letters had slight signs that the photocopier's glass plate had been scratched; this barest of clues led to the testing of dozens of copy machines in the Hamilton area and beyond, with no results. The perpetrator had also block printed all writing, erasing marks of personality or mood. In content, the two messages were about as informative as graffiti—seemingly al Qaeda hate messages, but not claimed by the group. FBI language and culture experts were put to the test: was the perpetrator a fanatical Islamic terrorist or someone posing as one?

The anthrax letters offered enough information for at least a rudimentary criminal profile of the sender. In 1972, when the FBI Academy created its Behavioral Science Unit, the Bureau began systematizing psychological assessments of serial killers and also rapists. Using interviews with convicted criminals like Ted Bundy and Jeffrey Dahmer, analysts hoped to create profiles that would help police track elusive suspects. The program grew and diversified, becoming in 1984 the National Center for the Analysis of Violent Crime. Assuming that a single terrorist had sent the anthrax letters (an assumption that not everyone in Washington accepted), analysts took all that was known about the letters, the targets, and the spore material, and began configuring the modus operandi, background, and personality of the anonymous killer. Granted, whoever sent the anthrax letters may not have originally intended to kill, only to scare; why else advise the target to take penicillin? Yet the Daschle letter had been postmarked three days after Bob Stevens' death, which suggested a willingness to put other targets in mortal danger, even if the second version of the letter warned, "THIS IS ANTHRAX."

Eventually, when the three anthrax letters were decontaminated and transferred from USAMRIID to Washington, they were analyzed by FBI fiber, paper, and ink experts. But it was the anthrax spores themselves that made the case unique and ultimately pointed to a new kind of forensic science. In the early days of the investigation, many thought the Ames strain was from Iowa and had been used in the U.S. biological warfare program, which meant it could have circulated for over forty years in hundreds of laboratories.[10] In addition, the extreme uniformity of the strain's genetic sequence made it seem a generic weapon, reproducible on petri dishes without any distinct features. For FBI investigators and anthrax experts alike, tracing a distinct genetic signature in the bacteria that had killed three people seemed a remote possibility. Yet Rita Colwell, the distinguished bacteriologist who headed the National Science Foundation, thought otherwise.

Colwell was holding an informal interagency meeting on bioterrorism when news of the Stevens diagnosis broke.[11] Sensing the potential for innovative input, she immediately contacted Claire Fraser, the president of TIGR (The Institute for Genomic Research), a Rockville, Maryland, company where the anthrax genome of a *B. anthracis* strain had already been sequenced.[12] Colwell asked if Fraser would be willing to begin a comparative genetic analysis of the Ames strain. Van Harp, heading the FBI investigation, was especially supportive of scientific input and took counsel from his WMD experts at Quantico. An agreement was reached, and in two days Colwell speeded TIGR's application for funding through the foundation's review process. To begin, Fraser and her scientists would compare the original 1981 "Ames Ancestor" strain, from a sample held by the U.S. Army at Dugway Proving Ground in Utah, with a derivative Ames sample from the British Defence Science and Technology Laboratory at Porton Down. The goal, a long shot, was to find a genetic signature in the letter spore material that could lead back to its laboratory source and perhaps the perpetrator.

✳

In the interim, anthrax contamination in the mail was still endangering human lives. On October 25, David Hose, a contract worker at the State Department mail annex in Winchester, Virginia, went to his physician after several days of feeling nauseous and weak. His chest x-ray looked normal and though his physician doubted he had anthrax he prescribed Cipro and ordered a blood sample analysis. The next day Hose's blood showed gram-positive rod-shaped bacilli. By that time Hose was gravely ill and had to be brought to the hospital by ambulance.

While Hose was being hooked up to intravenous Cipro, Brentwood manager Tim Haney was explaining to a CDC officer the possible routes that an anthrax letter could take from Brentwood's government mail bins to all the federal agencies, including the Winchester annex. Alerted to Hose's diagnosis, CDC officials speculated that Hose's infection might have been caused by cross-contamination from the Daschle letter—an acknowledgment of the danger of small-dose exposure.

But FBI analysts reasoned that more than one anthrax letter might have been sent to Congress. To track any additional anthrax letters, the Bureau decided to install the equivalent of a Biosafety Level 3 laboratory in a Virginia warehouse and transport to it the government mail accumulated from Brentwood and Capitol Hill.[13] Over 600 plastic bags of mail were sealed in 230 metal drums and delivered to the warehouse. FBI analysts advised Doug Beecher and others at the Bureau's Hazardous Materials Response Unit in Quantico that they should be looking for an envelope that closely resembled the three letters already discovered. The unit members reasoned that an unopened anthrax letter would shed spores, just as the others had done at postal facilities, and therefore it should be traceable by testing every bag for contamination. Once "hot spots" were discovered, they could conduct a manual search.

＊

In a more pressing effort, the FBI needed nearly instant feedback on the enormous number of environmental and clinical samples being turned in from known target sites and from suspected ones. The potential anthrax threat to the nation demanded exactly the kind of expertise, the high-containment laboratories, and the military security that USAMRIID's Diagnostic Services Division (DSD) offered. The choice of the institute seemed ideal. The Bureau already had a working relationship with John Ezzell at the Special Pathogens analysis lab within the DSD. The volume of samples would be enormous, but no other institution—whether in government, universities, or among defense contractors—matched USAMRIID's capacity.

When the FBI became a client of the Diagnostic Services Division, its project to analyze thousands of samples related to the anthrax letter investigation became part of Operation Noble Eagle, President Bush's special designation for the military's domestic response to the al Qaeda attacks. In the framework of 9/11, USAMRIID was assisting in national defense by helping the FBI track a terrorist or terrorists. The sample analyses, like the hundreds being done by Tanja Popovic at the CDC in Atlanta, where her team was working nonstop, would also confirm the scope of the letters' impact: the range of contamination and infection at the different crisis sites and whether the attacks were ongoing or not. At the rate of 2,000 per week, the FBI samples began arriving at Detrick daily by squad car and helicopter.[14]

Nearly every day, usually arriving by helicopter, the FBI's David Lee Wilson offloaded containers of samples to Ezzell and his crew, and then, with a friendly wave, flew away. From 1997 to 2000, the worst years of the anthrax hoaxes, Wilson had been the head of the FBI's Hazardous Materials Response Unit, based in Quantico. After too much time riding in helicopters on emergency call duty, he opted for a transfer to the Bureau's Washington office. At the time of the Daschle letter discovery, the Bureau's resources were still heavily concentrated on the 9/11 attacks. It was quickly realized, though, that the science part of the Amerithrax investigation would be crucial. Special Agent Wilson was picked to head its scientific wing, called Amerithrax 2.[15] Wilson was charged with bringing together scientists who, in addition to those at the FBI laboratory in Washington and the WMD brain trust in Quantico, could help solve the puzzle of the origin of the spore material in the letters. Ironically, his new posting also put him back in emergency response mode, riding helicopters to and from Fort Detrick.

In quick time, the laboratory staff at the Diagnostic Services Division swelled from 7 to over 70. Joining Operation Noble Eagle, Army scientists and technicians from Walter Reed Hospital and others hired as private contractors crowded into USAMRIID. To hasten analyses, a number of microbiologists from the institute's Bacteriology Division, including Bruce Ivins, were allowed to pitch in. The individual and group commitment to this national defense mission was extraordinary. In addition to lab analyses, the paperwork was enormous; each sample had its own file and needed to be securely stored, according to FBI evidentiary rules. For weeks Ezzell practically lived at the institute, camping out in his office, and dawn often found some researchers sleeping in their cars in the adjacent parking lot.

In the midst of this near frenzy, USAMRIID virologist Peter Jahrling, a senior scientist at the institute, introduced a political controversy that would endure for years. During his twenty-five years at the institute, he became best known for his research on the newly emerged Ebola virus and figured in more than one popular account of the Army's pursuit of defenses against the rare but deadly, incurable disease.[16] In the late 1990s, Jahrling subscribed to the growing perception that another virus, smallpox, globally eradicated by 1980, had reemerged as the new worst bioterrorism threat. In the climate of the times, Iraq's delay in meeting the terms of the Gulf War cease-fire agreement increased U.S. suspicions about Saddam's germ weapons. Furthermore, former Biopreperat deputy Ken Alibek, writing about Soviet smallpox virus production by the ton, also believed in past and possibly present genetic experiments to meld smallpox with hemorrhagic fever, creating a ghastly "chimera" weapon.[17] The specter of the Soviet Union persisted in concerns that, despite WHO supervision, Russia was unable to safeguard its repository of smallpox strains from sabotage. Like his former USAMRIID colleague Dick Spertzel, Jahrling was outspoken about the foreign threat; in a 1997 *Science* interview he proclaimed: "I hate to be accused of pushing the alarmist button, but for practical purposes, smallpox is back."[18]

After the Daschle letter was brought to USAMRIID, Jahrling did grow alarmed. Fearing that an Iraqi-assisted terrorist might have mixed the smallpox virus with the Daschle letter spores, he pressured John Ezzell to allow a younger colleague, virologist Tom Geisbert, to examine a Daschle sample under an electron microscope—right away, on October 16. On examination, the sample proved to be just the typical ovoid anthrax spores, containing no smallpox virus, but Geisbert brought Jahrling's attention to what looked to him a kind of "goop" or "fried egg" gunk apparently added to it.[19]

Concerned that this additive was the signature of a foreign perpetrator (either Iraq or al Qaeda), Jahrling went directly up the chain of command to General John Parker, the head of the Army's Medical Research and Materiel Command that oversees USAMRIID, who had briefed senators on the Daschle letter spores. Jahrling persuaded him and then the institute's commander, Colonel Edward Eitzen, that the Daschle letter material signaled some kind of special threat. In an example of how disjointed communication among the federal agencies was during the anthrax crisis, on October 24 Parker and Jahrling were called to two separate high-level meetings in Washington by two different cabinet members, Secretary Thompson and Attorney General Ashcroft, both exasperated by the lack of clarity about the Daschle spores as "weapons." At the first meeting, Jahrling displayed the "goop" photos and showed examples of the additive bentonite, a clay that had been used by the Iraqis to improve anthrax spore dispersal. After that first meeting, Parker and Jahrling spontaneously visited different offices at the Pentagon, to brief them on this discovery. Then, unexpectedly, they received a call that the attorney general wanted to speak to them—at the White House.[20] At that meeting, which included Governor Ridge, FBI Director Mueller, and Secretary Thompson, Jahrling showed just the Geisbert photos and speculated about an Iraqi source for the anthrax letters. Other FBI officials were also there, gritting their teeth—the Daschle material was to have been kept strictly under wraps at USAMRIID and here was Jahrling, on the basis of meager data, politicizing the investigation. The news of the Ashcroft meeting was leaked to the press and led to front-page stories in the *New York Times* and the *Washington Post* about new scientific evidence that Iraq was behind the anthrax letter attacks.

More media speculation about the spores' foreign origin was in the offing. Before the *Times* and *Post* stories broke, Geisbert had taken a sterilized sample of the Daschle spores to the Armed Forces Institute of Pathology, where experts examined it using their equipment—an energy dispersive x-ray spectrometer attached to a scanning electron microscope—for identifying particular chemical elements. The spores yielded a positive result; that is, spikes on a graph showed the presence of the elements silicon and oxygen, which could indicate the presence of silicon dioxide, also known as silica, a powdery coating that could be used to enhance the dispersion of anthrax spores. (Silica has broad commercial utility, used in everything from cosmetics to glassware manufacture and fiber optics.)

A consultant to ABC News, former USAMRIID scientist Dick Spertzel brought this inside-track information to the news team there, plus Jahrling's idea about a bentonite additive. Spertzel's input was considered highly authoritative and he had his Army contacts to back him.[21] On October 26, ABC anchor Peter Jennings began *World News Tonight* with the revelation that the Daschle anthrax spores contained an additive called bentonite, clay that was "a trademark of Saddam Hussein's biological weapons program." ABC news reporter Brian Ross went on to say that "four well-placed and separate sources have told ABC News that initial tests on the anthrax by the U.S. Army at Fort Detrick, Maryland, have detected trace amounts of the chemical additives bentonite and silica." Although Ross noted that the White House disputed these findings—Tom Ridge was listening to FBI director Mueller who was listening to his WMD and science experts—the broadcast was slanted toward Iraq (abetted by the Soviet Union) as the source of the anthrax letter material.

After 9/11, speculation that Saddam Hussein would arm terrorists with biological weapons had already been promoted by the major media. On October 7, *60 Minutes* on CBS, the most watched news show in America, gave center stage to Australian ambassador Richard Butler, a former head of the UN special WMD commission in Iraq—the commission was evicted in 1998 on his watch—and a strong proponent of regime change. Butler asserted that Saddam would not hesitate to give anthrax to anti-American terrorists and that Iraq's leaders wanted to use biological weapons "to kill Jews."[22] Host Mike Wallace added ominously that, according to the show's "intelligence sources," Saddam Hussein had secretly acquired smallpox, ostensibly from the Soviet Union or Russia.

In a *New York Times* op-ed published right after the Daschle letter discovery, Ambassador Butler proposed that al Qaeda leader Mohamed Atta had been given anthrax by an Iraqi intelligence official in June 2000, an idea just promoted by former CIA director James Woolsey in the British press.[23] The American media, brushing aside expert criticism that the story was based on flawed intelligence, continued to cede its pages to assertions of an Iraqi anthrax threat.[24] In the *Washington Post*, William Kristol ridiculed the FBI and intelligence agencies for not connecting the anthrax letters to bin Laden and warned against patience with Iraq.[25] *Wall Street Journal* editor Robert Bartley published a blistering criticism of federal agencies for their failure to realize that Iraq was obviously behind the anthrax attacks.[26]

Also in the media spotlight was Richard Perle, head of the Defense Policy Board that advised Secretary Donald Rumsfeld and a key neo-conservative analyst since the Reagan years. Although known as the "Prince of Darkness" for his behind-the-scenes influence, Perle, after the Daschle letter discovery, openly voiced his fears of an Iraqi anthrax attack—one that could kill tens of thousands of U.S. civilians—as part of the argument for forcibly ousting Saddam Hussein.[27] On PBS's *Frontline* in mid-October, Perle warned that Iraqi intelligence was poised for bioterrorist attacks against the United States:

> I can't tell you what form a new terrorist attack will take. The one that troubles me the most is the use of biological weapons, disseminated not by Iraqi intelligence officials, but by terrorists who are prepared to commit suicide, who cheerfully kill Americans, if they could do it. All that remains is to organize their entry into the United States together with those biological agents. And that is something that Saddam Hussein and his intelligence apparatus is in a position to do.[28]

When the ABC bentonite story broke, Captain Jim Burans was in Washington, visiting from the Navy's medical research lab in Lima, Peru, where he was then posted.[29] Burans knew the FBI's Dave Wilson—both in their forties, they were part of the same generation of 1990s bioterrorist threat experts—and telephoned him with a proposed solution to the bentonite controversy. During his time with the United Nations in Iraq, Burans had acquired the real thing, Iraqi anthrax spores with bentonite added, which were stored at the Naval Research Center in Silver Spring. Why not compare them to the Daschle spore material? When they examined the two side-by-side, Wilson and Burans found that the Daschle spores were clean, whereas the Iraqi samples clearly had been mixed with bentonite "clay."

In essence, as General Parker soon told a congressional committee, the Daschle material was "comprised solely of a high concentration of spores without debris or vegetative forms, suggesting this material was refined or processed."[30] After being shown electron micrographs of the Daschle letter spores by the FBI, two well-known outside experts—Ken Alibek and Harvard University's Matthew Meselson—agreed on that fact in a joint letter to the *Washington Post*.[31] Such a product required laboratory skills and equipment, but not necessarily a state biological weapons program.

The White House rejection of the bentonite story was quickly relayed to the media. Ari Fleischer, the White House press secretary, called Peter Jennings and Brian Ross at ABC to insist the bentonite additive story had no scientific basis.[32] Ross took the opportunity to ask if the Daschle material in any way pointed to Iraq. "Not yet," was Fleischer's cryptic reply. The Bush administration was then embroiled in attempting to destroy the Taliban in Afghanistan and chasing the elusive Osama bin Laden. At a National Security Council meeting where the anthrax letters were discussed—with George Tenet and others leaning toward an Iraqi source—Vice President Cheney stopped the speculation with the remark that there was no sense accusing Saddam of anthrax bioterrorism before the United States could "do something about it."[33] The implication was that such a time would come.

For some, the ambiguity about a nearly invisible silica coating on the spores—did it exist or not—kept the door open to suspicions of Iraq. On October 30, Director Ridge held a press conference to caution against jumping to conclusions about silica until more tests were done.[34] But as long as no tests proved otherwise—and as long as the anthrax terrorist was still on the loose—speculation about the mysterious goop in Geisbert's photos continued. As for more tests, FBI analysts realized that the instrument used by the Armed Forces Institute of Pathology measured only the gross characteristics of the anthrax spores, not their complete, layer-by-layer mineral composition. For that, the FBI had to find a laboratory with more sophisticated equipment.

＊

Meanwhile, the anthrax letters continued to have deadly consequences. On Sunday, October 28, sixty-one-year-old Kathy Nguyen stumbled into New York's Lenox Hill Hospital's emergency room. A slight figure, dressed in a sweater, jeans, and sneakers, she was almost too weak to describe her chest pains, which seemed to indicate heart failure. With the city's continued anthrax surveillance, though, Nguyen's case was flagged, and blood tests showed gram-positive bacilli that on October 30 were confirmed as *B. anthracis*. At this point her condition was beyond medical help; Nguyen died the next day.[35]

New York City's Joint Terrorism Team, with the CDC's Steve Ostroff helping at every step, did everything possible to discover the source of Nguyen's fatal infection. A 1977 immigrant from Vietnam, she worked as a clerk in a basement stockroom at Manhattan Eye, Ear, and Throat Hospital on East 64th Street. As a precaution, the hospital was closed and Cipro was distributed to employees. But the basement stockroom and the mail room adjacent to it yielded no signs of anthrax spores, nor did the apartment where she lived alone in the South Bronx. Investigators took environmental samples from virtually every place where Nguyen's co-workers, neighbors, and friends said she spent time: her normal subway routes, the several churches she attended, her favorite neighborhood shops and food stores in Chinatown, and her preferred Manhattan department store, Macy's. After weeks of searching, they found other pathogens but no *B. anthracis*.

With postal contamination still considered a threat, from November 2 to 6, Marci Layton's department and the CDC distributed antibiotics to another 4,000 New York City postal workers. Cipro and other antibiotics were in such short supply in the greater New York–New Jersey area that customers were purchasing them online from illegal vendors. In the Northeast Corridor, many people were either fearful of touching the mail or protecting themselves with gloves and masks or antibiotics.

Nguyen's case put an end to the CDC's idea of medically insignificant levels of anthrax spore exposure.[36] But the fears in post-9/11 New York ran to mass terrorist attacks. On the day of Nguyen's death, a front-page article in the *New York Times* conjectured that her illness was a possible "harbinger of something worse to come": an invisible anthrax aerosol.[37]

While speculations about coming threats dominated the media, the CDC learned that workers at the Brentwood facility had been in more danger from spore dispersal than ever imagined. On November 1, Brad Perkins at the CDC was finally able to read the Canadian DRES report simulating the opening of an anthrax letter. (Michael Osterholm at the University of Minnesota, one of the eight co-authors of the 1999 Johns Hopkins anthrax article, had received it and forwarded a copy to him.) Perkins immediately invited the Canadians for a joint testing of contamination at Brentwood. Together, in protective gear and carrying test equipment, the two teams entered the closed facility on November 7. As Bill Kournakakis, one of the Canadian scientists, recalled, the huge facility had a science-fiction look, as if its hundreds of workers had disappeared just minutes before.[38]

The Canadians were in charge of testing air in the vicinity of the infamous #17 digital bar code sorter. After the machine was switched on, to their surprise, they found that anthrax spores were still pouring from inside the machine—in small numbers, but even small numbers could kill. Around the clock, from October 11, when the Daschle letter was processed at Brentwood, until the afternoon of October 21, when the facility was shut down, workers had been routinely inhaling the lethal aerosol. This and other results of the November 7 tests, rather than being publicized, were published as a CDC technical update the following year.[39] It was an addendum to earlier tests with the sorting machines turned off that showed no airborne anthrax spores. Those tests revealed no contamination in the Brentwood administrative offices or customer service, but massive surface contamination in the processing area. Brentwood employees (some consistently taking antibiotics, others not) knew nothing specific about the anthrax aerosol hazards to which they had been exposed.

CHAPTER 7

LONE WOLF

How we wonder at the great amount of power used up,
in the case of many criminals! If we know the real
need behind the crime, we need no longer wonder at
the magnitude of the power. The relation between the
crime and the criminal is defined because we have
discovered his needs.

—HANS GROSS, *Criminal Psychology*, 1897

Tom Carey, chief of the FBI's Domestic Terrorism division, was completely focused on the 9/11 attacks when, just after the Daschle letter discovery, FBI director Mueller appointed him the Inspector-in-Charge for the anthrax investigation. Overnight, Carey, who knew a lot about terrorism and very little about anthrax, became responsible for the FBI's evolving strategies for apprehending the murderer who sent the letters.[1]

Before becoming an agent in 1983, Carey, a Boston native, had spent ten years as a policeman in a small town in Maine, and he still conveyed the wariness of a cop on the beat. His twenty-year counterterrorism portfolio was impressive: the investigation of Pan Am flight 103, the murder of Leon Klinghoffer, and the attacks on the Khobar Towers, plus intense Middle East hostage negotiations, and, in Washington, an instructive stint decoding foreign intelligence. When the first Justice Department TOPOFF (Top Officials) exercise was held in 2000, to test federal response to mass chem-bio terrorism, Carey held the imagined fort for the FBI while southern New Hampshire battled a virtual nerve gas attack, Washington, D.C., the explosion of a radiological bomb, and Denver succumbed to a fictional plague outbreak.[2]

Carey had worked for three previous FBI directors, but none quite as forceful as Mueller and not under the unique kind of pressure imposed by the 9/11 attacks. The usual routine in a major FBI investigation was to allocate primary authority to the Office of Origin, the jurisdiction within which the crime had been committed, and allow secondary authority to Auxiliary Offices less centrally involved. In reaction to 9/11, Mueller, breaking with tradition, took full charge of both the New York and Pentagon crime scenes, deploying agents and bureaucratic resources like a general at war. In the same way, he wanted the anthrax investigation run by central command in Washington, rather than sharing authority with New York City or Miami.

Carey was assigned to work with Van Harp, in charge at the Washington field office, as more Bureau resources were shifted to Amerithrax. Both men reported to the director every day at 6 a.m. and again at 6 p.m. A highly decorated former Marine and a practiced trial lawyer, Mueller had a reputation for unsparing toughness, with a style in meetings that verged on prosecutorial. When he asked questions, he expected his subordinates to be ready with correct answers or face excoriating criticism or even be replaced. Among staff, the ordeal was wryly referred to as "The Gong Show."

Carey, fortunately, had Mueller's respect and so too did Van Harp, a thirty-year veteran with a reputation for combining brains with a 70-hour work week.

In his new role, Carey became a participant in the daily interagency telephone conferences organized by Lisa Gordon-Hagerty at the White House. The constant round of communication was a challenge, and not just because he had to listen to Julie Gerberding, who was organizing response at the CDC, and USAMRIID's Art Friedlander talk about *Bacillus anthracis*. As a first in his career, Carey was required to make regular reports to the National Security Council—the anthrax case was about national defense as well as criminal justice. In one of the first telephone conferences, Carey realized that Ari Fleischer was on the line, although the discussion was supposed to include only federal officials, not the White House press secretary.

Carey, responsible for maintaining contact with Congress about the case, was sensitive to media relations. Senators, though, were celebrities, appearing frequently on news broadcasts and even late-night talk shows. For the FBI, Senator Patrick Leahy was a key figure and not exactly an ally. As chair of the Senate Judiciary Committee, he kept a critical eye on the Department of Justice and the FBI; he had argued unsuccessfully against the expanded authority both were given in the PATRIOT Act. The wall between policing and intelligence, which Leahy defended, Attorney General Ashcroft saw as an obstacle to national security.[3]

California Democratic Senator Dianne Feinstein, who chaired one of the Judiciary subcommittees and whose office had been contaminated in October, also wanted the FBI to keep her informed about the anthrax investigation. She had a question, for example, about how many laboratories in the United States possessed *B. anthracis* and how many microbiologists had access to it. The FBI didn't know, an embarrassing fact revealed at a November 6 subcommittee hearing that Feinstein chaired. The registration of potential pathogen weapons (called select agents) with the CDC, required in 1997, was erratic and, by another regulation, many diagnostic and other labs were exempted from the rule. The Bureau ventured an estimate that 20,000 individual labs could have the technical resources to produce purified spores—not outrageous given the hundreds of medical centers and universities engaged in microbial research. But Feinstein, who had just introduced a bill for stricter select agent regulation, went immediately on CNN to talk about the danger posed by these thousands of microbiology laboratories— not the message the FBI or the White House would have chosen.

The next day, after consultation with the Bureau, Governor Ridge held a press conference to set the record straight: the actual number of laboratories possessing anthrax, he said, was 80 to 90, a list that included those in defense facilities and several dozen universities and commercial laboratories. Officials from the FBI and Department of Justice, Ridge assured the nation, "have been in the process of talking to individuals associated with those laboratories to follow up and determine if there [are] any leads, any information they can glean from people who are participating in that research."[4]

Ridge's fundamental message was that American defense establishment researchers could be trusted to help the anthrax investigation. If that were so, the only plausible explanation for how the Ames strain spores were sent in the anthrax letters was subterfuge: a terrorist had stolen them from one of those presumed 80 or 90 sources.

＊

By working with the Bureau's congressional liaison and public relations offices, Tom Carey was expected to avoid bad press for the Bureau, no matter what agenda a senator or representative pursued. Carey's more pressing problem was how to proceed with Amerithrax and its new brand of terrorism. As far as clues, conventional terrorists had been relatively easy to track. In the 1993 bombing of the World Trade Center in New York, the FBI had quickly traced the al Qaeda perpetrators through the vehicle identification number on a rented truck. In the 1995 Oklahoma City bombing case, a vehicle identification number on a rented van led within a day to Timothy McVeigh. The 9/11 attackers left a trail of incriminating evidence—car and air travel receipts, suitcases, electronic surveillance photographs, bank and medical records—and a wealth of eyewitnesses.

For Amerithrax, as he put it frankly to the press, Carey was hoping for direct evidence, the equivalent of identified fingerprints on a letter, not circumstantial evidence, like the witness who says he saw the suspect at the crime scene, which could break down in a trial proceeding.[5] So far, Amerithrax lacked both. That left behavioral assessment of the anonymous perpetrator, not a science, but more than conjecture. In consultation with FBI analysts, Carey and Harp decided to follow up the October 18 offer of a million-dollar reward for information with a criminal profile that might lead to an identification by a relative or maybe a friend or colleague.

Working around the clock after the discovery of the letters, FBI behavioral assessment analysts checked the sparse letter evidence against what they knew about terrorists, bioterrorists, and hoax mailers. Experts familiar with Islamic culture were suspicious of the letters' texts, in which use of the phrase "Praise to Allah," especially combined with a death threat, seemed like comic-book language. The misspelling of penicillin as "penacilin" could be a ruse pointing too blatantly at al Qaeda operatives as illiterate in English—any microbiologist able to prepare a spore powder would almost certainly know how to spell penicillin.[6] A National Defense University study of attempted bioterrorist attacks of the past—most of them the 100-plus hoax anthrax letters of the late 1990s—suggested that a frustrated, angry "lone wolf" and not a group was likely to turn to anonymous threats.[7]

Drawing on the Unabomber case, on which the FBI and the U.S. Postal Inspection Service had cooperated for eighteen years, analysts speculated that once again they were confronted with a wily criminal who was at least one step ahead of federal investigators. The convicted Unabomber murderer, Ted Kaczynski, had targeted his victims with untraceable deadly weapons—the bombs were made from scrap materials—and he had left false clues to confuse investigators, traveling miles from his home, for example, to mail his bombs. Just as crafty, whoever sent the anthrax letters had left off a return address on the first set of letters and then, perhaps understanding that an obviously anonymous letter could be tossed aside, put a fake return address on the Daschle letter—the Fourth Grade at Greendale School in Franklin Park, New Jersey. The addition had a kind of brilliance: what Senate office would disregard a message from a civic-minded schoolchild?

Kaczynski's downfall proved to be his fanatical need to verbalize. His 35,000-word anarchic tract, published under threat in the *New York Times* and the *Washington Post* in 1995, alerted his brother David who, familiar with his diatribes, contacted the FBI. The anthrax criminal, in contrast, hid himself behind the mask of a foreign terrorist barely literate in English.

Covering the anthrax crisis for ABC News was journalist Gary Matsumoto, who blamed USAMRIID's AVA vaccine for Gulf War syndrome. Matsumoto argued early on that the anthrax letters were sent by foreign terrorists.[8] The main sources for his pieces, not surprisingly, were Dick Spertzel (also working for ABC) and Spertzel's friend from the U.S. biological warfare program, Bill Patrick. On November 1, Matsumoto wrote a commentary that, citing an unnamed federal official, gave the still confidential FBI behavioral assessment a catchy label—"Ted Kaczynski with a Petri dish"—and then presented the supposed silica coating on the Daschle spores as a sign of foreign state sponsorship.[9]

On November 9, at a press briefing and on its Web site, the FBI released its profile of the anthrax criminal, which did resemble the antisocial Kaczynski and, as a result, sat poorly with those who suspected

Iraq and al Qaeda. "He is likely older," the description went, "a loner living in the United States who has substantial laboratory and scientific skills. He has no ties to organized terrorists, but sought to use the September 11 attacks as a cover for the mailings." FBI analysts did not hesitate to stipulate the perpetrator's gender and laboratory access:

> Based on the selection of anthrax as the "weapon" of choice by this individual, the offender is likely an adult male. If employed, he is likely to be in a position requiring little contact with the public, or other employees. He may work in a laboratory. He is apparently comfortable working with an extremely hazardous material. He probably has . . . access to a sophisticated lab.

The profile noted that the criminal had been organized and rational in executing the letter attacks, acting with malice aforethought. Taking a step further, analysts speculated that he was "nonconfrontational" in his public life:

> He lacks the personal skills to confront others. He chooses to confront his problems "long distance" and not face-to-face. . . . Might hold grudges vowing that he will get even with "them" one day. There are probably other, earlier examples of this type of behavior. While these earlier incidents were not actual anthrax mailings, he may have chosen to anonymously harass other individuals or entities he perceived as having wronged him. He may also have chosen to utilize the mail on those occasions.

The assessment suggested that the September 11 attacks might have triggered his anger and made the attacker "mission-oriented." Throughout the course of the anthrax crisis, this person may have exhibited "significant behavioral changes" or "an unusual pattern of activity" or a noticeable tendency toward secrecy.

The profile intimated no ethnic identity, but after 9/11 many Americans suspected any men who looked Middle Eastern of being terrorists, and American government agencies apprehended dozens of terrorist suspects on the basis of their nationalities. Before the anthrax attacker profile was published, FBI agents had picked up on a "bioter-rorism conspiracy" tip from Chester, Pennsylvania—and blundered badly. It was exactly the kind of FBI response Director Mueller wanted to avoid, that is, decentralized, with a cursory review of the suspects' backgrounds, followed by raids in full media view.[10]

On November 13, thirty armed FBI agents raided two homes, one of Dr. Irshad Sheikh, his brother Mahsood, and their mother, and the other of Asif Kazi and his wife, Palwasha. Kazi's neighbors had reported seeing Kazi dump suspicious white liquid in his backyard, from a metal canister that the Sheikh brothers had delivered to him. After breaking down doors, armed Bureau agents put yellow tape around the houses and confiscated computers, documents, clothes, and Mrs. Sheikh's teddy bear collection.

In the context of the FBI's own intensive investigation of al Qaeda, the raids seemed justified. Both families were from Pakistan, although Kazi was an American citizen. But the suspicious liquid turned out to be a sudsy overflow from a broken washing machine and the metal canister was a large cooking pot for biryani, borrowed from the Sheikhs. The suspects had neither laboratory access nor microbiology skills. Dr. Sheikh, trained as a radiologist in Pakistan and with a doctorate in international health from Johns Hopkins University, was the city health commissioner, his post since 1994; in 2000, he began teaching part-time at Hopkins, where his colleagues, once contacted, protested his harsh treatment. His brother Mahsood Sheikh was the director of the lead-poisoning prevention program in Chester, and Asif Kazi was a town accountant. Most important, none had access to any Ames strain anthrax or any apparent motivation to set off a national anthrax crisis.

The FBI's legal pressure on the two families continued for months, effectively destroying the order of their lives. Soon denied a visa, Mrs. Sheikh had to leave the country; her two sons, committed to caring for her, left with her.

✦

In the small town of Oxford, Connecticut, Ottilie Lundgren, age 94, lived independently in her own home (her husband had died twenty-two years before), regularly visited the beauty parlor (her niece drove her), and enjoyed opening her mail every day, sorting her personal correspondence and bills and ripping up junk mail. On November 13, she felt feverish and short of breath, but stoically paid it no mind.[11] On November 16, very ill, she was admitted to the local hospital, where she was diagnosed with a viral infection and dehydration and a sample of her blood was taken for testing. Her blood culture revealed gram-positive "bacilli in chains" immediately recognized as anthrax—clinicians had come very far since Larry Bush first examined Bob Stevens' spinal fluid—and Lundgren was put on intravenous antibiotics and oral Cipro. Yet this intervention was too late; she died of inhalational anthrax on November 21.

A most unlikely terrorism target, Lundgren became the eleventh confirmed case of inhalational anthrax since Stevens' diagnosis, and the fifth fatality. No spores were detected at her home, but analysis of the codes on a contaminated envelope delivered to a neighbor showed that it had passed through the Brentwood facility at the same time as the Daschle letter. Anthrax contamination was discovered at the local post office and at the larger plant in Wallingford where Lundgren's mail was processed; both were quickly closed for decontamination and their employees given antibiotics. Uncertain about the risks, people all over the country and especially in the Northeast refused to touch their mail. It was Thanksgiving time, leading to Christmas, when U.S. postal revenues ought to have revived from the depressing impact of 9/11. Instead, they were falling.

As Ottilie Lundgren was dying, the efforts of the FBI's Hazardous Materials Response Unit to find another anthrax letter paid off. Setting up a high-containment environment to search the 642 bags of government mail and deciding on the most efficient methods for sample testing had taken time and much interagency collaboration. But once in gear, teams of investigators in protective garb took just five days to detect, through air and surface samples, the "hot" letter addressed in block print to Vermont Democratic Senator Patrick Leahy and, like Daschle's, postmarked October 8, at Hamilton, New Jersey.[12] As the progressive chair of the Senate Judiciary Committee, Leahy had received other dire threats; now, like Daschle, Leahy was a high official cast into the role of terrorist target. His situation, though, was more complex. As Judiciary committee chair, Leahy was in charge of making sure the FBI pursued justice; now he had a stake in the Bureau's finding the terrorist who had tried to murder him.

As Leahy told the press, the letter sent to him (not yet opened) held enough anthrax spores (perhaps two grams or two trillion) to kill 100,000 people.[13] Despite the sensational calculation, media attention to the anthrax letters had sharply declined. During the week of October 16 to October 22, 1,487 news articles on anthrax were published nationwide; during the week of Lundgren's death in November, which coincided with the discovery of the Leahy letter, only 146 appeared.[14] The opening of the Daschle letter and the two Brentwood postal deaths marked the height of the anthrax crisis. Once the shock was over, the American media and the public began looking for explanations. The FBI had intercepted the Leahy letter, in a sense defused it, but the Bureau could offer no answer to the question of why the letters had been sent—other than the suggestion that some lone wolf biologist had needed to vent his wrath.

Published with nearly miraculous timing just a few weeks before the Stevens diagnosis, the popular book *Germs* did present an explanation: the threat to Americans was foreign bioterrorism. Researched and written by three top-flight *New York Times* reporters—Judith Miller, Stephen Engelberg, and William Broad—*Germs* became a bestseller, reaching number one on the *New York Times* nonfiction list for the weeks of October 28 and November 4.[15]

The narrative of *Germs* essentially recapped the rising influence of the bioterrorism threat of the late 1990s, about which most Americans outside the Beltway knew very little. Now they could understand President Clinton's nightmares about annihilating "living weapons" that could be produced from a tiny vial and why he sought to protect the United States against bioterrorism by domestic legislation and international negotiation. The lingering menace of the old Soviet germ weapons program was revived by reiterations of Ken Alibek's suspicions that Russia was secretly perpetuating Soviet biological weapons, perhaps intent on creating supergerms. Or perhaps former Soviet scientists might be defecting to enemies like Iran, North Korea, Syria, or Libya. The colorful Bill Patrick, whose business card featured a Grim Reaper dispensing pathogens, was introduced to a wider audience, and *Germs* featured his mass attack speculations, including one that had the 1979 Sverdlovsk epidemic being caused by pounds of anthrax spores instead of the more scientific calculation of a few grams or less.[16] The Soviet threat, though, was counterbalanced by reporting on successful international efforts to dismantle the old Biopreparat facilities and find peaceful employment for hundreds of former Soviet biological warfare scientists.

For policy experts who tracked the biological weapons threat, the alarming news in *Germs* was the revelation that the United States had under Clinton embarked on at least three covert anthrax projects—reconstructing a Soviet anthrax bomb model, re-creating a Russian vaccine-resistant strain, and building a small spore production factory—that verged on violation of the 1972 Biological Weapons Convention.[17] The perceived bioterrorism threat seemed to justify this blurring of the line between defensive and offensive research. As described by the book's authors, even reputable scientists, like Joshua Lederberg, assisted in the covert projects, although Lederberg did request government legal assurance that no treaty violation was involved. Yet the same experiments conducted by another country (save perhaps the United Kingdom) would have raised an outcry in Washington.

According to *Germs*, the most significant biological weapons threat was Saddam Hussein's Iraq. Touting Dick Spertzel as "one of humanity's few natural-born weapons inspectors," *Germs* supported his claim that Saddam had maintained his biological weapons capability and even gone beyond it.[18] In 1995, United Nations inspectors had uncovered documentary evidence of Iraq's rudimentary biological arsenal, but little in the way of actual weapons, and in 1996 the presumed major Iraqi germ weapons plant, al Hakam, just south of Baghdad, had been destroyed under United Nations supervision. Nonetheless, following Spertzel's lead, the authors of *Germs* took the defeated Saddam, a constant bragger about his WMD capability, seriously. "If Iraq ever resumed making germ weapons," they concluded ominously, "they would be much more deadly."[19]

On November 13, PBS aired a documentary based on the *Germs* narrative—minus the allusions to possible U.S. violations of the 1972 Biological Weapons Convention. The accompanying Web site went further and imposed the al Qaeda–Iraq conspiracy on the anthrax letters:

> Tragically, as the recent anthrax attacks in the U.S. have demonstrated, terrorists will not hesitate to use such state-derived biological weapons—or crude versions of them secured from other sources—to further their deadly goals.[20]

The PBS site directed viewers to the restored Web site of the CDC and, as a second option, to that of the Johns Hopkins Center for Civilian Biodefense Studies, which featured "Dark Winter," a scenario of smallpox-infected Iraqi terrorists invading America and causing a pandemic and political chaos.

The bottom-line policy message of *Germs* was a holdover from the Clinton era, when advocates promoting the bioterrorism threat as existential, on a par with nuclear weapons, succeeded in increasing funding for domestic preparedness and anthrax and smallpox research. In that vision, the United States, dangerously unprepared for a mass germ attack, had to increase its biodefense budget or potentially be destroyed. "If we as a nation believe that the germ threat is a hoax," Miller and her colleagues reasoned, "we are spending too much money on it. But if the danger is real, as we conclude it is, then the investment is much too haphazard and diffuse."[21]

After 9/11 and the anthrax letters, members of Congress on both sides of the aisle agreed that the danger of bioterrorism was real and that almost no amount of money was too much. After the September 11 attacks, even before any anthrax letters were discovered, congressional leaders moved to make civilian biodefense a major priority, with a heavy emphasis on biomedical and other technological protection. The anthrax letter attacks then added to the momentum. In 2002 the budget for defenses against bioterrorism, in the millions when President Clinton left office, increased to over $3 billion.[22] Assuming a mass threat, basic research on anthrax, smallpox, plague, and other pathogens seemed the obvious route to effective, improved medical interventions for civilians. For that research, new high-containment laboratories needed to be built—nearly a billion dollars in 2002 were set aside for that construction alone. Many scientists who might never have dreamed of big research budgets or running their own laboratories could, like a few recruits to USAMRIID in the 1980s when it was flush, achieve that dream, but without joining a military enclave. National defense had appropriated microbiology, or at least a segment of it.

Similarly, local domestic preparedness funding went from $67 million at the time of the anthrax letters to $940 million in 2002, with more stringent state planning requirements. The budget for the Strategic National Stockpile, which had provided Cipro supplies after the anthrax letter attacks, went from $81 million in 2001 to $1.157 billion in 2002. In November 2001, Secretary Thompson awarded the pharmaceutical company Acambis/Baxter a $428 million contract to speed smallpox vaccine production—the goal was to have enough for the entire nation.

In reaction to the anthrax letters, the federal restraints on the controversial AVA vaccine also gave way. In mid-December 2001 the Food and Drug Administration, which had withheld accreditation from BioPort, gave permission for limited use of its AVA supplies (to be administered in three shots over four weeks), but only to allow postal and Capitol Hill employees on antibiotics another post-exposure option. After buying 200,000 doses from the Department of Defense (20,000 produced by BioPort and the rest from the 1992 stocks), Secretary Thompson was explicit that the vaccine was "experimental" and the government assumed no liability for adverse effects. Fewer than a hundred of the thousands eligible chose the vaccine.

Then, on January 31, 2002, the Food and Drug Administration approved the AVA stocks for general military use. The possibility of anti-American terrorism and perhaps a war against Iraq had shifted the perception of risks—discomfort from the inoculations seemed minor compared to an anthrax attack. The government then offered a billion dollars to any company that could present a reasonable plan for creating and manufacturing an improved vaccine, for soldiers and civilians alike.

✦

In late October, after lending Dave Wilson a hand in quelling the bentonite controversy, the Navy's Jim Burans regularly commuted from his post in Lima, Peru, to Washington, to consult on Amerithrax 2, the science part of the FBI's anthrax investigation. After the discovery of the Leahy letter, Wilson's highest priority was making sure the letter and its contents were carefully preserved as evidence.[23] Still sealed, it had been handed over to John Ezzell, who placed it with the three others in his division's BSL-3 suite, under secure 24/7 "card guard." The institute was under strict instructions: the Leahy letter would be opened only in the presence of designated FBI representatives, including Jim Burans. The Bureau wanted no repeats of the way in which the Daschle letter material had been made available to Geisbert and Jahrling and, as it turned out, to Bruce Ivins who, without Ezzell's direct supervision, had measured the concentration of those spores.[24] The institute's tradition of allowing its scientists their professional autonomy was, from a forensic perspective, a serious liability.

By early December 2001, the Ames strain's 1981 origin in Texas and its possession by Dugway and USAMRIID alerted the mass media to the possibility that the institute might be the source of the anthrax letter spores and that one of its scientists might have sent the letters. Art Friedlander, who had defended the institute during the controversy over Gulf War syndrome, again became the institute's spokesman. He told the *New York Times* that USAMRIID scientists used only "wet anthrax"—spores in a slurry—to develop vaccines and test their effectiveness. Regarding the production of the Daschle spore material, Friedlander said he believed that no one at the institute had "that kind of expertise."[25]

About this time, according to his later account, Bruce Ivins became concerned about powdery spore spillage from the Daschle letter. He did surface swabs in his office and in the adjacent men's changing room, and he said he found, after culturing the residues, what looked like anthrax spores. Telling no one, he decontaminated those areas and apparently felt he had done the institute a protective service.

⁑

The date for opening the Leahy letter was set for December 5, and, as the day approached, the excitement level in Building 1425, already high from Operation Noble Eagle, increased. By consulting with outside experts, Wilson and Burans had worked out ways to better control spore dispersal, which had troubled the examination of the Daschle letter. A triboelectric charge (the same that can happen when a comb is run through hair on a dry day) had sent the individual spores aloft. The solution was to place polonium, a radioactive element, in the cabinet to make the air electrically conductive; this would "discharge" the spores and reduce their tendency to fly into the air and deposit on surfaces.[26] The air in the BSL-3 cabinet and the entire room had to be kept as still as possible, again, to prevent dispersion.

As planned, Ezzell carefully went through the choreographed ritual of cutting the envelope open and gently removing the letter. Its pharmaceutical fold was identical to those in the three other letters. The letter proved to be a photocopy (a duplicate of Daschle's and also cut to make a square). The writing on the prefranked federal eagle envelope had also been photocopied. The perpetrator had again eliminated any overtly distinct clues that would reveal his identity. Using a spatula, Ezzell carefully transferred the spore powder, off-white and fine-grained like the Daschle material, into a special container. This time he made no comments about weaponization.

Jim Burans and Dave Wilson, watching from outside with a small group of institute officials, were relieved when the process was over. There was enough spore material to send to Paul Keim for strain identification. In addition, there was enough to irradiate and send to a new consultant, Joe Michael at the Department of Energy's Sandia National Laboratories in Albuquerque. A top-flight materials chemist, Michael with his research team was going to analyze the chemical composition of the spores with state-of-the-art equipment and put an end, one way or another, to the silica coating controversy. Photographs of the Leahy letter and envelope were posted on the FBI Web site later that day, as part of the Bureau's Amerithrax update. The general public and whoever sent the letters could now see four of those retrieved on display in full color.

In December, Operation Noble Eagle began to wind down. Nearly 90 percent of the over 30,000 samples tested were turning out negative—harmless powders or other materials. The positive results helped delineate the contamination trail and cross-check other lab results and show that the known letter attacks and those attacks alone had threatened the nation. The extra scientists from Walter Reed Hospital and elsewhere began to leave. After two months of intense lab analyses, John Ezzell was near exhaustion. Dave Wilson was grateful—one day he'd called out "We love you, John!" just before climbing into the helicopter—but Ezzell needed a break.

One more disruption, though, was in store for USAMRIID. Also in December, the USPS's Vice President of Engineering Tom Day arrived there to conduct a unique experiment, arranged as an interagency favor. Day wanted to test exactly how a digital bar code sorter forced spores out of an anthrax letter. To do that he had a small but exact replica of a DBCS installed at the institute in a good-sized room with a viewing window. His goal was to test the machine with facsimiles of the sealed anthrax letters, each packed with two grams of *Bacillus globigii*—the same spore type used by the Canadian scientists to test spore dispersal from letters.

On December 14, Day had his experiment filmed in slow motion under high-intensity light. The sealed envelope was fed upright into the machine where it was grabbed by pinch belts and, under the cover of a metal hood, wound around a spindle and passed through at 70 miles per hour, forcing spores through the pores of the envelope paper, which, like most envelopes, had openings of three to five microns. The inside of the machine became inundated with spores, which emerged from the hood with the letter in a great puff of powder.[27] In ordinary light, the aerosol would have been invisible, as it was at Hamilton and Brentwood and other facilities.

As the spores floated, a figure in a white coat hurried past the viewing window. In all their careers, who among USAMRIID microbiologists had ever thought how a contaminated mail sorter might lethally infect postal workers with anthrax?

◆

In January 2002, still hopeful that a tipster might move the Amerithrax case forward, the FBI increased the reward for information from $1 million to $2.5 million. The Bureau also picked up on leads involving former USAMRIID scientists. One was retired U.S. Army major Perry Mikesell, who in the 1980s and early 1990s had worked in the Bacteriology Division with Ezzell, Friedlander, Ivins, and others.[28] In the lead-up to the Gulf War, Mikesell was part of the effort to determine antibiotic protection for the troops.[29] After retirement, he took a job at Battelle in Ohio, in its National Defense and Security Division. Mikesell had the skills to produce the letter material and could have had access to Ames spores. Apparently, he harbored grievances against USAMRIID—about being passed over for promotion and about being excluded by colleagues from a patent application—and so might fit the "disgruntled scientist" characterization.

Another suspect was Lt. Colonel Philip Zack, a microbiologist who had left the institute in 1991 to work at Walter Reed and was rumored to have later violated lab security at Building 1425. Zack had been part of the "Camel Club," a group that had harassed an Egyptian-born colleague, Ayaad Assaad—such was the negative influence of the Gulf

War on the institute's workplace culture. A decade later, in late September 2001, the FBI received an anonymous letter describing Assaad (then an EPA toxicologist) as "a potential biological terrorist" with a vendetta against the U.S. government.[30] Called in for questioning, Assaad suggested the author of the letter might be one of his old USAMRIID antagonists. Assaad was quickly cleared of the allegation, and neither the lead to Zack as a suspect nor the one to Mikesell panned out.

While FBI agents traced other leads, Van Harp approached the officials of the American Society for Microbiology and received their permission to contact the society's 42,000 members, via its email listserv, to ask their help in identifying the anthrax murderer. Instead of focusing only on the defense establishment scientists who actually did research with Ames strain anthrax, the Bureau was casting the net wide, still seeking identification of a "lone wolf." In January 2002, Harp sent a letter stressing the likelihood that the killer was a single person, with "legitimate" access to biological agents and the technical expertise to produce "a highly refined and deadly product." Then he added:

> This person has exhibited a clear, rational thought process and appears to be very organized in the production and mailing of these letters. The perpetrator might be described as "stand-offish" and likely prefers to work in isolation as opposed to a group/team setting. It is possible this person used off-hours in a laboratory or may have even established an improvised or concealed facility comprised of sufficient equipment to conceal the anthrax.

One recipient of Harp's letter was Nancy Haigwood, a senior scientist at the Seattle Biomedical Research Institute and a professor at the University of Washington in Seattle. Attractive and outgoing, Haigwood knew one person who, based on her encounters with him, fit the FBI description: Bruce Ivins.[31]

Haigwood had met Ivins in the late 1970s when they were both at the University of North Carolina at Chapel Hill—she as a graduate student and he as a postdoctoral fellow. Ivins had made friendly overtures, but Haigwood wasn't interested. His reaction had been to persist with inquiries about her personal life and particularly about a sorority, Kappa Kappa Gamma, to which she had belonged. The same sorority had a chapter at the University of Cincinnati, where Ivins had received his undergraduate and graduate degrees. He seemed to have some kind of obsession with its sophisticated and, for him, unattainable coeds.

Over the years, without any encouragement, Ivins had kept intermittently in touch with Haigwood by telephone, letters, and emails—to which she responded tersely. It bothered her that he often referred to details about her and her family—the names and ages of her children, for example—which she herself had never told him. On September 21, 2001, after years without direct contact, he sent her an email about the importance of his institute and telephoned her office when she did not immediately reply. Once in the past he had sent her a message encouraging her to consider defense research, and then sent a complaining letter to her supervisor when she declined. The same urgency seemed to have returned. Most recently, on November 14, 2001, Ivins had included her in an email message to family members and a few friends that joked about anthrax and included two photos, one of Ames strain spores and another of Ivins in a white lab coat, apparently working with *B. anthracis* but without protective gloves.

After Haigwood contacted the FBI, two Bureau agents came to interview her in Seattle. She told them that in 1982, while she was living with her fiancé, biochemist Carl Scandella, in Gaithersburg, Maryland, they discovered one morning that a vandal had spray-painted the initials of her old sorority, KKG, on their fence, the sidewalk, and on the rear window of Carl's car. Haigwood couldn't think of anyone but Bruce Ivins who was in the least interested in her membership in the group. Scandella filed a police report about the vandalism.[32] At the time, he and Haigwood were unaware that Ivins, employed at USAMRIID, was living on the same street as theirs in Gaithersburg. Scandella and Haigwood were never sure if it was by happenstance or design that Ivins lived so close to them. At a chance meeting, Haigwood confronted Ivins about the vandalism, but he denied the accusation and hastened away.

In 1983, Haigwood came across a letter written in her name published in the *Frederick News-Post*. The letter identified her as a member of KKG who believed that the hazing of pledges was good for their character and group solidarity. Haigwood was sure that Ivins had impersonated her. She complained to the newspaper, but soon discovered that the letter had been widely circulated and led the sorority, which banned hazing, to publicly reprimand her.

The FBI report about Haigwood's suspicions of Ivins went to Washington, along with other responses from ASM members—and disappeared without a ripple.

The lapse was somewhat peculiar. Once Operation Noble Eagle ended, the FBI seemed more aggressive about scrutinizing every anthrax expert as a potential suspect. Not even Ken Alibek, Bill Patrick, or Jim Burans was excluded. Bruce Ivins, along with John Ezzell, Art Friedlander, and others at USAMRIID, submitted to a polygraph test and interviews. The institute's Peter Jahrling took the inquiry calmly, telling the press, "The one thing that is hard to grapple with is the possibility of a determined insider. We are being asked quite reasonably to take a hard look at the character of the people who have access to these pathogens."[33] But John Ezzell, for one, took umbrage. "I know that there's a certain amount of necessity for all this, but at the same time we're scientists—very dedicated, very loyal, very patriotic. And as hard as we've worked, to now be subjected to these kinds of observations is demeaning."[34]

There were signs of demoralization at the institute. Certain anthrax scientists like Ezzell in the Diagnostic Services Division and Patricia Worsham from the Bacteriology Division were working closely with the Bureau, while most others were excluded. One day Worsham found a sign "FBI Rat" affixed to her office door. She suspected that Bruce Ivins, feeling shut out, had put it there, which later turned out to be the right guess. On January 23, 2002, claiming to have "recently-obtained information," Ivins engaged one of the FBI special agents in a tutorial on how genetic mutations might arise when *B. anthracis* samples were cultured from plate to plate rather than from the original sample, which was actually Worsham's field. In fact, she and a few others at the institute had been examining the letter material for stable genetic mutations, without sharing that work with Ivins. Ivins told the agent that he himself worked with the original culture of Ames—one step away from the Texas cow—and brought out his records of transfers of that material to other labs and colleagues at the institute, as possible leads to suspects. Ivins, who had examined the highly purified Daschle letter spores after literally handling the letter in its ziplock bags, suggested they were "fermentation quality," implying the use of sophisticated equipment. He denied ever using dry anthrax spores, but he pointed out that scientists at the Army's Dugway Proving Ground in Utah did. To cap this discussion, Ivins gave the agent the names of two scientists he thought had "the knowledge and character required to have prepared and sent the anthrax letters."[35]

The Bureau was looking for a loner, but Ivins, as any of his colleague would attest, was a team player—helpful, generous with technical advice and willing to share his own equipment, and humorous, the kind of man who composed witty jingles for co-workers when they retired or moved on to other jobs. Haigwood's suspicions referred to incidents dating back nearly two decades. In 2001, to all outward appearances, Ivins was a solid member of the institute's scientific community.

CHAPTER 8

LAWS, REGULATIONS, AND RULES

> Where a defendant's conduct creates a foreseeable zone of risk, the law generally will recognize a duty placed upon the defendant either to lessen the risk or see that sufficient precautions are taken to protect others from the harm the risk poses.
>
> —*McCain v. Florida Power Corp.*, 1992

As the FBI pursued the Amerithrax investigation, Department of Justice lawyers already knew that if the FBI could find its prime suspect they would prosecute the accused under Title 18 of the federal law, the use of a weapon of mass destruction with malice aforethought, punishable by either the death penalty or life imprisonment. When the term "weapons of mass destruction" was first officially used—in a 1947 draft resolution submitted by the United States to the United Nations—biological weapons were included along with nuclear and chemical ones because the American military, above all, had pioneered their potential for indiscriminate, large-scale lethal impact.[1] Fortunately, the Cold War ended without either of the two superpowers, the United States and the Soviet Union, using the anti-civilian potential each had developed, and without lesser states that had tried to emulate them—for example, South Africa, Iraq, and Israel—daring to use their germ weapons in warfare. A combination of law, moral repugnance, and the relative unpredictability of germ weapons compared to conventional bombs seemed to restrain state use. But nothing had deterred the mailer of the anthrax letters from this particular WMD terrorism.

For the individuals most affected by the letters, the indiscriminate nature of the attacks was particularly frightening. It was difficult to say why, among the thousands exposed, one person should become sick and not another. As weeks passed and no more letters were discovered and no cases followed Ottilie Lundgren's, some commentators dismissed the anthrax letter attacks as mere disruptions. Yet those who survived infection, the families and friends of those who died, and those who fled contaminated workplaces had each, in varying degrees, lost the sense of personal safety that is vital to everyday life. How does one "breathe easily" if a lethal microbe might be in the air? And what does one do after the bioterrorist crisis is over—as far as others are concerned, but not for oneself?

In Florida, the displaced employees of American Media, Inc., were soon safely reunited at another office building in Boca Raton. The original, contaminated AMI off Route 95 remained closed—a company formed by now ex–New York Mayor Rudy Giuliani was under contract to clean it. A complete FBI crime scene investigation there had revealed heavy spore concentration at Stephanie Dailey's desk and in her wastebasket (which supported her account of opening the powder-filled envelope), plus significant contamination in the mail room and throughout the building's first floor. Surprisingly, very few spores were found on the third floor where Bob Stevens worked or elsewhere. Perhaps, in the ten minutes after Dailey opened the letter, he passed by her desk; or maybe he died simply from handling a contaminated piece of mail.

Ernesto Blanco, fully recovered—even better than before, he insisted— returned to his mail room job.[2] The role of anthrax survivor had its highs and lows, which Blanco bore with equal grace. To Bayer, the German manufacturer of Cipro, Blanco was proof their product belonged in the national stockpile. The company flew him and his wife to Manhattan, where Blanco opened the New York Stock Exchange. But in North Miami his neighbors kept their distance—a shunning that other AMI workers also experienced. The first time Blanco attended Sunday mass at his parish church, those standing near him refused to extend the traditional peace greeting handshake. At the new AMI workplace, co-workers who were once friendly avoided him, but Blanco blamed no one except the terrorists who sent the letters.

Maureen Stevens, still grieving the loss of her husband, endured a strange widowhood. Instead of being shunned, for a time she found it difficult to go out in public, even to shop for groceries, without a stranger approaching to express sympathy. The media soon left her alone, but the panic in New York and Washington and the discovery of the four letters revived terrible memories. Keeping the public and private separate seemed beyond her control. One night she was watching television when Senator Bill Frist showed an x-ray of her husband's devastated lungs to illustrate inhalational anthrax. The bacteria from her husband's spinal fluid, called *Bacillus anthracis Florida*, were being used in biodefense and forensic science.

Eventually, the anthrax letters faded from the news. The media focused instead on compensations being arbitrated for the families of 9/11 victims and the spirited demands of the New Jersey widows for an investigation of how the government missed the warning signs of the al Qaeda attack. No one from the FBI had bothered to update the Stevens family or other victims on the Amerithrax investigation; the idea that there were victims of the attacks seemed to have been overlooked.

On their own, the two Brentwood widows sought legal redress. The day after Mrs. Morris accepted the Medal of Freedom from Postmaster General Potter, the *Washington Post* announced that she was suing Kaiser Permanente for $37 million for negligence in failing to prescribe Cipro for her husband when the "weapons-grade" nature of the anthrax spores was publicly known. The suit also raised the possibility of racism.[3] Johnnie Cochran, the lawyer who had represented O. J. Simpson, joined the Morris team of lawyers. Not long after, Mrs. Curseen and her family threatened a similar suit against the hospital that fatally misdiagnosed his condition. Both claims were settled out of court for undisclosed amounts, on the condition the plaintiffs not discuss the terms or their complaints.

As the FBI investigation dragged on, Maureen Stevens made an appointment at the law offices of Schuler, Halvorson & Weisser, located in a neat white office building in West Palm Beach, with a discreet parking garage in the back. The founding partner, Richard Schuler, a native of Manhattan with a law degree from Syracuse University, specialized in personal injury claims and had behind him nearly two decades of trial experience. When Maureen Stevens came to see him, Schuler advised that she seek a wrongful death suit against the U.S. government. The claim would be that the federal government and specifically Fort Detrick had failed in their responsibility to keep "ultra-hazardous" anthrax spores from posing a risk to the public, of which Bob Stevens was a representative. In the history of Florida tort law, a 1912 decision affirmed the relevant principle, called "proportionate care":

> The reasonable care which persons are bound to take in order to avoid injury to others is proportionate to the probability of injury that may arise to others. And, where a person does what is more than ordinarily dangerous, he is bound to use more than ordinary care.[4]

"The updated concept," Schuler explained, "is called 'a foreseeable zone of risk.'" In the 1992 case of *McCain v. the Florida Power Corporation*, the court upheld the argument that whoever created a "foreseeable zone of risk" was responsible for injuries that occurred within it. The gist of the case was this: an underground cable laid by Florida Power caused injury to Mr. McCain, who was using a mechanical trench digger on private property that had been marked "safe" by a Florida Power employee. The court decided that Florida Power should have foreseen the broader "zone of risk" it had created, even if it could not predict the specific way in which McCain was injured.

In February, Schuler notified the Department of Justice of his intent to pursue a $50 million wrongful death suit on behalf of the Stevens family. For good measure, Schuler included Ohio defense contractor Battelle and BioPort, the Michigan anthrax vaccine company, in the suit; according to speculation in the press, they might also be sources of the Ames strain spores in the letters. Finding the criminal who sent the letters was less important than the fact that the federal government had lost control of a weapon of mass destruction and, under Florida law, might have to take responsibility for the damages suffered. The Stevens suit was a long shot and could take years to resolve. But if it moved to trial, Schuler looked forward to using the discovery process to open the door on the whole investigation.[5]

In Washington, the Hart Building staff and the senators they served began the year still camping out in annexes or buildings, like the one that housed the General Accounting Office on G Street, from which other federal employees had been bumped. Yet progress had been made in decontaminating the Hart Building and a reopening was planned for March. Far from contemplating lawsuits, the Daschle staff closed ranks. The name of the intern, Grant Leslie, who discovered the letter, was kept from the press and there was agreement in the office that no one would discuss the incident with outsiders. The barricade was also emotional. The Senate staffers present when the Daschle letter was opened felt a special bond to one another. Those who had been in serious danger of infection had difficulty relating with others who had not shared that brush with death, even close family members.[6]

In New York, Erin O'Conner and Casey Chamberlain, the two office workers most at risk from the Brokaw letter, also chose to stay out of the media spotlight; each dealt privately with personal fears. Journalist Johanna Huden at the *New York Post* could hardly hide. In October 2001, the glamorous thirty-one-year-old blonde had been photographed for the paper's front page raising the biopsied middle finger on her right hand—described in the headline as a defiant gesture to Osama bin Laden. Huden, like Brokaw, was struck by the unreality of a news reporter being the object of media attention. Judith Miller at the *Times*, although the letter sent to her was a hoax, had experienced the same odd sense of being a media target. Huden believed that she and others at the *Post*—op-ed editor Mark Cunningham and mail room worker William Monagas both later contracted cutaneous anthrax— had been lucky.[7] Had she bothered to open that oddly printed letter, instead of concentrating on her 9/11 reporting, the dispersed anthrax spores might have caused staff fatalities—and not just because of the primary aerosol released by the envelope. EPA tests at the Hart Building showed that, even after ordinary movement, spores could be detected in the air.[8]

No one disputed that the exposed postal workers in New Jersey and Washington had borne the brunt of the physical risks, but few realized the psychological costs. New Jersey social workers running the follow-up workshops for Hamilton employees noticed pervasive signs of distress and anxiety.[9] They were identical to the reactions that Jean Malecki and her staff confronted among dislocated AMI employees, whose workplace had given them an organized world of meaning and security.[10] With that world gone, postal workers reacted like many victims of disaster—they grieved.[11] The New Jersey postal workers in need were referred to therapists and counseling groups. The Brentwood employees in Washington were nowhere near as fortunate.

·

Terrell Worrell, the forklift driver who had questioned the delay in shutting down Brentwood, was assigned to the National Airport facility. In the weeks after the plant closed, he suffered from shortness of breath and his physician, although he knew his patient was a nonsmoker, told him that the x-ray of his lungs looked as if he had been smoking heavily for years. Worrell began spending much of his free time at the local library, surfing the Internet to learn about anthrax as a possible cause of his condition—like many Brentwood employees, he worried about what the government had failed to tell him. In the process of his search, he came upon the Cold War history of Fort Detrick and then discovered the 1979 Sverdlovsk outbreak and the Soviet program. After that he learned about the germ weapons program of apartheid South Africa, its use of pathogens in sabotage, and the role of the white Rhodesian Selous Scouts in attacking tribal groups. Along the way, he clipped or downloaded every article he could find on the anthrax letters and pasted them in a scrapbook.

When, in mid-December, Brentwood postal workers were offered the AVA vaccine, Worrell, familiar with the Gulf War syndrome controversy, had no trouble rejecting it. He and other Brentwood employees remembered the racist Public Health Service Tuskegee syphilis study of years past and bristled at the idea of government asking blacks to become the subjects of yet another medical "experiment."[12] When the CDC hired a survey contractor to find out if postal workers were complying with their antibiotic regimen, Brentwood workers, left on their own to take the antibiotics as they chose, resented the intrusion. Some, like Terrell Worrell, refused to cooperate when strangers knocked on their doors to talk about such private medical matters. One night, when his home phone rang, Worrell was treated to a new tactic—the race card. "Good evening, brother," a deep male voice said. "Have you a minute to talk about those antibiotics?" "Who says I'm your brother?" Worrell replied. "How do you know I'm black?" Irritated by the ploy, he hung up.

As Worrell filled up scrapbooks in his spare time, at work he bent the ear of anyone who would listen—did they think they'd been told everything about those anthrax letters? One day in February, a co-worker gave his telephone number to Helen Lewis, the government mail worker who had discovered the letter that Morris referred to in his 911 call. Lewis had just been featured on a local television special about the delayed Brentwood shutdown, which compared it to the privileged treatment of Capitol Hill employees. Lewis called Worrell and they arranged to meet at her apartment in Southeast Washington.

Former Brentwood mail sorter Dena Briscoe was also filling scrapbooks with articles about the anthrax letters and the Brentwood shutdown. Decontaminating the Hart Building, with its 100,000 cubic feet of space, was taking months.[13] The plans for decontaminating Brentwood, with its 17.5 million cubic feet, would use 20 tons of chlorine dioxide gas and cost an estimated $35 million. In community meetings, USPS vice president Tom Day assured postal workers that the goal was complete safety: "If there is any doubt, then we won't leave the machines there and we won't open the building." He also promised that DBCS #17 would be removed, for symbolic reasons.[14]

Briscoe, though, had a hard time imagining herself returning. After she was released from the hospital in late October, she was reassigned to one and then another facility and then a third. Unable to concentrate, she would fall into a kind of dream state and then have to be pulled off the job. Her voice remained raspy, making it hard for her to talk above a whisper. The first two psychiatrists she went to were no help explaining what was ailing her, although her symptoms—which started around the time of the Brokaw letter discovery—were classic responses to the twin traumas of mortal fear and cultural loss.[15] Finally, a third therapist recognized Briscoe's problem and helped her confront her anxieties.

After seeing Helen Lewis on television, Briscoe telephoned her and reintroduced herself, this time as someone concerned about the treatment of Brentwood workers. "This is some coincidence," Lewis replied. "Can you come here tomorrow? A fellow named Worrell from National Airport wants to talk about the situation."

Both women knew what the "situation" was. Other workers had reacted similarly to Briscoe after resuming their positions at the mail sorting machines—and been accused of malingering. Still others had trouble sleeping or eating or they had turned to drugs or alcohol to ease their pain. Some had retired or quit rather than work inside another postal plant. Adjustment to new work sites had been difficult, especially in the early days when Brentwood exiles were considered as "contaminated" as their facility. For example, on Monday, October 22, when a group of Brentwood mail handlers, in their usual uniforms and aprons, appeared in the cafeteria at a Maryland facility, every worker there immediately got up and left.

When Helen Lewis opened the door, Terrell Worrell recognized her as one of the shop stewards at Brentwood. When Dena Briscoe, carrying her scrapbook, arrived, he realized he also knew her from a distance. In the hierarchy of postal positions, these two mail sorters were a cut above those who, like Worrell, did the heavy lifting of mail handlers. That division no longer mattered. "I thought I was the only one who was collecting information," Worrell told them.[16]

That afternoon, Dena, Helen, and Terrell considered the many anthrax stories accumulated in the scrapbooks—the five deaths, the lawsuits (Leroy Richmond, disabled and living on 80 percent salary, was suing the Postal Service for compensation), various congressional hearings, and the stalled FBI case. For hours they traded stories about the personal difficulties the dispersed Brentwood workers were having and the efforts many were making to communicate with one another, relying on cell phones and emails to catch up with absent friends.

In this first get-together, the three decided to organize a group and to call it Brentwood Exposed. "It's a perfect name," Terrell commented. "We were all exposed to anthrax. But now we want to expose the facts that have been hidden from us."

Dena had another idea, about healing. She had kept the business card the D.C. social worker at Judicial Square had given her on October 21. Psychologically, Briscoe had traveled a great distance since that day. She still had occasional moments of fear, but not the paralysis she had suffered before. Her voice, though still hoarse, was returning to normal. "The government is offering therapy to Washington people affected by the attack on the Pentagon," she told Helen and Terrell. "Where is the help for Brentwood workers who are traumatized?" The three next agreed to hold a meeting—just to see if anyone would come. Among them, they had enough telephone numbers and emails to contact at least a hundred other Brentwood exiles. They consulted the calendar and picked Wednesday, February 6, at 10:30 a.m., to accommodate their evening shifts. If people showed enough interest, future meetings could be scheduled to suit other shifts. Worrell suggested they reserve the community meeting room at the Woodbridge Library, near the Brentwood facility, and that they think about inviting guest speakers to answer the community's questions about anthrax.

On February 6, several dozen people crowded into the library's second-floor meeting room. Helen, Dena, and Terrell introduced themselves and explained their concerns and then listened to the litany of worries from their audience—everything from the adverse side effects of the doxycycline they had taken for so long to fear they could never muster the courage to return to Brentwood, where they were sure to be assigned when it reopened. No one had heard from the CDC about post-exposure test results. Was the government keeping secrets from them? The consensus was that the group should meet again, in fact, that it should meet weekly. Throughout the spring of 2002, the Brentwood Exposed meetings continued, with growing numbers attending. The founders drew up bylaws. Dena Briscoe was designated president, Helen Lewis vice president, and Terrell Worrell secretary. For a brief interval, the group had a treasurer, but then eliminated the position to avoid the problems of money management.[17] With help from its members, it created a Web site that Dena Briscoe monitored and a listserv for broadcasting messages to the community.

As the membership of Brentwood Exposed grew, its leaders started organizing meetings in the large churches in Washington's northeast quadrant that often hosted community gatherings. The first was on May 3 at the beautiful Patmos Church, on Rhode Island Avenue, near Brentwood. Although the goal of "healing" was the top priority, Dena Briscoe added another item to the agenda. Judicial Watch, the legal watchdog group that specialized in suits against the government, had offered to represent Brentwood employees in a class-action suit against the Postal Service. Larry Klayman, a former Department of Justice lawyer who had founded the organization in 1994, had started by suing the Clintons—it went after the president in the Lewinsky affair—and then, with the new Bush administration, struck out against Vice President Cheney for his secret meetings on energy policy with industry leaders.[18] Starting with the Stevens diagnosis in Florida, Judicial

Watch began filing Freedom of Information Act requests about the attacks and staged media and television interviews about the government's response. After seeing one of those interviews, Briscoe contacted the office several times until, finally, a meeting was arranged with Judicial Watch staff and five of the Brentwood Exposed leadership. Their "compelling story" about the delayed closing of their postal facility persuaded Chris Farrell, the director of investigations and research for Judicial Watch, to become the group's most ardent supporter and guide. Larry Klayman's take on the case was that postal officials had violated a raft of regulations designed to protect worker safety, based on collective bargaining agreements with unions. In addition, the USPS had issued its own instructions in the event of an anthrax incident.

For example, instruction EL-860-1999-3, titled "Emergency Response to Mail Allegedly Containing Anthrax," went beyond notifying superiors and the FBI:

> Suspected bioterrorism threats or suspicious incidents require prompt action by health, safety, law enforcement, and laboratory personnel. Coordination and communication are essential to protect first responders and employees . . . [I]t is management's responsibility to minimize potential exposures through quick isolation and evacuation until emergency response and law enforcement can arrive and take control of the incident.

When anthrax exposure was suspected, USPS officials were directed to turn off machinery (including ventilation equipment) and evacuate and medically treat those at risk—which, in October 2001, happened only after days of delay.

Over six hundred people attended Brentwood's May 3 meeting at Patmos Church. After an introductory prayer, Dena Briscoe stepped aside to let Larry Klayman speak. The rumor had already spread that a lawsuit against the U.S. Postal Service could be in the offing—not a popular idea among employees hired to obey federal authority.

A slight man with a stern face, Klayman made his pitch succinctly. He had reviewed the circumstances of the deaths of Morris and Curseen, the illnesses of the two survivors, and the trauma the letters had caused among the relocated Brentwood employees. "As a lawyer," he said, "I advise you to pursue this case against the federal government, specifically the U.S. Postal Service, for criminal neglect. I can make no promises about the outcome. But Judicial Watch, I can assure you, is committed to our motto: No one is above the law."

As Klayman spoke, his African American audience was completely silent. When he was done, without entertaining questions, he picked up his briefcase from the front pew and, accompanied by Chris Farrell, left via a side door. They knew a core group was in favor of the suit. It was anyone's guess if others would sign up.

As Klayman exited, Dena Briscoe, without missing a beat, urged the assembly to welcome Shauna Spencer from Project DC and two other district social workers seated in the front pew. In response to her call, they had volunteered their services to Brentwood employees who might need them. Briscoe then called on those assembled to offer their experiences in the aftermath of the letters. At first there was hesitation, then the hands went up and the words flowed.

"I can't sleep. I got some pills but they don't work."

"My husband won't leave the house. He's too afraid."

More hands went up. The testimonies multiplied.

"I can't get rid of this fear. Am I still going to get sick and die?"

"After we have some praying and singing," Briscoe said, "our three counselors are going to be at the back of the church to take your names. They're going to put together groups so that all these problems can be talked about, to help with the pain."

Just then an older man in the audience stood and angrily blurted out, "Our safety wasn't their issue! I'm no soldier. I'm no guinea pig. I'm scared."

"We're here to heal," Briscoe advised calmly, "not to injure ourselves by hate and anger."

The next month, on June 2, Brentwood Exposed held another meeting of "healing and information," as Briscoe called them, at the Israel Baptist Church on Brentwood Road, another grand house of worship, which was filled to overflowing. The D.C. volunteer social workers were again there, as were Leroy and Susan Richmond. The Brentwood leadership had decided to go forward with Judicial Watch and file suit against the Postal Service.[19] Briscoe, Worrell, Lewis, and others took turns speaking. The church then filled with prayer and song.

To develop the Brentwood case, Chris Farrell, a former military intelligence officer, and the Judicial Watch staff needed documentation it lacked—that U.S. postal authorities understood there was a deadly anthrax risk and failed to inform the Brentwood workers and implement the emergency measures. By filing a barrage of Freedom of Information Act requests, Judicial Watch hoped to find proof of just when the fact of Brentwood's contamination became known. Meanwhile, a slow trickle of Brentwood employees began arriving at its office in southwest Washington to record their versions of what management had told them that final week before the plant was finally closed on October 21—that the facility was safe.

+

Just outside Washington, in Rockville, Maryland, the scientific team at The Institute for Genomic Research (TIGR) was making slow progress in its search for genetic clues to the anthrax murders. Its first accomplishment was to sequence the genome of the bacteria isolated from Bob Stevens' spinal fluid, *B. anthracis Florida*, and to compare it with a sample from the U.K.'s Porton Down defense laboratory and also with Ames samples from four other labs. The hope was to discover some defining characteristic of the Stevens genome and therefore the spores sent in the letters that might eventually be matched to a specific known source. Unfortunately, all the genomes appeared to be identical, except the one from Porton Down, probably because it had been intentionally stripped of its two plasmids.[20] When the genome of the original Ames Ancestor from Texas was sequenced, it too appeared identical to the Florida and other virulent strains. At this point, the genetic investigation ground to a halt. With no distinctive differences between the letter strain and other Ames strains, genomic DNA sequences offered no way to trace a signature back to the perpetrator.

Nonetheless, by the time the TIGR results were published in June 2002, the potentially limited availability of Ames strain anthrax within the U.S. defense establishment was an accepted fact. Spores from Dugway Proving Ground and USAMRIID had been shared with Porton Down and three unspecified U.S. laboratories. The widely accepted presumption—the FBI, the U.S. Army, and TIGR researchers did not contest it—was that some criminal had "stolen" the letter material from one of these legitimate sources.

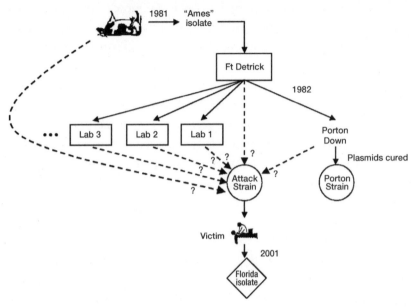

Suggested relationship of Ames isolates

Early estimates of the source of the anthrax letter material focused on USAMRIID and, indicated here with solid lines, a limited number of defense establishment laboratories with which it had shared the Ames strain. [Graph abridged from T. Read et al., *Science* (2002), 2029.]

Despite the setback at TIGR, the Bureau still sought a future match between the anthrax letter bacteria and another Ames sample, the source used by the perpetrator. To that end, it started an innovative project, the collection of an FBI Repository (called the FBIR) of Ames strains from every laboratory known to have possessed it. The Bureau's management of this venture—hundreds of virulent samples would be submitted—was far beyond the capacity of its own laboratory in Washington. Reasonably, the Bureau turned again to the obvious resource: John Ezzell and USAMRIID's Diagnostic Services Division. As a backup, Paul Keim at Northern Arizona University was asked to take responsibility for a duplicate repository. To get the ball rolling, the Department of Justice first subpoenaed laboratories registered as having anthrax to check their inventories for Ames strain samples. Then it followed up with a second subpoena for the twenty labs possessing the Ames strain to share two copies of it with the Bureau.

The approach was far from perfect. Some researchers were hoarders who kept culture samples for years on back shelves, while others either used them up in experiments or disposed of them. With pressure to meet the requirements of the PATRIOT Act and other new regulations to register select agents, research institutions had incentives to distance themselves from select agent research and even destroy stored *B. anthracis*, which is exactly what Iowa State University at Ames did with a single sample from the 1920s in the immediate aftermath of the anthrax letter attacks.[21] Confusion about the relatively recent discovery of Ames strain anthrax lingered for months. FBI submissions were never limited by date, although carbon-dating tests on the letter material later suggested that the spores had been produced some time after 1998.[22]

After consulting with the anthrax experts at USAMRIID, the Bureau issued fixed standards for submissions. First, the material submitted to the FBIR should be direct from the original container, not a regrowth. Two identical submissions should be provided, each in a standard slant, that is, a tube containing solidified growth medium set at a slant (hence its name). The submissions should be "a representative sample of each stock." That is, instead of a single colony grown from one spore, multiple colonies should be included and, if the spores were suspended in liquid, that suspension should be at a concentration of a billion spores per milliliter and "well mixed" before the sample was transferred to the slant.

Even before Operation Noble Eagle and his work with the anthrax letters, John Ezzell at USAMRIID was familiar with FBI evidentiary standards. For Paul Keim, converting a fairly relaxed academic research laboratory to a forensic lab proved a challenge.[23] The FBI rules were strict. Witnesses had to be on hand for every step of the process, from the ongoing delivery of samples through their testing and storage. Some initial tests had to be redone, with guidance from FBI scientists. As the project moved forward, Keim began to shift his perspective from academic research to forensics and the demands of defining "exclusionary evidence" for possible use in a high-profile murder trial—during which he might be cross-examined on the witness stand.

Building the FBIR, at face value a simple project, had its setbacks. In February 2002, for example, Bruce Ivins made a mistake and submitted the two Ames samples from a flask labeled RMR-1029 in the wrong slants, ones he had created, not slants commercially manufactured.

One of his submissions, identified only by a number, went to Paul Keim's lab, where the error was recognized and the tube set aside. The other sample, submitted to Ezzell, was destroyed. Advised of his error, Ivins submitted another sample in April, in the right kind of tube.

✦

In the interim, USAMRIID was involved in defense research on anthrax spurred by perceptions of the Iraqi threat. Recently retired from the Army, Art Friedlander was hired as a civilian scientist to manage a project on an antibiotic-resistant anthrax strain—which a skilled enemy might invent to subvert American troop protection. Patricia Worsham, a longtime colleague in the Bacteriology Division, was under his supervision.

The project was going smoothly until around 9 a.m. on April 8, 2002, when a microbiologist in Worsham's lab (which was in Bacteriology's Level 3 containment suite) took a large flask from a rotary shaker and noticed that hardened drips of media streaked its outside.[24] The flask, which contained 250 milliliters of Ames anthrax culture and had been in the shaker for 72 hours, showed no sign of cracks or breakage. Nonetheless, the junior scientist, who wore neither mask nor gloves, put the flask in a biological safety cabinet and decontaminated it with a bleach solution. Alerted to the problem, Worsham sent her to the institute dispensary for an anthrax booster shot and Cipro. Worsham then informed Friedlander about the accident. There was no panic; as many as forty such mishaps might occur at the institute in a year.[25] Friedlander signed the official record of potential anthrax exposure while Worsham went to the dispensary for her own supply of Cipro.

Worsham then tested her lab for contamination and found anthrax spore spillage—in Room 306 on the lab bench where the flask had been placed, on a centrifuge rotor in nearby Room 304, on the handle of the B-3 pass box (an air lock for transferring papers or small articles outside the lab), and on a pair of protective shoes left over from the previous year. She realized that most of the lab's contamination could be explained by minor incidents, for example, when researchers with contaminated gloves inadvertently touched a surface.[26] Worsham disinfected the area and then retested to make sure the lab was clean.

That minor incident was contained, but a larger crisis was just beginning. When Bruce Ivins heard about the lab accident a few days later, he advised Worsham to test for contamination in areas outside the B-3 suite—insinuating that a dangerous spore escape might have occurred. About a month before, he had casually told her that during Operation Noble Eagle he had detected and cleaned up just such contamination in his office (number 19 in Building 1425). Worsham recommended that Ivins talk with his superior, the head of the Bacteriology Division. Instead, on his own initiative, Ivins began swabbing "cool" as opposed to high-containment surfaces: his own office and the pass box from the B-3 suite, the external side of the men's changing room, and the exterior hallway adjacent to the suite. In his lab, he began culturing five samples to see if anthrax bacteria would appear.

On Tuesday, April 16, eight days after the accident in Worsham's lab, Ivins surprised his division supervisor with his suspicion of possible anthrax contamination outside the high-containment area. The next day, Ivins reported that all five of his samples showed *B. anthracis*–like colony morphologies on agar plates. The following day, while they waited for more conclusive PCR (polymerase chain reaction) results, Worsham did comparative surface swipes outside the B-3 suite, following Ivins' recommendations for where to test.

In the late afternoon, with the test results looking positive, USAMRIID's commander Colonel Edward Eitzen was finally informed that virulent anthrax may have escaped from the BSL-3 lab suite. By 6 p.m., the PCR results were conclusive: anthrax spores had contaminated unprotected areas of USAMRIID, which meant that unprotected workers might have been exposed to a dangerous aerosol. Within the hour, word of the risk was conveyed to the chief of the Army's commander of Medical Research and Materiel Command, Major General Lester Martinez-Lopez, who had replaced General John Parker.

The next morning, Friday, April 19, damage control began. Room 19 (the office of Bruce Ivins) and the men's changing room were locked pending further testing and disinfection, USAMRIID workers were counseled to seek testing and antibiotics at the clinic if they were concerned about exposure, and a team from the U.S. Army Center for Health Promotion and Preventative Health arrived to conduct a comprehensive sampling of Building 1425, including its ventilation system and the laundry and maintenance areas, and retest Bruce Ivins' office and the men's changing room.[27] Even as the institute's public affairs office was preparing a calming press release, word of the calamity spread.

Complaints poured in from the Department of Defense, the mayor of Frederick, and a group of Senate staffers who had recently toured the facility and who had already had their fill of anthrax scares. Congressman Roscoe Bartlett appeared in person at Detrick headquarters, heatedly declaring that by blowing the incident all out of proportion USAMRIID risked damaging Frederick's chances for federal biodefense funding—and then he asked to have soil from his farm tested. Nearly a hundred Detrick employees, including anxious laundry workers, crowded the base dispensary to receive their supplies of Cipro. On April 22, the institute staged a base-wide "town meeting" to calm employees' fears.

By Sunday, April 21, it was certain that the *B. anthracis* contamination was confined to Room 19 and the men's changing room and that the rest of USAMRIID was safe. Equally clear was that the detected spores were sensitive to erythromycin and therefore unrelated to Friedlander's project. So what was the origin of the contamination? After criticizing USAMRIID for having no written policy that would have prevented Ivins from unauthorized environmental testing, Major General Martinez-Lopez ordered an official inquiry by the Judge Advocate General's Corps (JAG). USAMRIID's command, safety officers, the Bacteriology Division, the Diagnostic Systems Division, and anyone involved in high-containment research could count on being interrogated.

To determine the strains of the escaped anthrax, samples from the 27 positive tests were sent to Paul Keim at Northern Arizona University. On May 8, JAG investigators had Keim's results, which indicated that an Ames strain spill in Ivins' office was the key problem.[28] Of the 25 conclusive identifications, 19 were Ames strain, and 15 were from Room 19—around the pass box or on Ivins' desk, the computer of his assistant, or files on shelves near the exhaust vent, where the spores had obviously dispersed. The remaining four Ames samples were from the cool side of the men's changing room. Two other strains used in anthrax experiments were also detected. The virulent Vollum IB, which had been supplied to BioPort, appeared in both Room 19 and the men's changing room; the innocuous Sterne vaccine strain, used in animal research, was found only in Room 19, on Ivins' desk. Although some USAMRIID officials conjectured that the contamination could have occurred years before, the stronger suspicion—and the one that

Bruce Ivins supported—was that the Ames spores had escaped from the Daschle letter, during its transfer from FBI custody to John Ezzell and the Special Pathogens lab. An alternative explanation was that Ivins or someone using his office had been careless in transporting Ames anthrax spores to Building 1412 for aerosol experiments.

The JAG investigators could have come on tough, with probing questions that linked the spill to the anthrax letters—not as they were examined at the institute, but as they might have been prepared there and caused contamination outside the B-3 suite. But instead of a biosecurity breakdown, the inquiry focused on biosafety failures. The investigators asked Bruce Ivins many questions—he had, after all, sounded the alarm—and he consistently responded by criticizing mistakes others made during Operation Noble Eagle. To make his point, he recounted how, the previous December, he had been obliged to disinfect his office. As he told the story, his contract technician (identified in the report as Kathy) told him she was worried about lax safety codes.[29]

"She was afraid she might have been exposed," he explained to JAG interrogators. "So I tested my office and I found suspicious colonies on test plates that could have been anthrax. So I used a bleach solution to clean her desk and the surrounding area."

Asked why he didn't alert his superiors, Ivins claimed that he acted to protect the institute. A formal record of the contamination would have created negative publicity during Operation Noble Eagle, or, he thought, some journalist might find out about it later through a Freedom of Information Act request, which was how, in 2001, Gary Matsumoto had sought access to Ivins' lab notes on his vaccine research.

Asked about the specific cause of the contamination, Ivins offered two explanations. One of them was Kathy. "The young people," he complained, "aren't trained in the proper safety standards." His other idea was that anthrax spills—ostensibly from the Daschle letter—affected the B-3 suite and contaminated the outside of ziplock bags or containers—maybe even some he had prepared. "I often put packages of anthrax material on my desk," he said, "before I take them to the shipping department. Maybe that caused the contamination."

Interviewed separately, the technician Kathy denied being anxious about safety standards or that she had ever transferred live anthrax agents out of the B-3 lab to the office. Others interviewed said they never saw packages of anthrax material on Ivins' desk—the institute norm was to bring such dangerous containers immediately to the shipping department, not to leave them around.

The JAG summary report overwhelmingly accepted Ivins' view that the problem was biosafety failures traceable to the previous fall. JAG concluded that it was "likely that some or all of the contamination occurred as a consequence of inadequate decontamination of the outside of shipping containers brought out of Suite B-3 in building 1425."

The report's second finding specifically linked the contamination to Ezzell and the Daschle letter, such that "opening evidentiary material (a letter containing powdered anthrax) in suite B-3 created conditions leading to contamination of the outside of ziplock bags used to transport material out of the B-3 pass box and led to contamination of areas near the pass box." Ivins or his technician might have contaminated his office, but, the report noted, "other workers cannot be excluded."

In keeping with Ivins' criticism of safety norms, the JAG report chided USAMRIID for "deficient housekeeping"—in the use of centrifuges and pass boxes.[30] "Junior personnel with inadequate training or survey instruments" were faulted for failing to detect the spore leaks earlier.

It took two and a half years for the JAG report to be made public. Although Ivins had withheld proof of virulent *B. anthracis* spills during Operation Noble Eagle and then again in April 2002, he received no reprimands. To the contrary, the report practically congratulated him for bringing the contamination problem to the fore. Apparently, Ivins was an expert above reproach—and above suspicion.

Not long after the JAG interrogation ended, in early June 2002, Ivins and scientists at the institute assembled in the auditorium for a presentation on the 1979 Sverdlovsk outbreak, caused by a release of lethal spores—possibly no more than a gram of aerosolized spores—from a military facility. Obscured for years by Cold War disinformation, the deadly accident was proof of the civilian suffering that the anthrax pathogen could inflict and the paramount importance of both biosafety and biosecurity—of which the institute was acutely aware.

CHAPTER 9

GONE AWRY

I am a loyal American, and I love my country. I have
had nothing to do in any way, shape, or form with the
mailing of these anthrax letters, and it is extremely
wrong for anyone to contend or suggest that I have.

—STEVEN HATFILL, August 11, 2002

The trail of postal contamination, at first a dreaded health hazard, later
became a way of imagining a route back to the perpetrator. In 2001,
every letter slipped into a mailbox in America was picked up by a carrier (whether on foot or by truck) whose adherence to a fixed schedule
was electronically monitored—by routine "punching in" at check stops
and destination points. Leroy Richmond, for example, knew that his
truck from National Airport to Brentwood should arrive every day at
8:27 a.m. because the route had been timed to the minute. Each letter,
once inside a processing plant and in the sorting system, became electronically loaded with information that documented its precise mechanical passage—starting with distribution into bar-coded trays and a
machine that electronically read addresses and zip codes, then into the
big bar code sorters and coded bins, and then on to the next destination
point, which could be a local mailbox or another, distant processing
plant, and from there to a home or office and into the reader's hands.

Examination of the Daschle and Leahy letters after they had been irradiated solved the mystery of exactly how the Leahy letter had gone off course. On October 9 at Hamilton, it had passed through an Automatic Flats Canceling and Sorting machine (which read the printed address) at 4:57 p.m.; the Daschle letter followed at 5:15 p.m. The machine correctly encoded the Daschle letter for zip+4 code "20510-4502" which directed it to the Senate, but the same zip code on the Leahy letter was encoded "20520-4502": the fourth digit was misread as "2" instead of "1." This error directed it to the Department of State mail annex, via Brentwood. There the error was noted; the letter was manually redirected to the Senate, via the P Street Station, where it was retrieved by the FBI. Spores leaking from the Leahy letter nearly killed David Hose at the mail annex and contaminated around a dozen overseas diplomatic mail pouches. (One was the pouch used to send mail to the U.S. consulate in Ekaterinburg, Russia, the former Sverdlovsk, where the local public health laboratory in November 2001 tested it and found the Ames strain spores.)

The Daschle letter followed a direct route. It arrived at Brentwood on October 11 and went from a bar-coded tray into an all-purpose automated carrier, from which it was manually fed into DBCS #17 at 7:10 a.m. on Friday October 12, reaching the Hart Building around noon that same day, just as Mayor Giuliani was announcing the O'Conner diagnosis in New York.

Postal codes also shed light on the mystery of New Jersey mail deliverer Teresa Heller's cutaneous infection, the case that shut down the Hamilton facility, by linking it to cross-contamination. At first the FBI suspected that she had picked up an anthrax letter along her suburban Trenton route, which prompted a name search for suspects there—the FBI after 9/11 developed an enormous terrorist database for cross-checking identities, which continued to increase during Amerithrax. But digital bar code information revealed that within three hours of each other the Brokaw and *Post* letters had been postmarked by the same machine at Hamilton and then passed through two sorting machines, exuding spores.[1] The week of September 18, Heller was delivering mail contaminated enough to give her cutaneous anthrax on her arm.

The same tracking information, taken in reverse and combined with contamination tests, pointed back to wherever the anthrax criminal had posted the letters. Conferring with postal inspectors, the

Bureau was able to locate the 600 mailboxes that fed into the Hamilton postal facility. This part of the investigation moved slowly, until, after two-plus months of swabs and testing, a single "hot" mailbox was found. It stood in front of 10 Nassau Street in the center of Princeton, across from the main university campus.

Why the perpetrator would twice choose the same mailbox in academic, elite Princeton was puzzling. The stretch of Nassau Street where the mailbox was located was lined with small-scale commerce—a bookstore, a souvenir shop, a shoe store, a traditional diner called the Pancake House, a women's clothing boutique—shops that closed early, maybe allowing an unseen late-night posting of the letters.

The monitored mail pickup schedules, plus the letters' digital bar code information, narrowed the windows of time during which the perpetrator must have mailed the letters. The first batch (the Brokaw and *Post* letters and probably the one delivered to AMI and lost), postmarked September 18, had to have been dropped in the mailbox between 9 a.m. Sunday, September 16, and 5 p.m. Monday, September 17. For the Daschle and Leahy letters, postmarked October 9, the window of time for posting was 9 a.m. Saturday, October 6, to 5 p.m. Monday, October 8.

Teams of FBI agents descended on Princeton, questioning local business owners, asking for surveillance tapes, and reviewing information about Princeton residents, university scientists, and students, but with no leads. The facts, though, conjured up two eerie scenes. In the first, a terrorist parks near the mailbox, carefully removes anthrax letters from a sealed container, ambles down Nassau Street, slips the letters into the mailbox, returns to his car, and drives away, perhaps jubilant to have pulled off the stunt unobserved. In the second scene, three weeks later, the terrorist knows he is a murderer—Bob Stevens is dead—and is willing to kill again: the purified spores in the letters addressed to Senators Daschle and Leahy are even more dangerous than those he posted to the media. The perpetrator lets the two "missiles" fall into the mailbox on Nassau Street and again escapes undetected. Within a week, both the Brokaw and Daschle letters are discovered. Pandemonium breaks out.

Cued by the identical return addresses on the Daschle and Leahy envelopes, Bureau agents also scoured other parts of New Jersey as well. There was no Greendale School in Franklin Park, the return address on the Daschle and Leahy letters, but there was a Greenbrook Elementary School in nearby South Brunswick. Again, using its database, agents combed the records of its graduates going back two decades, with no results. Oddly, the zip code for Franklin Park on the two letters was actually for nearby Monmouth Junction, a tiny community within South Brunswick township, a fact that offered investigators no leads. The anthrax terrorist had so far outwitted them.

＊

On June 18, 2002, the FBI's Tom Carey and Van Harp went to a meeting on Capitol Hill organized by Senator Leahy's staff. Several months into the Amerithrax investigation, the two men, who worked well together, reached an agreement, which Director Mueller approved. Carey would continue as liaison with Congress and the press—he kept his door open to journalists—and still offer oversight, while Harp, who controlled the Bureau's workforce and other resources, would take charge of the Amerithrax investigation.[2] In March, a *Washington Post* puff piece on Van Harp quoted him as saying the inquiry remained broad: "We're focused that it might be an individual, possibly with an accomplice, but we're not excluding a group, either domestically or internationally."[3]

That spring Senator Leahy was keeping close watch on the FBI and its tilt toward counter-terrorism intelligence. At a press conference in May, Mueller had announced that the Bureau's number one priority was "Protect the United States from terrorist attack." To better meet that goal, the Bureau had forged a new relationship with the Department of Defense that allowed it to send agents and analysts to Afghanistan to interview captives—a level of cooperation last permitted just after World War II in the search for Axis criminals. Down the list of FBI priorities were the protection of civil rights and the pursuit of criminal syndicates and white-collar crime—in the past the Bureau's stock in trade.[4]

Senator Leahy, one of the anthrax mailer's prime targets, was also impatient with the lagging Amerithrax investigation. To spur some action, his staff invited microbiologist Barbara Hatch Rosenberg, head of the Federation of American Scientists' working group on biological weapons, to share with Carey and Harp her strong opinions about who the anthrax murderer had to be, namely, a U.S. defense establishment insider. Rosenberg had a doctorate in microbiology and for nearly twenty years had devoted herself to one arms control issue: implementing the 1972 Biological Weapons Convention. Just after the end of the Cold War, at a time of spectacular advances in nuclear and chemical arms control, hopes ran high that the convention would be given a budget and a standing organization in The Hague to match the resources accorded the 1993 Chemical Weapons Convention. There was hope, too, for a protocol to promote compliance, including on-site inspections; if a nation declared that its military facilities were engaged in purely defensive research or that its pharmaceutical plants were dedicated only to medicine, it should allow international inspectors to visit those facilities.

But in a few years, the protocol negotiations bogged down, mainly around this transparency issue.[5] Despite President Bill Clinton's support for the treaty, the conservative U.S. Congress, backed by the U.S. military and the American pharmaceutical industry, remained firmly against international oversight that might jeopardize military and commercial secrets. In 1998, when Clinton convened his most high-level White House meeting on bioterrorism, Barbara Rosenberg was there—along with Nobel Laureate Joshua Lederberg, genetics entrepreneur Craig Venter (the founder of TIGR), and top national security advisors—as one of the few in the room who still saw the treaty's potential.

In 2001, the Bush administration destroyed any lingering hopes for an inspection regime that would strengthen the Biological Weapons Convention. In July of that year, Bush's envoy from the State Department, John Bolton, went to Geneva to announce that the United States was pulling out of the Ad Hoc Group of the states party to the treaty that had spent seven years negotiating the new protocol. From the administration's perspective, there were better ways to defend against biological weapons—trade sanctions against possible malefactors, intelligence sharing among allies, and military force against threatening "rogue nations."[6]

In December 2001, the Biological Weapons Convention's states parties had met as usual in Geneva. The mood was bleak; instead of inspections, they would be discussing export controls on select agents, the detection of unusual disease outbreaks, and codes of conduct for microbiologists—subjects the U.S. State Department approved. There as an observer, Rosenberg gave a talk that caused a stir. She claimed that the U.S. government was purposefully hiding the defense insider who was the anthrax terrorist. Soon after, she posted her manifesto of evidence and conclusions on the Web site of the Federation of American Scientists.[7] Although the federation soon backed off from any association with Rosenberg's idea, in a series of *New York Times* columns that spring and summer, Nicholas Kristof began describing a nefarious "Mr. Z" as the protected government insider who had sent the anthrax. Rosenberg's critique of the FBI's failure to arrest the insider culprit also found a receptive audience in Leahy's staff.

At the June meeting in the senator's Russell Office Building suite, Carey and Harp squirmed as Rosenberg outlined her suspicions—that the Amerithrax murderer was a scientist who had worked at USAMRIID and who had openly promoted himself as a bioterrorist expert. Exactly who introduced the name Steven Hatfill into this discussion is unclear, but the forty-eight-year-old virologist became the subject of the meeting.[8] The FBI already had a number of subpoenas out on Hatfill, as they did on other suspects, but Carey and Harp left the meeting without sharing any specifics.

To call Hatfill an insider stretched the facts. In the 1990s, he became part of the demimonde of counter-bioterrorism entrepreneurs and hopscotched from one contract position to another, building on a résumé that featured South African medical and science degrees, rough-and-ready field experience (he claimed he had been a Rhodesian Selous Scout), some study at Oxford University, training for the United Nations special committee to search Iraq for germ weapons, and a research fellowship at USAMRIID. His career mentor was Bill Patrick, who considered him like a son; they shared billing at counter-bioterrorism conferences, and did each other favors. In 1999, when Hatfill became a bioterrorist threat consultant to SAIC, the giant consulting company known for its top-secret national security projects, he asked Patrick to write the report about anthrax attack risks, the one that described a lethal anthrax letter as "futile."[9] That report flagged Hatfill to the FBI. So, too, did his tendency to promote himself in the media as a bioterrorism expert, photographed in high-containment lab gear.

Although his affiliation at USAMRIID had ended more than a year before, Hatfill kept an apartment in the small complex that abutted Detrick's main gate, at the corner of Military Road and West Seventh

Street—a stone's throw from Bruce Ivins' house. At the time Hatfill was being discussed in Leahy's office, he had just found a new niche. For $140,000 a year, he would be teaching first-responder techniques at Louisiana State University, which had established a small counter-bioterrorism enterprise, partially underwritten by Department of Justice funds. A former USAMRIID commander ran the Louisiana program, so it seemed the contact had paid off for Hatfill. In truth, known as short-tempered and aggressive, Hatfill had made few friends there. When his former USAMRIID colleagues were interviewed by the FBI, they voiced suspicions of him—offering up, for example, the rumor that he had once left the base carrying lab equipment to his apartment.

A week after the meeting in Leahy's office, FBI agents at the Bureau's regional office in Frederick asked Hatfill to meet with them. By the end of their conversation, he agreed to have his apartment next to Detrick searched, without a warrant. On his return, Hatfill found a media blitz of television vans and circling news helicopters covering the arrival of the FBI search team. The Washington news audience, as well as curious neighbors and people from the base, watched as Hatfill's computer and personal effects were hauled out of the apartment. Tom Carey emphatically denied that the FBI was the source of the leak to the media.[10] Nonetheless, leaks about Hatfill continued to trouble the inquiry.

On August 1, with the media again tipped off, the FBI arrived at Hatfill's apartment for a second search and found, among other things, a draft of a Tom Clancy–type novel (titled *Emergence*) about a mass bioterrorism attack—a terrorist in a wheelchair gains entry to the White House in order to spray plague germs. Simultaneously, the Department of Justice informed Louisiana State University that none of its program funds could be used to pay for Hatfill's services—which meant his job offer was canceled. In Princeton, FBI agents began circulating Hatfill's picture on Nassau Street, seeking but not finding anyone who had ever seen him there.

Throughout these episodes, Rosenberg emphatically denied ever identifying Hatfill by name. Kristof had also held off naming him. Then on August 6 on CBS's *The Early Show* Attorney General Ashcroft, ignoring the FBI's rules against releasing information involving an ongoing investigation, identified Steven Hatfill as "a person of interest" in Amerithrax. The term, without any legal import, may have just popped into Ashcroft's head. Later, on NBC's *Today*, Ashcroft repeated that Hatfill was "a person that—that the FBI's been interested in." Director Mueller was not pleased, nor were Carey and Harp. But their boss Ashcroft was a performer—known as a talented gospel singer—and a politician who relished the media spotlight.

Five days afterward, on Sunday, August 11, an emotional Hatfill fought back with his own press conference. "I am a loyal American," he told reporters, "and I love my country. I have had nothing to do in any way, shape, or form with the mailing of these anthrax letters, and it is extremely wrong for anyone to contend or suggest that I have."[11]

Hatfill did not object to being investigated; he objected to the media presumptions of his guilt, which were destroying his reputation. The same day, the text of his bioterrorism novel was leaked to ABC News, which made Hatfill look like something of a mad scientist. The next day columnist Kristof joined the chorus and identified Steven Hatfill as the possible anthrax attacker.[12] In response, Hatfill hired a well-regarded Washington law firm to represent him and filed a formal complaint with the FBI and Department of Justice. In an August 22 press conference, Ashcroft ignored this shot across the bow and repeated that Hatfill was "a person of interest to the Department of Justice." For Hatfill, this was the last straw. His lawyers turned to the 1972 *Bivens* decision whereby the Supreme Court allowed individuals to sue the federal government if their basic rights had been violated; for example, by unwarranted search and seizure or other violations of their right to due process.[13] Using that precedent, they filed suit against Attorney General John Ashcroft and a list of other Department of Justice and FBI defendants, most notably Van Harp, head of the Amerithrax investigation.[14]

The media insinuations of Hatfill's guilt continued, an infringement on his civil rights that Leahy's staff—which the FBI blamed for media leaks—could now blame on the FBI. The Bureau would continue to investigate Hatfill for months. In December, in search of the equipment Hatfill was rumored to have lifted from USAMRIID, the FBI arranged for the dredging of a pond in Gambrill State Park, close to Fort Detrick's main gate. The event became another media circus, complete with footage of sniffing bloodhounds. Only a plastic box that looked like a turtle trap was discovered. Oddly, Bruce Ivins observed the dredging. A committed Red Cross volunteer, he answered a request to help with a food canteen for the FBI and the muddied divers. While the evidence search went on, Ivins dutifully served coffee—until an agent recognized him and, to Ivins' chagrin, asked for his removal.

With few prospects, living behind shaded windows, Hatfill began drinking heavily.[15] The strain of being an Amerithrax suspect was extreme. During this same time, former USAMRIID scientist Perry Mikesell, another suspect, died quietly in Ohio. A relative later claimed that, unable to withstand the pressure, he drank himself to death.[16]

✣

In Washington, Dena Briscoe and the leadership of Brentwood Exposed were having their own new experience contending with government. A few days after Carey and Harp met with Leahy's staff, Briscoe, wearing a business suit and high heels, went to the office of Eleanor Holmes Norton, the District of Columbia's House delegate. Spurred by the energy of Brentwood Exposed, Briscoe, Helen Lewis, and Terrell Worrell decided their constituency needed to garner broad political support. Norton had already expressed an interest in a hearing on Brentwood, which they hoped would address the delayed closure and the difficulties with adjustment the displaced workers were facing.

Added to those difficulties was a series of eight sudden deaths in the community of Brentwood employees. All apparently healthy men, they had passed away in the weeks and months following the October crisis. Briscoe wrote a June 10 press release from Brentwood Exposed calling for better government assessment:

> Each of the employees suffered similar symptoms of respiratory, renal, swollen joints, liver and/or kidney damage. Stress-related heart attack was also noted. Federal investigators have reported that the deaths are not linked to Cipro/doxycycline or anthrax without giving supporting clinical studies or statistics from which they base their opinion. We are concerned.[17]

Initially, Norton's chief of staff was cool to Briscoe's concerns. Norton was wary of any outraged outbursts at the hearing, like some featured on television just after the Brentwood closing. But Briscoe explained that the Brentwood postal workers simply needed to feel protected and that their goal was therapeutic assistance.[18]

Nonetheless, as events proceeded, Brentwood Exposed leaders were denied their chance to speak at the hearing. On July 19, Terrell Worrell circulated a group email announcing that instead of Norton's holding a hearing, Maryland's Representative Connie Morella would chair a special subcommittee meeting of the House Committee on Government Reform, at which only union officials, largely silent about Brentwood workers, and USPS authorities would be allowed to make statements.

Leery of the subcommittee's intentions, Judicial Watch also imposed constraints. Morella's staff had offered to meet in private with the leaders of Brentwood Exposed. But, Worrell told the group, "Judicial Watch has informed us that they only want information because of the lawsuit. So we were asked not to meet with them, but rather to go and to listen and to record the session if possible."[19]

After seeing Larry Klayman on CNN talking about the Brentwood suit, mail handler Bob Unick in New Jersey called Judicial Watch, which put him in touch with Dena Briscoe. Judicial Watch had no interest in representing the Hamilton workers. The facility had been closed quickly and clinics mobilized, giving its workers little cause to sue the USPS, health care providers, or the drug companies whose antibiotics, despite negative side effects, had likely saved lives. Still, when Briscoe told Unick about the hearing, set for July 26 at 10 a.m., he decided to drive down.

The House hearing took place in a large auditorium at Gallaudet University in northeast Washington.[20] In front were several rows of men and women in conservative suits. U.S. Postal Service Vice President Tom Day was there, along with representatives from the D.C. Department of Health and the EPA and several senior postal union officials. Behind them was clustered a small African American contingent from Brentwood Exposed, with Bob Unick, burly and fair, seated with them.

Ignoring the October 2001 disaster, the federal officials told Morella about plans for future safety: about the decontamination process, about the planned installation of biosensors, and about how, once they returned to Brentwood, postal workers would be monitored closely for illness or any adverse effects, physical or emotional "for as long as it takes for workers and the public to feel safe."[21]

Having submitted questions in advance to the committee staff about the eight unexplained deaths, Briscoe and the others waited expectantly for a response, which came only as the hearing drew to a close. With undisguised scorn, an official from NIOSH (the CDC's National Institute for Occupational Safety and Health) dismissed the additional Brentwood deaths as nothing unusual. Her agency, she said, had reviewed the cases and found nothing statistically out of the ordinary.

Afterward, over lunch, Briscoe and the others felt even more strongly that Judicial Watch should proceed with their suit. Bob Unick, driving back to New Jersey to make his shift, felt he'd had an important civics lesson and that he would return to learn more.

That summer and into the fall, Brentwood Exposed kept up a busy schedule of weekly meetings and more large gatherings for healing and information, along with spontaneous barbecues and potluck dinners. With new money allocated by Congress to help those traumatized by 9/11 terrorism, Washington's Project DC was able to fund social workers to counsel Brentwood workers and their families who were still troubled. Briscoe and the other leaders also introduced themselves to allies within easy reach: the Congressional Black Caucus, the NAACP, the National Council of Negro Women, and the National Association of Black Social Workers.

As part of their educational mission, they contacted experts who had been in the news and invited them to give one of the weekly library talks. Ken Alibek, who had a position at George Mason University in Virginia, said yes to his invitation. Although more used to giving congressional testimony or lecturing biosecurity graduate students, Alibek expounded on his ideas for a wonder drug that could give generalized immunity to infectious diseases. Before he left, he encouraged Briscoe and the others to keep questioning the government. (A link to Alibek's biotech company, Hadron Advanced Biosystems, Inc., quickly appeared on the Brentwood Web site.)

The first anniversary of 9/11 was a national day of mourning, but Briscoe and the others in the Brentwood community felt a memorial for Morris and Curseen should also be held. After much planning, the event took place on Sunday, October 20, 2002, at the grand Cathedral of the Immaculate Conception at Catholic University, in northeast Washington.

Another tragedy nearly overshadowed the Brentwood ceremony, which was scheduled to start at 5:30 p.m. Since October 2, nine people in the D.C. area had been randomly shot dead by a cruising sniper.

People were afraid to drive their cars, stop for gas, or walk across a mall parking lot. Outside the cathedral, the streets of the capital were nearly empty.

Inside, close to a thousand Brentwood employees and their families and friends gathered for the memorial. Large photos of Morris and Curseen were displayed in front of the altar, along with those of the eight Brentwood men who had died suddenly in the past year.

To begin the ceremony, everyone stood and sang "Amazing Grace." Then Dena Briscoe started to read an inspirational poem by Sufi teacher Hazrat Inayat Khan. "We asked for strength," she said, "and God gave us difficulties to make us strong." Her voice was slightly husky, but encouraged by the "Amens" from her audience, she continued to the end: "We asked for courage and God gave us dangers to overcome. We asked for love and God gave us people to help."

Then the music started—solos and duets backed by guitar, drum, and electric piano. At his keyboard, Terrell Worrell poured out his heart in two gospel-pop songs he had composed about hope overcoming adversity. A choir of postal workers, the Sounds of Redemption, brought the crowd, clapping in rhythm, to its feet.

Interspersed with the musical performances were statements from invited speakers. Maryland Democratic Senator Barbara Mikulski (small in stature, she stood on a box to reach the microphone) praised the heroism of Morris and Curseen; her office was in the Hart Building and she had taken Cipro for two months. Ivan Walks, who had been head of the D.C. Department of Health during the crisis, offered his condolences, as did Vincent Orange, the local D.C. councilman. Senator Daschle sent a written message of praise, which one of the Brentwood workers read to the community.

By far, the best speakers were the postal workers themselves, who shared their affectionate remembrances of Morris and Curseen. One of them, minister Carl Tillman, addressed the problem of fear: "I grew up in the ghetto. I know what street shootings are like, how the fear takes over. But I also know the difference between living *with* fear and living *in* fear. We can choose. We from Brentwood have chosen not to live in fear, not to bow down to it."

Two days later, on October 22, the anonymous sniper shot another victim. This time, a witness reported a license plate and car description. On October 24, alerted by an observant truck driver, the police apprehended a vagrant man and a teenager in a 1990 Chevy sedan with a gun hole cut next to the trunk lock. They had fallen asleep in the car at a rest stop in suburban Maryland. The Beltway sniper siege was over.

That same day, under a court order to respond to a Judicial Watch Freedom of Information Act request, the U.S. Postal Service delivered a document that was crucial for the Brentwood case: the work diary of plant manager Timothy Haney. In it, he recorded that tests confirming anthrax spore contamination were known to him and higher postal officials on October 18, three days (and ten working shifts) before the facility was closed and workers were offered antibiotics.[22]

Brentwood Exposed leaders reacted with a mixture of astonishment and disillusion. They knew the system had failed them, but they had not known about the early test results. Dozens of postal workers who had been sitting on the fence about the lawsuit went to the Judicial Watch office to join the plaintiff list and have their accounts of that final week at Brentwood recorded.[23]

In December, on behalf of approximately 2,200 Brentwood workers, Judicial Watch, drawing, like Hatfill, on the 1972 *Bivens* decision, filed a suit against the U.S. Postal Service. The claim was for $100 million in damages for deprivation of the workers' rights of due process. The Postal Service had failed them "by providing false and/or misleading information and/or failing to provide accurate information" that would have allowed them to invoke the protective procedures called for by their union contracts.[24]

The defendants in the case were Postmaster General John E. Potter, Vice President of Engineering Thomas Day, and Processing and Distribution Center Plant Manager Timothy C. Haney, along with ten "U.S.P.S. Unknown Officials," all sued in their individual capacity and "for acting under color of federal law."

Six Brentwood workers signed up as plaintiffs—not without trepidation, for they were challenging the top authorities at the powerful, enormous corporation that employed them. The first was Dena Briscoe, as the class representative of Brentwood facility employees represented by the American Postal Workers Union. Terrell Worrell became the class representative for employees represented by the National Postal Mail Handlers Union. Others represented the National Association of Letter Carriers and the National Association of Postal Supervisors.[25]

✦

Meanwhile, the FBI contracted with USAMRIID for another Amerithrax project in addition to the Ames strain repository. It was based on a simple question: If individual spores from the letters were allowed to germinate and multiply to form individual colonies on agar plates, would they exhibit any distinctive shape or color differences—that is, morphotypes? USAMRIID's Terry Abshire had noticed just such minor irregularities on October 17, 2001, while examining colonies of bacteria grown from the Daschle letter material. To answer the question thoroughly required conducting "visual differential tests"—that is, seeding bacterial cultures on agar plates and carefully looking for colonies that differed from the majority in shape, size, or color. Patricia Worsham in Bacteriology had pioneered the technique for discerning these minor deviations.[26] As with Operation Noble Eagle, the institute seemed to offer the perfect resources—the scientists, high-containment laboratories, and security—for cooperation with the FBI. This low-tech approach to discovering rare morphotypes soon revealed that a small percent of the colonies generated by the letter spore samples were consistently yellow or yellow-gray, compared to the gray-white of the majority of colonies.

The next phase, started at TIGR in December 2002, was to find distinctive DNA signatures associated with the particular morphotypes, signatures that could provide a more specific test than mere visible appearance. Eventually four morphotypes, coded A1, A3, D, and E, were selected for screening the FBIR samples. All four were found by DNA tests in samples from the Leahy letter; three of the four (A1, A3, and E) were found in samples from the *Post* and Daschle letters. (The material from these two letters was not tested for D and no tests were done on the Brokaw letter spores.)[27]

The FBI now had a scientific project with promise. If the technical means could be found to match these distinct genetic sequences against the repository samples, together the four irregularities might trace back to a specific laboratory sample and perhaps even to the perpetrator. The goal was the discovery of the same four morphotypes in any of the approximately 1,000 samples in the FBIR, in such a way that the evidence would be decisive—like identified fingerprints—and trial-worthy. No institution that had submitted samples to the repository could be involved in the analyses to come, and that included USAMRIID. For security's sake, the FBI arranged for the anthrax strain repository to be moved to another U.S. Army facility with BSL-3 labs, in Edgewood, Maryland. Ezzell, promoted to senior scientist in September 2002, later recalled he felt some relief at the change; he didn't feel it was his job to answer to the FBI.[28] Paul Keim in Arizona, the strain expert, stayed in charge of his FBIR collection and became even more involved in the scientific branch of the investigation.

After consulting with scientists within and outside the Bureau, the decision was made to divide the process of morphotype identification among separate contract laboratories: TIGR in Maryland, Commonwealth Biotechnologies in Richmond, Virginia, the Midwest Research Institute in Palm Bay, Florida, and the Illinois Institute of Technology Research Institute (IITRI) in Chicago. The analyses would be blind— only coded numbers marked the FBIR samples—and independent, with no sharing of information about results. Each lab team would look for a match to the morphotype designated to it, whether A1, A3, D, or E. The results as they came in would be reviewed only by the top levels of the FBI scientific staff, certain field agents with science backgrounds, and trusted consultants.

Despite its promise, the morphotype project presented the same problems of adapting new-age science to forensic purposes that the FBI had confronted in the 1990s, when the revolutionary potential for DNA identification of criminal case material was first recognized, argued over, and then improved. Special Agent Mark Wilson, a biologist at the FBI's Counterterrorism and Forensic Science Research Unit in Quantico in 2002, had spent most of his career refining DNA analyses to the point where he could testify with high confidence about the genetic identification of hair and bone samples. In 1999, he articulated the basic standards for valid evidentiary results, that is, the protocol for DNA testing:

> The protocol is a basic recipe, if you will, for conducting an examination in the laboratory. It lists all the reagents, all the suppliers, all the companies where you buy the materials, the solutions that you make, the steps you go through to obtain a result from a sample, the comparison process, the interpretation, the published articles you rely on for the underlying science and the general description, the methodology.[29]

No such protocol existed for the kind of genomic identification the FBI was seeking. The chosen laboratory teams would have to learn by doing and by paying close attention to experienced Bureau scientists like Mark Wilson and others who had pioneered DNA forensics. The scientific challenges were enormous, no less than tracking the ultimate origins of a microbial weapon.

In addition, genetic sequencing was slow and costly; the unprecedented project could take years and cost the Department of Justice and other involved federal agencies many millions. Yet consulting experts from the National Institutes of Health, the Department of Defense, the Department of Homeland Security, the CIA, and Justice itself, brought together in large measure by the efforts of Rita Colwell, head of the National Science Foundation, and Bruce Budowle, one of the FBI's leading forensic scientists, saw no alternative but to begin. As Colwell observed later, "We were, in effect, serving as midwives to this new discipline."[30] The hope was that the scientists under contract to the FBI would develop the necessary assays to test the FBIR samples for the four morphotypes and develop a microbial forensic protocol that would stand up in federal court, and that larger technological advances would speed the process.

CHAPTER 10

TO WAR

We must take the battle to the enemy, disrupt his plans
and confront the worst threats before they emerge.

—PRESIDENT GEORGE W. BUSH, West Point, June 1, 2002

In the spring of 2002, at the Department of Defense, Deputy Secretary
Paul Wolfowitz requested clarification from the FBI about the possible
foreign source of anthrax letter attacks. Wolfowitz, Secretary Donald
Rumsfeld, and others at Defense had been public about their suspicions of
al Qaeda and Iraq's germ weapons threat. The Bureau complied, offering
assurances that it was diligently investigating possible foreign sources,
with all its legations worldwide on alert for al Qaeda or other terrorist
connections. The Bureau's agents and WMD intelligence analysts had
been traveling the globe—to South Africa, the Pacific, South Asia, and
Western Europe in search of clues. (In South Africa, they checked the
credentials of Steven Hatfill and were updated on the truth and recon-
ciliation hearings involving former biowarfare scientists.)[1] They had
found nothing to implicate foreign terrorists, and government intelligence agencies were no wiser on the subject than the Bureau.

Earlier that year, there had been a dust-up caused by Tara O'Toole
and Tom Inglesby at the Johns Hopkins Center, after they circulated a
memo in the intelligence community to the effect that one of the al

Qaeda terrorists on Flight 93 had been treated for cutaneous anthrax in Florida some weeks before the 9/11 attacks.[2] In the immediate aftermath of Bob Stevens' death, the FBI interviewed an emergency room physician who identified Ahmed Ibrahim Al Haznawi as having sought help for a lesion on his leg, explained as the result of bumping hard into a suitcase. Reportedly, a black scab had formed, but no biopsy was done. In a bizarre twist, an FBI official not connected with Amerithrax asked O'Toole and Inglesby for their opinions. Their joint conclusion was that Al Haznawi had suffered from cutaneous anthrax, which was interpreted as a link between al Qaeda and the anthrax letters. In the *New York Times* article that broke this story of suspicion, D. A. Henderson, referred to as the "top bioterrorism expert" at the Department of Health and Human Services, agreed with his two protégés. Yet months before, Bureau agents had put enormous energy into testing the terrorists' cars, personal possessions, and apartments for any signs of *B. anthracis* and found nothing. Coincidences abounded in Florida—al Qaeda operatives had rented an apartment through a real estate agent married to the editor of *The Sun*—but no evidence of a foreign source for the letters had surfaced.

Still, to pursue the lead, FBI investigators had gone to the site of the Flight 93 crash in Pennsylvania, where, unlike the New York City and Pentagon sites, the FBI was in full charge of the crime scene and of identifying those who died. The crash site was gory, with body parts scattered over the field; one victim's face, slipped from the skull, was found hanging from a tree. Investigators again searched for signs of al Qaeda anthrax, this time by excavating the cockpit, buried 90 feet below ground, and taking samples from the remains of the terrorists, including from a severed leg. They also sampled the rest of the plane and the surrounding field. The results, tested by the U.S. Army, eventually proved negative.

Nor was there anything to the claims about a silica coating on the spores that, for some, could have linked them to Iraq. It was by no means knowledge the Bureau could share, but Joe Michael and his colleague Paul Kotala at Sandia National Laboratory had analyzed the spores from the *Post*, the Daschle, and the Leahy letters (there were not enough to share from the Brokaw letter) and found that they had no glassy silica coating. The proof that Dick Spertzel had assured ABC News linked the anthrax letters to a foreign source simply did not exist.

Instead, there was silicon inside the spores, as part of their layered composition. The Armed Forces Institute of Pathology, with limited equipment, had detected the element and mistakenly reckoned it was on the surface of the spores, where an artificial coating might be expected. Michael had signed a non-disclosure agreement; by FBI rules, his analyses had to remain secret until the case went to trial, whenever that might be.

The Bureau was continuing to pursue a list of possible suspects with means and motive, but so far none had ties to Iraq or al Qaeda. The Bureau's access to foreign intelligence was improving—Attorney General Ashcroft and the FBI's Mueller were determined to bring down "the wall" between policing and intelligence, even as it existed between Bureau divisions. Still, the FBI's commitment to trial-worthy evidence, as opposed to connecting data dots, remained firm, as did its faith in the "lone wolf" profile.

An advisor to Wolfowitz at this time was Laurie Mylroie who, in 1990, had co-authored a bestselling book on Iraq with Judith Miller, the lead author of *Germs*.[3] The conclusion of that book, written on the brink of the Gulf War, quoted commentator Kevin Phillips to the effect that the U.S. involvement in the Persian Gulf conflict "looks like the classic overreach of a declining superpower going into debt to maintain yesteryear's prestige."[4] But perceptions of Saddam's threat had only grown. Linking Iraq and al Qaeda as partners in terrorism, Mylroie staunchly advocated regime change, and Miller, along with other journalists writing for the *New York Times* and others at the *Washington Post*, was relying on administration insiders with the same unilateral agenda.

Members of Congress, evacuated from the Hill on 9/11 and then thrown into chaos during the anthrax crisis, were listening to experts on biological weapons who saw little but foreign threats. Ken Alibek, a former deputy head of the Soviet Biopreparat program, and Dick Spertzel, onetime Fort Detrick scientist and former United Nations investigator in Iraq, together gave congressional testimony insisting on the combined threat of the Soviet specter and Iraqi menace.[5] Although self-exiled for nearly ten years, Alibek claimed that Russia was engaged in dual-purpose or outright offensive biological weapons work and that former Soviet weapons scientists had gone to Asia or "disappeared" to work for terrorists. In his statement, Spertzel suggested that in the late 1980s Iraq may have acquired silica and the Ames strain, implying it was behind the anthrax letter attacks. He also asserted that Iraq's past experience with smallpox epidemics (its last outbreak was in 1972) made it likely it had smallpox strains and the necessary facilities, expertise, and equipment to achieve a dangerous capability. In a single two-day period in early June 2002, Bill Patrick briefed senior senate staffers, conferred at length with the FBI, and was interviewed by the BBC—all on the threat of mass foreign bioterrorism.[6]

With the exception of Tony Blair, the U.K. prime minister, the heads of the other major powers were reluctant to use force against Iraq. Although Secretary of State Colin Powell wanted the backing of an international coalition, Vice President Cheney argued for unilateral military action, and it was Cheney who was winning.[7]

As a U.S. invasion of Iraq loomed, the Pentagon began mobilizing its vaccinations of American military personnel with the controversial AVA (anthrax vaccine adsorbed) from the BioPort company in Michigan. In the interests of national security, the Food and Drug Administration had cleared the way for the company. From the point of view of troop morale, the campaign was helped by a new report from the Institute of Medicine at the National Academy of Sciences that disputed any causal connection between the AVA vaccine and Gulf War syndrome. After reviewing vaccination records from 1990 on, a committee of experts found no proof "that life-threatening or permanently disabling immediate-onset adverse events occur at higher rates in individuals who have received AVA than in the general population."[8] USAMRIID and particularly its Bacteriology Division and Bruce Ivins were vindicated. This time, in contrast to the rushed Gulf War inoculations, the Pentagon started this effort early and kept careful records. Battlefield risk perceptions were more heightened than they had been in 1990: Iraq not only had an anthrax arsenal but Saddam might be crazy enough to use it.

Meanwhile, FBI investigators, following a 32-item interview schedule, kept questioning staff at USAMRIID about the big problem: How did the Ames spores "escape"?[9] No employees at Dugway Proving Ground, which possessed the Ames Ancestor strain, or the institute seemed likely suspects. Some of the polygraph test results revealed a certain amount of volatility and stress—but nothing unusual in a military defense community. The security at Dugway looked tight; in contrast, USAMRIID was a busy, more open environment. Exploring the idea of sabotage there, the FBI interviewers asked if any foreigners had been in or near the B-3 suites where Ames strain anthrax spores were stored and used for research. The answers came back consistently negative: foreign visitors were allowed only in conference rooms and were never left unsupervised. Was it possible to "piggyback" to gain access to a high-containment laboratory, that is, for one person to key open a door and let another unauthorized person through? Some staff mentioned that it used to be easy to gain entry to Building 1425, but that after 9/11 and the anthrax letters, security had improved. As for piggybacking into the B-3 or B-4 labs, no one had ever witnessed any such violations. Even if someone had covertly entered, the process of exiting from the B-3 suite with any dangerous pathogen would be more difficult than the facile "vest pocket" scenarios featured in the press. Yet, without camera surveillance or a buddy system, USAMRIID scientists were relying heavily on mutual trust.

Dozens of scientists and technicians, including some who were former institute employees, were asked if they could think of any worker who might have been motivated to send the anthrax letters, for example, someone with a grudge against the government or the media. No one could—or almost no one. An exception was Bruce Ivins who, in January 2002, had called the FBI to identify two suspects, former employees who had had access to Ames strain anthrax who, Ivins felt, had the skill and character to send the letters. Later he added another name. All three individuals were eventually cleared of suspicion. Ivins also suggested that the FBI should investigate the personnel at laboratories with which he had personally shared his store of Ames strain anthrax. Foremost among them were facilities at the U.K.'s Porton Down, Canada's DRES in Alberta, the U.S. Army's Dugway Proving Ground in Utah, and Battelle Memorial in Ohio.[10]

FBI agents also had technical questions to ask institute scientists about how they conducted their anthrax experiments. The questioning was to determine whether they could make anthrax powder or if they ever possessed it. Art Friedlander had insisted that only wet spores were used at the institute and, in a series of discussions, Bruce Ivins vouched for this fact. His Ames spores, for example, were kept in a solution containing phenol, which preserved them without destroying them. Many of the anthrax experiments required subjecting lab animals to aerosols. The aerosol equipment in Building 1412 was suited only to wet spores, not powders. Injecting animals with the bacilli likewise required a solution. Growing and processing *B. anthracis* wasn't usually done at USAMRIID. When it came to anthrax spores, USAMRIID researchers were the users—Dugway in Utah was the provider. For example, as Ivins explained, in 1997 Dugway had sent him the Ames strain spores in the flask RMR-1029; and before the switch to Ames— which came in the 1990s—Dugway used to supply him with less virulent Vollum spores. Therefore, institute researchers didn't use fermenters. Although there was a lyophilizer available that might have been used to freeze-dry spores, it served no purpose—the machine sat idle in a hallway.

During the interviews, a number of USAMRIID researchers told FBI agents that they were dismayed to learn that Dugway had experimented with *B. anthracis*, as if reverting to before 1969. Just after the anthrax crisis, the *New York Times* broke the story that in 1998 Bill Patrick had taught Dugway scientists how to produce powdered anthrax in bulk. Patrick was quoted as saying, "We made about a pound of material in little less than a day. It's a good product."[11]

‡

When Governor Jeb Bush asked his first question about Bob Stevens' diagnosis—is the disease contagious?—he aptly defined the characteristic most likely to send the public into a panic. Inhalational anthrax has a brutally high mortality rate, but in human history it is the devastating plagues that are most remembered and feared. Smallpox, once a colossal incurable killer, is foremost among them, a loathsome scourge that devastated entire communities. In 1999, Ken Alibek claimed that, during the former Soviet Union's biological weapons program, "We stockpiled hundreds of tons of anthrax and dozens of tons of plague and smallpox."[12] And Alibek was vocal about his suspicions that the Russians, who had inherited the Soviet repository of 170 Variola strains, were secretly developing new, perhaps genetically manipulated, smallpox weapons.

At this time, D. A. Henderson, for a decade the leader of the successful smallpox eradication campaign, had just started his new think tank, the Johns Hopkins Center for Civilian Biodefense Studies in Baltimore. Resonating to Alibek's suspicions, he warned that Russia might be continuing the Soviet quest for more virulent and contagious pathogens.[13] Not surprisingly, Henderson added smallpox to the center's short list of the most likely bioterrorism agents—anthrax, plague, tularemia, and botulinum toxin.

From the global smallpox campaign, Henderson had learned a crucial public relations lesson. In the classic "Big Red Book" that summarizes its achievements, he reflected, "Those who decide policy and the allocation of funds must perceive the disease problem to be serious enough to warrant expending additional funds; but, no less, the populations which are most affected must be motivated to cooperate."[14] Washington officials who held the domestic preparedness purse strings had to believe that the bioterrorism threat was serious—that was the new challenge for Henderson. To persuade them, his staff created scenarios that dramatized the chaotic system-wide impact of different disease agents. The formula was simple: predicate a mass attack followed by inflated casualty rates and show how poor decisions by unprepared, unfunded officials lead to ruination, ending with the National Guard being summoned to quell public panic. The center's 1999 scenario on anthrax and another on plague presented in 2000 followed this narrative arc.[15] Such scenarios, hardly unique to the center, were never intended to be scientifically accurate. As one commentator put it, the apocalyptic bioterrorism exercises that sprang from the domestic preparedness program were "magic shows" staged by public health conjurers.[16] But coming from Henderson and Johns Hopkins, these apocalyptic scenarios had credibility.

In July 2001, at Andrews Air Force Base, the center staged its third scenario, about a potential smallpox attack. Associate director Tara O'Toole, a physician who had formerly worked on nuclear safety at the Department of Energy, and Tom Inglesby, another physician at the Johns Hopkins Center, composed a tabletop exercise to illustrate how Saddam's terrorists might invade America with a frightening disease. The intent of "Dark Winter," the title of the scenario, was to boost funding for biodefense, in decline after President Clinton left Washington. Condensing 13 days of crisis into two days of interactive game-playing, Dark Winter pitted actors playing federal officials against smallpox-infected Iraqi terrorists, whose invasion quickly precipitates a national catastrophe. The cast included former Senator Sam Nunn as the American president, Donna Shalala, Clinton's head of Health and

Human Services, reprising her former role, and other former agency heads and government advisors taking part, plus Judith Miller as the White House press secretary. As the bewildered officials lose control, the pandemic spreads across twenty-five states, political mayhem breaks out, and the National Guard is called in. On the last day, 15,000 cases have been reported, and a million Americans are projected to die in three months; simultaneously, the pandemic goes global to kill more millions.

Shortly after Dark Winter was performed, Senator Nunn and Tara O'Toole testified about its dire predictions to Congress, to bolster the argument that the nation needed more emergency medical and pharmaceutical defenses against mass bioterrorism.[17]

When details of the Dark Winter exercise became public, physicians who had worked with smallpox patients during the eradication campaign—as well as British military defense experts—objected strenuously to its exaggerations of risk.[18] But members of Congress were not reading articles in the *New England Journal of Medicine* and *Nature*. Henderson's reputation as the hero who saved the world from smallpox lent legitimacy to his center and to the Dark Winter apocalypse. Immediately after 9/11, Congress was pressuring Secretary of Health and Human Services Thompson to increase smallpox vaccine reserves to protect all Americans. Thompson immediately called Henderson and put him in charge of the Secretary's Council on Public Health Preparedness.[19]

The repercussions of Dark Winter might have ended there, with a congressional mandate to increase smallpox vaccine supplies, had it not been for Vice President Dick Cheney. Before 9/11, Cheney, whose policy strength had been nuclear threat issues, said that of any potential terrorist attack, he most feared one with a dirty bomb, a crude nuclear device that could have mass consequences.[20] But al Qaeda's attacks had made Cheney a "doomsday expert" who shared the intelligence community's conviction "that a second wave of even more devastating terrorist attacks on America was imminent."[21] On September 20, Cheney's chief assistant, I. Lewis "Scooter" Libby (dubbed "Germ Boy" by the president for his concerns about bioterrorism), brought his boss a videotape of the Dark Winter exercise.[22] Deeply impressed—here was a disease attack of nuclear proportions—Cheney immediately brought the tape to a National Security Council meeting and had everyone, including President Bush, watch it. Cheney wanted the Iraqi smallpox threat taken seriously and, from that day forward, it was.

Dark Winter originated as a policy ploy, the equivalent of banging a few drums to wake up committee chairs on Capitol Hill. But the Bush administration was preoccupied with a much more serious agenda: persuading the American public to back a war to oust Saddam Hussein. The Johns Hopkins scenario planted the seeds of how the fear of smallpox might aid that endeavor. Speaking of the bioterrorism threat just after the Stevens diagnosis, one of the center's associates commented on national television: "What is important is to scare people into positive action."[23] Positive action for the Bush administration meant taking the battle to the enemy, Iraq.

After 9/11 it was almost easy to persuade the American public that a new terrorist threat would emanate from the Middle East. On October 3, 2001, the popular CNN health commentator Sanjay Gupta introduced the Dark Winter scenario to viewers and gave Henderson and O'Toole new national exposure. Henderson, now a federal official, argued that the exercise represented a reasonable threat. "There are some," he grimly declared, "who said this is an extreme example of what might happen in a worst-case scenario. I wish I could say that, but I can't." Agreeing, O'Toole contributed gory details: "The rash is very painful, usually causing scarring for life, some people go blind and about thirty percent of the people who get smallpox die."[24]

In the popular press, Richard Preston, a master of disease thrillers, revived the specter of the Soviet smallpox weapons—promoted by Ken Alibek and D. A. Henderson. Preston rolled the story toward the future, describing Peter Jahrling's successful attempt at the CDC to kill otherwise immune monkeys with smallpox in order to develop medical countermeasures against a terrorist attack on Americans—as in the Dark Winter scenario. Preston also turned to Dick Spertzel for his familiar take on Saddam's WMD: "Their biowarfare program continues and the chance that the Iraqis are continuing research into smallpox today is high."[25] The evidence for this assertion was minimal; Iraq in 1995 had put "camel pox" on its list of select agents, with no further comment, while their other documents described in detail their anthrax, botulinum toxin, and aflatoxin weapons. Spertzel meant what Charles Duelfer, the former deputy executive chairman of the U.N. special commission on Iraq, had said elsewhere: "So long as this regime remains, the Iraqi WMD threat, in some form, will also remain."[26] Saddam's capabilities might be weak, but his intentions were patently clear.

Following suit, in his 2001 book on smallpox, Washington policy analyst Jonathan Tucker also relied on Henderson, Spertzel, and Alibek and their threat perceptions.[27] Characterizing the Dark Winter scenario as "realistic," Tucker described in detail the fictional pandemic inflicted by Saddam's terrorists and then how analysts connected the dots from the Soviet Union and Russia to the Iraqi smallpox threat. Yet the intelligence seemed far from compelling:

> A declassified DIA intelligence report from May 1994, citing a source of unknown reliability, stated that virologists from one of the Soviet Ministry of Defense's military microbiology institutes had transferred smallpox virus cultures to Iraq in the late 1980s or early 1990s and had assisted the Iraqis with their biological warfare program. In addition, the British Secret Intelligence Service (MI6) had reportedly spotted a [Soviet] Vector scientist in Baghdad in 1991.[28]

Although this evidence was "circumstantial," Tucker noted that the relevant Interagency Working Group (which included representatives from the Pentagon, Health and Human Services, State, the Department of Energy, and the intelligence community) "could not simply dismiss it."

In early November 2002 the *Washington Post* reported a CIA assessment of the smallpox threat that seemed ominous but, again, thin on intelligence. As a data point, the agency cited blood tests from seven Iraqi Gulf War prisoners that showed immunity to smallpox.[29] For unspecified reasons, the CIA put al Qaeda on a smallpox terror list that included Iraq, North Korea, and Russia. The agency also added France, which at the time, like Russia, was objecting to the United States' plan for a military invasion of Iraq. The CIA asserted with "high confidence" that a French BSL-4 military defense laboratory harbored a live smallpox virus, in violation of the 1980 international resolution banning all but the United States and Soviet strain repositories. The French foreign minister firmly denied the allegation.[30]

According to polls, Americans were showing mounting apprehension about a return of smallpox. At this juncture, Henderson had a dilemma. The previous spring he had allocated $500 million to add smallpox vaccine to the national stockpile, well before he realized it might be used in a mass civil defense campaign. As he tried to convince Vice President Cheney and Scooter Libby, his preferred approach was to vaccinate in a "ring" around communities where cases had already broken out, which was how the global eradication campaign was won. In early May 2002, Henderson stepped down as interim director of the Office of Public Health Preparedness and, although still an advisor to Secretary Thompson, it was the vice president, not Thompson, who controlled the momentum for mass smallpox vaccinations, to counter a Dark Winter order of threat.

If there were mass vaccinations, there would be risks. The government would be using Dryvax, a vaccine that could have adverse side effects, even death. Dryvax relied on the Vaccinia virus (from the poxvirus family) to provoke immunity and, made from a process involving the scrapings of calf skins, the vaccine was generally regarded as "dirty." Certain populations were especially vulnerable—those who were HIV-infected or otherwise immuno-compromised, the very old, the very young, and women in the early weeks of pregnancy. Rashes from scabs caused by the inoculation could spread, with serious consequences; those with eczema or other skin diseases were at high risk. The National Institutes of Health was funding new vaccine prototypes, but these were far from ready.[31]

Health safety expert Julie Gerberding, who had in 2002 replaced Jeff Koplan as director of the CDC, bore the responsibility of helping American health authorities evaluate the smallpox terrorism threat and response. The perception of the smallpox threat had changed radically since June 2001 when, under Koplan and before 9/11, the CDC Advisory Committee on Immunization Practices had recommended limiting vaccinations to the few laboratory scientists working with other virulent pox viruses—just as a precaution.[32] A year later, the advisory committee recommended that vaccinations extend to 20,000 civilians nationwide, but remain restricted to dedicated smallpox response teams and staff from hospitals designated for intensive clinical treatment in the event of attacks. Experts from the RAND Corporation agreed: only those at the front lines of national response should be vaccinated and only if the epidemic threats were imminent.[33]

But Vice President Cheney, believing that a mass bioterrorist attack was likely, advised that the vaccine should be broadly available to all Americans as they chose.[34] A Harvard School of Public Health poll, conducted from October 8 to December 8, 2002, made it seem the public agreed with Cheney. The Harvard researchers concluded that "the current view held by many public health officials and leaders of the medical community—that the smallpox vaccine should not be widely available to the general public—is at odds with the public's desire for access to the vaccine."[35] Yet, quite reasonably, that public "desire" depended greatly on risk perception—how people balanced the likelihood of the disease versus the harm the vaccine might cause. Sixty-one percent of those polled in the Harvard study approved vaccine availability on a voluntary basis if there were an actual bioterrorism threat, and 88 percent approved if smallpox cases actually emerged in their community. But their approval sank to 33 percent if respondents heard someone had died from the vaccine.

By October 2002, CDC advice conformed to Cheney's mass vaccination plan. Its advisory committee now recommended that 500,000 first responders be vaccinated on a voluntary basis. The CDC rapidly broadcast the campaign's operational details to state governments. On December 13, 2002, President Bush announced that the National Smallpox Vaccination Program would start in approximately a month. The CDC set a timetable of 30 days after that start date to vaccinate 500,000 volunteer first responders, mainly medical and National Guard personnel. Then the vaccine would be offered to another 10 million health care workers, police, and firefighters. A possible additional phase—in the event of a nationwide pandemic—would make the vaccine available to all Americans.

"Smallpox is a serious disease and we know that our enemies are trying to inflict serious harm," the president told the country. "Yet," he added, "there is no evidence that smallpox imminently threatens this country." The mixed message was perplexing. If no imminent threat existed, why the urgent need to vaccinate half a million civilians? To show his commitment, though, President Bush was himself revaccinated.

Well before the president's announcement, the Department of Defense had accepted the Iraqi smallpox threat as a serious risk to soldiers, enough to warrant mass vaccination of 500,000 U.S. troops, with the CDC assisting. The Pentagon, burned by protests against the anthrax vaccine, managed the campaign cautiously, starting with four pilot sites where procedures could be tested and adverse health reactions monitored.[36] The two-pronged inoculation was known to produce mild, usually temporary discomfort—muscle ache, fatigue, swollen lymph nodes. In rare cases, the vaccine could also cause brain inflammation and even death. To reduce the risks of spreading skin rashes to unvaccinated spouses and family members, the plan was to advise bandaging the site of the inoculation.

Around a third of the military to be vaccinated in 2003 had already been vaccinated, either in childhood or by the military, which had kept vaccinating against smallpox until 1990. The rest were, in Pentagon parlance, "Vaccinia-naïve" recruits. The troop population as a whole was young and healthy, but it was also vulnerable to HIV infection. As a precaution, the Pentagon required an accurate 24-hour HIV test to exclude soldiers whose immune systems might be compromised. In mid-January, confident that the Dryvax vaccine would be safe, the Pentagon began full implementation of the campaign.

On January 24, 2003, the civilian phase of the smallpox vaccination campaign began—just after the president's State of the Union address in which he emphasized Iraq's WMD threat. War was definitely on the horizon. Thousands of first responders lined up to be vaccinated, although many were not covered by insurance against the risks of adverse reactions and the vaccine manufacturers and the medical providers administering it were protected from legal liability.[37]

Secretary of State Colin Powell was scheduled to argue the U.S. case for an armed invasion of Iraq to the United Nations Security Council in early February. Beforehand, Powell found himself doubting the facts about Saddam's germ weapons, including anthrax and smallpox. But CIA director George Tenet forced Powell's hand by insisting that he had reliable intelligence from a top-level informant that both the biological and the chemical threats were real. Tenet, however, omitted mentioning that the Defense Intelligence Agency had discredited that source.[38] Powell had also talked with Hans Blix, head of the UN Monitoring, Verification and Inspection Commission then searching for WMD in Iraq. Blix assured Powell that his teams had investigated every CIA lead and found no evidence of chemical or biological weapons.[39] Absence of proof, though, was not proof that Saddam, who continued to be uncooperative, had met the United Nations' cease-fire agreement.

On February 5, on national television, Secretary Powell described in detail the WMD threat that Iraq posed to the world. He emphasized mobile biological weapons fermenters, chemical weapons stocks, and Saddam's likely nuclear arsenal. Somewhat awkwardly (it was not his finest moment), Powell held up a small vial of white powder and reminded his audience that just a few grams of anthrax had shut down the U.S. Senate in the fall of 2001—as if Iraq had perpetrated the anthrax letter attacks and deposing Saddam would protect America from bioterrorism.

On February 23, the smallpox vaccine campaign seemed to be going smoothly. The CDC and the Department of Defense released information indicating that the negative reactions were minimal.[40] About 100,000 members of the military had been vaccinated, with only five cases of serious illness. On the civilian side, just over 4,000 people had received their shots, with only a few, relatively minor reactions—fevers, rashes, hypertension, and throat inflammations. Optimistic, the CDC estimated that if a million people were inoculated, between 15 and 50 could suffer serious side effects and, of these, one or two might die. More first responders lined up for inoculation. Meanwhile, the anthrax vaccination of soldiers, begun the previous year, continued into 2003 without a hitch.

The American invasion of Iraq began on March 20. As the missile attacks continued, three civilian volunteers, two women and a man, all in their midfifties, fell sick and died after being inoculated with the Dryvax vaccine.[41] One died on March 23 and the other two on March 26. The three deaths stopped the vaccination campaign in its tracks. Eleven states, including New York and Florida, ceased cooperating and, across the nation, dozens of hospitals followed suit. From a peak of 5,000 inoculations per week, the numbers sank to a few hundred.

The three deaths might have been unrelated to Dryvax, yet somehow the CDC and USAMRIID as well had downplayed the risks of the Vaccinia virus—the vaccine's essential component—to heart health, which had been reported in the older medical literature. For example, the virus was known to cause inflammation of the myocardium, the heart's muscle, and the pericardium, the sac surrounding the heart. (Since the second inflammation usually accompanies the first, the term *myopericarditis* is often used.)[42] The condition can have serious, long-term, or fatal consequences. Yet, as Julie Gerberding told the press immediately after the first death, the campaign had to continue because "we are at a time in the history of our country when the potential for terrorism has probably never been higher."

Caught off guard, the CDC quickly revised its vaccination guidelines to exclude anyone with heart disease or with multiple cardiovascular risk factors, such as smoking, hypertension, or a family history of heart problems. A longtime smoker and on the heavy side, the seventy-four-year-old Henderson himself was in this risk category, but he had chosen nonetheless to be reinoculated. The sixty-two-year-old Dick Cheney, an advocate of individual choice, had declined vaccination, which, given his history of heart ailments, was a wise or perhaps lucky decision.

Although the CDC changed its guidelines, it was reluctant to conclude that the vaccinations had killed the three first responders. Instead it pointed out that all three who died had been smokers and their autopsies revealed "extensive arteriosclerosis." It could have been that preexisting health risks, not the smallpox vaccine, had caused their deaths. In the next weeks, the CDC investigated 18 cases of cardiac complications among 25,000 vaccinated health workers, but wavered on drawing conclusions about the relationship between the vaccine and heart problems. The Department of Defense also reported unpredicted cases of heart-related illness following the smallpox inoculation.[43] Of 230,734 previously unvaccinated soldiers, 18 (all healthy men between ages 21 to 33) unexpectedly came down with myopericarditis. As it proceeded with another 100,000 troop inoculations, the Pentagon warned the clinicians to be on the alert for this side effect. In time, 184 soldiers (of 501,946 vaccinated against smallpox) showed serious adverse reactions. In addition to the 18 early cases, another 40 cases of myopericarditis were reported, none fatal. Another five deaths occurred among those vaccinated, but the CDC hesitated to attribute them to the vaccine.

The American invasion of Iraq ended on May 1, 2003. Afterward the CIA-directed Iraq Survey Group, assisted by teams of other government experts, combed the country for WMD arsenals.[44] By September 2003, David Kay, the head of the group, was sure the search for weapons of mass destruction was in vain. As he later put it, concerning pre-invasion intelligence on Iraq's WMD capability, "We were almost all wrong."[45] The group's full report, which took nearly a year to complete, added some investigative details, but Kay's conclusion remained.[46]

In the aftermath of the Iraq invasion, the subject of Iraq's anthrax arsenal disappeared and the smallpox threat evaporated—like magic shows that had ended. Gerberding, still with millions of dollars to offer states to continue smallpox vaccinations, lacked takers. The participating states had already borne the costs of the vaccine—at $250 per inoculation—and had paid in other, unanticipated ways. Although short in duration, the campaign seriously disrupted routine medical services, shunting aside, for example, prenatal care and screenings for infectious diseases, which increased medical problems and disease incidence, mainly among inner city populations.[47] Prominent public health physicians concluded, "In the absence of any smallpox cases worldwide or any scientific basis for expecting an outbreak, these deaths and other serious adverse events are inexcusable."[48] Much later, an Institute of Medicine panel criticized the CDC for failing to weigh the risks of smallpox terrorism against the risks of the vaccine. The panel faulted Gerberding personally, stating that her ability to speak authoritatively, on the basis of the best scientific reasoning, was "severely constrained" by her willingness to accommodate the vice president's agenda.[49]

Despite criticism, Gerberding had correctly reckoned that the CDC's future lay in national security, counter-bioterrorism, and emerging infectious diseases. Like Tanja Popovic, Brad Perkins, and others involved in responding to the anthrax letters, she had weathered a surreal month of eighteen-hour workdays and midnight phone calls from the White House, with thirty or more people pressing for the results of crucial tests and eager for CDC analyses of the cascading crisis. Improved communication with Washington, with states, and with overseas public health institutions was vital—the CDC Web site should never again fail—if her organization was to be ready for catastophe. State and local domestic preparedness funding administered by the Centers went from $67 million at the time of the anthrax letters to $940 million in 2002.[50] The CDC's Strategic National Stockpile, funded at $81 million in 2001, had its budget increased to $1.157 billion in 2002. Funds to upgrade CDC facilities went from $22 million at the time of the letter attacks to $141 million in 2002 and $157 million in 2003. After 9/11 and the anthrax letters, the new CDC shifted its attention to emergency response to potentially catastrophic diseases, from whatever source. In late 2003, when the SARS (severe acute respiratory syndrome) outbreak spread from China, Gerberding and her organization received high praise for the kind of central command proficiency that had been missing at the time of the anthrax crisis. CDC management of vital international communication, travel alerts, public outreach, and U.S. state and local disease reporting kept a dreaded epidemic from affecting the United States.[51] Yet like bioterrorist attacks, such emergencies were rare and, for some, hardly seemed to justify the national security culture—heightened secrecy, restricted access, bomb checks, and increased control by Washington—that became routine at the CDC.

While focusing on emergency response, the CDC was also losing hold of its traditional public health mission to protect Americans from everyday health problems. In 2002, its chronic disease prevention and health promotion departments were slated to lose $57 million. Public health improvement was losing $31 million; occupational safety and health $28 million; emergency recovery $20 million; and ironically, infectious disease control programs $10 million.[52] In 2002 and 2003, the Institute of Medicine was warning that the infrastructure of U.S. public health was suffering from years of neglect—everything from childhood immunizations to emergency preparedness varied drastically from state to state—and that public health physicians were in short supply.[53]

At the Johns Hopkins Center in Baltimore where Dark Winter had been invented, critiques of the politicization of the scenario and its link to the disastrous smallpox vaccination campaign were scrupulously avoided. A 2004 overview by a staff member, for example, erased the episode from an account of the center's activities.[54] In his autobiography, Henderson avoided mentioning his own role or his center's in the Bush-Cheney promotion of Iraq's WMD threat. His brief description of the 2003 campaign as "an abject failure" referred to how few people participated—not to the vaccine-related deaths or harmful side effects or the displacement of vital public health services.[55] As a corrective to Dark Winter's hyperbole, with Henderson's help, a group of experts in biostatistics later showed that, even in the event of a large smallpox terrorist attack, the isolation of diagnosed cases and "ring" vaccination of known contacts would quickly contain an outbreak and limit deaths to more like hundreds than thousands or millions.[56]

But little of this mattered. Civilian biodefense was an entrenched policy goal, part of the larger post-9/11 directive. In November 2002, the Bush administration had created the Department of Homeland Security, with Tom Ridge as its first secretary. Within it, fostering protection against foreign bioterrorism played a major role. Instead of networks of individual experts—the contacts at the White House that Lisa Gordon-Hagerty had relied on in October 2001—entire institutions were cooperating in the joint mission to defend all Americans against germ weapon attacks. The federal biodefense budget rose and, under Tara O'Toole's capable leadership, the Johns Hopkins Center continued as a powerful lobbying group, a nexus of information and expertise. It was so powerful, in fact, that it was soon bought out by the University of Pittsburgh. Without having to relocate from Baltimore, the center accepted a $12 million endowment (over five years) with guaranteed professorships for its qualified staff, in exchange for a name change: the Center for Biosecurity at the University of Pittsburgh Medical Center.[57]

Despite the limits of Dark Winter, O'Toole and her staff staged an international version of it, called "Atlantic Storm," based on simultaneous smallpox attacks in Istanbul, Rotterdam, and Frankfurt. Former Secretary of State Madeleine Albright played the American president, while former diplomats and high government officials from eastern and western Europe struggled with the inevitable chaos.[58] Participants were advised that, although the table-top exercise was based on smallpox, it could be about the newly looming threat of avian influenza, with perhaps even more drastic consequences. In any event, Europe and the world—not just the United States—were at catastrophic risk and would have to be prepared with emergency medical response and effective vaccines.

Despite the absence of biological weapons in Iraq, the U.S. investment in biodefense continued to grow, as a defense against other potential hostile states and terrorists. Overall, excluding special appropriations and covert Defense Department projects, the federal budget for civilian biodefense research and development grew from $271 million in 2001—the Clinton-era level—to $2.940 billion in 2002, then to $3.738 billion in 2003, with more increases to come.[59] Compared to the U.S. Defense spending or what the National Institutes of Health invest yearly in drug research, these were modest amounts, but in the world of infectious disease research, which saw the greatest percentage increases, it was a windfall like no other.

＊

Just days before the Iraq War commenced on March 14, 2003, the Pentagon awarded Bruce Ivins and two of his colleagues, Louise Pitt and

Steven Little, each a medal, the Decoration for Exceptional Civilian Service, the highest award granted civilians, equivalent to the Distinguished Military Service Medal for members of the armed forces. The award was for the work they had done as members of the Anthrax Potency Integrated Product Team from April 2000 to February 2002, which resolved the AVA production problems at BioPort. A fourth member of the team, Patricia Fellows, who had left USAMRIID to work at the Southern Research Institute in Frederick, also received the medal. Each recipient's contribution was commended—Ivins for testing vaccine lots on rabbits, Pitt for her comparative aerosol test models, Little for comparative serological testing, and Fellows, who had worked for Ivins, for her expertise on spore storage, production, harvesting, and purification. Through no fault of her own, that last noted expertise would prove troublesome, although she was by no means the only institute employee able to produce purified anthrax spores.[60]

Ivins accepted the award proudly. It was a personal validation, coming just as Gary Matsumoto was about to publish his book suggesting that Ivins' early vaccine formulas were linked to Gulf War syndrome.[61] Modestly discounting the team's accomplishments, Ivins commented, "Awards are nice but the real satisfaction is knowing the vaccine is back on line."[62]

Ivins' life was also "back on line." He had reconnected with his brother Charles, who was seven years his senior; the two started taking a yearly vacation, a fishing, hunting, or boat trip. His productivity at work had increased; with his experiments on vaccines going well, he anticipated co-authoring a half-dozen new articles in the near future. One of his two vaccine patents was showing commercial promise.

Still, Ivins remained irked that the contamination discovered in April 2002 in his office and outside his B-3 suite had been, however tentatively, attributed to him by Army investigators. He believed that the Diagnostic Services Division should take the blame for mishandling the Daschle letter. But, Ivins felt, the Diagnostic Division, its scientists acting superior to those in Bacteriology, shunned the responsibility for spillage. To a former colleague, he argued, "I firmly believe that if I had been allowed to swab DSD labs and offices as thoroughly as I swabbed initially in Bacti Division, that I would have found 'hot' spores. It was (and still is) an incredible cover-up."[63]

CHAPTER 11

THE STRONG DESIRE FOR JUSTICE

Let's be clear about the consequences here. People are sick to this day and some are dead, and the courts are saying, "Tough luck."

—Tom Fitton,
president of Judicial Watch, November 19, 2004

In mid-December 2003, an FBI agent was dispatched to visit Bruce Ivins at USAMRIID. The objective: to go with him into the walk-in cold storage area of his BSL-3 lab to search among the vials and flasks on its shelves for any stray Ames samples that still needed to be included in the FBI repository. When the two men discovered several aliquots (precisely measured samples) not on the FBIR list, Ivins promised to prepare them in slant tubes, according to the required protocol—but since he was busy it would take a while. Some weeks later, three FBI agents appeared and asked him for some of his lab notebooks, which Ivins gave willingly. Having second thoughts, he checked with an administrator who told him the FBI was not allowed to remove documents without special permission—the institute would provide photocopying access as needed. Ivins made a note to remind Bureau agents of the rule, if they ever returned.[1]

The Bureau reportedly was still pursuing Steven Hatfill as a suspect and USAMRIID was a trusted FBI partner, its mission increasingly integrated into Washington's overall "war on terror." A transformation right next to Ivins' office was proof of that partnership and a sign of even bigger plans ahead. The Diagnostic Services Division (along with the Special Pathogen analysis lab) had been moved. In its place was a new tenant: the National Bioforensic Analysis Center, a technologically upgraded resource for microbial crime scene analyses. Its sponsor was the new Department of Homeland Security, headed by Secretary Tom Ridge. The bioforensics center's designated chief customer was the FBI.

If the Amerithrax investigation had taught the Bureau one thing it was that the techniques for tracking dangerous pathogens at a crime scene were behind the curve and that any future microbial terrorism would require a dedicated staff and laboratories.[2] The FBI was grateful for USAMRIID's assistance—John Ezzell, promoted to senior scientist, was still a bioforensics advisor—but the institute's mission was troop defense, not criminal investigation, and its organizational culture was ill-suited to FBI demands for keeping evidence under wraps. For example, the silica controversy generated by Peter Jahrling in October 2001 continued to feed conspiracy theories about the foreign source of the anthrax letters.

Ivins' new hall mate, the associate director of the new bioforensics center, called NBFAC, was none other than Jim Burans, his onetime anthrax apprentice who'd led the Navy's development of a hand-held anthrax assay, the prototype for the one used to test the Daschle letter at the Hart Building. Now his job was to promote methods that would prevent the gaffes that marred the early days of the anthrax investigation—just thinking about the spores spilled from the Brokaw letter made him wince. An FBI consultant, Burans was also advised on the pioneering effort to trace the morphotypes from the letter material to samples in the FBI repository.

The intrusion of Burans and the new center into Building 1425 was only temporary. The future plan was to house the bioforensics center in a brand-new high-security building at Detrick and equip it with enough BSL-3 and BSL-4 laboratories and expert staff to crack any bioterrorism case. Homeland Security would pay a private company to manage the enterprise; bids were out for the contract. Ever loyal to the Navy, Burans dreamed of having the center's new building resemble a glittering battleship and, aboard that ship, disciplined teams would work within a culture of both accountability and "reportability." Following Homeland Security regulations, projects would be reviewed beforehand and while in process to ensure safety and legality, that is, staying in compliance with the 1972 Biological Weapons Convention.[3] Burans wanted an organizational culture in which the staff could bring the inevitable lab snafus to light without fear of penalty.[4]

The NBFAC with its bioforensics mission was just one part of revolutionary institutional change being planned for Fort Detrick, which was being reconfigured as a national center that combined civilian and troop biodefense. A vast increase in federal funds for the National Institute of Allergy and Infectious Diseases (NIAID), one of the National Institutes of Health in Bethesda, was the force propelling Detrick into a twenty-first century of advanced select agent research. In 2001 its director, Dr. Tony Fauci, a world expert on AIDS, had $199 million allocated for NIAID's 2002 biodefense grants. In the wake of 9/11 and the anthrax letters, Congress increased that amount to $687 million. In 2003, the funding for Fauci's institute grew to $1.629 billion and continued to rise.[5] Fauci twinned the crusade against biological select agents with the battle against emerging infectious diseases.[6] Both had the potential of being unending threats; either nature or scientists could design lethal pathogens to successfully overcome human resistance. His game plan, which proved successful, was to promote basic research aiming at broad-spectrum therapies for entire categories of disease, not just twenty or so select agents. Still, the perceived national security threat and the funding surge were, without contest, about foreign terrorists with germ weapons capability.

The expansion of biodefense projects required new research facilities and laboratories. The NIAID budget for furnishing these new spaces with costly high-containment laboratories went from zero in 2001 to $92 million in 2002, then to $495 million in 2003.[7] BSL-4 laboratory space was projected to increase from around 16,000 square feet in 2002 to 150,000 square feet by 2009. A new national BSL-4 laboratory was planned at Galveston and another in Boston, at the inner-city Boston University Medical Center, with a national total of Level 4 labs that could reach 15. The number of BSL-3 labs was also increasing to meet project demands, so quickly that the CDC lost count.[8]

With the surge in NIAID funds, Fauci's plan was to create a nation-wide research network, with ten National Centers of Excellence for Biodefense and Emerging Infectious Diseases. Each center would offer "core facilities for other NIAID biodefense researchers in the region"—everything from research animals and BSL-3 laboratories to select-agent research training and product development—to integrate them into area complexes.[9] The chosen sites were Harvard Medical School, Columbia University, University of Chicago, University of Maryland, University of North Carolina, University of Texas Medical Branch in Galveston, Washington University, Colorado State University, University of California at Irvine, and the Oregon Health and Science University (where, coincidentally, Nancy Haigwood worked).

To crown this biodefense achievement, the Department of Defense and federal agency officials envisioned a National Interagency Biodefense Campus—a concentration of high-containment laboratories—located at Fort Detrick, which offered open land, high security, and USAMRIID's defense establishment reputation. In addition to the Department of Homeland Security and NIAID, the Department of Agriculture would have its own new biodefense building for research on plant and animal diseases. Finally, a grand new building for USAMRIID—which developed a formal cooperative relationship with Fauci's NIAID—would complete the research quadrangle. A new age was dawning. Building 1425, home for thirty years to the scientists of Bruce Ivins' generation, would either be torn down or used for training. Depending on how quickly the expansion plans could be implemented, Ivins would likely cross over to that promised land with his generation of USAMRIID researchers—Ezzell, Friedlander, Worsham, Jahrling, and others.

In addition to funding government initiatives, Congress sought to engage commerce in the biodefense venture. Senator Joe Lieberman (then a Democrat), whose home state of Connecticut had been directly affected by the anthrax letters, articulated the vision:

> We will know that we've established a biodefense industry when hundreds of millions of dollars in company and investor capital are available to fund countermeasure research and investors see a reasonable opportunity to profit to the same degree they do on investments in other biomedical research.[10]

To encourage commercial involvement, in 2004 Congress enacted Project Bioshield, legislation that guaranteed pharmaceutical companies at least ten million dollars in biodefense funding over a six-year period.[11] As an enticement, the project allowed the Secretary of Health and Human Services to short-circuit funding approval, for example, by buying products still in development (as long as eight years before their estimated delivery) and distributing medical countermeasures considered vital to defense that lacked Food and Drug Administration approval.[12] In Congress, support for the measure was bipartisan. Democratic Senator Ted Kennedy, mindful of his state's growing biotechnology industry, was as enthusiastic as Republican Senator Bill Frist, who came from a family of health care entrepreneurs (his father and brother had started the for-profit hospital chain Hospital Corporation of America).

The goal was to move quickly to microbe-specific countermeasures, "from bugs to drugs." Larger pharmaceutical companies, whose profits came largely from drugs to counter chronic conditions, were generally uninterested. Thirty mostly small companies (start-ups with names like Dynavax, Diversa, Chiron, Dynport, Chemocentryx, Cangene, Alphavax, Human Vaccines, and Surface Logix) won the first funding infusions, which covered three years of research, with renewal options.

In 2004, Project Bioshield contracts for industry reached $5.6 billion, with about a billion allocated for anthrax vaccines.[13] BioPort still had its hat in the ring, but a major competitor, VaxGen, Inc., in San Francisco, with great promise for a new, safer product, won a contract for $877 million. As reports of adverse reactions and even deaths associated with the 2003 AVA campaign rose, the Pentagon allowed military personnel to be inoculated on a voluntary basis—and critics deplored the idea of subjecting civilians to the vaccine's health risks.

Attracting scientists to work on biodefense projects—academic, military, or commercial—proved no problem. The screening process, its groundwork established by the PATRIOT Act, required a Department of Justice database check of each individual's background, to weed out felons, the mentally unstable, and those from nations hostile to the United States. Thousands, very few with any previous experience in select agent research, filled the positions. At the same time, the institutional committees that were supposed to oversee risky research were barely functioning—microbial research in the early years of the new century did not seem dangerous enough to need policing.[14] At the same time, with the twenty-first century being heralded as the century of biology, it was impossible to ignore advances that could be used for harm—the engineering of microbes or the synthesis of new life forms—as well as good. And it was even more impossible to confine these advances to U.S. laboratories.

◆

In 2003, the anthrax letter attacks seemed forgotten—but not by Maureen Stevens in Florida. In September, after the Department of Justice refused to negotiate, her lawyer Richard Schuler decided to file suit against the U.S. government. The Stevens complaint was that the U.S. government and specifically Fort Detrick had failed to meet its responsibility to keep "ultra-hazardous" anthrax spores from posing a risk to the public. "We have not been told of any suspects or where the investigation has led in terms of ultimately who did this," the dapper Schuler told the press. In any event, the FBI's criminal prosecution was only tangential to the case. If security had broken down at USAMRIID or a U.S. government contractor's laboratory, it did not matter which murderer took advantage. Only the source of the Ames strain anthrax in the letters was crucial. "Under Florida law, all we have to prove is where it came from."[15]

By this time, Van Harp, head of the Amerithrax investigation, and Tom Carey, the Bureau's inspector for Amerithrax, had retired. Harp's successor in running the investigation, Rick Lambert, continued to pursue the case against Steven Hatfill. In addition to his suit against the attorney general and the FBI, Hatfill went after the press, suing the media he claimed had slandered him: the New York Times and columnist Nicholas Kristof, as well as the magazine Vanity Fair for an incriminating article by Don Foster, a Vassar professor and some-time FBI profile consultant, who was convinced of Hatfill's guilt. Hatfill subsequently brought a third lawsuit against Foster, Vassar, the publisher Condé Nast, and the Reader's Digest Association, which had distributed the article. Still broke and without job prospects, Hatfill remained determined to defend his innocence.[16]

More than two years into the Amerithrax investigation, the FBI was still pursuing leads to possible "lone wolf" suspects among a pool of entrepreneurs who, like Hatfill, had emerged in the 1990s as self-made bioterrorism threat experts. In early 2004, the Bureau set its sights on Dr. Kenneth Berry, an emergency room physician in a small town in western New York State who had developed an alternate career as a consultant on biological attack threats, especially ones involving anthrax.[17] Since 1997, when federal funds for counter-bioterrorism took a sharp rise, Berry had been organizing conferences and seminars on biological and chemical weapons and even picked up a part-time consulting contract with the Defense Department. In public lectures, press interviews, and on his Web site, he joined the chorus warning about apocalyptic bioterrorism. In one seminar, he predicted a million deaths from an enemy attack with B. anthracis spores. Right after the anthrax letters were discovered, Berry had applied for a patent for an outdoor chemical and biological weapons sensor, which was granted early in 2004. His financial interest in an elevated bioterrorism threat level seemed clear. Earlier, in 2000, he had persuaded Bill Patrick to give him a two-day course on using pathogens as weapons, another red flag for FBI investigators.

In the spring of 2004, the Bureau began interviewing Berry's neighbors and friends, unearthing details about his apparent obsession with the civilian biodefense mission. On August 5, the FBI deployed fifty of its agents to stage parallel commando-style searches, one at Berry's home and an apartment he had once occupied in Wellsville, New York, and another at his parents' beach house at the New Jersey Shore, where he was vacationing with his family. Berry had a temper—his physical attacks that same day on his wife and two stepdaughters put him under a restraining order—but he was never formally accused of mailing the anthrax letters. In a replica of Hatfill's more publicized dilemma, Berry lost his job, his wife divorced him, and he spent years struggling to rebuild his life and retrieve his reputation.

On another front, in response to CIA intelligence, FBI investigators traveled to the site of the rudimentary bioweapons laboratory that al Qaeda operatives had attempted to start in the Afghan city of Kandahar. Yazid Sufaat, trained in chemistry at California State University in Sacramento, had set up a makeshift enterprise near the city's airport and apparently experimented with local strains of anthrax. When the U.S. bombings began in October 2001, Sufaat fled to Pakistan and then to his native Malaysia, where he was arrested and held for questioning.[18] If there were an al Qaeda connection to the anthrax letters, the

Bureau's hazardous response experts might find it in Kandahar. In addition to environmental samples, they shipped back furniture and plumbing for thorough anthrax testing. On the first go-round (using polymerase chain reaction), two samples yielded one of five possible genetic markers that could indicate anthrax and possibly the Ames strain. But no *B. anthracis* could be grown from any sample. Two more missions were conducted, with more test samples acquired, but none of these tested positive for anthrax.

On April 7, 2004, nearly four months after the FBI request, Bruce Ivins submitted his promised Ames samples to the FBI. That day, FBI agents secured the original sources of Ivins' new samples in a safe in the cold room and sealed it with yellow evidence tape. After hours, they returned and locked up the flask labeled RMR-1029 in the same safe and replaced the evidence tape. The plan was to have all the Ames material shipped to the Naval Medical Research Center for inclusion in the FBIR. But were all the USAMRIID Ames samples accounted for? Apparently not, as just a few days before his FBIR submission, Ivins signaled to a colleague that five milliliters of spores in a 50-milliliter plastic tube had gone missing from inventory. Had it been autoclaved? "It will be more than embarrassing if I can't account for it," he wrote.[19] Further FBI inquiries would show that these spores were not the only ones missing from Ivins' inventory.

＋

While the anthrax murderer remained free, Brentwood employees were instructed to return to their old facility, which had reopened in December 2003 as the Curseen-Morris Federal Processing and Distribution Center. As USPS Vice President Tom Day had promised, the infamous DBCS #17 had been removed. As further safety provisions, biosensors were installed and employees processed only mail posted from the District, not to it.

Still, the Postal Service gave leeway to workers who preferred to work elsewhere. Dena Briscoe, assigned to the National Airport postal facility, decided not to return. With no government mail coming into Curseen-Morris, Helen Lewis continued at another Washington facility, on V Street, where it had been diverted. In a significant turn, Briscoe and Lewis both became more involved with the local chapter of the

American Postal Workers Union. Terrell Worrell opted for mail delivery rather than work inside a plant. He and his wife, Jen, had three young children with another on the way. Worrell's health improved, and in his spare time, he composed church musicals whose themes, echoing Lazarus, were about resurrection from death.

Tim Haney, commended by the Postal Service for his handling of the Brentwood closure, returned as plant manager, which was upsetting to some workers but to others a necessary resumption of order. "When the Postal Service invests in training a manager," Leroy Richmond (on permanent disability) sagely reflected, "it can't afford to just let him go."[20] The USPS was by no means blaming Haney for the crisis of October 2001.

On April 29, 2004, Judge Rosemary Collyer, trim with gray-blond hair, took her place on the bench of the U.S. district court at Judicial Square, across from the building where two and a half years before Brentwood employees had picked up their packets of doxycycline. Collyer frowned as she looked out on the racially divided courtroom. On her right were a half dozen U.S. Postal Service lawyers, all white men except for one young African American man who looked uncomfortable. On her left were nearly a hundred African American postal workers, represented by the two white male lawyers seated in the front row.

"If there is any commotion," Collyer warned, "I'll clear the court."

Dena Briscoe and Terrell Worrell, seated near the front, sat a bit straighter, as did many of the other plaintiffs. Although practically none had ever set foot inside a federal courtroom, they were more sophisticated than perhaps the judge knew. Chris Farrell and the other Judicial Watch staff had taught the Brentwood community a good deal about federal law. Brentwood Exposed had continued to host weekly seminars by guest speakers, among them members of Congress, District officials, physicians, scientists, historians, the head of the Washington chapter of the NAACP, and Tom Day. At Day's talk, one Brentwood worker asked him to justify the delay in closing the facility. Surprised, Day spontaneously replied what he believed: "If the CDC had told us to, we would have shut it down."[21]

While Judge Collyer listened to the two sides argue their points, the Brentwood Exposed community kept politely silent. Briscoe, Worrell, and the others noticed that the judge was patient with the young Judicial Watch lawyers, who, in their enthusiasm, occasionally veered off-script or jumbled their notes. In contrast, the lawyers from the Department of Justice, older and experienced, smoothly argued their defense, which was that existing labor laws were sufficient to compensate for any injuries incurred at Brentwood. When the lead attorney, a portly man in an expensive suit, used the phrase "a workplace accident," a faint rustle of dissent went through the Brentwood group. Seated toward the back of the courtroom, Leroy Richmond, who had lost his suit against the USPS, exclaimed softly, "But anthrax is a weapon!"[22] The Judicial Watch lawyers, as they argued about precedents—was anthrax contamination different from toxic chemical spills?—lost sight of the military source and nature of the deadly spores.

Afterward, sensing the judge was sympathetic to their side of the argument, Briscoe and the others had high hopes for victory. But Chris Farrell advised them that the battle was far from over; either Judicial Watch or the Postal Service would appeal the judge's ruling, which would take months before it was announced. "We're in this for the long haul," he said, as both a warning and a promise.

Through the spring and summer, the activities of the Brentwood community continued, with more meetings and invited speakers, but attendance was down. As Dena Briscoe put it, "We have moved on with our lives."

✣

In New Jersey, Eddy Bresnitz, the state public health official who had handled the October 2001 response, became chair of the Environmental Clearance Committee, overseeing the long cleanup project of the Hamilton facility. Hamilton was smaller than Brentwood, but all the anthrax letters had been processed there, and nearly every inch of it was contaminated. Meanwhile, Bob Unick and the other workers were still being rotated as needed from one distribution center to another. When he could, Unick drove down to Washington for Brentwood Exposed events. Deciding to become a more active member of his local mail handlers union, he counted Briscoe and Brentwood Exposed as his inspiration. "Brentwood people," he recalled, "came together as a community. It didn't happen for us in New Jersey." Ethnically diverse and scattered throughout the suburbs, the Hamilton workers kept their traumas private. Although they had quarrels with postal officials, they united only occasionally, to protest the delay in reopening their workplace.

✤

Decisive evidence—the "fingerprints" that would clinch the anthrax case—continued to elude the FBI. The tape that had sealed the anthrax envelopes yielded no distinctive fiber, hair, or other substances. Analysts' conclusion that the ink used was fluid (rather than from a ballpoint pen) meant little, as did the special pressure exerted on some letters (the *A*'s and *T*'s) in the messages. Rita Colwell's brainstorm to rely on genomic analysis seemed almost too futuristic. Even after the visual discovery of the morphotypes at USAMRIID in 2002, the technology for rigorously comparing the FBIR samples to the letter material needed development. Each of the four morphotypes in the letter material required a reliable assay in order for any of them to be detected in the FBIR samples. Jacques Ravel and his team at TIGR and scientists at the three other companies contracted by the Bureau for the Amerithrax investigation set to work. On an organizational level, partially in response to the anthrax letter attacks, in 2003 the FBI created the Chemical, Biological, Radiological, and Nuclear Sciences Unit to rationalize the lines of authority as the microbial forensic part of the investigation proceeded. Until the assays were perfected, one sample of Ames strain remained practically indistinguishable from another, which meant the perpetrator still had the advantage.

In Flagstaff, at Northern Arizona University, Paul Keim continued as guardian of the growing FBI repository. He had an FBI contract to prepare the DNA from each number-coded sample and ship it to TIGR in Maryland, where it would be sequenced for comparison with the letter material. His lab had received hundreds of samples in slant tubes, eventually numbering 1,070, with around 600 from USAMRIID. The pressure to churn out DNA almost led to a lab workers' revolt, until a method using PCR (polymerase chain reaction) was devised to speed the analyses. Every step in the process had to be meticulously recorded as trial-worthy evidence. The entries in laboratory notebooks had to be legible, not scribbled in haste, and continually reviewed for accuracy.

Fifteen domestic labs and three foreign ones—in the United Kingdom, Canada, and Sweden—had submitted samples of Ames cultures. Each sample had a written genealogy—the laboratory record whereby it could be traced to the original source, Dugway's Ames Ancestor strain, either directly or via the intermediary sources, that is, the measured samples (aliquots) shared among laboratories.

On June 29, 2004, Bruce Ivins handed over all his lab notebooks for FBI agents to photocopy. For years he had been in charge of distributing small spore amounts to his institute colleagues for use in vaccine and other experiments on mice, guinea pigs, rabbits, and monkeys, experiments usually performed by using an aerosol, which involved going to the separate specially equipped Building 1412, or by injections.

The RMR-1029 flask, which the FBI had in its possession, had been a source for a number of samples submitted to the FBIR. In sole charge of it, Ivins kept a "Receipt Log" itemizing each transfer of material, its amount, the date of transfer, and the recipient's name. Occasionally, he had also used the spores for his own experiments. Most of the distributions noted in the log went to USAMRIID projects, including one on behalf of a Veterans Administration Hospital in southern Pennsylvania. The exceptions were three aliquots sent to Battelle in the spring and summer of 2001.

As for microbial genealogy, FBI investigators correctly understood that the contents of the flask had originally come from Dugway Proving Ground in 1997, at the request of USAMRIID—to allow testing of Ivins' new vaccine prototype, which contained RPA, a genetically recombinant form of the B. anthracis protein protective antigen (PA). The spores had arrived in "seven shipments containing the concentrated product of 12 ten-liter, fermenter-grown lots—the 'Dugway Spores,'" as he had labeled his April 2002 submissions to the FBIR.[23] But when investigators read Ivins' lab notebooks, they realized that RMR-1029 was very much his personal creation. Unknown to them (he had never mentioned it), he had reformulated the final contents of the RMR-1029 flask after all the shipments reached USAMRIID from Dugway. Some of those shipments, in Ivins' judgment, contained debris that would only hinder research, for example, by clogging aerosol equipment. He either cleaned the material by centrifuging it through a dense liquid or, in the case of the seventh shipment of spores, he destroyed it by autoclaving because it was too dirty.

Ivins' cleanup of the spores, though, left less material than might be needed for active research. With the help of a laboratory technician, Ivins prepared 22 batches of spores in two-liter flasks that were purified and then concentrated to a high level and combined with the Dugway ones. This wet preparation was contained first in two flasks and then reduced to just one. The completed October 1997 result was, as Ivins wrote in the receipt record, a 1,000 milliliter suspension of "highly purified," unclumped spores with less than 1 percent debris.

On examination, Ivins' log of transfers from this flask—dating from its creation to the time of the anthrax mailings—was inaccurate: trace material seemed to be missing. To follow up, Bureau agents began cross-checking the lab notebooks of other anthrax researchers at USAMRIID for evidence of unrecorded transfers. Fourteen unrecorded transfers were discovered, including some Ivins made to himself. As far as could be determined, around 200 grams, potentially many trillions of spores, had been lost.

Unknown to Ivins, the Naval Medical Research Center had prepared his cold storage anthrax samples according to FBIR standards, including spores taken directly from the RMR-1029 flask, and submitted them to the repository for future comparison with the four morphotypes.

In mid-October 2004, to mark the third anniversary of the Curseen-Morris deaths, Brentwood Exposed leaders organized a luncheon at a downtown Washington Holiday Inn. Only around sixty people attended. Two guests, Chris Farrell and Tom Fitton, the photogenic policy analyst who had replaced Larry Klayman at Judicial Watch, urged the group to keep fighting for justice.

A month later, on November 19, representatives of Brentwood Exposed again gathered at the federal courthouse. From the bench, Judge Collyer ruled that Dena Briscoe et al. could not sue the U.S. Postal Service. Not without sympathy, she agreed that federal officials showed deliberate indifference to worker safety by failing to close the plant for nearly four days after anthrax contamination was known. She appreciated that the medical protection given Senate employees in the Hart Building was superior to that accorded Brentwood workers.[24] But the events of October 2001 were so unusual that USPS officials, including manager Tim Haney, could not be held legally responsible for knowing how dangerous anthrax contamination might be. As Collyer wrote in her opinion: "Because the law was insufficiently clear in October of

2001 to alert the Defendants to possible constitutional liability for their conduct surrounding the alleged misinformation to Brentwood employees, Defendants are entitled to qualified immunity."

Outside the court, in the bright sunshine, the Brentwood plaintiffs milled about in shock and dismay. Judicial Watch's Tom Fitton vented his frustration to a cluster of television reporters: "We can't imagine that in the end that courts will sanction government supervisors lying to workers about biological toxins infecting their workplace. Let's be clear about the consequences here. People are sick to this day and some are dead, and the courts are saying, 'Tough luck.'"[25]

Then Dena Briscoe, wearing a tailored white suit, faced the cameras. "For us federal employees who serve the citizens of this country," she said with dignity, "I think it's very unfair for no one to be held accountable for how we were mistreated."

The discouraging news of the ruling spread quickly through the Brentwood community. Accountablity, as Briscoe had said, was the confounding issue. No government agency had taken responsibility— not the CDC, the U.S. Postal Service, the American military or, for that matter, the Department of Justice. The identity of the anthrax terrorist, whose attacks had long since ceased, was still unknown. Judicial Watch filed a petition, but, after losing this first round, hopes of finding justice through the courts had diminished.[26]

✦

Having exhausted other inquiries, FBI analysts and postal inspectors took a harder look at the four pre-franked federal envelopes in which the anthrax letters had been mailed. The paper used in their manufacture, with holes as large as 5 microns, had been porous enough to allow clumps of spores to escape, but the real importance of the envelopes lay in the microscopic irregularities in their printing, recognized only in January 2005. Thereafter began the laborious process of trying to trace the four retrieved anthrax envelopes back to the exact post office where they had been purchased.[27]

The *New York Post* and Daschle envelopes shared identical print defects, which, because each printing machine alternated between two plates, differed from the slight irregularities on the Brokaw and Leahy envelopes. Although the plates were good for about a million impressions, wear-and-tear or fluctuations in the ink supply caused variations that gradually appeared and then disappeared. A part of any run, therefore, could share the signature defects. The problem was that 31 million envelopes had been printed in 37 print runs that took place from January 9, 2001, when a new ink formula was used, to October 9, 2001, the date of the last anthrax mailings. Bundled in packets of five, they had been shipped to thousands of post offices around the nation.

It was a long shot, but by examining shipping records, federal investigators hoped to track the delivery route. First they collected as many federal eagle envelopes as possible, nearly 300,000, from the stocks of post offices nationwide and searched for similar or identical defects, with the vending locations secretly coded.

The envelopes used in the anthrax mailings were finally traced to a February 14–15, 2001, production run that had been shipped on March 2, 2001, to the Dulles Stamp Distribution Office just outside Washington, which served all of Virginia and part of Maryland. On March 21, 2001, federal eagle envelopes from this run were shipped to eighteen Maryland post offices and three in northern Virginia.

The main post office in Frederick, Maryland—nearest to Fort Detrick—had received a shipment of a thousand envelopes from this run. But by 2005 the chance to check its stock had passed. In June 2002, when the first-class postal rate increased from 34 to 36 cents, the Frederick post office returned its unsold federal eagle envelopes to Dulles, where they were destroyed.

Nonetheless, on March 21, 2001, just before the Frederick drop-off, envelopes from the same run were delivered to two other Maryland post offices, in Cumberland and Elkton. Just after the Frederick delivery, the truck made three more local deliveries (to Severna Park in Maryland and to Machipongo and Fairfax in Virginia). The stocks from all those offices matched the imperfections on the 2001 anthrax envelopes. The existing stocks from the other area shipping destinations that day—for example, to Baltimore, Hagerstown, and Annapolis—had no matches.

✤

In 2005, while the search for the post office that sold the anthrax envelopes was under way, the matching of the four morphotypes in the letters with the FBI repository samples was at last progressing. The assays for each of the signature variants had gradually been developed and verified as reliable according to the standards of the FBI's own laboratory which now had a brand-new, 50,000-square-meter facility at Quantico.[28] After the 2003 creation of a new organizational unit for WMD science investigation—the Chemical, Biological, Radiological and Nuclear Sciences Unit—the Bureau was evolving a more rational approach to its Amerithrax bioforensics, with weekly meetings between the science team and criminal investigators. Mark Wilson, the DNA hair and bone specialist, was moved from counterterrorism to become the Biology Program manager in the CBSU (the Chemical-Biological Sciences Unit) there. Along with his supervisor, Dave Wilson, who had overseen Operation Noble Eagle at USAMRIID in 2001, geneticist Bruce Budowle, another DNA pioneer, and a new recruit, microbiologist Jason Bannan, plus a "Red Team" of consulting experts, he monitored the reports of morphotype matches. As Rita Colwell at the National Science Foundation and the other interagency "midwives" of the project had hoped, advances in genetic sequencing were making the testing process faster and less expensive and the laboratories under contract were meeting protocol standards. The assays for the A1 and A3 morphotypes were developed before those for D and E. Not all the 1,070 repository samples were testable (some were dead on arrival); eventually only 947 (of them, 598 from USAMRIID) yielded definitive results. For those inside the investigation, there was no single "eureka" moment when a clear pattern emerged. Instead, it gradually became clear that few of the FBIR samples had even the A1 or A3 morphotypes and that those that did were from USAMRIID. The reports of separate analyses were being sent to the FBI, where only a few top analysts saw the combined results.

Soon, a confounding result emerged, the kind that had to be double-checked. When tested, the sample from the RMR-1029 flask prepared by the Naval Medical Research Center proved positive for all four signature morphotypes. Yet the samples that Bruce Ivins had submitted in April 2002, ostensibly from the same flask, had tested completely negative. Summoned for an interview on Friday, March 31, 2005, Ivins insisted that for the April submission he had taken the spores from the RMR-1029 flask.

This pivotal interview marked a turning point in the FBI investigation—Ivins' innocence was under question. For the April submission, he may have picked an individual spore colony from the flask, rather than offering the required representative mix, but this was his second failure to contribute to the FBIR. Was he just "eccentric," as some of his co-workers affectionately described him, or had he been consistently trying to throw the FBI off course? When investigators told him that the flask spores contained the same morphotypes as found in the letter material, Ivins replied that one of the Bureau's special agents, Darin Steele, had told him that news a year or so before, in 2004. But Steele, assigned to John Ezzell's lab during Operation Noble Eagle and well known at the institute, denied having had any such conversation with Ivins about FBIR results.

The March interview continued with a wide range of questions. When investigators asked Ivins to explain why, in the immediate aftermath of 9/11, he spent so many nighttime hours alone in his high-containment laboratory, he explained that he had been escaping from a stressful home situation. Asked if he was familiar with Princeton, New Jersey (where his father had been an undergraduate), he replied that he had been there only once as a child, when his family made a brief visit. When asked to explain why all his 2001 emails were missing from his hard drive (which the Bureau had copied in January), Ivins replied he was "highly surprised" at their absence and suggested they might have been backed up on the Fort Detrick server. Ivins then went willingly with agents to his house, where he allowed them to copy the hard drive on his home computer. There, in reference to a computer file of church music, he described how, since 1996, he and his wife had led the music group at St. John the Evangelist in Frederick, where they had been parishioners since 1981. Other files stored Ivins' original music (called "Reach for the Stars") memorializing Christa McAuliffe, who had died in the 1986 *Challenger* launch disaster. Preoccupied with the young teacher's tragedy, he had played his composition at memorial services for her. As the FBI agents worked, Ivins asked if a person could be incriminated if, for example, child pornography were found on a home computer. Their answer was yes.

Retrieved from the Detrick server, Ivins' computer records, especially his emails, revealed a deeply troubled man. Reliant on antidepressants, he had also been obsessed with a former technician—once driving ten hours to anonymously drop off a special wine and a bottle of Kahlua at her home in upper New York State. Questioned about this, Ivins volunteered that he often drove long distances just to relax, setting back the odometer so his wife wouldn't know. The FBI's report summarizing the entirety of this interrogation noted that "[Ivins] is devastated that someone might have used his Ames material to commit a crime and that people are dead because of it."[29]

Ivins later characterized this March interview as one of the worst experiences of his life—the FBI might learn enough about him to jeopardize his job. For years, Ivins had signed waivers allowing the U.S. Army access to his private medical records, including his mental health history, but USAMRIID authorities never inquired deeply into them or saw Ivins' problems as a security risk—not even after 9/11, when the 2002 Department of Defense Biological Personnel Reliability Program and other regulations put mental disability restrictions on select agent access. Alarmed by the interrogation, on April 4, Ivins gave the FBI the name and telephone number of his lawyer in Frederick. Then he took a stress-related leave from BSL-3 research, which a letter from his Frederick psychiatrist, Allan Levy, supported. Within three months, having kept his secret clearance, he was back in his lab, after Levy judged him fit to return.

＊

That same April, as Bruce Ivins sought legal protection, Maureen Stevens received a surprise call from her lawyer, Richard Schuler. He had great news: the first hurdle to her case against the federal government had been cleared. In Palm Beach, U.S. District Judge Daniel T. K. Hurley had just upheld the Stevens family's right to sue the federal government for negligence in its handling of the anthrax spores that killed Robert Stevens. The possibility of a major, lethal security failure at Fort Detrick might be argued in court. As expected, Department of Justice lawyers quickly filed an appeal, mixing a variety of arguments. They denied that the federal government could be held liable for the criminal acts of a third party or that the crime was "foreseeable." They protested that this litigation could imperil the FBI investigation and "sensitive national security interests" as well as advances in clinical medicine, and might encourage anti-business abuses of Florida tort law.[30] Fundamentally, though, the Justice lawyers argued that the federal government had no duty to protect the general public against USAMRIID's anthrax research:

> Without explanation, the [Stevens] complaint asserts that
> the United States "owed a duty of care and in fact, the

highest degree of care," in virtually every facet of the work (including hiring, security screening, and workplace security, as well as the handling of and experimenting with anthrax bacteria) performed at a U.S. Army research laboratory located in Fort Detrick, Maryland. . . . The complaint does not identify any class or category of individuals to whom the government owed this asserted duty of care, nor does the complaint identify any special relationship between Mr. Stevens and the Army laboratory, nor any other component of the government, that could give rise to such a duty.[31]

The appeals court could dismiss the case—giving Justice lawyers a victory—or return it to the Florida federal court for trial, a decision that might force the Department of Justice to enter negotiations with the Stevens family for a settlement.

Maureen Stevens had heard nothing from the FBI since her husband died. Avoiding all limelight, she continued to live in the same house, shop at the same stores, and attend mass at her local parish in Lantana, and she kept her husband's voice on the answering machine, sometimes calling her own number just to hear him again. She found it hard to understand why the Bureau had not caught the person who sent the anthrax letters. It was obviously an inside job, a "failure of security," as her case put it. When her lawsuit drew media attention, Maureen Stevens kept her comments brief. Her life, she explained, was held together by her faith, her family, her friends—and her "strong desire for justice."[32]

✦

In late October, to commemorate the fourth anniversary of the deaths of Thomas Morris and Joseph Curseen, Brentwood Exposed leaders organized a small luncheon, a repeat of last year's, with the same few loyalists attending. The operation of the Morris-Curseen plant and the opening the previous March of the Hamilton facility—safely fumigated and renovated, as Tom Day had promised—made it seem almost as if the anthrax deaths had never happened.

On the opening day, Hamilton employees, including manager Joe Sautello, and their families and union leaders, congressional representatives, and local officials gathered in the parking lot for a celebration.

Bob Unick was there; newly active in local 308 of the progressive National Postal Mail Handlers Union, he returned to his old workplace with a new role: shop steward. Dr. Eddy Bresnitz was there. As chair of the environmental health committee that oversaw the long cleanup project at Hamilton, he had witnessed the behind-the-scenes problems—from the discontent of the workers to the metal erosion caused by the decontamination chemicals. "To have the facility opened," he said, "was like a rebirth."[33]

On November 7, 2005, the District of Columbia Court of Appeals upheld Judge Collyer's ruling that USPS officials deserved "qualified immunity" regarding the delayed closing of the Brentwood postal facility in October 2001. Chris Farrell at Judicial Watch explained to Dena Briscoe and other Brentwood Exposed leaders that the organization would appeal the decision to the Supreme Court, but that they should definitely not expect the case would be selected for review. This quest for justice was more or less over. On the positive side, which Briscoe and the others always emphasized, it had helped unite the community when it was most dispersed and demoralized. It had made many (among them USPS management) aware of the need to be vigilant, rather than passive, about workplace safety. As predicted, on May 11, 2006, the Supreme Court declined to hear the Brentwood case.

To date, the FBI's investment in Amerithrax had been enormous: hundreds of thousands of agent hours, over 9,000 interviews, 6,000 grand jury subpoenas, and 67 searches, plus the convening of eight panels of scientific experts; the expansion of hazardous materials response capability; the creation of a new forensic unit, the Chemical-Biological Sciences Unit; and great improvement in international liaison capability.[34] But the number of FBI agents on the Amerithrax Task Force had recently dropped from 31 to 21 and the number of postal inspectors from 13 to 9. Had the Bureau resigned itself to a cold case? Many thought so, but the investigation was headed for a breakthrough.

CHAPTER 12

LIVING PROOF

Contrary to popular belief, what is important in science is as much its spirit as its product: it is as much the open-mindedness, the primacy of criticism, the submission to the unforeseen, however upsetting, as the final result, however new that may be.

—NOBEL LAUREATE FRANÇOIS JACOB, *The Logic of Life*, 1982

In August 2006, in an obscure journal, the FBI's Doug Beecher published an article about the discovery and analysis of the Leahy letter. Cleared at the highest FBI levels, Beecher's overview ended with a brief discussion of the letter material that dismissed "a widely circulated misconception," namely, "that the spores were produced using additives and sophisticated engineering supposedly akin to military weapon production."[1] With a pointed reference to a 2002 *Washington Post* article co-authored by Gary Matsumoto, Beecher expressed concern that such errors detracted from the magnitude of hazards that simple spore preparations presented. The search for the Leahy letter showed extensive cross-contamination, with the protective garb of nearly all the crew members covered with spores from mail items and from the air. Beecher's implication—that there was no silica coating on the letter spores—was a summary of Joe Michael's analysis at Sandia, completed nearly four years before, but held secret as possible trial evidence. This rebuke in the Beecher article, picked up by the media, reignited the "foreign source" controversy surrounding the anthrax letters.[2] Ignoring the fact that the data from the Armed Forces Institute of Pathology, which had generated the silica coating theory, remained unpublished, incensed critics faulted the FBI for not revealing its TEM (Transmission Electron Microscopy) data in full detail.

Word of the controversy, plus rumors that Amerithrax was taking a new turn, reached Congress, where New Jersey Representative Rush Holt Jr., whose district included Princeton, had followed the case closely. With a doctorate in physics (his campaign bumper stickers read, "My congressman IS a rocket scientist"), Holt was a member of the House Permanent Select Committee on Intelligence. When he asked the Bureau for a closed briefing on the investigation, the FBI's Congressional Affairs office flatly refused. In a reference to the Hatfill fiasco, an official wrote to Holt, "After sensitive information about the investigation citing Congressional sources was cited in the media, the Department of Justice and the FBI agreed that no additional briefings to Congress would be provided."[3] Holt, incensed, contacted Charles Grassley, the Republican head of the Senate Finance Committee, who, equally appalled, was about to hold hearings calling the FBI to account about the millions invested in Amerithrax with no discernible result.

The direction of Amerithrax was changing, but not because of Joe Michael's findings. The exciting news, known only at the top echelon, was that progress was being made in identifying the signature morphotypes in the FBIR samples. The four teams assigned to test the FBIR samples for the four morphotypes (A1, A3, D, and E) had been independently submitting their results, the great majority of them negative. Any one finding that was positive, from their vantage, could not be matched to the other three, nor did they know where any of the FBIR samples originated. But others at the FBI did, and the field agents there were watching the returns with particular interest.

At the Chemical-Biological Sciences Unit, Mark Wilson, who had pioneered the Bureau's mitochondrial DNA forensics in the 1990s, remained in charge of monitoring the morphotype matches. The consulting experts for the project met under top security conditions, such was the import of the findings by the start of 2006, when the pieces of the puzzle seemed to fit together. Of the 947 valid FBIR samples, only eight contained the four morphotypes that matched the letter material. Seven were from USAMRIID's RMR-1029 flask, which had been Bruce Ivins' responsibility since 1997. The eighth was from Battelle Memorial laboratory in Ohio, sent there by Ivins from the same flask. A preliminary list of individuals with possible legitimate access to the signature spores for the two years prior to the 2001 letter attacks numbered over 200. Any one of them could have violated Army security.

✢

On September 11, 2006, the fifth anniversary of the al Qaeda attacks, President Bush and Vice President Cheney attended a memorial service at St. John the Evangelist Church in Washington and then went to the Pentagon for another ceremony, at the site of the outdoor monument to its 184 victims. At Ground Zero in New York City, a great crowd gathered and tearful families and friends read the list of over 2,700 victims' names. Still fighting in Afghanistan and Iraq, the United States, the world's lone superpower, had failed to capture Osama bin Laden or the terrorist who had sent the anthrax letters.

Three weeks later, on October 19 at 10:30 a.m., the Brentwood community reunited for its "Five Year Anthrax Crisis Memorial"—organized by Dena Briscoe, still head of Brentwood Exposed, and the other faithful supporters. The setting was the majestic Israel Baptist Church on Saratoga Avenue, in the Brentwood neighborhood. Members of the Curseen and Morris families spoke first. Both widows were present: Celestine Curseen had remained in the Washington area and Mary Morris returned for the ceremony from Chicago. Leroy Richmond spoke next, followed by Joe Paliscak, a postal inspector likely infected with anthrax at Brentwood on October 19, 2001, although his near-fatal illness remained unconfirmed by the CDC. Three postal union vice presidents offered condolences; then D.C. Representative Eleanor Holmes Norton and Senator Barbara Mikulski added theirs, as did Judicial Watch President Tom Fitton. No grudges were held about the failed lawsuit. U.S. Postal Service Vice President Jerry Lane, the Washington area's postal manager in 2001 and a defendant in the case, praised Curseen and Morris for the service they had rendered.

Last on the program was a surprise speaker: FBI Special Agent Joseph Persichini Jr., the ADC (Assistant Director in Charge) of the

Washington field office. Together, he and four junior agents—all in suits and ties, they arrived wearing sunglasses—sat attentively through nearly two hours of speeches, prayers, hymns, and a rousing performance by the Baba Ngoma-Narafiki Drummers. When it was finally his turn, Persichini took the podium to assure the Brentwood community that the Bureau was giving its all to catch the criminal who had killed two of their fellow workers. "Despite the frustrations that come with any complex investigation," he said, reading from his notes, "no one in the FBI has, for a moment, stopped thinking about the innocent victims of these attacks, nor has the effort to solve this case in any way been slowed."[4]

To skeptics at the memorial, Persichini's words sounded like empty promises. But Dena Briscoe took the assurances at face value. For the first time, the FBI had paid attention to Brentwood's victims—that in itself was heartening.

Five days later, FBI Director Robert Mueller arrived on Capitol Hill to give testimony on Amerithrax to the Senate Finance Committee. Impeccable in a crisp white shirt, dark suit, and tie, he was prepared for a grilling, but unlikely to be intimidated. Mueller was one of the few high-ranking federal officials who had not been pink-slipped after President Bush won his second term in 2004. Attorney General Ashcroft, Secretary Thompson, Secretary Ridge, CIA Director Tenet, Defense Secretary Rumsfeld, Secretary of State Powell, EPA Secretary Whitman—the Bush broom had swept them from power. The taciturn, media-averse Mueller had survived, and respect for him at the Oval Office had only increased. In line with the Bush-Cheney "war on terror," he had shifted the Bureau's top priority from crime solving to intelligence. At the same time, he kept the FBI protected from the turmoil of intelligence reorganization that was affecting Bush's second term. Intent on centralizing FBI authority, he was assigning more agents than ever to Washington, either as new recruits or relocated from field stations, and modernizing the Bureau's famously outmoded communication systems.

As he sat before the Senate Judiciary Committee, Mueller had in his briefing folder the excoriating letter rebuking the FBI that the committee chair, Senator Grassley, had sent Attorney General Alberto Gonzales, the docile substitute for John Ashcroft. Grassley and other committee members took turns berating Mueller for an investigation that had cost millions and yielded no conviction.[5]

Mueller, his big jaw set, left the hearing unchastened. With the shift of Amerithrax to the defense establishment, Mueller had decided on a change of guard. He sent Rick Lambert, in charge of the investigation, to head the Knoxville, Tennessee, FBI office. In the Bureau's culture, this assignment was a reward: it offered more authority than working in Washington—it was like being given your own duchy, as one former agent described it. Plus, it avoided any demoralizing critique of Lambert, whom some inside the Bureau faulted for persisting too long in the pursuit of Steven Hatfill as a suspect.

That fall, Mueller put two experienced special agents, Vincent Lisi and Ed Montooth, in charge of Amerithrax. Lisi became the case supervisor, while Montooth took on responsibility for reinvigorating the field investigation. A veteran of the difficult Bosnian genocide investigation, Montooth had a stellar reputation for inspiring effective teamwork and working long hours, two necessary qualifications as the chase narrowed.

Montooth's approach was to roll up his sleeves and review from scratch the files of every scientist with the requisite skills, access to RMR-1029 spores, and no alibi for the days when the anthrax letters were posted in Princeton. The criminal investigation formula was straightforward: determine access, knowledge, experience, and motive. Yet the new turn in the Amerithrax case reminded Bureau officials of the Wen Ho Lee espionage case, which in the late 1990s, under director Louis Freeh, it had unsuccessfully and, to its public embarrassment, pursued.[6] Leaked to the press, the main accusation against Lee, a physicist at Los Alamos National Laboratory, was that he had given top-security nuclear missile information to the Chinese; after eight months in solitary confinement, Lee was cleared. In pursuing the anthrax attacker, the Bureau was back in the realm of national security and science. But rather than involving treason, the anthrax attacks had worked well for the defense establishment by promoting protection against a foreign threat. The perpetrator, therefore, could be motivated by group loyalty and patriotism, not at all a "lone wolf." Far from being isolated, perhaps he worked in a highly cohesive setting—a scientific laboratory with esprit de corps. Rather than being a Unabomber hermit, he could be living in suburban western Maryland near Detrick or in Ohio, near Battelle.

The possibility of someone from inside USAMRIID being the perpetrator of the anthrax letter attacks raised another sensitive issue at the Bureau: the discovery in late 2000 that for nearly twenty years one of its trusted agents, Robert Hanssen, had been a double agent, selling secrets first to the Soviet Union and then to Russia. He was an oddball (he always dressed in black suits), yet his co-workers excused his foibles. After all, he was a respectable family man whose children attended the same school as those of the director and he was a devout Catholic. Robert Mueller was a Justice Department lawyer when the Hanssen case broke in 2001 and, in his opinion, the traitor deserved the death penalty. (Wiser heads prevailed; double agents are more valuable alive and telling what they know.) John Ashcroft, among others, was furious about this national security failure.[7]

If the FBI caught the "determined insider"—as Peter Jahrling once phrased it—it would inevitably be demonstrating another major national security breach: the U.S. Army's failure to prevent the use of the Ames anthrax for murder, as well as its blind inclusion of the killer within its ranks for years afterward. Heads at the Pentagon, Fort Detrick, and USAMRIID would certainly roll, and the institute would be damaged.

But the FBI's and the Department of Justice's sole goal was a successful criminal prosecution, no matter what the consequences. The charge would be murder in the first degree, defined in U.S. Title 18, Section 1111, as "the unlawful killing of a human being with malice aforethought." Under Section 2332, concerning the lethal use of a biological weapon, the law was that the guilty party "shall be punished by death, or by imprisonment for any term of years or for life."[8] When credible evidence pointed to a criminal suspect, the U.S. Attorney General's Office would request a federal grand jury to meet in the District of Columbia—and hope that the jurors, persuaded by the case evidence, would issue an indictment. The defendant would then stand trial and the government's prosecution would either succeed or fail, as the court decided. That was the process of justice.

Given the high stakes for the Pentagon, military authorities might prefer that the criminal worked for Battelle, a defense contractor, and not at USAMRIID, poised for a bright future as part of the new Detrick biodefense campus. In 2004, the FBI had obtained a search warrant to make sure that samples were taken from each stock of the Ames strain anthrax at Battelle, to avoid ambiguity about what the company possessed. (At Dugway and USAMRIID, the Bureau conducted what it referred to as "consent searches" to guarantee the same compliance.)[9] When FBI investigators examined Battelle's workplace norms, they found that its security rules in 2001 were much more rigorous than those at USAMRIID. At Battelle, forty-two employees had access to the RMR-1029 spores after they were sent there in the spring and summer of 2001. Twenty employees were identified as having the skills and equipment to prepare and dry the spores. The Bureau checked not only them but everyone else for alibis—administrators, scientists, technicians, and animal handlers. Battelle work hours were regular, limited to daytime hours, and efficiently recorded, with a buddy system in effect. From 7:30 a.m. to 4:30 p.m., no researcher was ever alone in the laboratory. During a unique phase of after-hours work (June 13 to 16, 2001), researchers worked in rotating pairs.

On the key dates for the Princeton mailings, everyone in the Battelle group had an alibi; to be doubly sure, the FBI name-checked air travel records between Ohio and the East Coast. During the times the letters had been mailed, no one from Battelle with access to the spores had been remotely near Princeton.

At USAMRIID, where anthrax researchers had more autonomy, investigators reviewed the files of those who had access to RMR-1029 spores from 1999 until the letter mailings—the estimated window of time during which the letter spores had been produced. In the early phase of the investigation, most of these researchers had been interviewed and had their alibis checked. Many, including Bruce Ivins, Art Friedlander, and John Ezzell, had been polygraphed—without any alarms going off.

With time, though, Friedlander's claim that only wet spore preparations were available at USAMRIID could not be sustained. Although he had kept quiet about it, in 1999 John Ezzell had indeed made powdered Ames anthrax spores in his institute unit, for a special Department of Defense project to test weapons threats, researched at Johns Hopkins University under the auspices of DARPA (Defense Advanced Research Projects Agency). But Ezzell emphasized that the spores he produced were then irradiated and "dead" and prepared in accordance with all regulations.[10] More important, arguments that critics like Dick Spertzel had been making that the institute lacked the technology for powdered spore production also crumbled. Ezzell and others knew that putting a suspension of spores in a centrifuge would create a pellet of graded purity: shave off and dry the whiter layer and you had a powder similar to the anthrax letter material. It was by no means a mass production method, but it would have been sufficient for the five anthrax letters.

As all the former suspect files were reopened and reconsidered, Bruce Ivins made the short list. His failure in February 2002 to submit a proper first sample from the flask to the FBIR raised a red flag. That February, the sample Ivins submitted to the FBIR at the institute, then in John Ezzell's charge, was destroyed. But at Northern Arizona University, Paul Keim had saved the submission. When in late 2006 the FBI requested it—using the number code that blinded its source—Keim turned it in. Genetic analysis showed that the sample matched the RMR-1029 spores and contained three of the four signature morphotypes—consistent with other samples from the flask. Yet, as already discussed with Ivins in March 2005, all of the morphotypes were missing from Ivins' second submission to the FBIR, in April 2002. Ivins' label for that second submission, "Dugway Ames spores-1997" instead of RMR-1029, could have been just a minor confusion—or it could have been subterfuge.

In retrospect, Bureau interviews with Ivins showed a pattern of inconsistencies and even lies. For instance, on May 7, 2007, Ivins told FBI agents that within three months of the letter attacks he knew that RMR-1029 showed morphological similarities to the attack spores. He claimed he had learned this from three USAMRIID colleagues who had participated in the forensic analysis, which all three emphatically denied. If he did know the connection so far in advance, Ivins never raised it in his many conversations with Bureau agents. To the contrary, his file was full of suggestions he made about other researchers as possible perpetrators and even a claim that the anthrax letter spores resembled those used by another researcher at USAMRIID, which differed from the *B. anthracis* in the RMR-1029 flask.[11]

Since accessing Ivins' emails in 2005, FBI investigators knew that he suffered not just from bipolar depression but from a possible split personality or dissociation between a good and a bad self. The man his colleagues described as "quirky" but "law abiding and a caring person" might actually be struggling with a dual persona.[12]

Ivins had apparently experienced a mental health crisis in mid-1999, after his assistant Mara Linscott, an attractive, accomplished young woman—not unlike Nancy Haigwood—left the institute for medical school. Ivins had convinced himself that Linscott and a more senior collaborator on the BioPort project, Patricia Fellows, were the only people to whom he could talk about his special "sensitivities." In a November 1999 email, he tried to engage the two in a three-way confrontation of his problems. He offered the "full exposition, including some VERY dark family material." Ivins' alcoholic father, it emerged later, had often been physically abused by his wife who, at one point, kept a loaded gun and threatened to use it.[13]

Neither woman took up the offer and about this time Ivins' relationship with Fellows soured—one has to imagine a workplace atmosphere in which one's boss makes psychotherapeutic demands. After stealing Fellows' computer password, Ivins began reading her emails and found she was saying "some very negative things" behind his back, to the effect that he was either "mentally ill or just mean."

Wounded by Linscott's leaving USAMRIID—he described it as "dreadfully painful"—Ivins inundated her with lengthy emails describing his mental turmoil and rounds of unsuccessful therapies. When her replies were delayed and diffident, Ivins recriminated her, but he remained fixated. It was for Linscott that he drove ten hours to leave wine and Kahlua on her doorstep, at a time when he had, as he explained to the FBI in 2005, two herniated disks in his back that caused him great pain.

Ivins' unsolicited emails to Linscott from April 2000 through December 2001 vividly described his depression, paranoia, delusion, and anger—his self in anguish—although he tried to keep a light touch. On April 3, 2000, for example, he wrote about his dissociative experiences, but playfully: "Other times it's like I'm not only sitting at my desk doing work, I'm also a few feet away watching me do it. There's nothing like living in both the first person singular AND the first person singular!" In June 2000 he complained to her that even "with Celexa and the counseling, the depression episodes come and go. That's unpleasant enough. What is REALLY scary is the paranoia." He described these episodes as feeling as if he were "a passenger on a ride." His weekly sessions with a counselor, he reported, offered no help. In July Ivins described his precarious state: "The thinking now by the psychiatrist and counselor is that my symptoms may not be those of a depression or bipolar disorder, they may be that of a 'Paranoid Personality Disorder.'" A few days later he joked to her that he didn't want to see a tabloid headline, "PARANOID MAN WORKS WITH DEADLY ANTHRAX!!!" Toward the end of the month—in a message that could only startle—he described trouble with a counselor who thought he should be "jailed."

The revealing emails to Linscott continued through the summer, full of complaints about failed therapies and insinuations that his marriage was troubled. His mental problems, which he was careful to hide from colleagues, caused him shame and fear; stoic resolve alternated with desperation. On March 4, 2001, Ivins wrote to her, "I'm down to a point where there are some things that are eating away that I feel I can't tell anyone." In April, Ivins took a break from work and spent a month in a rehabilitation hospital. For his superiors at the institute, as long as while on the job he posed no physical threat to his co-workers or to himself, Ivins' disturbances were a private matter.

Bureau investigators also began scrutinizing Ivins' behavior in December 2001—the time of his alleged cleanup of his contaminated office—and his role in the April 2002 discovery of Ames spore contamination outside his B-3 suite, which the Army had interpreted as a "housekeeping" problem. His account of how he secretly disinfected his office in December 2001 and his later discovery of more "escaped" anthrax spores outside the B-3 suite could constitute an elaborate cover-up of earlier Ames spore spills, perhaps from preparing and transporting the anthrax letters.

A review of his emails also revealed a disconcerting "split personality" problem well before 9/11, a problem that persisted during the stressful time of Operation Noble Eagle.

On December 10, 2001 (around the time USPS vice president Tom Day was at USAMRIID testing spore dispersal from a bar code sorter), Ivins emailed Mara Linscott a disturbing jingle that mimicked the old "I'm a little teapot" nursery song:

> I'm a little dream-self short and stout.
> I'm the other half of Bruce—when he lets me out.

When I get all steamed up, I don't pout.
I push Bruce aside, then I'm free to run about!

Ivins' jingle continued playfully:

Hickory dickory Doc—Doc Bruce ran up the clock.
But something then happened in very strange rhythm.
His other self went and exchanged places with him.
So now, please guess who
Is conversing with you.
Hickory dickory Doc!

He ended the rhyme with macabre cheer:

Bruce and this other guy, sitting by some trees,
Exchanging personalities.
It's like having two in one.
Actually it's rather fun![14]

This strange playfulness was difficult to reconcile with the meticulous rationality of whoever sent the anthrax letters. Investigators zeroed in on Ivins' solitary nighttime use of his laboratory—which they had already questioned him about in March 2005. A combination of pass card use and coded key punch entries, electronically recorded for security purposes, revealed Ivins' patterns of access over the course of months in 2000 and 2001. The weeks just after 9/11 and before the letter mailings showed a striking pattern.

The first aberration in Ivins' schedule began on Friday, September 14, when he entered his office at Building 1425 at 8:54 p.m. and left at 12:22 a.m. Two hours and 15 minutes of this time he spent by himself in the B-3 suite. For the next two nights, Saturday, September 15, and Sunday, September 16, he repeated this pattern: three to four hours in his office, with two hours plus some minutes spent in the B-3 suite.

The first set of anthrax letters—to mass media targets—was posted in Princeton sometime between 7 p.m. Monday, September 17, 2001, and 7 a.m. Tuesday, September 18.

After September 16, Ivins stopped his nighttime visits to his lab and office. Then, on Friday, September 28, he returned to his pattern of

2001 Night Hours in Suite B3

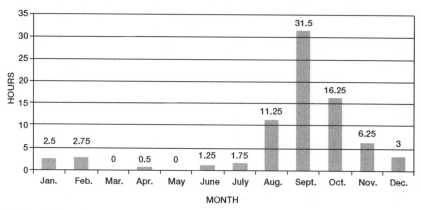

Using USAMRIID security records, the FBI plotted the nighttime use Bruce Ivins made of his BSL-3 laboratory during 2001.

solitary evening visits. That night, Ivins went to his lab for an hour and 42 minutes, and returned the next two nights, Saturday and Sunday, September 29 and 30, for about the same amount of time. At this point, the three anthrax letters mailed to the media had been received but ignored. To the perpetrator, it could have seemed they had missed their marks.

On Wednesday night, October 3, Ivins spent 2 hours and 59 minutes in his laboratory. He returned the next night, October 4, when the Bob Stevens diagnosis dominated the news. How Stevens had contracted the disease was ambiguous, with Secretary Thompson and others suggesting a natural source. The terrorist who sent the letter to AMI might have felt that, without its message, the missile was a dud and needed a more concerted attack.

That October 4, Ivins spent four hours in Building 1425, from 6:10 p.m. to 10:12 p.m., the longest period so far, and of that time he was alone for three hours and 33 minutes in the BSL-3 lab. The next night, Friday, October 5, Bob Stevens' death was featured on the news, again with no mention of a terrorist letter. At 7:40 that evening, Ivins returned to Building 1425, spent three hours and 42 minutes in the B-3 suite, and left his office at 12:43 a.m. on Saturday.

That Sunday, as news broke of anthrax spores at the AMI building, Ivins went to his office and clocked in at 2:34 p.m., spent 21 minutes alone in his lab, and clocked out at 3:26 p.m.

Sometime between 3 p.m., Saturday, October 6, and noon on Tuesday, October 9, the anthrax attacker dropped the letters to Daschle and Leahy in the Princeton mailbox, after which they were delivered to the Hamilton facility.

By FBI reckoning, Ivins could have used both crucial time periods, one in September and the other in October, to prepare first the anthrax spores that were put in the letters that targeted the media and second the more purified ones sent to Daschle and Leahy. Ivins no doubt had the skills. But was this technically possible with existing equipment, in that lab context, and within those time periods? The Bureau consulted with over a dozen experts with experience in this area and the answer came back a unanimous affirmative.[15]

With little traffic, the round-trip drive from Frederick might be done in less than six hours. Had Ivins an alibi? He had left work in the late afternoon on Monday, September 17, and then reported in at 7 a.m. on the eighteenth to make a vaccine delivery to a VA hospital in southern Pennsylvania. If he had gone for an overnight ride, he could have made the trip to Princeton and back in time.

During the October window of time for the mailings, he had been in and out of USAMRIID. He left his lab at nearly 1 a.m., Saturday, October 7, and on Sunday was back at his office in the afternoon. (Presumably he attended church as usual that morning.) Nonetheless, he could have disappeared from home that Saturday or Sunday night or the night of Monday, October 8, driven to Princeton, mailed the letters and returned in due time the next morning. His wife, Diane, as Ivins had assured FBI agents in 2005, could corroborate nothing. He insisted that they led separate lives.[16]

During September 2001, Ivins' emails to Mara Linscott revealed his strong reactions to the 9/11 attacks. On September 15, he wrote: "I am incredibly sad and angry at what happened, now that it has sunk in. Sad for all the victims, their families, their friends. And angry. Very angry. Angry at those who did this, who support them, who coddle them, and who excuse them."

Right after 9/11, the press was full of warnings of bioterrorism. On September 12, in the *Washington Post*, former Defense Secretary William Cohen (who had promoted universal AVA vaccinations for the military and the BioPort deal) announced that "the next terrorist attack could well involve a contagious agent carried to our soil or airspace in a briefcase or a bottle."[17] Five days later, on September 17, the *Post* ran a story on the "devastating threat" of bioterrorism.[18]

On September 19, the day after the first mailings, Ivins wrote Linscott that he was feeling well for the first time in a long while, because he had gotten some "exercise." A week later, though, his mood again darkened. On September 26, he sent her this message: "Of the people in my 'group' everyone but me is in the depression/sadness/flight mode for stress. I'm really the only scary one in the group. Others are talking about how sad they are or scared they are, but my reaction to the WTC/Pentagon events is much different. Of course, I don't talk about how I really feel with them—it would just make them worse." Ivins then continued: "I just heard tonight that Bin Laden terrorists for sure have anthrax and sarin gas. . . . Osama Bin Laden has just decreed death to all Jews and all Americans."

Fears of terrorists launching a "second blow" against America became a fixation in the mainstream media. For example, in a September 30 article in the *Washington Post*, a government consultant proposed a rationale that fit the second set of anthrax letters:

> The chance of a large attack that affects tens of thousands
> or hundreds of thousands is very small. But is that what
> the terrorist cares about? Inducing enough disease to pro-
> duce panic or disrupt life is probably enough. I would
> posit that one or two cases of pulmonary anthrax in
> downtown Washington would achieve that goal.[19]

The FBI began theorizing that 9/11 had moved Bruce Ivins, in righteous wrath, to simulate just such an attack, perhaps to patriotically warn the nation or perhaps simply because the "bad Bruce" pushed the good Bruce aside.

※

As the FBI's Ed Montooth revived Amerithrax, the investigation circled back to Nancy Haigwood and her 2002 response to the FBI letter that had circulated to the American Society for Microbiology members. Her suspicions of Ivins' weird vandalism related to her Kappa Kappa Gamma (KKG) sorority and his stalking her over the years began to make sense. With some misgivings, Haigwood agreed to initiate direct email contact with Ivins, which the FBI monitored. She was afraid of Ivins, feeling she had experienced something his colleagues had not: a dark, manipulative side.[20]

The FBI contact with Haigwood opened a door to Ivins' long-term habit of hiding behind fake identities to express his anger, as well as his obsession with KKG. Using the name of Carl Scandella, Haigwood's then husband, for a post office box, Ivins in the 1980s sought contact with others interested in the sorority and he assumed an email pseudonym for online discussions where he could vent about his love-hate relationship with it. He emailed one correspondent that although Kappas were noted for being "lovely, highly intelligent campus leaders," they had decades before labeled him as an enemy, pronouncing a "Fatwah" on him. "I like individual Kappas enormously," he wrote, "and love being around them. I never choose an enemy, but they've been after me since the 1960s, and REALLY after me since the late 1970s." In the 1990s, he assumed an anonymous email identity to wage an acrimonious battle with the KKG executive director about the sorority's Wikipedia description. It emerged that years before, armed, he had broken into a KKG sorority house to steal cipher and rule books. In still another episode, he put ads in the magazines *Mother Jones* and *Rolling Stone* representing himself as "Carla Sanders," a disaffected KKG member willing to give away the sorority's secret codes.

Did Ivins' KKG obsession matter? Although no direct evidence linked him to the Princeton mailings, investigators discovered that a KKG office was located on Nassau Street, a short block from the contaminated mailbox, which the murderer had twice chosen to use.

In June 2007, Ivins emailed Haigwood expressing irritation that he had to hire a lawyer to defend himself against FBI questioning. His situation was worse than he let on. That summer he was called to testify before a federal grand jury in Washington. The questions put him on the defensive, and it was explained to him that, if convicted, whoever sent the anthrax letters could face the death penalty. Interviewing Ivins' co-workers, Bureau agents heard how depressed he had become about his career, complaining to them that "I am just a technician." "I am not attractive," he told one of them at this time. "I'm a nerd and a science geek."[21]

Ivins sought counsel at the pricey law firm of Venable LLP at its Rockville, Maryland, office. There he was assigned Paul Kemp, who specialized in white-collar crime cases; in 2002, he had been listed as one of Washington's top 75 lawyers in *Washingtonian* magazine. Though about Ivins' age, Kemp, with his ruddy complexion, trim physique, and perfect smile, looked much younger. He understood little about microbiology or anthrax, but he was following the Hatfill case, which was in negotiation—a good sign, he felt, for Ivins, who he presumed was innocent.

By the time the FBI honed in on Ivins, he was a sixty-year-old alcoholic, suffering from chronic back and leg pain, and still in therapy and taking prescription medicine for his bipolar disorder and depression. To escape the pain, he was mixing pills and alcohol, usually vodka, in alarming quantities. His children had flown the nest; Andrew was at a local college, Amanda lived a few towns away. He and his wife, Diane, had separate bedrooms, hers on the first floor and his upstairs. From one vantage, Ivins was hiding his "bad self," his Mr. Hyde, from her, revealing only his good Dr. Jekyll. He told close colleagues that when Diane was away, he drank tequila in combination with Ambien, after which he could not remember what he did.[22] From another vantage, he was protecting his wife—and his children, too—who had always depended on him.

At the Bacteriology Division, Ivins hinted to colleagues that he might retire in a year—or that he might die of "the big one," a heart attack, before that. Yet he still showed up regularly for work, continued his animal research on anthrax, and helped others expose cages of rabbits and guinea pigs to anthrax aerosols. Yet, when Bureau agents persisted in fishing for suspects at the institute, Ivins himself suggested to them that his former assistants, Linscott and Fellows, could have mailed the anthrax letters—a vicious gesture at best. Then he pointed the FBI to a microbiologist at Battelle to whom he had sent RMR-1029 spores in the spring of 2001.

On October 31, 2007, the FBI and the U.S. Postal Inspection Service applied for two search warrants from the District of Columbia federal court. One sought permission to obtain evidence from Ivins' office at USAMRIID, the other to search his home on Military Road and his three automobiles: a red 1996 Dodge van and a 2002 Saturn, plus a 1993 Honda Civic, used primarily by his wife. Although the anthrax letter mailings had been meticulously planned and executed, the Amerithrax Task Force (as it was called) took a chance that Ivins, after six years, might have been unable to destroy all evidence.

The warrant application, which was sealed, succinctly laid out the case against Ivins as it then stood.[23] He had been in charge of the flask from which the letter spores had originated; he had spent suspicious night hours in the high-containment lab just prior to the mailings; his state of mind, by his own admission, had been unstable; the potential failure of BioPort threatened his research future; and his post–September 11, 2001, emails echoed the phrases used in the four anthrax letters. (Not mentioned in the warrant was an FBI misstep. Ivins had been polygraphed while he was possibly on Valium, which because of its physical effects would cancel out signs of anxiety during the questioning.)

The warrants were granted—and this time there were no leaks to the media, no helicopters over Military Road, no vans blocking the street, the way they had when Hatfill's apartment was searched in 2002. Instead, the two-part search—this time involving a USAMRIID employee—was discreetly planned and executed.

On November 1, 2007, at 5 p.m., the FBI presented the search warrant to USAMRIID Commander Colonel George W. Korch Jr., informing him that Ivins was under suspicion of mailing the anthrax letters. Ivins was immediately barred access to the BSL-3 and BSL-4 laboratory suites, although not from other labs or his office.

At the Bacteriology Division, Ivins was confronted by FBI agents (some of whom he knew) who explained that his office and home would be searched and that, for his convenience, hotel rooms had been reserved for him and his family for the night. The agents then led Ivins to a nearby conference room for a grueling discussion about the samples Ivins had submitted to the FBIR. When Ivins asked if he should have a lawyer present, the agents replied that they asked only that he listen—they wanted him to hear why they were rejecting all of his excuses for fumbling both the February and April 2002 sample preparations. The bottom line, as it was put to him, was that Ivins knew that RMR-1029 was "the largest, most pure, most concentrated, batch of *Bacillus anthracis* Ames spores at USAMRIID"—already linked to the letter attacks—and yet, because of him, its contents could not be analyzed until after April 2004, when the flask was seized by the Bureau. At one point, when Ivins began to cry, the agents thought he was about to confess, but he did not.

Meanwhile, investigators started a thorough sweep of Ivins' office, swabbing every surface and seizing research records and correspondence, a Dell computer and disks, a list of personal codes, a safe deposit key, and old income tax files.

After 8 p.m., the interview with Ivins over, an FBI agent and a postal inspector drove him to the local Hilton Garden Inn where he and his wife waited for lawyer Paul Kemp to arrive. When he did, Kemp urged Ivins to keep his temper and not attract a media blitz.[24] So far, the FBI and the postal inspectors were treating Ivins with kid gloves, at least compared to the Hatfill debacle. Still, according to a friend at work, Ivins was furious that the Bureau had interrogated his wife and children and felt "backed into a corner."

That evening at 6:50, Bureau agents had entered the Ivins home on Military Road and began removing his personal effects: VHS and cassette tapes, family photos and documentation of the Ivins family lineage, Ivins' University of Cincinnati transcripts, a copy of Albert Camus' novel *The Plague*, and two boxes of documents marked with Paul Kemp's name. They also took away two computers and extra hard drives.

Ivins, who occasionally hunted, had a small shooting gallery in his basement. There investigators seized three handguns (a Glock 34, a Glock 27, and a Beretta), which, since 2005, the Bureau had known he owned, and a sawed-off shotgun, eight boxes of ammunition, and a bulletproof vest.

At 3:50 a.m., the team that had been swabbing Ivins' office arrived to do the same at his home. Two hours later they finished, leaving with 22 environmental samples, none of which tested positive for anthrax.

Among Ivins' papers, the Bureau found a single page of notes he had scrawled, perhaps shortly after his grand jury questioning. At the top, ambiguously, he put the word *Themes* and then continued with a terrible litany of purported motives: his psychiatric problems, his wanting to get the PATRIOT Act passed, and his wanting to make money off a new anthrax vaccine; each "made me do it."

Bureau agents returned to Military Road to continue round-the-clock surveillance. On November 8, at one in the morning, they observed Ivins (clad in long underwear) come out of his house to check that the city trash pickup was on time, which it was. Afterward, the agents retrieved Ivins' trash and found what he had thrown away: books on composing complex ciphers based on DNA sequences. Bureau analysts began combing them for clues that Ivins might have hidden in the texts of the letters. What they discovered—or thought they discovered—in highlighted letters in the anthrax texts were coded derogatory references to Linscott and Fellows—just weird enough to be true.

The November searches and the continuing investigation unnerved Ivins and upset some of his co-workers, who were still being interviewed by the FBI. On November 4, one authority at USAMRIID circulated a strict order: "At this time you are absolutely not to contact Bruce by any methods or means. In addition, absolutely nothing is to be said about the investigation, what has happened or comments about anything related to Amerithrax or anthrax to anyone inside or outside the institute."[25]

That fall Ivins turned to alcohol, anti-anxiety drugs, and sleeping pills to relieve his misery and physical pain. Still, he stuck to his old routine—working in his office and on lab projects that did not require high containment. But being barred access to his BSL-3 lab, where all his significant research had been done, was a humiliating restriction. Alerted to his problems, USAMRIID officials requested that his psychiatrist of the last five years, Dr. Allan Levy, send them Ivins' records. After Levy sent three months of minimal documentation, the authorities let the matter drop. As far as the institute was concerned, Ivins had lost his secret clearance, although that same November, on a separate track, the Department of Defense Biological Personnel Reliability Program had approved it and even allowed Ivins the option of applying for top secret clearance.

In January the FBI advised Ivins that he and his lawyer should appear for another interview at the office of the U.S. Attorney General in Washington. After the November search, the Bureau had obtained permission from America Online and MSN Hotmail to access Ivins' multiple email accounts. Its agents now knew volumes about five fake email identities he had been using to indulge his obsession with the KKG sorority and, as a surprise twist, with women blindfolded and in bondage.

In addition, the Bureau's analysts had been piecing together facts they believed pointed to Ivins as the prime suspect.[26] He had a predilection for using the U.S. mail to send anonymous "surprise" packages addressed in block print. The return address on the Daschle and Leahy letters might connect to a lawsuit, reported in the American Family Association journal, to which Ivins subscribed, about a fourth grader at the Greendale Baptist Academy in Greendale, Wisconsin, who was interrogated about corporal punishment by teachers without his parents' consent. The use of the zip code for Monmouth Junction, New Jersey, might be linked to Ivins' troubled father and his family, which in the eighteenth century had settled as farmers in nearby Monmouth, and also to Monmouth College in Illinois, where in 1870 the KKG sorority was founded. According to co-workers, Ivins read and commented on issues of the *National Enquirer* left lying around the BSL-3 suite. Ivins' files revealed numerous letters of complaint to public figures, including members of Congress. Ivins likely knew that in June 2001 Senator Daschle wrote a letter critical of the Pentagon's anthrax vaccine program; displeased by political obstruction of the PATRIOT Act, Ivins might have chosen Senator Leahy as a worthy target. He had a particular disdain for New Yorkers, which might explain his targeting of the *New York Post*; after 9/11, he thought too much attention was paid to al Qaeda victims there, compared with those at the Pentagon.

A possible link between Tom Brokaw and Ivins' KKG obsession also surfaced. In 1982, in a televised interview with a woman whose daughter had died in a hazing accident, Brokaw mentioned that his co-anchor Jane Pauley was a KKG member. Subsequently, as he later admitted, Ivins wrote the Nancy Haigwood letter defending hazing and mailed a printed copy of it to the grieving mother. She, in turn, showed it to an author writing a book on hazing, after which it circulated widely as Haigwood's opinion and led to her reprimand by her sorority.

To friends, Ivins ranted about his persecution, claiming that he was another Richard Jewell, the man who had been wrongly accused by the FBI of the 1996 Olympic Games bombing in Atlanta. The previous August, Jewell, long in poor health, had died, after battling in the courts and media to be recognized as the hero who had discovered the terrorist bomb and saved lives by quickly sounding the alarm. A hero in broken health who had altruistically sounded an alarm—that was the image Ivins projected.

CHAPTER 13

ODD MAN OUT

The man's interior is a battleground for what he feels to
be two deadly hostile selves, one actual, the other ideal.

—WILLIAM JAMES, *The Divided Self,* 1902

After Ed Montooth took charge of the investigation, the FBI began to invite the victims of the anthrax letters—the three widows and the survivors—to Washington for case updates. The meetings were difficult. Little information could be revealed, and in addition the victims each had widely different reactions to the experience. Mary Morris refused to have the anthrax attacks define her life and, similarly, Celestine Curseen, Qieth McQue, and Jyotsna Patel wanted their privacy. In contrast, the eloquent Leroy Richmond appeared on Oprah Winfrey's show in 2002 and spoke at a national postal convention, where he met Jack Potter in person. Some, like Norma Wallace and David Hose, grew disillusioned with government authorities and refused the FBI invitations. Ernesto Blanco, approaching eighty, still worked at American Media, Inc., had total faith in his country, and never missed any of the briefings.

Maureen Stevens was not sure what to believe. At the FBI's first meeting with victims, in late 2006, Ed Montooth gave her his card, with his FBI cell phone number written on it. "Call me if you have any questions," he told her kindly. Yet the Department of Justice had imposed delay after delay on her lawsuit. "It's been like a merry-go-round that just doesn't stop," she told reporters.[1] Justice lawyers were hoping that the appeals court in Atlanta would dismiss the Stevens case, but in early 2007, finding no precedent in Florida tort law, the Eleventh Circuit Court tossed the ball back to the Florida Supreme Court, asking it to decide if the case should go forward. The unexplained 1992 loss of dangerous pathogens at USAMRIID had resonated. The circuit court judge wanted this question answered:

> Under Florida law, does a laboratory that manufactures, grows, tests or handles ultra-hazardous materials owe a duty of reasonable care to members of the general public to avoid an unauthorized interception and dissemination of the materials, and, if not, is a duty created where a reasonable response is not made where there is a history of such dangerous materials going missing or being stolen?[2]

In response, lawyers at the Department of Justice again denied that the federal government had any special relationship to the public concerning protection against select agents in research laboratories.[3] Moreover, they raised a new objection: if the Stevens case prevailed, it would vastly expand the scope of Florida's negligence law, "subjecting a research laboratory (whether private or governmental) to potential liability if any substance from the facility is later used as a weapon in a criminal attack." Did Florida want to obstruct civilian biodefense research with liability claims? With the annual U.S. biodefense research and development budget at around $5 billion, the stakes were high. As a further complication, unknown to the public, the entire FBI repository of Ames anthrax strains was being analyzed at the Midwest Research Institute in Palm Bay, Florida.

✦

On January 16, 2008, of his own volition, accompanied by Paul Kemp and another lawyer from Venable, Bruce Ivins went to the attorney general's office in Washington to answer questions. Many of them were about his solitary nighttime visits to his lab, his alibis for the Princeton mailing dates, and his interest in the KKG sorority. Ivins freely admitted that he had burgled two KKG chapter houses and searched out others, some of them hundreds of miles from his home. About Nancy Haigwood, he explained that he had emailed her on September 21, 2001, after the anthrax attacks, "to refresh our acquaintance," not realizing that on that date no one but the sender would have known about the letters to the media. But he added nothing about his lab use or possible alibis for the Princeton mailings.

Federal investigators posed another question: What post offices did Ivins usually rely on? He told them he usually used the College Estates station in Frederick, near his house, a branch of the main post office. Perhaps this fact seemed insignificant, but the FBI and the Postal Inspection Service had gone all out to trace the four anthrax envelopes with their distinctive printing defects back to where they had been purchased. In December 2006, they had arranged a full-scale simulated production run of 525,000 federal eagle envelopes in order to trace how print defects arose and waned.[4] Months of photographing and analyzing the printed envelopes led to two conclusions: first, such defects were rare, and second, any defect duration was limited to about 2,000 consecutively printed envelopes. The thousand federal eagle envelopes delivered to Frederick's main post office on March 21, 2001, almost certainly bore the imperfections found in the several hundred envelopes shipped to nearby Cumberland and Elkton just before the Frederick delivery and in those shipped to the four other Maryland and Virginia post offices right after. Unfortunately for the investigators, almost certain results were suggestive, not conclusive.

In February, Ivins and Kemp were back at the Justice Department for another interview. This time, Ivins was grilled about his relations with Patricia Fellows and Mara Linscott—as reflected in email messages.

On March 11, 2008, Patricia Fellows, who had left the institute but still worked nearby, confronted Ivins about the email—discovered by the FBI and shared with her—in which Ivins reasoned that she and Mara Linscott had sent the anthrax letters. His email apology to her blamed "Crazy Bruce" and mental illness, and added with self-pity, "I have been selected as the 'blood sacrifice.'" In his group therapy sessions, which he attended weekly, he made the same claim that he had become a martyr in the investigation.

On March 17, 2008, Bruce Ivins was in a BSL-2 lab, preparing samples of the live but harmless Sterne vaccine strain, when apparently he accidentally spilled several milliliters of spores on his pants. In a repeat of his past behavior, he decontaminated the spill without informing his supervisors. Then he went across the street to his home, washed his pants with hot water and bleach, and dried them in the dryer. That done, he returned to the base and reported the incident, which reprised the way he overstepped his authority in December 2001.[5] This time, the institute command blocked him from all lab access. "Dr. Ivins will be assigned to administrative duties immediately and for the indefinite future," its notice read. "His badge access has been deactivated for laboratory areas of USAMRIID." Angry, Ivins blamed subordinates. "Don't clean up technicians' messes in BSC [biological safety cabinet]," he responded to an incident report query about how to prevent such problems in the future.

In despair, Ivins berated Mara Linscott in a March 18 email message:

> You were the one person I knew I could bare my soul to and tell everything to, and now you have abandoned me. You have put me on your dark list. . . . I lose my connections. I lose my years. . I lose my health. I lose my ability to think. I lose my friends. What have I left but eternity?[6]

Then, in a follow-up email to her on the morning of March 19, he bemoaned what he called his "long-distant and non-productive past."

Just after 2 p.m. that same day, in response to a 911 call, patrolman Ryan Forrest arrived at 622 Military Road and found that paramedics had already put the semiconscious Ivins in the ambulance.[7] They told Forrest to go upstairs in the house, where the victim had collapsed, and find his driver's license or other identification and any medications he might have taken. As the ambulance left, Forrest entered the house, where he was met by an angry and apprehensive Diane Ivins. She confronted him by insisting that the police were not needed, that her husband Bruce had done nothing wrong, that he was just sick.

"I'm here to make sure Mr. Ivins was not trying to harm himself," Forrest explained. "Do you believe he was attempting suicide?"

"No, my husband would never do such a thing," she answered. "He was on a new medication. He probably took the wrong pill by mistake."

Mrs. Ivins ordered Forrest to leave, which he did, making no report of the incident, which was just a routine assist to the fire department.

Taken to the emergency room at Frederick Memorial Hospital, Ivins was released several hours later. He was later briefly an inpatient at the Suburban Hospital in Bethesda for psychological problems.

Having joined up as a Red Cross volunteer just after 9/11, Ivins had faithfully attended its monthly meetings, sometimes with his wife. By reputation, he was a "great volunteer," a "worker bee" who took directions well.[8] He had a great sense of humor and sometimes entertained the group by playing the piano or juggling. The previous November, just after the FBI searched his home and office, Ivins took a medical leave from the chapter, saying that he expected to return in a few months. In April 2008, he applied for reinstatement, filling out the required update of his medical restrictions, a repeat of the previous two years' ailments: anxiety, depression, sleep disorder, back and leg pain. As for drugs, he reportedly relied on Celexa once daily for depression, the antidepressant Cymbalta twice daily, and during the day, diazepam for anxiety. He might have added that he was in weekly group therapy and had a serious dependency on vodka. In late April, his condition deteriorating, Ivins began a four-week stay at the Massie Unit of the Finan Center, a psychiatric hospital in Cumberland.

◆

On May 14, 2008, Paul Keim was in Washington, D.C., attending a meeting of the FBI's Scientific Working Group on Microbial Forensics. The technology for genetically fingerprinting different strains had progressed light years beyond what had been available in early October 2001, when he identified the Ames strain from the bacteria in Bob Stevens' spinal fluid. The same identification could now be done in minutes, not days. From a legal perspective, these rapid technical advances bore watching. According to federal rules, a judge acted as the gatekeeper regarding the admissibility of scientific evidence in court—and whether the scientific methods could be trusted.[9] When expert witnesses testified, their data had to be backed up by proof that their methods met rigorous standards, that rates of error were explicit, and that any new science had been validated in peer-reviewed journals. As potential expert witnesses, Paul Keim and Jacques Ravel knew that the cutting-edge methods they used were scientifically valid, but the FBI wanted absolute assurance.

At the Washington meeting, five unsmiling FBI and Justice officials approached Keim in the hotel corridor and asked to speak to him privately.

"I've greased up my wrists," he joked, "just so I can slip out of my handcuffs when you throw me in the back of the van."[10]

Not amused, the group led him to a private room where they asked for help in assessing Bruce Ivins' behavior, the first hint Keim had heard that Ivins might be a suspect. The agents showed Keim reprints of email conversations that had circulated among the small coterie of anthrax experts in 2001, at the time of the anthrax crisis. Did he see anything in the messages that suggested Ivins was trying to cover his tracks?

Keim was of little help. As far as he remembered, everyone in the anthrax expert community at that time had been tossing out ideas about the possible source of the letters. Back in Arizona, he rummaged through his files and found an old email from Ivins dated February 7, 2002. "The only place I know of that makes anthrax powder," Bruce had written the group, "is Dugway Proving Ground." Keim could not tell if Ivins had been simply stating a fact—Dugway was the production source of the Ames Ancestor and a longtime test site—or directing suspicion away from himself.

About a month later, in June 2008, a team of FBI agents came to Keim's lab at Northern Arizona University, packed up the FBIR collection, and flew it away on a government plane. Keim understood that an important phase of the investigation was over, but knew nothing about the decisive evidence it had yielded.

＊

In early June, at the Venable office in Rockville, Maryland, Bruce Ivins and his lawyer Paul Kemp had an "off-the-record" meeting with FBI and Justice officials.[11] Kemp listened to the questions posed to Ivins and considered his client's defense. Ivins' connection to RMR-1029 was worrisome but far from decisive evidence. Someone could have stolen the spores, run a covert "midnight requisition," or secreted some away by sleight of hand.

Another weakness in the FBI case, Kemp thought, was its lack of any proof that Ivins had been in Princeton when the two sets of letters were mailed. To test how long it would take to drive from Frederick to

Princeton and back, Kemp made the trip himself. It took him seven hours and he estimated that with traffic it could take longer. Kemp thought he could cast serious doubt on the argument that Ivins could have prepared the spores and loaded the letters, driven to Princeton, and still showed up ready for work as usual. Any jurist who saw Ivins, obviously frail, would have to question whether he would have had the stamina for such an arduous plan.

After the meeting, Ivins asked Kemp point-blank, "What can they do to me? What is the worst-case scenario?" Kemp gave it to him straight, perhaps too bluntly. "It looks as if an indictment is coming. You should be prepared to face the death penalty. Once you are indicted, the charge is so serious that you'll likely be jailed right away."

"For how long?"

"It could be six months, maybe longer. It depends on the trial date."

"What about legal fees?" Ivins asked.

"They could be two to three million dollars." Kemp, though, would petition for legal assistance allowed defendants in federal capital cases.

Shaken, Ivins drove back to Frederick. That same day, June 5, he emailed a friend about these dire predictions. Then he spoke frankly with another confidant, in a conversation that was tape-recorded and passed to the FBI.[12] Asked to consider if his "dark side" implicated him in the anthrax letters, Ivins admitted that he might have done something wrong unconsciously, without remembering. In response to the suggestion that he try hypnotism, Ivins asked, "What happens if I find something that, that is like buried deep, deep, deep?" Then he added, "I don't think of myself as a vicious, a, a nasty evil person." To the contrary, he saw himself as someone who didn't "like to hurt people, accidentally, in, in any way." If he felt guilty about anything, it was that the RMR-1029 flask hadn't been "locked up" before the letter attacks.

That same June 2008, the Department of Justice reached a settlement with Steven Hatfill for $5.8 million, which included restitution for the salary he would have been paid, with Justice Department funding, for teaching at the University of Louisiana: $140,000 per year for twenty years. On June 27, the FBI finally exonerated Hatfill, declaring him no longer a suspect in the anthrax letters case.

That summer, Ivins' onetime colleagues saw him wandering the streets, an odd man out. Jim Burans, aware of the morphotypes in RMR-1029, saw him at the local coffee shop, a shadow of his former self.

Meanwhile, the USAMRIID staff was contemplating a rosy future. The new building (with a total of 1.3 million square feet of space) was next in line for construction at Fort Detrick. To be built in two stages, it would house four times the BSL-4 space of the Department of Homeland Security's National Biodefense Analysis and Countermeasures Center (NBACC) and eight times the BSL-3 space. Its workforce would increase from 750 to over a thousand. In addition, it would house a new Joint Center of Excellence, in cooperation with the Walter Reed Army Institute of Research and the Naval Medical Research Center.

To fill his time, Ivins began posting messages at the Web site for the television reality show *The Mole*, whose 2001 season was rebroadcast that summer. Ivins' hostility was directed at a contestant, a lawyer named Kathryn Price; using a fake email, he also tried to meet her. Exposed in the last episode, Price was the secret mole whose goal was to sabotage the other nine players. Her own test was to sit blindfolded while a hatchet was hurled at her. In fact, the hatchet was only stuck in the wall behind her. Ivins urged that it should have been brought down "hard and sharply across her neck, severing her carotid artery and jugular vein." He himself would gladly do it, he said, adding, "The least someone could do would be to take a sharp ballpoint pen or letter opener and put her eyes out, to complete the task of making her a true mole."[13] "The Mole" seemed a particularly violent addition to the list of Ivins' angry obsessions.[14]

On the evening of July 9, Ivins went to his usual group therapy session, which counselor Jean Duley, a novice practitioner in her early twenties, had been co-running for six months. Duley asked everyone to focus on father-child issues. At first reluctant to speak, Ivins let loose a tirade against FBI investigators, the government, and "the whole system" that was persecuting him.[15] He declared that he wasn't going to let the government indict him on five counts of capital murder. With a strange smile, he described how, protected by a bulletproof vest and armed with a Glock handgun (he would get it from his son, he said) and a 22-caliber rifle, he was going to "take out" co-workers who had wronged him. Making a jabbing gesture with his pen, he talked about how he walked Black neighborhoods looking for someone to fight. With the group growing upset, Duley cut him off. She knew that Ivins popped pills and drank and that the FBI investigation was a strain—he'd told her privately that the real criminal was one of his institute colleagues—but she had never seen him like this.[16]

After the meeting Duley called her supervisor, Allan Levy, and followed his advice to contact the Frederick police first thing the next morning. That same morning, Ivins was at USAMRIID, attending a conference on the plague pathogen, unaware that the police and Duley's supervisor were about to warn Detrick authorities that he might pose a danger to his co-workers—especially the ones he had threatened to "take out"—and perhaps to himself. Ivins' ultimate degradation came at two that afternoon, when military police escorted him out of Building 1425—his workplace for twenty-seven years—to the main gate. From there two police officers brought him to Frederick Memorial Hospital for overnight observation. The next day, Ivins was involuntarily admitted to a Sheppard Pratt health facility in Frederick for psychiatric care.

In touch with Duley while Ivins was confined, the Amerithrax Task Force obtained another search warrant and on July 12 again inspected his house and cars.

After two weeks, on Thursday, July 24, Ivins was discharged from Sheppard Pratt—he had convinced therapists there and Levy that his crisis was over—and FBI agents began tailing him. One of the first things he did was go to a public library and log on to the Amerithrax Web site for an update. Then he drove to a Frederick supermarket, Giant Eagle, where he renewed three of his antidepressant prescriptions and bought a 70-count bottle of Tylenol PM and some groceries—grape juice, orange juice, 2% fat milk, and wheat bread.[17]

The Thursday Ivins was discharged, Jean Duley filed a Protective Order with the Frederick Police Department's Victim's Services Unit. Ivins had made three threatening phone calls to her, two on July 10 while he was at Frederick Memorial and another the day he was admitted to Sheppard Pratt. In her petition Duley wrote: "Client has a history dating to his graduate days of homicidal threats, actions, plans, threats and actions toward therapist." She added that his psychiatrist agreed and that the FBI was going to charge Ivins with five counts of murder. In addition, she mentioned that she had been summoned to testify before a federal grand jury on August 1.[18]

On Ivins' first day out of the clinic, his wife, Diane, wrote him a note full of despair and recriminations and placed it on the bedside table in his upstairs bedroom for him to find.

> Bruce,
>
> I'm hurt, concerned, confused, and angry about your actions over the last few weeks. You tell me you love me but you have been rude and sarcastic and nasty many times when you talk to me. You tell me you aren't going to get any more guns then you fill out an online application for a gun license. You pay Paul Kemp an enormous amount of money then ignore his advice by contacting Pat and Mara, going into work at odd hours, and walking in the neighborhood late at night. You are jumpy and agitated from the extreme amount of caffeine you drink each day. [Our accountant] asked us not to cash any more EE bonds because we pay so much tax on them and you cashed one in June. The FBI is convinced you are having an affair with Mara [and] every time you mail her they are more suspicious. Can you honestly say you are following the plan you developed at the Massie Clinic for stress reduction and coping with this?

After he found the note and read it, Ivins scrawled a terse response on the back: "I have a terrible headache. I'm going to take some Tylenol and sleep in tomorrow—Bruce." (He also wrote but then scratched out, "Please let me sleep. Please.")

On Saturday, July 26, Ivins spent most of his time upstairs in bed. At 7 p.m. and again at nine, Diane Ivins checked and found him asleep, although at one point he groggily acknowledged her presence.[19] She eventually went downstairs to read a book, and dozed off. Then, at 1 a.m., she awoke—maybe she heard a noise—and went upstairs to check on her husband. She found him collapsed on the floor of the bathroom in his underwear, in a pool of urine. He had a pulse and was breathing, but when she tried to rouse him by pinching his arm, he made no response. She called 911 to report an attempted suicide.

In minutes the fire department ambulance pulled up to the curb in front of the Ivins house, followed by Frederick police officer Robert

Pierce. As Pierce got out of his cruiser, one of the FBI agents watching the Ivins house asked him what happened. "Attempted suicide," Pierce told him and dashed up the front walk.

Inside the house, Pierce talked to Diane Ivins while, upstairs, the paramedics evaluated her husband's condition—he was cold to the touch, breathing rapidly, and both his eyes responded to light. They secured him on a stretcher, carried him downstairs, and transferred him to the ambulance, where he was put on oxygen. Wakened by the commotion, the neighbors on Military Road watched from their windows and porches. Its siren blaring, the ambulance took off, followed by the FBI agents.

As the ambulance left, Diane Ivins and Officer Pierce began counting each pill of her husband's newly filled prescriptions. They found only one missing, a tablet of Seroquel, to treat bipolar depression. Downstairs, they checked her store of pills and found none missing and no sign that her husband had ingested anything toxic. Throughout the ordeal Mrs. Ivins was, as Pierce noted in his report, "emotionless" but "cooperative."[20]

The inventory done, Pierce drove to Frederick Memorial and arrived before Diane Ivins. (She later explained that she thought one of the neighbors was following her, so she took a detour.) In the parking lot outside the emergency room, two FBI agents asked Pierce if he would find out about Ivins' condition and report back to them. In a few minutes, he returned with the news that the ER physician, who recognized Ivins as the FBI suspect, thought he had either overdosed on a drug or suffered a stroke.

As Pierce recounted in the incident report, "The agents advised that they knew that Ivins, his wife and many members of the general public were aware of their operations." Then they drove away, leaving Ivins to his physicians and family.[21]

At the hospital, Diane Ivins took up her vigil as her husband, still unconscious, was moved to the intensive care unit. At around 3 a.m., laboratory tests showed that his body was overloaded with acetaminophen, the main active ingredient of Tylenol, at almost two hundred times above normal, plus elevated levels of codeine.

At 8 a.m., when Ivins regained consciousness, the nurse on duty asked him if he had attempted suicide. He nodded in assent. Then he struggled to pull out his nasal tube and other life-support lines and had to be restrained. At this point, his wife asked that no staff talk about his being a suspect in the anthrax investigation, a request that was passed on to the nursing administrator.

Ivins was dying. His liver, already severely damaged, was barely functioning, his kidneys were failing, his heartbeat was irregular and his blood pressure dangerously low. His wife was empowered to make all decisions regarding extraordinary medical interventions to save him—and she declined each of them. At 3 p.m. on July 28, an attending physician asked her if she wanted her husband transferred to another hospital as a candidate for a liver transplant. She refused, replying, "He wouldn't want to live like that." She also declined having him resuscitated if his heart stopped. She wanted routine life support continued, including drugs to increase his blood pressure, but only temporarily—until the children, Andrew and Amanda, were prepared to bid their father farewell.

The next morning around 7:30, Mrs. Ivins had the blood pressure medication discontinued, and later, after the children arrived at the hospital, the life support lines were removed. Ivins' wife and children were at his bedside when he passed away at 10:47 a.m.

Many people in Frederick may have known that Ivins was an Amerithrax suspect. But on August 1, when the story of his "apparent suicide" broke in the *Los Angeles Times*, the public at large and even people who knew him were shocked.[22] Predictably, television vans and reporters crowded Military Road. The media world, though, had changed since the press had descended on the Stevens home in Florida in 2001 and in 2002 on Steven Hatfill's apartment down the street. The last of the celebrity broadcasting icons were gone. Tom Brokaw and Dan Rather had retired; Peter Jennings had died of cancer. Judith Miller had become front-page news, spending 85 days in federal detention for not revealing a White House source on a story relating to CIA operative Valerie Plame and WMD in Iraq.[23]

News about the news—that is, stories about the rapidly changing media landscape—had become commonplace. The major news networks and the print media were competing with faster electronic sources of information; the breaking stories from the *New York Times*, the *Washington Post*, and ABC News, transmitted via multimedia Web sites, had become fodder for the Internet, where citizen journalists and bloggers ruled.[24] Long before Ivins' death, the stalled Amerithrax investigation had generated conspiracy theories into which his sudden death was easily incorporated: either he was the victim of an international plot or the FBI had scapegoated him to protect the dark secrets of the American government.[25] The U.S. Postal Service, a victim of changes in communication, lost business to email transactions, social networks like Facebook, and cell phone texting. But its real problem was the economic downturn that started in 2008; despite great strides in biosafety and electronic package tracking and the cutting of over 50 million work hours, Postmaster General Potter had to report a loss of $2.8 billion for fiscal year 2008.[26] As plants closed and mechanization increased, union leaders like Dena Briscoe, who had become the president of the D.C. area American Postal Workers Union, went toe-to-toe with management to hold on to jobs, pensions, and benefits. So, too, did Bob Unick at the Hamilton facility in New Jersey, where he had been appointed shop steward and was increasingly active, like Steve Bahrle, in the National Postal Mail Handlers Union.

On August 3, the USAMRIID community at Detrick closed ranks around Ivins and held a memorial for him at the base chapel. An overflow crowd of two hundred colleagues and friends attended and the testimonies to his long years of service to the institute's mission and to his personal generosity were sincere and many. Some who believed the FBI had persecuted Ivins struggled to contain their anger. Others who had cooperated with the Bureau kept silent.

On August 5, a second memorial service for Ivins was held at the family's parish church, the historic St. John the Evangelist in Frederick where two stone angels hover at the entrance.[27] His widow, Diane, selected quotes from the Bible about forgiving one's enemies and achieving glory in the afterlife. Father Richard Murphy, the pastor, gave a homily that emphasized Bruce's "dedication to quiet service." Others echoed this theme of "selflessness," speaking of a patriotic scientist who avoided ambitious self-promotion. Still others memorialized him as a loyal friend who loved pop music and offbeat humor, like the comic strip *The Far Side*.

His friends also admitted Bruce could be "a character." One described Ivins asking to borrow his twelve-year-old daughter for a juggling practice. Later, he found Ivins and his partner tossing knives around both sides of the girl. Ivins' older brother Charles emphasized that he was "a darn good father." He had known little of Bruce's recent difficulties and had been shocked by the suicide. With tears in his eyes, he ended his eulogy with "I'm glad your torment has ended!"

At the reception after the service, a display of photographs showed Ivins at his happiest—with his young children, at town festivals, and with friends. His lawyer Paul Kemp described him the way his community saw him, as a "devoted husband and father who worked for more than thirty years [sic] to defend his nation and soldiers against the terrible effects of anthrax."[28]

In an August 5 op-ed in the *Wall Street Journal* Dick Spertzel—still believing the anthrax letters had a foreign source—rushed to Ivins' defense. His claim was that Ivins and USAMRIID lacked the sophisticated scientific disciplines and technologies necessary to produce the letter spores—which Spertzel contended had a silica coating and a special electrical charge.[29] Although long retired from the institute, Spertzel refused to believe that Ivins could work alone there for hours. And despite common knowledge about the use of a centrifuge to make pure spore powder, Spertzel still refused to believe that USAMRIID had the equipment to create "essentially pure spores."

Others at USAMRIID, certainly John Ezzell and Art Friedlander, knew better but remained silent and let the Spertzel claim stand. Adding to the confusion, on August 4, a *USA Today* interview with former USAMRIID commander Dave Franz misquoted him, making it seem he agreed with Spertzel. Franz quickly emailed the reporter: "We [at USAMRIID] absolutely had, and they still have, the equipment to produce dried anthrax spore preps . . . as do many laboratories in academe, industry and the rest of government."[30] Still, the controversy continued—with no word from USAMRIID, the U.S. Army, or the Pentagon on the FBI investigation and its national security implications.

Three days after Ivins' death, the FBI began posting case material on its Web site, but it was far from comprehensive and, with Hatfill exonerated, many in the public were skeptical that the Bureau this time had the right man.

On August 6, FBI Director Mueller gave a closed briefing on Amerithrax for the widows and survivors of the anthrax letter attacks—describing Ivins' mental instability, as well as his possible motives; for example, to revive the anthrax vaccine enterprise and consequently his career. Most of all, Mueller emphasized the scientific evidence that matched the spores in the letters with those in the RMR-1029 flask kept by Ivins in his lab at USAMRIID.

Ernesto Blanco was convinced by the case presentation.[31] Leroy Richmond considered the FBI evidence "good enough."[32] Persuaded, his wife, Susan, posed a fundamental question: "If Ivins didn't do it, why did he kill himself?" Steven Hatfill, with few resources, fought to prove his innocence and won. Why did Ivins, with a community to back him, give up? The question was unanswerable.

Of all the victims, Maureen Stevens, who found the FBI case credible, was in the most unusual situation. By scientifically tracing the letter spores to the flask at USAMRIID, the FBI had actually bolstered her "zone of risk" case still pending against the U.S. Army.

To showcase its scientific findings, on August 18, 2008, the FBI assembled five key advisors to give a press briefing at the Washington office.[33] Jacques Ravel was on the panel, along with his boss Claire Fraser-Liggett and his mentor Rita Colwell. After TIGR dissolved in a merger, Fraser-Liggett became director of the Institute for Genome Sciences at the University of Maryland Medical School, and Ravel was an associate professor there. In 2004, Colwell had stepped down as head of the National Science Foundation and now had professorships at both Maryland Medical and the Johns Hopkins School of Public Health. Paul Keim from Northern Arizona University and Jim Burans from the National Bioforensic Analysis Center at Detrick (part of NBACC) were on the panel, too, to help field press questions.

Sandia's Joe Michael was also there, to put the silica coating theory to rest. Until August 1, when the news of Ivins' suicide broke, Michael had never heard his name. Released from his nondisclosure agreement, he was able at last to announce what he and Paul Kotala had discovered in 2002 through TEM analysis of the letters' spores: there was absolutely no "fused silica" on the letters' spores. Silicon was found beneath the spores' outermost coating (called the exosporium), not in it.[34]

The genomic signature (the four morphotypes linking the letter spores to RMR-1029) was equally simple to explain. And, as one Justice official stressed, Bruce Ivins created and controlled those Ames strain spores:

No one received material from that flask without going through Dr. Ivins. We thoroughly investigated every other person who could have had access to the flask and we were able to rule out all but Dr. Ivins.[35]

Brentwood Exposed's Dena Briscoe had a front-row seat at the briefing. She recognized FBI assistant director John Persichini Jr., who had spoken at the 2006 Brentwood memorial, and listened hard when, commenting on Bruce Ivins, he said, "It appears, based on evidence, that he was acting alone." Briscoe took notes and asked questions. Although her mind was not completely made up, she found consolation in hearing the FBI case, which at least proposed a reasonable solution to the crime.

Senator Leahy, Senator Grassley, and Representative Rush Holt—the FBI's staunch critics—were even more skeptical of Persichini's assertion and of the FBI evidence. They wanted an investigation of Amerithrax, whether by Congress or by some other arm of government.

The conspiracy theories multiplied, as Amerithrax became a new version of the Kennedy assassination puzzle. Had Ivins acted alone or was a terrorist group, specifically al Qaeda, responsible for the anthrax letters?[36] One bone of contention among conspiracy theorists was whether Ivins had committed suicide or been secretly murdered. The day Ivins died, Frederick police detective Loumis Gene Alston began his investigation of Ivins' death.[37] On November 4, 2008, Detective Alston reported his conclusion that it was a suicide. Based on interviews with Ivins' wife and the hospital records, there seemed little doubt that Ivins meant to kill himself. Two empty packages of Tylenol PM had been found by the FBI in his trash, disposed of a day or so before his collapse. Yet Ivins' body had not been autopsied to rule out lingering suspicions; it had been cremated, following instructions. (In the summer of 2007, he added a requirement to his will: his wife had to make sure that after he died his body would be cremated—or $20,000 from his estate would go to her nemesis, Planned Parenthood.)

Guilty or innocent, Bruce Edward Ivins' torment had ended. By committing suicide, he spared himself and his family the shame of his standing in the dock accused of murder. If convicted, his name would have lived in infamy as a real-life Dr. Jekyll and Mr. Hyde, one who had threatened a nation already shaken by the 9/11 attacks. Despite the accusations against their father, Ivins' children remained steadfast in their devotion. On his Facebook page, Ivins' son, Andy, wrote, "I will miss you Dad. I love you and I can't wait to see you in Heaven. Rest in peace. It's finally over." On her page, Amanda Ivins also expressed her affection: "forever my hero, forever in my heart, forever my daddy. rest in peace I will always love you!!"

In addition, consistent with his selfless sense of service, Ivins had saved USAMRIID from the ordeal of a trial that, unprecedented in the history of national security or science, could have destroyed its image as a research institute capable of assuring protection against dangerous infectious diseases and monitoring its own employees. Had it for years, as the FBI case concluded, harbored a murderer? One could argue that Ivins, if guilty, had fooled nearly everyone, ingratiating himself like a true psychopath with colleagues and FBI investigators. But if not Ivins, had some other scientist with access to RMR-1029 done the same—fooled the authorities and, in so doing, demonstrated the precarious nature of biosecurity at Fort Detrick?

For those who had suffered because of the anthrax letters—they numbered in the thousands—Ivins also destroyed the hope that the FBI investigation would bring the closure of due legal process and, perhaps ultimately, justice for the crimes committed. Had he been indicted and stood trial, Ivins might have been acquitted—the case against him was less than airtight—but the criminal evidence against him would have been presented and deliberated. Instead, the victims were left with the same doubts and questions that arose in the early days of the anthrax crisis: Could their government protect them?

CONCLUSION

Surprise, when it happens to a government, is likely to be a complicated, diffuse, bureaucratic thing.

—NOBEL LAUREATE THOMAS SCHELLING, 1962

The fear generated by the 2001 anthrax letter attacks intensified federal resolve to fight terrorism. Yet the primary problem that the letters precipitated was distrust in government, especially in the realm of justice: a deadly bioterrorist attack had occurred without any legal retribution. After Bruce Ivins' death, the FBI considered the Amerithrax case closed, but critics would have none of it. Advocates for civilian biodefense and congressional leaders alike were skeptical about the evidence.[1] Conspiracy theorists saw international terrorist plots and al Qaeda connections they claimed the FBI had missed, intentionally or through incompetence. Others who had cherished Ivins as a colleague came out publicly to defend him against the humiliations inflicted by the investigation.[2]

Taken separately, some aspects of the FBI case evidence seemed far from decisive. The sale of the four federal eagle envelopes in Maryland, the location of the KKG office near the Princeton mailbox, Ivins' penchant for nocturnal drives, his multiple false identities, his anger against al Qaeda after 9/11, and the possible secret codes in the letters—all these were circumstantial, critics said, or unrelated to the letter attacks. Ivins' extended hours in his BSL-3 lab might have been just what he claimed, a respite from stress at home or maybe he had been checking up on mice used in an experiment—a time sheet had surfaced suggesting this justification. His cleanup of the December 2001 spore spill could have been what the JAG report assumed, that he innocently responded to failed biosafety measures during the handling of the Daschle letter. Maybe, despite their inquiries about "piggybacking" and other possible security violations at USAMRIID, the FBI had overlooked security breaches or been less than diligent in investigating other scientists with access to RMR-1029. Or, not included in the thousand-plus samples in the FBIR, another Ames culture possessed by terrorists contained the same morphotype signature as RMR-1029. As his lawyer pointed out, the FBI had no proof that Ivins had traveled to Princeton during those two crucial windows of time when the letters were mailed. Case investigators had found no anthrax spores in Ivins' cars or in his home. Was Ivins innocent or was he, from years of experience, both a master at handling spores and an expert in decontamination?

In response to critics, the Bureau attempted to make public the case evidence. On its Web site it posted thousands of pages of documents—emails, personal interviews, newspaper and journal articles—potentially incriminating Ivins, or not. Emails exposing his secret hostilities and obsessions were revelations of a troubled psyche, yet hardly evidence for murder. Many documents on the site were workaday emails about his preparing laboratory animals for research (twenty guinea pigs one day, forty rabbits another), angling for grants, preparing articles, or organizing anthrax conferences—he had particularly enjoyed a workshop held in 2003 in southern France. Visitors to the site could and did cherry-pick facts according to their own ideas about the investigation. By themselves the documents hardly affected the widespread reaction, reinforced by speculation in the national media and on the Internet, that the field evidence was inconclusive—not beyond a reasonable doubt.

The FBI's strongest suit was its science-based evidence—the "living proof" that had led the investigation to Ivins and the RMR-1029 flask in his charge. Feeling that these data deserved to be presented in detail in a legitimate public forum, rather than just an FBI press briefing, Paul Keim asked the American Society for Microbiology (ASM) to devote a plenary session to the subject at its February 2009 "Biodefense and Emerging Infectious Diseases Research" meeting, to be held in Baltimore. Initially, the society's program board was reluctant—why should the ASM be a showcase for the FBI investigation?[3] Keim replied that the purpose of the panel was simply to explicate the bioforensics side of the investigation, without drawing conclusions. The speakers agreed to voice no opinion about Ivins' guilt or innocence—to just stick to the science.

On February 23, 2009, to an audience of nearly a thousand scientists, the FBI's Jason Bannan, who had played a major role in overseeing the science behind the Amerithrax investigation, introduced the key players. Bannan, Paul Keim, and Jacques Ravel were already known from the FBI press briefing the previous August. Ravel's team at TIGR had tested the FBIR for the A1 and A3 morphotypes. Two newcomers joined the panel: Tom Reynolds from Commonwealth Biotechnologies in Richmond, Virginia, whose team tested for morph D in the collection, and Valorie Ryan from the Midwest Research Institute in Palm Bay, Florida, where morphotype E was tested. The PowerPoint shows began, starting with Keim on the Ames strain and moving on to stunning multicolored visuals of the signature morphotypes that identified the RMR-1029 samples. Each of the three scientists describing the search for the signature—Ravel, Reynolds, and Ryan—gave their personal accounts of what it was like to have FBI vans deliver high-security vials of Ames *B. anthracis* samples—and have not the slightest notion of what the other labs were finding. Until the August 18, 2008, briefing in Washington, in fact, none of them knew that the anthrax letter spores were from the RMR-1029 flask.[4]

After the morphotype presentations, Joe Michael from Sandia took the stage to present his physical-chemical analyses of the letter spores. In a series of striking photos, he took viewers inside the sample spores to reveal the composition of the interior layers, where silicon was present. For comparison, Michael included scans of other bacteria that also incorporate silicon within their spores—as random uptake from the environment. It had been frustrating for him to wait seven years to have his team's work made public, and especially difficult to keep silent as the silica controversy persisted unchecked.[5] In one of the many ironies of the Amerithrax investigation, information that might have swayed public opinion about Saddam's anthrax menace was held secret as evidence for a trial that never happened.

Michael's findings convinced two major proponents of the silica coating theory—USAMRIID virologist Peter Jahrling and journalist Gary Matsumoto—to change their minds. In addition to an earlier statement to the press, Jahrling took the microphone at the ASM meeting and affirmed Michael's research to the audience. Matsumoto, who was also at the meeting, waited until the press briefing afterward, when a critic challenged Michael's results. The dissenter was not alone. A contingent of about a dozen USAMRIID scientists, unhappy with the session, crowded at the open door to the small, windowless briefing room, and one young institute microbiologist, without a press pass, had wangled a seat inside. But the burly Matsumoto intervened with a raised hand. "No, his research stands," he said, indicating Michael, who stood tensely before the group, his back literally against the wall. "There's no coating."[6]

Michael appreciated Matsumoto's vote of confidence—his reputation and Sandia's depended on top-flight science. At that same press briefing, though, Paul Keim had to admit that the microbial analyses were incomplete. Once the Amerithrax case was closed, FBI funding stopped and this prevented, as Keim put it, "crossing the t's and dotting the i's the way we would have wanted."[7]

Senator Patrick Leahy, doubtful that Ivins acted alone, Representative Rush Holt, and others in Congress called for an independent evaluation of Amerithrax. In April 2009, to forestall a congressional investigation, the FBI contracted with the National Academy of Sciences for an independent panel of experts to review the scientific evidence. The sixteen members of the committee included Tom Inglesby, from the University of Pittsburgh Center for Biosecurity, where Tara O'Toole was director. Unlike other members, whose backgrounds were more academic and research-oriented, Inglesby had crossed swords with the FBI in 2002 when he and O'Toole circulated their memo to the effect that one of the al Qaeda operatives in Florida had cutaneous anthrax. (During the committee's inquiry, O'Toole became the Under Secretary for Science and Technology at the Department of Homeland Security, and Inglesby replaced her as the director at the Pittsburgh center.) Other committee members came from backgrounds as diverse as biochemistry, nuclear chemistry, physics, statistics, and jurisprudence.

Initially, the committee's dealings with the Bureau foundered on questions about the FBI's process of data collection, which evolved over time, as did the field of microbial forensics it was pioneering. The narrowness of their assignment also prevented committee members from knowing the extent to which the Bureau had checked the history of each FBI repository sample, reviewed lab records, and investigated the alibis of everyone with access to the Ames strain. On February 19, 2010, while the committee was still deliberating, the Department of Justice, the FBI, and the U.S. Postal Service officially declared that the case against Ivins was closed; simultaneously, the Department of Justice issued a report summarizing the Amerithrax investigation.[8] The summary, written by Justice staff, argued the case against Ivins beyond what the committee as a whole found supportable, based on the information it had been given. Its final report, released on February 15, 2011, concluded skeptically: "The results of the genetic analyses of the repository samples were consistent with the finding that the spores in the attack letters were derived from RMR-1029, but the analyses did not definitely demonstrate such a relationship."[9] For example, the signature morphotypes might have been present in other samples not included in the FBIR.

Although the evidence presented by Joe Michael and his colleagues at Sandia was left unchallenged, the committee report revived the possibility of a foreign source for the anthrax letter attacks. In the process of reviewing the FBI's science, its members asked for more information about its cooperation with the broader intelligence community during the investigation. Advised that the first draft of the NRC report was highly critical of Amerithrax methods, Director Mueller decided that transparency might improve the assessment. In December 2010, the Bureau supplied more than 600 pages of new material. Far from being fully appeased, the committee expressed its discontent with both the thoroughness of the FBI's scientific approach and the gaps in information about the investigative process overall—leaving the door open for a 9/11-type commission that members of Congress were proposing. In the NRC report, a skeptical allusion was made to the FBI investigation of the al Qaeda operative with the suspicious scab who had died in the crash of Flight 93. Note was also made that the FBI had not tested for anthrax in the remains of the terrorists in New York City and at the Pentagon. Another tantalizing reference was made to the al Qaeda hideout in Kandahar, which the CIA had identified as a prototype anthrax lab. Between May and November 2004, the FBI had conducted three missions there with no conclusive *B. anthracis* findings. Still, the committee urged that this testing should be explored in more detail.[10]

The report's skepticism generated headlines that faulted the Bureau's scientific case evidence and satisfied conspiracy theorists and believers in Ivins' innocence.[11] The *Frederick News-Post*, for example, ran the story under the banner, "Conclusion on Anthrax Origins Not Possible with Available Scientific Evidence."[12] From the perspective of those who had suffered from the letter attacks, the report was a step backward. As Dena Briscoe put it, "It opened old wounds, raised doubts and revived fears. The scientists, instead of offering a conclusion, have just asked more questions. They will go on to new projects, but we have to live with the uncertainty."[13] The killer might still be on the loose.

As a result of the investigation, questions were raised about whether USAMRIID and, by implication, the U.S. Army, could be trusted with safeguarding national security. Even if Ivins were innocent, his mental instability had made him unfit to work on virulent anthrax. The 2001 PATRIOT Act had specifically excluded anyone with a history of mental problems from access to select agents. Yet Ivins, with his long history of instability, was barred from high-containment research only in November 2007, when FBI search warrants were submitted to the USAMRIID commander.

In July 2009, a federal judge authorized an expert panel of behavioral analysts, most of them psychiatrists or psychologists, to review Ivins' unsealed mental health records, along with the FBI investigative files, to determine what lessons could be learned to prevent future bioterrorism attacks. The panel's report was published (with redactions) in 2011, shortly after the National Research Council report evaluating the FBI's science. In contrast to the NRC report, the expert panel unambiguously supported the FBI case against Ivins, finding in the materials it examined long-term, obsessive patterns of devious aggression—especially involving the KKG sorority and women—and proof of means and motivation.[14]

The report came down especially hard on the failure of USAMRIID authorities to detect Ivins' mental problems before the 2001 anthrax attacks, as well as their subsequent turning of a "blind eye" to his later breakdowns. A review of Ivins' sessions with a psychiatrist in Maryland just before he was hired by USAMRIID and, much later, his therapeutic record from 2000 to 2007 might have raised alarms about his secret crimes and misdemeanors: the KKG burglaries, his 1979 theft of Haigwood's lab notebook at the University of North Carolina, the 1982 Gaithersburg vandalism, and multiple anonymous deviant identities. Yet, just as he masked his worst problems at work—at his best, he was an intelligent, lively, humorous man—Ivins was selective in what he told his therapists. Not even his long-term psychiatrist Dr. Allan Levy connected Ivins' dangerous pathogen research to national security risks or saw him as violent.

If nothing else, the FBI case against Ivins showed USAMRIID officials that its approach to biosecurity was stuck in the Cold War of the 1980s, when the major threat was the Soviet Union and possible saboteurs, and the institute relied on patriotic group solidarity as its main guarantee of security. In the 2002 Bioterrorism Act, a new framework emphasizing the control of access to select agents was clearly delineated; across the board, from government labs to those in universities and industry, individuals had to be cleared. But the institute had obviously lagged in its adherence to the new regulations, remaining more protective of Ivins than was safe. There were also suggestions that its organizational culture had displayed the military tendency to dismiss psychological problems and substance abuse as shameful and weak, hence Ivins' concerted, stoic efforts to hide his mental anguish.

The case against Ivins aside, the strong evidence for the morphotype signature posed an undeniable problem for USAMRIID as it faced a future of interagency and commercial collaboration. A criminal—either Ivins or someone else—had used the institute's Ames anthrax spores to commit murder. Within the new National Interagency Biodefense Campus, USAMRIID would be cooperating closely with its new neighbors, the Department of Health and Human Services, the Department of Agriculture, and the Department of Homeland Security, to integrate research on troop defense with civilian defense projects. A dispersed network of individuals from different government sectors was already crossing institutional lines. (Peter Jahrling, for example, was now affiliated with NIAID, which had a branch on the Detrick campus.) Commercial partnerships were fundamental to the federal agenda, and a new generation of biodefense researchers was in the making; since 2002, over 12,000 of them had been cleared for access to select pathogens. In August 2009, at the groundbreaking ceremony for USAMRIID's new building, one of its spokesmen declared, "We can't support our fighting force if we don't protect the whole nation."[15] But could the institute protect the nation if it had allowed its WMD pathogens to be used by a terrorist?

Even though the Ivins case would never go to trial, U.S. Army officials at Detrick had to respond to its implications, especially to local citizens who were concerned that the new, grand-scale USAMRIID facility could pose a threat to their safety. Required by law to posit a worst-case biohazard scenario, in 2006 the institute had downplayed any risks that might be generated by its enormous expansion.[16] Optimistically, it hoped that Frederick County residents would agree and invited them for cookies and coffee and an update. The meeting went badly. Locals raised questions about waste management, the disposal of animal carcasses, water and air pollution, increased traffic, and the possibility of escaped infectious disease agents.[17] Above all, they wanted transparent project evaluations, with Frederick residents included in the process. In response, Army officials affirmed the institute's open mission and adherence to the 1972 Biological Weapons Convention and pointed to its safety committees and safety records. With the FBI known to be interrogating its laboratory scientists, USAMRIID acknowledged public concern about "the threat from disgruntled employees."[18] But it claimed that "each person who has access to BSAT [biological select agents and toxins] meets the highest standards of reliability."[19] In April 2008, urged by the Frederick County Commission, Senator Barbara Mikulski requested a National Research Council review of the new USAMRIID lab's risks to public safety.[20] That evaluation was still in process when Ivins committed suicide. To the local community, it seemed obvious that the institute had misled it.

Four months after Ivins' suicide, in December 2008, Detrick officials publicly announced tightened security screening of biodefense laboratory employees, equivalent to top-secret clearance. Borrowing from the nuclear weapons establishment, the measure incorporated into its mandate the term "personnel reliability"—the criteria of high integrity, patriotism, and mental, physical, and professional competence. In the nuclear weapons world, such standards act to deter sabotage or other malfeasance.[21] Only those who are emotionally stable and physically capable and who have demonstrated reliability (including sound finances), professional competence, and loyalty to the United States can be defense employees. Anyone who fails the standard is a potential threat to national security. For the first time, USAMRIID supervisors in charge of assessing employee performance would receive formal training to make them more aware of employees who might pose security threats. Major General Robert Lennox, the Army's point man for the announcement, expressed the goal: "In order to stay in this business, we have to ... change the culture of the scientists and the workers in the labs to be more vigilant after each other."[22]

Not addressed were the long-term problems: how the Army would balance secrecy against openness, mission dedication against scientific freedom, or, perhaps most important, civilian workforce commitment against future destabilizing changes in threat perception and funding. The new, larger, and younger cadre of microbiologists at Fort Detrick might have much lower expectations about institutional support than the older generation. Still the question remained: How would USAMRIID adjust to future change given its record of the past?

As critics noted, the Army's lack of vigilance regarding laboratory security had been nothing short of dangerous. Somehow, before the anthrax letter attacks, it lost control of spores from RMR-1029. For seven years after the letter attacks, until Bruce Ivins' suicide, USAMRIID seemed mired in adamant denial of its security problems. The identification of Ames strain spores in the letters, Ivins' unique control of RMR-1029, his considerable scientific skills, and his late-night pattern of solitary time in his lab just prior to the letter mailings—all these were facts of record, but what Army authority had taken account of them? In April 2002, through internal reports and then the JAG investigation, Ivins' superiors learned about the December 2001 anthrax cleanup episode and knew the details regarding contamination in his office. But, maintaining group solidarity, they gave him the benefit of the doubt, helped reward him with a medal for valorous service, and upon his death held a memorial service in his honor.

Reflecting on why disasters happen in government, Nobel Laureate Thomas Schelling described the problem of failed threat perceptions within bureaucracies:

> The danger is not that we shall read the signals and indicators with too little skill; the danger is in a poverty of expectations—a routine obsession with a few dangers that may be familiar rather than likely.[23]

This problem of institutional blindness was by no means unique to USAMRIID. There were FBI field agents and analysts who at first never suspected the institute staff could be the source of the letter attacks. In a world divided into "good guys" and "bad guys," anthrax scientists working for the U.S. Army were definitely the good guys. Most modern terrorists were young, foreign ideologues, lacking self-esteem and dependent on clandestine groups. The Amerithrax case inverted that model by proposing that an aging defense microbiologist, fearing exclusion, had used the lethal *B. anthracis* against U.S. civilians. For many at USAMRIID, the crime was unthinkable.

To move ahead, the Army was willing to improve surveillance in high-containment laboratories—with video cameras and a buddy system, but responsibility for the past could not be avoided. In Florida, in November 2009, Judge Daniel T. K. Hurley in Palm Beach ruled that the Stevens family's suit against the federal government, charging that the institute's negligent handling of its anthrax spores had created "a foreseeable zone of risk," could proceed to trial. Department of Justice lawyers soon arrived at Fort Detrick for serious talks with USAMRIID officials. Difficult as it was, the U.S. Army had to accept the validity of the FBI investigation: one arm of the federal government could not dispute another over the core issue of where the letters' spores originated. Justice lawyers might negotiate a settlement with the Stevens family or proceed to trial in defense of USAMRIID, but they could not repudiate the Bureau's case.

Every federal response to the 2001 anthrax attacks was meant to protect civilians. The November 2001 Frist-Kennedy Bioterrorism Preparedness Act set the agenda, requiring more federal assistance to state and local governments in the event of a biological attack, improvements in local institutional response, the rapid development of technical interventions—therapies, vaccines, and medical supplies—and the protection of the nation's food supplies and agriculture.[24] But the overall government approach to protecting Americans was based on the pursuit of technological solutions—not local institutional reinforcement. For a billion dollars, the smallpox vaccine supply for the national stockpile was increased to protect all 350 million Americans. The development of an effective, safe anthrax vaccine kept absorbing millions of dollars; it remained the Holy Grail of bacteriology that it had been in Bruce Ivins' youth and for years before. As an alternative to the

AVA vaccine, over a million doses of antibiotics were available through the stockpile, with the stocks continually updated and ready to deliver in hours anywhere in the nation.

To develop new medical interventions to protect Americans, the U.S. government began investing an average of $6 billion a year in civilian biodefense research and development, with much of that continuing to go to academic research centers through the National Institute of Allergy and Infectious Diseases.[25] In addition to this funding, the National Centers of Excellence and new Level 4 laboratories were the major biodefense investments. By 2008, the projected number of BSL-4 laboratories nationwide had increased to 15—a tripling of the pre-9/11 number—to conduct research on dangerous select agents or to serve as resources in an unusual disease outbreak. The number of Level 3 laboratories was certainly in the hundreds, but, in October 2007, an official from the General Accountability Office told Congress that, due to recent growth, no one federal agency could identify the exact number of approved BSL-3 laboratories in the United States.[26] The great scale and diversity of the biodefense enterprise posed obvious obstacles to oversight, which the CDC promised to improve with more in-depth inspections.[27] Some biodefense labs were small. Others were set in impressive new conglomerates. For example, in addition to the three BSL-3 laboratories adjacent to its BSL-4 laboratory, the University of Texas Medical Branch at Galveston maintained an additional 21 BSL-3 labs in the surrounding medical complex.[28]

The more the biodefense research initiative expanded, the more questions arose about the risks that it posed to American health and safety—not from insider terrorism, although that could be a threat—but from accidents and safety violations involving dangerous pathogen research and the reluctance of institutions to be totally transparent about possible hazards.[29] In 2004, the accidental distribution of virulent anthrax (originally obtained from USAMRIID) to an institute at an Oakland, California, hospital resulted in the exposure of unprotected researchers.[30] In late August 2005, Hurricane Katrina flooded the Galveston complex, forcing its scientists to evacuate and leave their deadly microbes behind for days; its officials assured the public that no harm was caused. In July 2007, the CDC suspended all select agent research at Texas A&M University after two unreported accidents there exposed lab workers to infectious diseases.[31] In September 2009, a sixty-year-old University of Chicago geneticist researching a new vaccine for plague died of the disease after being accidentally infected in his laboratory.[32]

In the high-alert national security atmosphere that followed 9/11 and the anthrax letters, most biodefense research projects got a free pass. Over time, with a growing awareness of the risks that high-containment laboratory research might pose, the restraints on new facilities increased. In Boston, local community activists fought having a BSL-4 laboratory in the city's densely populated South End, a project approved in 2003 by the National Institutes of Health. In 2011, the project remained stalled. The risk scenarios that Boston University Medical Center had submitted as part of the required environmental impact statement had been rejected in two court decisions and by a National Academy panel of experts.[33] Another National Academy panel gave thumbs down to a planned Level 4 high-containment laboratory for large animal research in Kansas. Critics pointed out that since roughly 9.5 percent of the U.S. cattle industry was within a 200-mile radius of the planned facility, an accidental release of the highly contagious foot-and-mouth disease could be economically devastating, in the billions of dollars.[34] The bad news about laboratory risks, circulating by Internet to towns and cities adjacent to high-containment biodefense facilities, produced a new kind of community activism and unified calls for more transparency and safety guarantees. From Frederick to Boston to towns in California, North Carolina, and Washington State, citizens expressed their concern about health and environmental hazards if dangerous pathogens were suddenly to escape, by accident or deliberate malice.[35]

Throughout the biodefense research enterprise, what stood out was the erratic definition and implementation of biosecurity measures—every institution had its own rules and organizational culture. In military style, USAMRIID could top-down impose personnel reliability measures, but the academic centers, where much of the funding for select pathogen research was going, resisted deep background checks and surveillance.[36] In 2010, only one government agency, the Department of Homeland Security, had a comprehensive oversight policy, called the Compliance Review Group, that made an independent committee and principal investigators responsible for keeping projects safe and legal and also required site visits.[37] Other institutions, including USAMRIID, relied on internal review.

Another problem was the potential growth of secrecy around biodefensive projects. As the troop defense mission expanded to the civilian defense mission, so too did presentiments that the once open, beneficent areas of microbiology were turning to secret or "sensitive" research, a trend that most microbiologists disdained.[38] Historically the line between defensive and offensive research in this area has been difficult to control, especially when scientists are drawn into great national projects in the name of national defense.[39] Theodore Rosebury, the man who for all practical purposes invented the U.S. biological weapons program in 1942, commented later that if scientists concern themselves with nothing but unnatural disease—pathogens in forms that have been selected or designed for maximum virulence— then they become used to the ways in which, as Rosebury put it, bacteriology can be turned upside down for destructive ends.[40] Imagining the weapons advantage that a foreign enemy might pursue can drive defensive research, but in those imaginings, new germ weapons were pioneered in the past and could be in the future.

The post-October 2001 mission to combat bioterrorism had a profound impact on the Centers for Disease Control and the federal concept of public health. The CDC, after absorbing much of the responsibility for emergency bioterrorism response during the anthrax crisis, changed from a national public health institution with relatively free access to a high-security agency geared to emergency response and increasingly answerable to Washington. At its traditional base on Clifton Road in Atlanta, the CDC's heavily guarded new entrance was the size of a small airport terminal, complete with identity checks and electronic package scanners. By 2008, its main campus boasted a second Level 4 laboratory and it had two "command central" briefing rooms wired for emergency White House communication. Its misunderstandings about anthrax dose response were in the past. Its Web site offered information on the history, diagnosis, and treatment of the disease and how clinical samples should be prepared for analysis, in cooperation with the Laboratory Response Network. It had increased its staff on the alert for bioterrorism, and the modeling of unusual disease outbreaks was growing sophisticated. CDC officials were unlikely ever again to underestimate the risks of exposure to any dangerous pathogen.

Some analysts approved of what they called the "militarization" of the CDC.[41] Its ability to collect and analyze statistical information remained a major strength—if its organizational structure was more centralized and corporate, so much the better. Still, others in public health worried about the resources for preventive health care—prenatal checkups, early intervention for diabetes and obesity, HIV/AIDS, and children's vaccinations—which vary widely from one state to another. During the anthrax crisis and the 2003 smallpox campaign, public health services had been interrupted, increasing disease rates. Would those breakdowns occur again? There were questions, too, about the next generation of local public health officers, physicians dedicated to serving in the trenches, yet capable of the kind of leadership that Jean Malecki, George DiFerdinando, Eddy Bresnitz, Marci Layton, and others demonstrated during that tumultuous October of 2001. Could hard-pressed states and cities afford them? Could they afford to do without them?

In a different realm, that of basic research, the National Institute of Allergy and Infectious Diseases had created a large, decentralized network, its Centers of Excellence and their offshoots. A wise steward, director Tony Fauci had followed through on his commitment to divide the funding of biodefense projects with support for countering emerging and re-emerging infectious diseases and also for broad-spectrum biomedical solutions. Time had favored a practical, globally oriented assessment of disease risks. By 2010, $961 million of NIAID's biodefense budget was being invested in research on AIDS, SARS, drug-resistant tuberculosis, malaria, influenza, and other known scourges, with $466 million allotted for projects on select agents. Another $252 million was allocated to what Fauci called "cross-functional research," that is, discovering defenses against entire categories of bacteria, viruses, and other infective organisms.[42] If one took the view that the constantly changing microbial world poses major threats to the health of people worldwide—whether from deliberate or accidental outbreaks or those that we call natural—there was little to fault in NIAID's definition of biodefense.

The sense that we are in an age of rapid technological advance permeated all the new federal efforts to defend the nation against bioterrorism. The Department of Homeland Security, for example, turned to technical surveillance as its antidote to bioterrorism. Its BioWatch program used air sensors to monitor thirty U.S. cities and other target areas for possible germ attacks or unusual pathogens; the department also coordinated input on attack alarms from twelve different federal agencies. One of them was the U.S. Postal Service, which installed real-time BDS (Biohazard Detection Systems) based on PCR analysis in over a hundred facilities nationwide. BioWatch was a part of the comprehensive DHS system inaugurated in September 2008 to integrate clinical data—the early detection of disease—with intelligence data about suspected biological attacks. As former Secretary of Homeland Security Michael Chertoff put it, "In a very real way, intelligence is a critical element in promoting public health in the twenty-first century."[43] The more we know about select agents—how to detect them, how to defend against them, how to cure the infections they can cause—the safer we will be.

From the FBI to the CDC and DHS, military-style intelligence models based on the rapid, high-tech acquisition and analysis of data were being used to forestall the bioterrorism threat. The Bureau forged ahead with microbial forensics to investigate possible attacks in the context of its improved electronic communications and partnerships with the intelligence community. The CDC and the FBI developed a standard protocol for joint bioterrorism response, complete with more advanced methods for environmental and clinical tests and for surveillance. In 2009, for example, the CDC quickly tracked the global spread of H1N1, the "swine flu" that erupted in Mexico and soon invaded the United States. Although it usually caused only mild symptoms, it was related to the 1918 flu that had killed millions, and it could mutate into a more virulent form; infants and school-age children were at special risk.

The 2001 anthrax attacks showed the importance of public health readiness, as well as follow-up with those affected. But every sudden outbreak seems different. After the CDC and the World Health Organization declared an H1N1 pandemic in June 2009, the vaccine supply and local organizational response in the United States could not meet demand. Anxious parents lined up at drug stores, and physicians and health care providers were caught up in the chaos. Fortunately, the pandemic proved even less dangerous than ordinary flu cycles. Then, further eroding trust, an international controversy broke out about whether the WHO and CDC had been influenced by pharmaceutical companies that profited from the stockpiling of vaccines and drugs.[44] Learning about disease on the Internet and involved in virtual communities through Facebook and Twitter, the public has been largely educating itself on threat assessments.

In 2009, with a new president, Washington's primary defense against bioterrorism, as against terrorism in general, remained intelligence.[45] President Barack Obama's first policy statement addressing the bioterrorism issue posited that fanatics who seek "to harm free societies" were the world's greatest threat, and that "enhanced intelligence to thwart bioterrorist incidents" was the best approach to countering it. If bioterrorist attacks should occur, effective criminal investigation and prosecution were the next goals.[46]

The Obama strategy went further than the previous administration's to make the bioterrorism problem a global "health security" issue, but it simultaneously de-emphasized the potential role of state-sponsored weapons, and thereby rejected any pursuit of international monitoring under the auspices of the Biological Weapons Convention. The foreign terrorist remained the unshakable image of what Americans had to fear, and thus the rationale for civilian biodefense stood firm.

In December 2009, Ellen Tauscher, Obama's Under Secretary for Arms Control and International Security, went to Geneva and told the representatives of the states party to the Convention why bioterrorism demanded international cooperation. Such an attack in any of the world's cities, she explained, would cause as much death, economic damage, and psychological harm as a nuclear event—the world community was at risk. The U.S. congressional representative from California's tenth district when the Daschle letter was opened on October 15, 2001, she offered the conclusion that she and others in Washington had drawn from the anthrax letter attacks:

> Years later, no one has been brought to justice and it appears that a single person may have perpetrated these attacks. This underscores the fact that significant capabilities for harm are already available to small groups and individuals and the prospect of bioterrorism represents a growing risk for the global community. Already we have

seen terrorist groups like Al Qa'ida seek biological materials and expertise in order to conduct a biological attack.

American policy has for ten years and more been fixated on the
idea of foreign bioterrorism—almost as if no greater threat to national
health existed. An evaluation of the entire biodefense initiative is
due, not necessarily because it is extravagantly out of proportion to
known threats—which is likely—but because it prevents us from
moving beyond a "war on terror" mentality to more positive policies.
In writing about terrorism in 1998, Harvard law professor and former U.S. Deputy Attorney General Philip Heymann cautioned:

> One of the great dangers of terrorism in every democracy
> is that it may lead, as is often intended by the terrorists, to
> self-destructive actions. We must learn never to react to
> the limited violence of small groups by launching a crusade
> in which we destroy our unity or our trust in the fairness
> and restraint of the institutions of the U.S. government
> that control legitimate force.[47]

The caution was ignored after 9/11, perhaps because the nation was
caught so off-guard. Americans hardly guessed then that the September 11 terrorists would strike or that the nation's sense of vulnerability
would be amplified by anthrax letters. The expanded use of military
force abroad has led to scorching criticisms of the perpetual war
against terrorism and its ruinous cost in dollars and in trust in government.[48] Yet there is no turning away from the threat of terrorism or
from that of bioterrorism. The challenge lies in defining the means to
the end of national security that reinforces public confidence and
dispels cynicism. Specifically for bioterrorism, the difficulties lie in
understanding the different cultures of defense research institutions
regarding morale and mental health; in standardizing the norms of
oversight and accountability in select agent research, not just nationally but internationally; and in aligning biodefense measures more
prudently with public health goals and resources.

The history of biological weapons—and of lethal infectious
diseases—will continue, with threat perceptions and government priorities certain to shift and change. Eventually the perpetual war that has

supported the biodefense initiative will wind down, especially under economic pressures that force federal budget cuts. In this time of transition, our hope must be that the standards for public protection will be consistently high and that fanatics, whatever their beliefs, are prevented from using the life sciences—a source of pride and hope—to cause harm. If they succeed, one can only hope that investigators will use all possible legitimate resources—from old-fashioned technology to bioforensics, from personality assessments to sophisticated group analysis and intelligence—to achieve swift justice. The victims—they could be any of us—and society deserve no less.

NOTES

Author's Note

1. France, Japan, the United Kingdom, the United States, and the Soviet Union all invested in anthrax weapons. Jeanne Guillemin, *Biological Weapons: From the Invention of State-sponsored Programs to Contemporary Bioterrorism* (New York: Columbia University Press, 2005).

2. Sheldon Harris, *Factories of Death: Japanese Biological Warfare, 1932–1945, and the American Cover-Up* (New York: Routledge, 2002); Jeanne Guillemin, "Imperial Japan's Germ Warfare: The Suppression of Evidence at the Tokyo War Crime Tribunal, 1946–1948," in *Terrorism, War, or Disease?: Unraveling the Use of Biological Weapons*, ed. Anne L. Clunan, Peter R. Lavoy, and Susan B. Martin (Stanford, Calif.: Stanford University Press, 2008), 165–85.

3. Matthew Meselson, Jeanne Guillemin, Martin Hugh-Jones, Alexander Langmuir, et al., "The Sverdlovsk Outbreak of 1979," *Science* 266/5188 (1994): 1202–8; Jeanne Guillemin, *Anthrax: The Investigation of a Deadly Outbreak* (Berkeley: University of California Press, 1999).

4. Veterinarian Martin Hugh-Jones, quoted in Delthia Ricks, "Scientists Hope to Track Anthrax to Its Origin," *Newsday*, October 11, 2001.

5. Early on, dozens of journalists covered the anthrax crisis. At the *Washington Post*, Marilyn Thompson offered a book-length account, *The Killer Strain: Anthrax and a Government Exposed* (New York: HarperCollins, 2003); see also Leonard A. Cole, *The Anthrax Letters: A Medical Detective Story* (Washington, D.C.: John Henry Press, 2003). In his book on the smallpox threat, Richard Preston interwove a narrative of the 2001 anthrax crisis, *The Demon in the Freezer* (New York: Random House, 2002); and Robert Graysmith dramatized the early phase of the investigation in *Amerithrax: The Hunt for the Anthrax Killer* (New York: Jove Books, 2002). One of my overviews of the letter attacks appears in *Biological Weapons: From the Invention of State-sponsored Programs to Contemporary Bioterrorism* (New York: Columbia University Press, 2005), 172–78; another is "The Deliberate Release of Anthrax Spores through the United States Postal System," in *Public Health Response*

to Biological and Chemical Weapons: WHO Guidance (Geneva: World Health Organization, 2004), 98–108. Ed Lake's self-published book, *Analyzing the Anthrax Attacks: The First Three Years* (2005), based on his Web site; http://anthraxinvestigation.com, deserves special mention for its data gathering and review.

Prologue: The Bioterrorism Threat

1. Sinclair Lewis, *Arrowsmith* (New York: New American Library edition, 2008), 120.
2. John Ezzell interview, May 28, 2009, Frederick, Md. The first choice was Susan Welkos, who was hired a year later and became Ivins' research collaborator.
3. After 1969, 70 acres of the base was allotted to a branch of the National Cancer Institute and Detrick's new tenants included sub-offices of the Defense Intelligence Agency, the U.S. Army Signal Command (which maintained the Washington-Moscow "hot line"), the U.S. Army Reserve, the Army's Medical Materiel Agency, which oversaw USAMRIID, and the Department of Agriculture. On weapons defense enclaves, see Hugh Gusterson, *Nuclear Rites: A Weapons Laboratory at the End of the Cold War* (Los Angeles: University of California Press, 1998).
4. Maxime Schwartz, "Dr. Jekyll and Mr. Hyde: A Short History of Anthrax," *Molecular Aspects of Medicine* 30 (2009): 347–55.
5. Susan Welkos, Arthur Friedlander, Patricia Worsham, and Stephen Little, "Bruce Edward Ivins" [obituary], *Microbe*, November 2008; http://forms.asm.org/microbe/index.asp?bid=61457.
6. Robert Kadlec interview, June 2, 2009, Washington, D.C.
7. Daryl J. Kelly, Jeffrey D. Chulay, Perry Mikesell, and Arthur M. Friedlander, "Serum Concentrations of Penicillin, Doxycycline, and Ciprofloxacin during Prolonged Therapy in Rhesus Monkeys," *Journal of Infectious Diseases* 166/5 (1992): 1184–87; Arthur M. Friedlander, Susan L. Welkos, Margaret L. M. Pitt, John W. Ezzell, Patricia Worsham, Kenneth J. Rose, Bruce E. Ivins, John R. Lowe, Gerald B. Howe, Perry Mikesell, and Wade B. Lawrence, "Postexposure Prophylaxis against Experimental Inhalational Anthrax," *Journal of Infectious Diseases* 167/5 (1993): 1239–43.
8. Jack Dolan and Dave Altimari, "Anthrax Missing from Army Lab," *Hartford Courant*, January 20, 2002. These two journalists broke the story of the 1992 U.S. Army inquiry into these problems.
9. U.S. Court of Appeals for the Fourth Circuit, *Kulthoum A. Mereish v. Robert M. Walker* (No. 02-2366), *Ayaad Assaad v. Louis Caldera* (No. 02-2367), and *Richard D. Crosland v. Louis Caldera* (No. 02-2369), February 20, 2004.
10. David Franz interview, May 27, 2009, Frederick, Md.
11. Gary Matsumoto, "The Pentagon's Toxic Secret," *Vanity Fair*, May 1999, 82–98; *Vaccine-A: The Covert Government Experiment That's Killing Our Soldiers and Why GIs Are Only the First Victims* (New York: Basic Books, 2004), 53–54.
12. Anthony H. Cordesman, *Terrorism, Asymmetrical Warfare, and Weapons of Mass Destruction* (New York: Praeger, 2001); Jeanne Guillemin, "Inventing Bioterrorism: The Political Construction of Civilian Risk," in *Making Threats: Biofears and Environmental Anxieties*, ed. Betsy Hartmann, Banu Subramaniam, and Charles Zerner (New York: Rowman & Littlefield, 2005), 197–216.
13. Daniel Benjamin and Steven Simon, *The Age of Sacred Terror* (New York: Random House, 2002), 230.
14. Lawrence Wright, *The Looming Tower: Al Qaeda and the Road to 9/11* (New York: Vintage, 2006), 233–35. The author notes, "In the web of federal agencies concerned with terrorism, Clarke was the spider" (p. 233).

15. Department of Justice, *Five-Year Interagency Counterterrorism and Technology Crime Plan*, September 1999, 1–3.
16. The 1996 Defense Against Weapons of Mass Destruction Act established the Domestic Preparedness Program.
17. Guy Oakes, *The Imaginary War: Civil Defense and American Cold War Culture* (New York: Oxford University Press, 1994), 78–129.
18. Graham S. Pearson, *The Search for Iraq's Weapons of Mass Destruction: Inspection, Verification and Non-Proliferation* (New York: Palgrave Macmillan, 2005), 210–21.
19. Cordesman, *Terrorism*, 270.
20. Rosabeth Moss Kanter, *Men and Women of the Corporation* (New York: Basic Books, 1993), 164–205.
21. Judith Miller, Stephen Engelberg, and William Broad, *Germs: Biological Weapons and America's Secret War* (New York: Simon & Schuster, 2001), 223–34.
22. Paul Jackson, M. Hugh-Jones, D. M. Adair, G. Green, K. K. Hill, L. M. Grinberg, F. A. Abramova, and P. Keim, "PCR Analysis of Tissue Samples from the 1979 Sverdlovsk Anthrax Victims: The Presence of Multiple *Bacillus anthracis* in Different Victims," *Proceedings of the National Academy of Sciences of the United States of America* 95 (1998): 1224–29.
23. Ken Alibek with Stephen Handelman, *Biohazard: The Chilling True Story of the Largest Covert Biological Program in the World—Told from the Inside by the Man Who Ran It* (New York: Random House, 1999).
24. D. A. Henderson, *Smallpox—The Death of a Disease: The Inside Story of Eradicating a Worldwide Killer* (Amherst, N.Y.: Prometheus Books, 2009), 22–24.
25. Elizabeth Fee and Theodore M. Brown, "Preemptive Biopreparedness: Can We Learn Anything from History?" *American Journal of Public Health* 91/5 (May 2001): 721–26; Elizabeth W. Etheridge, *Sentinel for Health: A History of the Centers for Disease Control* (Berkeley: University of California Press, 1992), 41–42.
26. Berton Roueché, *The Medical Detectives* (New York: Plume/Talley, 1988). Between 1954 and 1984, Roueché published nine books on medical detection, with many stories provided by the CDC's Alexander Langmuir, founder of EIS.
27. Thomas V. Inglesby, Donald A. Henderson, John G. Bartlett, Michael S. Ascher, et al., "Anthrax as a Biological Weapon: Medical and Public Health Management," *JAMA (Journal of the American Medical Association)* 281/22 (1999): 1735–45; Donald A. Henderson, Thomas V. Inglesby, John G. Bartlett, Michael S. Ascher, et al., "Smallpox as a Biological Weapon: Medical and Public Health Management," *JAMA* 281/22 (1999): 2127–37. With essentially the same team of about 20 collaborating authors, led by its staff, the center went on to publish three more articles in the series: Thomas V. Inglesby, David T. Dennis, Donald A. Henderson, John G. Bartlett, et al., "Plague as a Biological Weapon: Medical and Public Health Management," *JAMA* 283/17 (2000): 2281–90; Stephen S. Arnon, Robert Schechter, Thomas V. Inglesby, Donald A. Henderson, et al., "Botulinum Toxin as a Biological Weapon: Medical and Public Health Management," *JAMA* 285/8 (2001): 1059–70; and David T. Dennis, Thomas V. Inglesby, Donald A. Henderson, John B. Bartlett, et al., "Tularemia as a Biological Weapon: Medical and Public Health Management," *JAMA* 285/21 (2001): 2763–73.
28. Amy E. Smithson and Leslie-Anne Levy, *Ataxia: The Chemical and Biological Terrorism Threat and the US Response* (Washington, D.C.: Henry L. Stimson Center, 2000).
29. Miller, Engelberg, and Broad, *Germs*, 216–17.
30. Victor Sidel, Meryl Nass, and Todd Ensign, "The Anthrax Dilemma," *Medicine*

and Global Security 2/5 (1998): 97–104; Institute of Medicine, *Anthrax Vaccine: Does It Work? Is It Safe?* (Washington, D.C.: National Academy Press, 2002).

31. Jeanne Guillemin, "Medical Risks and the Volunteer Army," in *Anthropology and the United States Military: Coming of Age in the Twenty-First Century,* ed. Pamela Frese and Margaret Harrell (New York: Palgrave, 2003), 29–48.

32. Arthur M. Friedlander, Philip R. Pittman, and Gerald W. Parker, "Anthrax Vaccine: Evidence for Safety and Efficacy Against Inhalational Anthrax," *JAMA* 282/22 (1999): 2104–6.

33. Leonard A. Cole, "Risk of Publicity about Bioterrorism: Anthrax Hoaxes and Hype," *American Journal of Infection Control* 27 (December 1999): 470–73.

34. W. Seth Carus, *Bioterrorism and Biocrimes: The Illicit Use of Biological Agents Since 1900* (Washington, D.C.: Center for Counterproliferation Research, National Defense University, 2002), 170.

35. Ezzell interview, May 28, 2009.

36. Miller, Engelberg, and Broad, *Germs,* 240–41.

37. The United States Department of Justice, *Amerithrax Investigative Summary.* Friday, February 19, 2010; http://www.justice.gov/amerithrax/docs/amx-investigative-summary.pdf, 39.

38. Jim Dwyer and Kevin Flynn, *102 Minutes: The Untold Story of the Fight to Survive Inside the Twin Towers* (New York: Henry Holt, 2005); Charles B. Stozier, *Until the Fires Stopped Burning: 9/11 and New York City* (New York: Columbia University Press, 2011).

39. Alfred Goldberg, Sarandis Papadopoulos, Diane Putney, Nancy Berlage, and Rebecca Welch, *Pentagon 9/11* (Washington, D.C.: Office of the Secretary of Defense, 2007).

40. Wayne Barrett and Dan Collins, *Grand Illusion: The Untold Story of Rudy Giuliani and 9/11* (New York: HarperCollins, 2006), 16.

41. Frederick Police Department, "Supplemental Report," Incident Date 7/27/2008, OCA 2008044096 Review of American Red Cross Records, November 4, 2008@1046hrs, 1–5.

1. The Diagnosis

1. Ernesto Blanco interview, April 21, 2009, West Palm Beach, Fla.

2. These and other details were provided by Maureen Stevens in email correspondence with the author, January 19–28, 2010.

3. Jean Malecki interviews, April 18, 2009, and May 15, 2010, West Palm Beach, Fla.; Larry Bush interview, April 16, 2009, Atlantis, Fla.

4. Jean Malecki, personal communication, March 19, 2009.

5. Tanja Popovic interview, April 2, 2009, Atlanta, Ga.

6. Governor Jeb Bush interview, November 17, 2010, Cambridge, Mass.

7. Amanda Riddle, "Area Man Infected with Anthrax in Critical Condition," Associated Press, October 5, 2001.

8. Ari Fleischer, *Taking the Heat: The President, the Press, and My Years at the White House* (New York: William Morrow, 2005), 190–91.

9. Jane Mayer, *The Dark Side: The Inside Story of How the War on Terror Turned into a War on American Ideals* (New York: Doubleday, 2008), 2–4.

10. P. S. Brachman, S. A. Plotkin, F. H. Bumford, and M. M. Atchison, "An Epidemic of Inhalation Anthrax: The First in the Twentieth Century," *American Journal of Hygiene* 72 (1960): 6–23. The five reported cases were against a background of 141 cutaneous cases reported from 1941 through 1957.

11. Yudhijit Bhattacharjee, "Paul Keim on His Life with the FBI During the Anthrax Investigation," *Science* 323/5920 (March 13, 2009): 1416.

12. Paul Keim interview, December 8, 2009, Washington, D.C.

13. Doug Beecher interview, May 28, 2010, Washington, D.C.

14. Richard A. Falkenrath, Robert D. Newman, and Bradley A. Thayer, *America's Achilles' Heel: Nuclear, Biological, and Chemical Terrorism and Covert Attack* (Cambridge, Mass.: MIT Press, 1998), 9.

15. As an example, the 1984 Tylenol murders in Chicago—seven people died randomly from cyanide-laced tablets—had not been solved.

2. The Crime

1. CDC Office of Communication, "Update on Anthrax Investigations with Dr. Bradley Perkins," November 2, 2001; http://cmbi.bjmu.edu.cn/news/0111/8.htm.

2. Jean-Marie Maillard, Marc Fischer, Kelly T. McKee Jr., Lou F. Turner, and J. Steven Cline, "First Case of Bioterrorism-Related Inhalational Anthrax, Florida, 2001: North Carolina Investigation," *Emerging Infectious Diseases* 8/10 (2002): 1035–38.

3. Brad Perkins interview, April 2, 2009, Atlanta, Ga.

4. These and other reactions of Ivins to ongoing events are recorded in FBI Amerithrax interviews, case #279A-WF-222936-BEI.

5. John Ezzell interview, May 26, 2010, Frederick, Md.

6. Richard Preston, *The Demon in the Freezer* (New York: Random House, 2002), 7; Sherif Zaki interview, April 2, 2009, Atlanta, Ga.

7. Marc S. Traeger, Steven T. Wiersma, Nancy E. Rosenstein, Jean M. Malecki, et al., "First Case of Bioterrorism-Related Inhalational Anthrax in the United States, Palm Beach County, Florida, 2001," *Emerging Infectious Diseases* 8/10 (October 2002): 1029–34, 1031.

8. Ernesto Blanco interview, April 21, 2009, West Palm Beach, Fla.

9. David Pecker, personal communication to author, June 22, 2009.

10. Marc S. Trager et al., "First Case," 1032.

11. CNN.com, "Third Person Shows Exposure to Anthrax," October 10, 2001.

12. Delthia Ricks, "Scientists Hope to Track Anthrax to Its Origin," *Newsday*, October 11, 2001.

13. Paul Lamartire and Meghan Meyer, "Handling of Probe Angers Workers," *Palm Beach Post*, October 12, 2001.

14. Antigone Barton and Scott McCabe, "Scares from Powder, Threats Ensnare Entire Region," *Palm Beach Post*, October 13, 2001; Antigone Barton and Dani Davies, "Reports Snowball of Anthrax That Isn't," *Palm Beach Post*, October 16, 2001.

15. Chuck McGinness, "Officials: Tabloids No Health Threat," *Palm Beach Post*, October 11, 2001.

16. "NBC News Employee Tests Positive for Anthrax Exposure," http://transcripts.cnn.com/TRANSCRIPTS/0110/12/bn.08.html.

17. Kathy Nellis and Kay Golan, "Anthrax Anniversary Reaffirms CDC's Hard Work and Health Mission," *Inside Story*, October 5, 2004, 2; http://intranet.cdc.gov/ecp/insidestory.asp?stlD=164.

3. New York

1. Joel Akelsberg email, April 16, 2010.

2. Brigitte L. Nacos, *Mass-Mediated Terrorism: The Central Role of the Media in Terrorism and Counterterrorism* (Lanham, Md.: Rowman & Littlefield, 2007), 65.

3. "Newsweek Poll: Americans Fear Biological Attacks," *Newsweek*, September 29,

2001. "The poll shows that 85 percent think the use of such weapons is at least somewhat likely"; http://www.newsweek.com/2001/09/28/newsweek-poll-americans -fear-biological-attacks.html.

4. Michael Isikoff and David Korn, *Hubris: The Inside Story of Spin, Scandal, and the Selling of the Iraq War* (New York: Crown, 2006), 120–24.

5. Layton participated as a co-author in four of the five Johns Hopkins consensus group articles on biological weapons, but not the one on anthrax.

6. Interview with Marci Layton and Don Weiss, May 4, 2009, New York City; follow-up email correspondence, April 16, 2010; Don Weiss and Marci Layton, "Eschar: The Story of the New York City Department of Health 2001 Anthrax Investigation," in *Outbreak Investigations Around the World: Case Studies in Infectious Disease Field Epidemiology*, ed. Mark S. Dworkin (Sudbury, Mass.: Jones and Bartlett, 2009), 291–321.

7. Casey Chamberlain, "My Anthrax Survivor's Story," September 19, 2006, NBC News; http://www.msnbc/msn.com/id/14785359/.

8. Jeannette Guarner, John A. Jernigan, Wun-Ju Shieh, Kathleen Tati, et al., "Pathology and Pathogenesis of Bioterrorism-Related Inhalational Anthrax," *American Journal of Pathology* 163/2 (2003): 701–7.

9. Laurie Garrett, "The Anthrax Crisis," *Newsday*, October 8, 2002.

10. Quoted in Marilyn Thompson, *The Killer Strain: Anthrax and a Government Exposed* (New York: HarperCollins, 2003), 102.

11. Judith Miller, Stephen Engelberg, and William Broad, *Germs: Biological Weapons and America's Secret War* (New York: Simon & Schuster, 2001), 142.

12. Wayne Barrett and Dan Collins, *Grand Illusion: The Untold Story of Rudy Giuliani and 9/11* (New York: HarperCollins, 2006), 288. At this time, Giuliani was a national hero, despite the city's organizational failures before and after 9/11 that the authors describe.

13. CNN News, "Giuliani Gives Press Conference on Woman Infected with Anthrax," October 12, 2001.

14. Sanjay Bhatt, "Anthrax Probe Focuses on Mail," *Palm Beach Post*, October 13, 2001.

15. Weiss and Layton, "Eschar," 304–5.

16. Associated Press, "Brokaw Says NBC News Still Shaken," October 15, 2001.

17. Weiss and Layton, "Eschar," 303.

18. William C. Patrick, *Risk Assessment of Biological Warfare Primary and Secondary Aerosols and Their Requirements for Decontamination*, SAIC (Science Applications International Corporation), February 1999, 3.

19. Ibid., 2.

20. H. N. Glassman, "Discussion," *Bacteriologic Review* 30 (1966): 657–59.

21. Lorry G. Rubin, "Bacterial Colonization and Infection Resulting from a Multiplication of a Single Organism," *Reviews of Infectious Diseases* 9/3 (May–June 1987): 488–93. Rubin cites studies going back to 1954. Small doses are definitely not safe.

22. B. Kournikakis, S. J. Armour, C. A. Boulet, M. Spence, and B. Parsons, *Risk Assessment of Anthrax Threat Letters*, Defence Research Establishment Suffield, Technical Report TR-2001-048. One version in English (lacking any French translation) was approved and distributed on September 20, 2001. The full bilingual version was approved on October 4, 2001. The DRES team reduced the amount of material in later tests to one-tenth of a gram and still achieved similar dispersion results.

23. Dr. Camille Boulet, email to Richard Meyer, CDC, January 12, 2001. Subject: Laboratory Response Network.

24. Stephen A. Morse interview, May 30, 2009, Atlanta, Ga.

25. Kournikakis et al., *Risk Assessment*, 13.

26. The full list of authors on the anthrax article is as follows: Thomas V. Inglesby, Donald A. Henderson, John G. Bartlett, Michael S. Ascher, Edward Eitzen (then USAMRIID commander), Arthur Friedlander, Jerome Hauer (then a Washington consultant, formerly with Mayor Giuliani as a counter-terrorism expert), Joseph McDade, Michael T. Osterholm (an environmental scientist from the University of Minnesota), Tara O'Toole, Gerald Parker (a former USAMRIID commander), Trish M. Perl, Philip K. Russell (another former Army medical commander), and Kevin Tonat.

27. CNN.com, "New Anthrax Exposure in New York," October 14, 2001; Jonathan Tucker interview, "Plague Fears," Salon.com, October 9, 2001.

28. Before 2001, CDC phrasing was: "Inhalation anthrax results from the inspiration of 8,000–50,000 spores of *B. anthracis*." Brad Perkins, David A. Ashford, and Lisa D. Rotz, "Use of Anthrax Vaccine in the United States. Recommendations of the Advisory Committee on Immunization Practices (ACIP)," *Morbidity and Mortality Weekly Report* 49/RR-15 (2000): 1–17, 3. See also CDC teleconference transcript, "Update on Anthrax Investigations with Drs. Jim Hughes and Julie Gerberding," November 14, 2001; http://www.cdc.gov/media/transcripts/t011114.htm.

29. Graphic chart, *Palm Beach Post*, October 14, 2001. Associated Press, New York City Department of Public Health, *New York Times*, Centers for Disease Control, and *Post* wire services cited as sources.

30. Stephen Ostroff interview, October 16, 2003, Atlanta, Ga.

4. "We Have This Anthrax"

1. "Text: Government Briefing on Latest Anthrax Case, October 12, 2001"; http://www.washingtonpost.com/wp-srv/nation/specials/attacked/transcripts/ashcroft_101201.html.

2. Colleen Matony and Antigone Barton, "Abortion Clinics Become Target of Anthrax Threats," *Palm Beach Post*, October 16, 2001.

3. Eddy Bresnitz interview, May 24, 2009, Philadelphia, Pa.

4. "Memorandum from USPS to Vice Presidents, Area Operations Manager, Capital Metro Operations, Re: Emergency Action Plans (October 10, 2001)," USPS Management Instruction EL-860-1999-3; John B. Flood, "Revisiting the Right to Refuse Hazardous Work Amidst the Anthrax Crisis of 2001," *University of Pennsylvania Journal of Labor and Employment Law* 5/3 (2003): 545–84.

5. The 2001 American Public Health manual, for example, recommended that if first responders discovered a sealed letter or package associated with an anthrax threat, they should notify the FBI but not require either building quarantine or evacuation or mandatory antibiotics. American Public Health Association, *Control of Communicable Diseases Manual*, ed. James Chin (Washington, D.C.: American Public Health Association, 2001), 25.

6. Helen Lewis interview, February 21, 2011, Washington, D.C.

7. Bresnitz interview, May 24, 2009.

8. Ibid.

9. Bob Unick interview, May 24, 2009, New Brunswick, N.J.

10. Tom Daschle with Michael D'Orso, *Like No Other Time: Two Years That Changed America* (New York: Three Rivers Press, 2003), 147. Daschle's account of the incident is detailed, revealing for the first time Grant Leslie's name.

11. Ibid., 152–53. As Daschle describes it, the fifth-floor contingent had to insist on nasal swabs and Cipro.

12. Ibid., 147.

13. Ibid., 181–82.

14. Ibid., 152.

15. U.S. District Court for the District of Columbia, Search Warrant 07-524-M-01, 14. The warrant, requested by Postal Inspector Thomas F. Dellafera and granted on October 31, 2007, includes texts of emails by and about Bruce Ivins, cited here.

16. Postmaster General John Potter interview, June 2, 2009, Washington, D.C.

17. Associated Press, "Post Office Forms Anthrax Task Force," October 15, 2001.

18. Dena Briscoe email to author, June 13, 2006.

19. Terrell Worrell email to author, September 19, 2005.

20. Briscoe email.

21. Vice President Cheney, *Newshour with Jim Lehrer*, October 12, 2001; http://www.pbs.org/newshour/bb/terrorism/july-dec01/cheneya_10-12.html.

22. Bob Woodward, *Bush at War* (New York: Simon & Schuster, 2003), 247–49.

23. Tom Ridge with Lary Bloom, *The Test of Our Times: America Under Siege and How We Can Be Safe Again* (New York: St. Martin's Press, 2009), 48–49.

24. Tom Ridge interview, April 22, 2009, Cambridge, Mass.

25. Steve Bahrle, telephone interview, April 11, 2011.

26. Daschle, *Like No Other Time*, 160.

5. The Postal Victims

1. Eddy Bresnitz interview, May 24, 2009, Philadelphia, Pa.

2. Steve Bahrle, NPMHU Grievance no. 308-56-96-01, October 17, 2001, Trenton, N.J., P&DC.

3. George DiFerdinando email to author, January 13, 2010; Eddy Bresnitz email to author, January 17, 2010.

4. DiFerdinando email to author, January 13, 2010.

5. A local hospital, St. Francis, also assisted but was never compensated because, unlike the Robert Wood Johnson Hospital, it had no contract with the USPS.

6. Daniel B. Jernigan, Pratima L. Raghunathan, Beth P. Bell, Ross Brechner, et al., "Investigation of Bioterrorism-Related Anthrax, United States, 2001: Epidemiologic Findings," *Emerging Infectious Diseases* 8/10 (October 2002): 1019–28; Leonard A. Cole, "Risk of Publicity about Bioterrorism: Anthrax Hoaxes and Hype," *American Journal of Infection Control* 27 (December 1999): 470–73, 82–88.

7. Tom Carey, telephone interview, August 3, 2010.

8. Brentwood events are summarized in Civil Action No. 03-2084, *Dena Briscoe et al., Plaintiffs, v. John E. Potter, United States Postmaster General et al., Defendants*, U.S. District Court for the District of Columbia, 1–9. Through a FOIA request, Judicial Watch, which led the prosecution, obtained a copy of Brentwood manager Tim Haney's office diary, which documented the discovery of contamination and shutdown of the facility. The author's conversations with Brentwood employees over the years reiterated the same events.

9. Jack Potter interview, June 2, 2009, Washington, D.C.

10. Steve Twomey and Justin Blum, "How the Experts Missed Anthrax," *Washington Post*, November 19, 2001.

11. Munition Expenditure Panel, "Preliminary Discussion of Methods for Calculating Munition Expenditure, With Special Reference to the St Jo Program," August 11, 1954, Camp Detrick, Frederick, Maryland.

12. Bill Frist, *When Every Moment Counts: What You Need to Know About Bioterror-*

ism from the Senate's Only Doctor (Lanham, Md.: Rowman & Littlefield, 2002), 14–15.

13. Andrew Pollack, "U.S. Moving to Buttress Defense Against the Bioterrorism Threat," *New York Times*, October 15, 2001.

14. Qieth McQue (full name McQureerit) remained anonymous until being interviewed by Leonard A. Cole, *The Anthrax Letters: A Medical Detective Story* (Washington, D.C.: John Henry Press, 2003), 62–63.

15. Dena Briscoe email communication, March 6, 2006.

16. Ibid.

17. Leroy Richmond interview, September 21, 2009, Stafford, Va.

18. Terrell Worrell email communication, September 19, 2005.

19. Brad Perkins interview, April 2, 2009, Atlanta, Ga.

20. PBS, *NewsHour*, October 22, 2001; http://www.pbs.org/newshour/bb/terrorism/july-dec01/postal_10-22.html.

21. Jacob Weisberg, *The Bush Tragedy* (New York: Random House, 2008), 191.

6. Threat Perceptions

1. PBS, *NewsHour*, "The Anthrax Threat," October 24, 2001.

2. Steven Greenhouse, "A Nation Challenged: New York Region; Sorting Machines at Mail Center Are Contaminated," *New York Times*, October 26, 2001; Jane Fritsch, "A Nation Challenged: The Post Offices; One Center Staying Open; Anthrax Found at 4 Others," *New York Times*, November 10, 2001.

3. Suzanne Miro and Sean G. Kaufman, "Anthrax in New Jersey: A Health Education Experience in Bioterrorism Response and Preparedness," *Health Promotion Practice* 6 (2005): 430–36.

4. Christina G. Tan, Hardeep S. Sandhu, Dana C. Crawford, Stephen C. Redd, Michael J. Beach, James Buehler, Eddy A. Bresnitz, Robert W. Pinner, Beth P. Bell, the regional Anthrax Surveillance Team, and the Centers for Disease Control and Prevention New Jersey Anthrax Surveillance Team, "Surveillance for Anthrax Cases Associated with Contaminated Letters, New Jersey, Delaware, and Pennsylvania, 2001," *Emerging Infectious Diseases* 8/10 (2002); http://www.cdc.gov/ncidod/EID/vol8no10/02-0322.htm.

5. Tom Day interview, June 2, 2009, Washington, D.C.

6. *2002 Annual Report of the Investigations of the United States Postal Inspection Service*; http://postalinspectors.uspis.gov/radDocs/pubs/ar02_04pdf.

7. Tom Day interview, June 2, 2009, Washington, D.C.

8. U.S. Congress, *Making Appropriations for the Department of Defense for the Fiscal Year Ending September 30, 2002, and for Other Purposes,* 107th Congress, 1st sess., H. Rept. 107-350 (Washington, D.C.: U.S. Government Printing Office, 2001), 452.

9. *2002 Annual Report of the Investigations of the United States Postal Inspection Service.*

10. Joby Warrick, "One Anthrax Answer: Ames Strain Not from Iowa," *Washington Post*, January 9, 2002.

11. Rita Colwell interview, February 24, 2009, Baltimore, Md.

12. Entrepreneur geneticist Craig Venter created TIGR and then in 1998 passed its direction to Fraser-Liggett, then his wife, in order to start another company, Celera Genomics, devoted solely to the race to map the human genome. Nicholas Wade, *Life Script: How the Human Genome Discoveries Will Transform Medicine and Enhance Your Health* (New York: Touchstone Books, 2001); Kevin Davies, *Cracking the Genome: Inside the Race to Unlock Human DNA* (New York: Free Press, 2001).

13. Douglas Beecher, "Forensic Application of Microbiological Culture Analysis to Identify Mail Intentionally Contaminated with *Bacillus anthracis* Spores," *Applied and Environmental Microbiology* 8 (August 2006): 5304–10.

14. John Ezzell interview, April 23, 2009, Frederick, Md.

15. Special Agent John Hess was put in charge of the field investigation, Amerithrax 1.

16. C. J. Peters and Mark Olshaker, *Virus Hunter: Thirty Years of Battling Hot Viruses Around the World* (New York: Anchor Books, 1997), 120; Richard Preston, *The Hot Zone* (New York: Anchor, 1994).

17. Ken Alibek with Steven Handelman, *Biohazard: The Chilling True Story of the Largest Covert Biological Weapons Program in the World—Told from the Inside by the Man Who Ran It* (New York: Random House, 1999).

18. Jon Cohen, "Is an Old Virus Up to New Tricks?" *Science* 277/5 (July 18, 1997): 324.

19. Richard Preston, *Demon in the Freezer* (New York: Random House, 2002), 203. Preston also extended the "silica" additive to the Brokaw letter spores, describing them as "glassy chunks" (220).

20. Ibid., 222–35.

21. Brian Ross telephone communication, June 20, 2010.

22. Richard Butler, *The Greatest Threat: Iraq, Weapons of Mass Destruction, and the Crisis of Global Security* (New York: PublicAffairs, 2000), 86–87.

23. Richard Butler, "Who Made the Anthrax?" *New York Times*, October 18, 2001; Jason Vest, "Saddam in the Crosshairs," *The Village Voice*, November 20, 2001.

24. Responding in *The Guardian*, Scott Ritter, former U.N. chief WMD investigator in Iraq, advised Butler, his onetime boss, against "unsubstantiated speculation," but Ritter's response only intensified a growing media campaign, led by CNN, to personally discredit him. Scott Ritter, "Don't Blame Saddam for This One," *The Guardian*, October 19, 2001; Antonia Zerbisias, "CNN's Hatchet Job on Scott Ritter," *Toronto Star*, September 12, 2002. See also Scott Ritter, *Frontier Justice: Weapons of Mass Destruction and the Bushwhacking of America* (New York: Context Books, 2003), 159–84.

25. William Kristol, "The Wrong Strategy," *Washington Post*, October 30, 2001.

26. Robert L. Bartley, "Anthrax: The Elephant in the Room," *Wall Street Journal*, October 29, 2001.

27. "The Battle for Ideas in the U.S. War on Terrorism," American Enterprise Institute, October 29, 2001; http:/aei.org/event/364. The panel, moderated by Perle, included Michael Ledeen, Newt Gingrich, Natan Sharansky, and R. James Woolsey—all in favor of regime change in Iraq.

28. Richard Perle, PBS *Frontline* interview series "Gunning for Iraq," October 2001; http://www.pbs.org/wgbh/pages/Frontline/shows/gunning/interviews/perle.html.

29. James Burans interview, May 27, 2009, Frederick, Md.

30. Committee on Governmental Affairs and the Subcommittee on International Security, Proliferation, and Federal Service, October 31, 2001.

31. Matthew Meselson and Ken Alibek, letter to editor, *Washington Post*, November 5, 2002.

32. Ross, June 20, 2010; Ari Fleischer email to author, April 14, 2011.

33. Bob Woodward, *Bush at War* (New York: Simon & Schuster, 2003), 200.

34. International Information Programs, "Transcript: Tom Ridge, Other Federal Officials Brief on Anthrax," October 29, 2001; http:/www.iwar.org.uk/homesec/resources/anthrax/briefing.htm.

35. Bushra Mina, J. P. Dym, Frank Kuepper, Raymond Tso, et al., "Fatal Inhalational

Anthrax with Unknown Source of Exposure in a 61-Year-Old Woman in New York City," in *Bioterrorism: Guidelines for Medical and Public Health Management*, ed. Donald A. Huenderson, Thomas V. Inglesby, and Tara O'Toole (Chicago: AMA Press, 2002), 33–41.

36. Laurie Garrett, "Scientist Warns of Underestimating Anthrax Levels," *Newsday*, October 31, 2001.

37. William J. Broad, Stephen Engelberg, Judith Miller, and Sheryl Gay Stolberg, "Hospital Workers' Illness Suggests Widening Threat; Security Tightens Over U.S.," *New York Times*, October 31, 2001.

38. Bill Kournikakis, telephone interview, June 10, 2009.

39. Peter M. Dull, Kathy E. Wilson, Bill Kournikakis, Ellen A. S. Whitney, Camille Boulet, Jim Y. W. Ho, Jim Ogston, Mel R. Spence, Megan M. McKenzie, Maureen A. Phelan, et al., "*Bacillus Anthracis* Aerosolization Associated with a Contaminated Mail Sorting Machine," *Emerging Infectious Diseases* 8/10 (2002); http://www.cdc.gov/ncidod/EID/vol8no10/02-0356.htm.

7. Lone Wolf

1. Tom Carey, telephone interview, August 3, 2010.

2. Sponsored by the Department of Justice and FEMA, the 2000 exercise is described at http://www.globalsecurity.org/security/ops/index_topoff1.htm.

3. John Ashcroft, *Never Again: Securing America and Restoring Justice* (New York: Center Street, 2006), 128–29.

4. Press briefing by Homeland Security Office director Tom Ridge, November 7, 2001. Office of the White House Press Secretary Collection.

5. Brigid Glanville interviewed Tom Carey for "Anthrax: A Political Whodunit," ABC Radio National Australia, November 17, 2002.

6. BBC News, "Anthrax Killer Is US Defence Insider," August 18, 2002; Don Foster, "The Message in the Anthrax," *Vanity Fair*, October 2003, 180–200.

7. I. Seth Carus, *Bioterrorism and Biocrimes: The Illicit Use of Biological Agents Since 1900* (Washington, D.C.: Center for Counterproliferation Research, National Defense University, 2002), 25. In 43 of the 69 identifiable modern cases Carus describes, a lone individual perpetuated the plots. "Significantly," Carus observes, "the lone perpetrators successfully acquired biological agents in 19 of these cases, and used the agent in 12 of them."

8. Gary Matsumoto, "State Sponsor? Anthrax Suggests Scientific Expertise," ABC News, October 16, 2001.

9. Gary Matsumoto, "Terror Tests: Additive Search Requires More Study," ABC News, November 1, 2001.

10. Michael Powell, "Probe of Anthrax Attacks Casts Shadow on Brothers," *Washington Post*, October 7, 2006.

11. Lydia A. Barakat, Howard L. Quentzel, John Jernigan, David L. Kirschke, Kevin Griffith, Stephen M. Spear, Katherine Kelley, Diane Barden, Donald Mayo, David S. Stephens, et al., "Fatal Inhalational Anthrax in a 94-year-old Connecticut Woman," *JAMA* 287/7 (2002): 863–68.

12. Douglas Beecher, "Forensic Application of Microbiological Culture Analysis to Identify Mail Intentionally Contaminated with *Bacillus anthracis* Spores," *Applied and Environmental Microbiology* 8 (August 2006): 5304–10.

13. Kevin Johnson, "Authorities Will Use Robot to Open Letter Sent to Sen. Leahy," *USA Today*, November 29, 2001. No robot was used.

14. Michael T. Osterholm, "Framing the Debate: Applying the Lessons Learned," in

Institute of Medicine, *Biological Threats and Terrorism: Assessing the Science Capability* (Washington, D.C.: National Academies Press, 2002), 34–37.

15. Judith Miller, Stephen Engelberg, and William Broad, *Germs: Biological Weapons and America's Secret War* (New York: Simon & Schuster, 2001).

16. Ibid., 144; Matthew Meselson, Jeanne Guillemin, Martin Hugh-Jones, Alexander Langmuir, et al., "The Sverdlovsk Outbreak of 1979," *Science* 266/5188 (1994): 1202–08; Dean Wilkening, "Sverdlovsk Revisited: Modeling Human Inhalation Anthrax," *Proceedings of the National Academy of Sciences* 103/2 (2006): 7589–94.

17. Miller, Engelberg, and Broad, *Germs*, 223–34.

18. Ibid., 145.

19. Ibid., 188.

20. NOVA/PBS, "Bioterror," November 13, 2001; http://www.pbs.org/wgbh/nova/bioterror.

21. Miller, Engelberg, and Broad, *Germs*, 320.

22. Ari Schuler, "Billions for Biodefense: Federal Agency Biodefense Budgeting, FY2001–FY2005," *Biosecurity and Bioterrorism* 2/2 (2004): 86–96.

23. James Burans interview, January 19, 2010, Frederick, Md.

24. Anonymous source.

25. William J. Broad and Judith Miller, "Inquiry Includes Possibility of Killer from a U.S. Lab," *New York Times*, December 2, 2001.

26. Matthew Meselson offered this suggestion at a November 29, 2001, FBI consultation.

27. Frank Gottron, "Project Bioshield: Authorities, Appropriations, Acquisitions, and Issues for Congress," Congressional Research Service Report for Congress 7-5700, July 7, 2010, 9.

28. Perry Mikesell, Bruce E. Ivins, Joseph D. Ristroph, Michael H. Vodkin, Thomas M. Dreier, and Stephen Leppla, "Plasmids, Pasteur, and Anthrax," *ASM News* 49/7 (1983): 320–23.

29. Daryl J. Kelly, Jeffrey D. Chulay, Perry Mikesell, and Arthur M. Friedlander, "Serum Concentrations of Penicillin, Doxycycline, and Ciprofloxacin during Prolonged Therapy in Rhesus Monkeys," *Journal of Infectious Diseases* 166/5 (1992): 1184–87; Arthur M. Friedlander, Susan L. Welkos, Margaret L. M. Pitt, John W. Ezzell, Patricia Worsham, Kenneth J. Rose, Bruce E. Ivins, John R. Lowe, Gerald B. Howe, Perry Mikesell, and Wade B. Lawrence, "Postexposure Prophylaxis against Experimental Inhalational Anthrax," *Journal of Infectious Diseases* 167/5 (1993): 1239–43.

30. Laura Rozen, "Fort Detrick's Anthrax Mystery," Salon.com, January 26, 2002; http://www.salon.com/news /feature/2002/01/26/assaad/print.html.

31. Nancy Haigwood, email to author, February 6, 2011.

32. Carl Scandella, telephone interview, February 3, 2011.

33. Scott Shane, "Breakthrough in Research with Smallpox," *Baltimore Sun*, January 26, 2002.

34. Marilyn Thompson, *The Killer Strain: Anthrax and a Government Exposed* (New York: HarperCollins, 2003), 209.

35. FBI Amerithrax case #279A-WF-222936-BEI, January 23, 2002.

8. Laws, Regulations, and Rules

1. The U.S. definition of WMD was "atomic explosive, radioactive material, lethal chemical and biological weapons, and any weapons developed in the future which have characteristics comparable in destructive effect to those of the atomic bomb

or other weapons mentioned above." Benjamin C. Garrett and John Hart, *The Historical Dictionary of Nuclear, Biological and Chemical Weapons* (Lanham, Md.: Scarecrow Press, 2009), 229–30; on WMD and dread, see Jessica Stern, *The Ultimate Terrorists* (Cambridge, Mass.: Harvard University Press, 2000).

2. Ernesto Blanco interview, April 21, 2009, West Palm Beach, Fla.

3. Avram Goldstein, "Postal Worker's Family Suing Over Death," *Washington Post*, November 14, 2001. Manny Fernandez and Ruben Castaneda, "Anthrax Victim's Family Sues Md. Medical Center," *Washington Post*, March 27, 2002. The Curseen case against Southern Maryland Hospital Center dragged on for years before a settlement was reached.

4. *J. G. Christopher Co. v. Russell*, 63 Fla. 191, 58 So. 45 (1912).

5. Robert Schuler interview, April 21, 2009, West Palm Beach, Fla.

6. Brian W. Sugden and Rosemary Katchmar, "Bioterrorism and Its Aftermath: Dealing Individually and Organizationally with the Emotional Reactions to an Anthrax Attack," *International Journal of Emergency Mental Health* 7/3 (2005): 203–12.

7. Johanna Huden, "Anthrax—Still No Answers: Five Years After," *New York Post*, October 18, 2006.

8. Lawrence K. Altman, "New Tests Confirm Potency of Anthrax in Senate Office Building," *New York Times*, December 11, 2001.

9. Suzanne Miro and Sean G. Kaufman, "Anthrax in New Jersey: A Health Education Experience in Bioterrorism Response and Preparedness," *Health Promotion Practice* 6 (2005): 430–36.

10. Yi-Fu Tuan, *Space and Place: The Perspective of Experience* (Minneapolis: University of Minnesota Press, 1977), 3.

11. Martha Wolfenstein, *Disaster: A Psychological Essay* (Glencoe, Ill.: Free Press, 1957); Kai T. Erikson, *Everything in Its Path: Destruction of Community in the Buffalo Creek Flood* (New York: Simon & Schuster, 1976); Patricia J. Fanning, *Influenza and Inequality* (Boston: University of Massachusetts Press, 2010).

12. Sandra Crouse Quinn, Tammy Thomas, and Supriya Kumar, "The Anthrax Vaccine and Research: Reactions from Postal Workers and Public Health Professionals," *Biosecurity and Bioterrorism: Biodefense Strategy, Practice, and Science* 6/4 (2008): 321–33. Like many other postal workers, Worrell was college educated and had read the classic book about the forty-year government study of untreated Alabama sharecroppers: James Jones, *Bad Blood: The Tuskegee Syphilis Study* (New York: Free Press, 1981).

13. Steve Twomey, "Crowd Seeks Details of Brentwood Cleanup," *Washington Post*, March 28, 2002.

14. Francis X. Clines, "Contaminated Mail; Officials Try to Soothe and Inform in a Meeting on Anthrax Cleanup at Postal Building," *New York Times*, March 28, 2002.

15. Erikson, *Everything in Its Path*, 200.

16. Terrell Worrell, email to author, September 19, 2005.

17. Terrell Worrell, email to Brentwood Exposed, July 19, 2002.

18. Funding for Judicial Watch began with conservative sources. David Korn, "Klayman Watch," *The Nation*, March 29, 2004; http://www.thenation.com/article/klayman_watch. In September 2003, Klayman left Judicial Watch to run for elected office in Florida. He subsequently sued the new leader, Tom Fitton. Judicial Watch press release, "Founder Sues Judicial Watch President Tom Fitton," April 13, 2006.

19. Judicial Watch made its first move by filing a complaint on December 6, 2002, to the Washington Office of Equal Economic Opportunity, in Dena Briscoe's name.

20. Timothy D. Read, Steven L. Salzberg, Mihai Pop, Martin Shumway, et al., "Comparative Genome Sequencing for Discovery of Novel Polymorphism in *Bacillus anthracis*," *Science* 296/5575 (2002): 2028–33.

21. Susan Lilly, "Citing 'Extreme Concern,' Iowa State University Destroys Anthrax," CNN.com./Health, November 9, 2001; http://edition.cnn.com/2001/HEALTH/11/09/rec.iowa.anthrax/index.html.

22. David Johnston and William J. Broad, "Anthrax in Mail Was Newly Made, Investigators Say," *New York Times*, June 23, 2002; Guy Gugliotta, "Anthrax Spores from Hill Said to Be Made Recently," *Washington Post*, June 24, 2002.

23. Yudihijit Bhattacharjee, "Paul Keim on His Life with the FBI During the Anthrax Investigation," *Science* 323/5920 (2009): 1416.

24. Memorandum for the Commander, USAMRMC7FD, Subject: Legal Review-AR 15–6 Investigation Into Anthrax Contamination at USAMRIID, May 15, 2002.

25. Ibid., 228.

26. Ibid., 82.

27. "Beyond the Breach: Timeline," *Frederick News-Post* (undated); http://www.fredericknewspost.com/breach/timeline.htm.

28. Memorandum for the Commander, 33.

29. Ibid., 89.

30. Ibid., 6–14.

9. Gone Awry

1. Steve Twomey, "Letters Left Trail of Contamination," *Washington Post*, November 11, 2001.

2. Tom Carey telephone interview, August 3, 2010.

3. Allan Lengel, "Experience at Work in FBI Anthrax Case," *Washington Post*, March 4, 2002.

4. U.S. Department of Justice, *The FBI: A Centennial History, 1908–2008* (Washington, D.C.: U.S. Government Printing Office, 2008), 100.

5. Jez Littlewood, *The Biological Weapons Convention: A Failed Revolution* (Aldershot, U.K.: Ashgate, 2005).

6. Susan Wright, "Introduction" in *Biological Warfare and Disarmament: New Problems/New Perspectives*, ed. Susan Wright (New York: Rowman & Littlefield, 2002), 3–24.

7. Barbara Hatch Rosenberg, "A Compilation of Evidence and Comments on the Source of the Mailed Anthrax," Federation of American Scientists, December 10, 2001; http://www.ph.ucla.edu/epi/bioter/compilationofanthraxevidence.html.

8. Tom Carey, telephone interview, August 3, 2010.

9. William C. Patrick III, "Risk Assessment of Biological Warfare: Primary and Secondary Aerosols and Their Requirements for Decontamination," prepared for Science Applications International Corporation, February 1999. The names of Joseph Soukup and Steven Hatfill are noted on the cover page.

10. Brigid Glanville, "Anthrax: A Political Whodunit," ABC Radio National Australia, November 17, 2002.

11. Steven Hatfill, "I Am a Loyal American," the title of his prepared press statement, August 12, 2002.

12. Nicholas Kristof, "The Anthrax Files," *New York Times*, August 13, 2002.

13. *Webster Bivens, plaintiff-appellant, v. Six Unknown Named Agents of the Federal Bureau of Narcotics, defendants-appellees*, United States Court of Appeals, Second Circuit-456 F.2d 1339. Argued December 3, 1971, decided March 8, 1972, 34–42, with thanks given to Steven A. Grant, Esq. Thereafter, a citizen could sue the federal government for violation of rights—as when its officials deprive an individual of due process.

14. *Steven J. Hatfill, M.D., v. Attorney John Ashcroft et al.*, in the United States District Court for the District of Columbia, August 26, 2003.

15. David Freed, "The Wrong Man," *The Atlantic*, May 2010, with video interview of Hatfill; http://www.theatlantic.com/magazine/archive/2010/05/the-wrong-man/8019.

16. William J. Broad and Scott Shane, "Anthrax Case Had Costs for Suspects," *New York Times*, August 10, 2008.

17. "Revised Press Release from Brentwood Exposed," June 10, 2002.

18. Dena Briscoe email to Brentwood Exposed, "Congressional 'Field' Hearing," June 22, 2002.

19. Terrell Worrell email to Brentwood Exposed, July 19, 2002.

20. Subcommittee on the District of Columbia of the House Committee on Government Reform, "Cleanup of the U.S. Postal Service's Brentwood Processing and Distribution Center," July 26, 2002.

21. Ibid., testimony of John F. Hegarty, president, NPMHU.

22. Judicial Watch, Inc., to Roscoe C. Howard Jr., Esq., U.S. Attorney's Office, District of Columbia, "Complaint for Criminal Investigation—Anthrax Attacks," December 6, 2002. The narrative of events Judicial Watch presented in this and subsequent case arguments was based largely on interviews with members of the Brentwood plaintiffs, plus documents obtained through FOIA requests, which the USPS, as the case proceeded, had no opportunity to refute.

23. Part of the Judicial Watch investigation team, retired Marine JAG Lieutenant Colonel Geoff Lyon conducted hundreds of Brentwood interviews.

24. Civil Action 03–2084, United States District Court for the District of Columbia. *Dena Briscoe et al. v. USPS Postmaster General John E. Potter et al.*, October 13, 2003; ruling on appeal, November 7, 2005.

25. Postal supervisor Ossie Alston, who on October 15 had refused to read a USPS notice declaring Brentwood safe, was another plaintiff. Vincent Gagnon co-represented the mail handlers, and Vernon Porter represented the mail carriers in the case.

26. Patricia L. Worsham and Michele R. Sowers, "Isolation of an Asporogenic (spoOA) Protective Antigen-producing Strain of *Bacillus anthracis*," *Canadian Journal of Microbiology* 45 (1999): 1–8.

27. National Research Council, *Review of the Scientific Approaches Used During the FBI's Investigation of the 2001 Anthrax Letters* (Washington, D.C.: National Academies Press, 2011), 88–109.

28. John Ezzell interview, May 26, 2010, Frederick, Md.

29. Testimony of Mark Richard Wilson, *R. v. Murrin*, Between Her Majesty the Queen, and Shannon Leonard Murrin [1999] B.C.J. No. 2715, Vancouver Registry No. CC9711114, British Columbia Supreme Court, 22; http:/www.nlada.org/Defender/forensics/for_lib/Documents/1114546309.23/document_info. Wilson's expertise was in mitochondrial DNA, the genetic information that, unlike nuclear DNA, is inherited through the maternal line.

30. Rita Colwell, "Foreword," in *Microbial Forensics*, ed. Bruce Budowle, Steven E. Schutzer, Roger G. Breeze, Paul S. Keim, and Stephen A. Morse, (Burlington, Mass.: Academic Press, 2011), xv–xvii, xv.

10. To War

1. Chandré Gould and Peter Folb, *Project Coast: Apartheid's Chemical and Biological Warfare Program* (Geneva: United Nations Institute for Disarmament Research, 2002), 223–30.
2. William A. Broad and David Johnston, "Report Linking Anthrax and Hijackers Is Investigated," *New York Times*, March 23, 2002.
3. Judith Miller and Laurie Mylroie, *Saddam Hussein and the Crisis in the Gulf* (New York: Times Books, 1990); Craig Unger, *The Fall of the House of Bush: The Untold Story of How a Band of True Believers Seized the Executive Branch, Started the Iraq War, and Still Imperils America's Future* (New York: Scribner, 2007), 215–16.
4. Miller and Mylroie, *Saddam Hussein*, 230.
5. Committee on International Relations, House of Representatives, *Hearings on Russia, Iraq, and Other Potential Sources of Anthrax, Smallpox and Other Bioterrorist Weapons*, 107th Congress (Washington, D.C.: U.S. Government Printing Office, December 5, 2001), 31; http://commdocs.house.gov/committees/intlrel/hfa76481.000/hfa76481_OFHTM. Elisa Harris, formerly on the Clinton National Security Council staff, also testified at this hearing, arguing for political rather than military solutions.
6. Bill Patrick letter to Matthew Meselson, June 1, 2002.
7. Bob Woodward, *Bush at War* (New York: Simon & Schuster, 2003), 354–57.
8. Institute of Medicine, *Anthrax Vaccine: Is It Safe? Does It Work?* (Washington, D.C.: National Academy Press, 2002), 128.
9. FBI Amerithrax case #279A-WF-222936-USAMRIID Sections; http://www.fbi.gov/about-us/history/famous-cases/anthrax-amerithrax/foia-documents.
10. Amerithrax Exhibit M, #2 Ivins Hand Sketch; http://justice.gov/amerithrax.
11. William J. Broad and Judith Miller, "US Recently Produced Anthrax in a Highly Lethal Powder Form," *New York Times*, December 13, 2001.
12. Ken Alibek with Stephen Handelman, *Biohazard: The Chilling True Story of the Largest Covert Biological Program in the World—Told from the Inside by the Man Who Ran It* (New York: Random House, 1999), x.
13. Donald A. Henderson, Thomas V. Inglesby, John G. Bartlett, Michael Ascher, et al., "Smallpox as a Biological Weapon: Medical and Public Health Management," *Journal of the American Medical Association* 281/22 (1999): 2127–37, 2128.
14. Donald A. Henderson, "Chapter 31. Lessons and Benefits," in *Smallpox and Its Eradication*, ed. F. Fenner, D. A. Henderson, L. Arita, Z. Ježek, and L. D. Ladnyi (Geneva: World Health Organization, 1988), 1345–70, 1367.
15. Thomas V. Inglesby, "Anthrax: A Possible Case History," *Emerging Infectious Diseases* 5/4 (1999): 556–601; Tara O'Toole and Thomas V. Inglesby, "Epidemic Response Scenario: Decision Making in a Time of Plague," *Public Health Reports* 116 (2001): Supp. 92–103. These scenarios were also presented at the Second National Symposium on Bioterrorism, November 28–29, 2000, Washington, D.C., cosponsored by the Johns Hopkins Center for Civilian Biodefense Studies, the U.S. Department of Health and Human Services, and the Infectious Diseases Society of America.
16. Philip Alcabes, *Dread: How Fear and Fantasy Have Fueled Epidemics from the Black Death to Avian Flu* (New York: PublicAffairs, 2009), 188.

17. U.S. Senate Government Affairs Subcommittee for International Security, Proliferation and Federal Services, Hearing on FEMA's Role in Managing Bioterrorist Attacks and the Impact of Public Health Concerns on Bioterrorism Preparedness, July 23, 2001.

18. Martin I. Meltzer, Inger Damon, James W. LeDuc, and J. Donald Millar, "Modeling Potential Responses to Smallpox as a Bioterrorist Weapon," *Emerging Infectious Diseases* 7/6 (2002): 959–69; Thomas Mack, "A Different View of Smallpox and Vaccination," *New England Journal of Medicine* 348/5 (January 2003): 460–63. For a critique from U.K. military defense scientists, see Raymond Ganl and Steve Leach, "Transmission Potential of Smallpox in Contemporary Populations," *Nature* 414/13 (2002): 748–51. In defense of the exercise, see Tara O'Toole, Michael Mair, and Thomas V. Inglesby, "Shining Light on 'Dark Winter,'" *Clinical Infectious Diseases* 34/7 (April 2002): 972–83.

19. Henderson later took over the new Office of Emergency Preparedness, also within Health and Human Services.

20. Steven F. Hayes, *Cheney: The Untold Story of America's Most Powerful and Controversial Vice President* (New York: HarperCollins, 2007), 320–21.

21. Jane Mayer, *The Dark Side: The Inside Story of How the War on Terror Turned into a War on American Ideals* (New York: Doubleday, 2008), 3.

22. Judith Miller and Sheryl Gay Stolberg, "Sept. 11 Led to Push for More Smallpox Vaccine," *New York Times*, October 22, 2001.

23. Michael Osterholm, *60 Minutes*, October 7, 2001.

24. Sanjay Gupta and Rhonda Rowland, "Smallpox, Anthrax: What Could Happen?" CNN News, October 3, 2001; http://articles.cnn.com/2001-10-03/us/rec.smallpox .anthrax_1_smallpox-outbreak-bio-terrorist-attack-civilian-biodefense?

25. Richard Preston, *The Demon in the Freezer* (New York: Random House, 2002), 111.

26. Charles Duelfer, "The Iraqi WMD Arsenal Today," in *The Future of Iraq*, ed. Lyle Goldstein and Ahmed Hashim (Newport, R.I.: Center for Naval Warfare Studies, 2002), 73–80.

27. Jonathan B. Tucker, *Scourge: The Once and Future Threat of Smallpox* (New York: Atlantic Monthly Press, 2001).

28. Ibid., 205, 232–42.

29. Barton Gellman, "Four Nations Thought to Possess Smallpox, Two Officials Say," *Washington Post*, November 5, 2002.

30. ABC News, "France Denies It Possesses Smallpox Virus," November 7, 2002.

31. Jon Cohen, "Looking for Vaccines That Pack a Wallop Without the Side Effects," *Science* 298/5602 (December 20, 2002): 2314.

32. Institute of Medicine, *The Smallpox Vaccination Program: Public Health in the Age of Terrorism* (Washington, D.C.: National Academies Press, 2005), 66–67.

33. Samuel A. Bozzette, Rob Boer, Vibha Bhatnagar, Jennifer L. Brower, Emmett B. Keeler, Sally C. Morton, and Michael A. Stoto, "A Model for a Smallpox-Vaccination Policy," *New England Journal of Medicine* 348/5 (2003): 416–25.

34. Lisa Gordon-Hagerty interview, June 1, 2009, Washington, D.C.

35. Robert J. Blendon, Catherine M. DesRochers, John M. Benson, Melissa J. Hermann, Kalahn Taylor-Clark, and Kathleen J. Weldon, "The Public and the Smallpox Threat," *New England Journal of Medicine* 348/5 (2003): 426–32; Judith Miller, "Threats and Responses: Germ Weapons; CIA Hunts Iraq Tie to Soviet Smallpox," *New York Times*, December 3, 2002.

36. U.S. General Accounting Office, *Military Smallpox Vaccination Program* (Washington, D.C.: Government Printing Office, 2003).

37. AFL-CIO, "State and Federal Smallpox Compensation"; http://www.aflcio.org/issues/safety/smallpoxcomp.cfm; U.S. General Accounting Office, *Smallpox Vaccination: Implementation of the National Program Faces Challenges* (Washington, D.C.: Government Printing Office, April 30, 2003). Secretary Thompson and CDC Director Gerberding thought that individual health insurance would cover treatment for side effects and state workers' compensation plans would cover disability or death. In fact, not all first responders were fully insured, and only fourteen states had clear guarantees for compensating smallpox-related injuries or deaths.

38. Mayer, *The Dark Side*, 136–38. The intelligence Tenet was referring to was from Ibn al-Shaykh al-Libi, the al Qaeda leader taken by the CIA from the FBI just after 9/11. Defense Intelligence Agency analysts had warned that al-Libi was a suspect source. Others were as well; see Bob Drogin, *Curveball: Spies, Lies, and the Con Man Who Caused a War* (New York: Random House, 2007), 151–61.

39. Hans Blix, *Disarming Iraq* (New York: Pantheon, 2004), 145–50.

40. Associated Press, "No Serious Civilian Reactions to Smallpox Vaccine," February 23, 2003.

41. "Update: Adverse Events Following Civilian Smallpox Vaccination—United States, 2003," *Morbidity and Mortality Weekly Report* 53/5 (2004): 106–7. Five days after receiving her smallpox vaccination, Andrea Deerheart Cornitcher, age 56, a nurse of American Indian descent living in Connecticut, died of a heart attack on March 23. On March 26, Lloyd Clements, age 55, a National Guardsman in Florida, died of a heart attack two days after his inoculation. Virginia Jorgensen, age 57, a nurse's aide in Florida, also suffered a heart attack immediately after being vaccinated on February 26, and died on March 26.

42. Jack F. Woodruff, "Viral Myocarditis," *American Journal of Pathology* 101/2 (1980): 427–84.

43. Jeffrey S. Halsell, James R. Riddle, J. Edwin Atwood, Pierce Gardner, Robert Shope, Gregory A. Poland, Gregory C. Gray, Stephen Ostroff, Robert E. Eckart, Duane R. Hospenthal, et al., "Myopericarditis Following Smallpox Vaccination Among Vaccinia-Naïve US Military Personnel," *JAMA* 289/24 (2003): 3283–89.

44. The Navy's Jim Burans, in Iraq at this time, discovered that containers on trucks presumed to be mobile fermenters—a discovery the CIA was with relish about to report to the president—were not equipped for fermentation. Robert Kadlec interview, June 2, 2009, Washington, D.C.

45. U.S. Senate Armed Services Committee, Hearing on Iraqi Weapons of Mass Destruction and Other Programs, January 28, 2004.

46. Charles Duelfer, *Hide and Seek: The Search for Truth in Iraq* (New York: PublicAffairs, 2009), 441–60.

47. H. W. Cohen, R. M. Gould, and V. W. Sidel, "The Pitfalls of Bioterrorism Preparedness: The Anthrax and Smallpox Experiences," *American Journal of Public Health* 94/10 (2004): 1667–72.

48. Ibid., 1672.

49. Board on Health Promotion and Disease Prevention (IOM), *The Smallpox Vaccination Program: Public Health in an Age of Terrorism* (Washington, D.C.: National Academies Press, 2005), 82.

50. Ari Schuler, "Billions for Biodefense: Federal Agency Biodefense Budgeting, FY2001–FY2005," *Biosecurity and Bioterrorism* 2/2 (2004): 86–96; "Federal Funding for Biological Weapons Prevention and Defense, Fiscal Years 2001 to 2007,"

Center for Arms Control and Non-Proliferation, Washington, D.C.; http://www
.armscontrol.org.

51. U.S. Senate Committee on Health, Education, Labor and Pensions, statement
by Julie L. Gerberding, M.D., M.P.H., *CDC Response to Severe Acute Respiratory
Syndrome (SARS)*, April 7, 2003.

52. Greg Siegle, "U.S. Response: Despite Budget Cuts, CDC Up to Challenge of Bioterrorism, Official Says," Nuclear Threat Initiative Global Security Newswire, February
8, 2002.

53. Institute of Medicine, Board on Global Health, *Microbial Threats to Health: Emergence, Detection, and Response* (Washington, D.C.: National Academies Press,
2003). See also Institute of Medicine, Committee on Assuring the Health of the
Public, *The Future of Public Health in the 21st Century* (Washington, D.C.: National
Academies Press, 2002).

54. Monica Schoch-Spana, "Bioterrorism: US Public Health and a Secular Apocalypse,"
Anthropology Today 20/5 (2004): 1–6.

55. D. A. Henderson, *Smallpox—The Death of a Disease: The Inside Story of Eradicating
a World Wide Killer* (Amherst, N.Y.: Prometheus Books, 2009), 296–97.

56. Donald S. Burke, Joshua M. Epstein, Derek A. T. Cummings, Jon I. Parker, et al.,
"Individual-based Computational Modeling of Smallpox Epidemic Control Strategies," *Academic Emergency Medicine* 13 (2006): 1142–49; Ira M. Longini Jr., M.
Elizabeth Halloran, Azhar Nizam, Jang Yang, et al., "Containing a Large Bioterrorist Smallpox Attack: A Computer Simulation Approach," *International Journal
of Infectious Diseases* 11 (2007): 98–108.

57. Martin Enserink, "Johns Hopkins Biodefense Pioneers Depart en Masse," *Science*
301/5641 (2003): 1824.

58. Bradley T. Smith, Thomas V. Inglesby, Esther Brimmer, Luciana Borio, et al., "Nav-
igating the Storm: Report and Recommendations from the Atlantic Storm Exercise," *Biosecurity and Bioterrorism* 3/3 (2005): 256–67.

59. Center for Arms Control and Non-Proliferation, "Federal Funding for Biological
Weapons Prevention and Defense, Fiscal Years 2001 to 2007," Washington, D.C.;
http://www.armscontrol.org.

60. Caree Vander Linden, "USAMRIID Employees Earn Top Civilian Award," *Fort
Detrick Standard*, March 19, 2003; http://www.dcmiliatary.com/dcmilitary_archives/
stories/031903/22098-1.shtml.

61. Gary Matsumoto, *Vaccine-A: The Covert Government Experiment That's Killing
Our Soldiers and Why GI's Are Only the First Victims* (New York: Basic Books,
2004), 53–54.

62. David Willman, "Suspect Stood to Gain from Anthrax Panic," *Los Angeles Times*,
August 2, 2008.

63. Bruce Ivins email, Saturday, February 15, 2003, 10:47 a.m.; subject: Our conversa-
tion. Ivins insinuates that someone in the Diagnostic Services Division is blaming
Bacteriology, presumably for the 2002 contamination. He urges the recipient of
this message to tell the FBI to find certain information on a form—a data sheet
Ivins and two others signed—before it is destroyed. FBI Amerithrax case 279A-
WF-222936-BEI.

11. The Strong Desire for Justice

1. Email from Ivins, Bruce E., Dr. USAMRIID; Subject: Notebook policy;
Date: Thursday, February 19, 2004, 8:57:47 AM. FBI Amerithrax case #279A-WF-
222936-BEI.

2. James P. Burans, "The National Bioforensic Analysis Center," in *Microbial Forensics*, ed. Bruce Budowle, Steven E. Schutzer, Roger G. Breeze, Paul S. Keim, and Stephen A. Morse (New York: Elsevier, 2010), 619–25, 620.

3. Matthew Meselson, "Vast Biosecurity Expenditures Require Better Oversight and Monitoring," *Nature* 457/15 (January 2009): 259–60.

4. James Burans interview, April 22, 2010, Frederick, Md.

5. Ari Schuler, "Billions for Biodefense: Federal Agency Biodefense Funding, FY2001–FY2005," *Biosecurity and Bioterrorism: Biodefense Strategy, Practice and Science* 2/2 (2004): 86–89.

6. Anthony Fauci, Foreword, in *Bioterrorism: Guidelines for Medical and Public Health Management*, ed. Donald A. Henderson, Thomas V. Inglesby, and Tara O'Toole (Chicago: AMA Press, 2002), vii–viii.

7. Schuler, "Billions for Biodefense"; Clarence Lam, Crystal Franco, and Ari Schuler, "Billions for Biodefense: Federal Agency Biodefense Funding, FY2006–FY2007," *Biosecurity and Bioterrorism: Biodefense Strategy, Practice, and Science* 4/2 (2006): 113–27.

8. Keith Rhodes, "High-Containment Biosafety Laboratories: Preliminary Observations on the Oversight of the Proliferation of BSL-3 and BSL-4 Laboratories in the United States." Testimony Before the Subcommittee on Oversight and Investigations, Committee on Energy and Commerce, U.S. House of Representatives, October 4, 2007 (GAO-08–108T).

9. See http://www.niaid.nih.gov/labsandresources/rce/pages/sites.aspx.

10. Senators Joe Lieberman (D-Conn) and Orrin Hatch (R-Utah), "Move on Bioshield to Aid Biodefense Industry," *The Hill*, May 19, 2004.

11. Project BioShield Act of 2004. The 2006 Pandemic and All-Hazards Preparedness Act (Public Law 109–417) continued the commitment to commerce.

12. Frank Gottron, "Project Bioshield: Authorities, Appropriations, Acquisitions, and Issues for Congress," *Congressional Research Service Report for Congress* 7–5700, July 7, 2010.

13. Thomas Maier, "Anthrax: A Shot in the Dark?" *Newsday*, November 20, 2005.

14. Margaret S. Race and Edward Hammond, "An Evaluation of the Role and Effectiveness of Institutional Biosafety Committees in Providing Oversight and Transparency at Biocontainment Laboratories," *Biosecurity and Bioterrorism* 6/1 (2008): 19–35.

15. William Cooper Jr., "Anthrax Victim's Family Sues U.S. Government," *Palm Beach Post*, September 25, 2003.

16. *Steven J. Hatfill, M.D., v. Attorney General John Ashcroft et al.*, United States District Court for the District of Columbia, August 26, 2003.

17. Detective Ed Lake on his Web site gives a complete overview of Berry's background and possible reasons for FBI interest in him; http://www.anthraxinvestigation.com/DrBerry.html.

18. Lauren Johnston, "Is Al Qaeda Making Anthrax?" *CBS Evening News*, October 9, 2003; http://www.cbsnews.com/stories/2003/10/09/evening news/main577395.shtml.

19. Email from: Ivins, Bruce E. Dr.; Subject: Very Important, Date: Saturday, April 03, 2004, Amerithrax case #279-WF-222936-BEI.

20. Leroy Richmond interview, September 21, 2009, Stafford, Va.

21. Tom Day interview, June 2, 2009, Washington, D.C.

22. Author's notes on the hearing, April 29, 2004.

23. U.S. Department of Justice, *Amerithrax Investigative Summary*, February 19, 2010, 26; http://www.justice.gov/amerithrax/docs/amx-investigative-summary.pdf.

24. *Dena Briscoe et al., Plaintiffs, v. John E. Potter, United States Postmaster General et al.*, Civil Action No. 03–2084 (RMC), U.S. District Court for the District of Columbia, 31.

25. Carol D. Leonnig, "Workers Can't Sue Postal Officials Over Anthrax, Judge Rules," *Washington Post*, November 20, 2004.
26. *Dena Briscoe et al. vs. John E. Potter et al.*, Appeal No. 04-5447, in the U.S. Court of Appeals for the District of Columbia, May 17, 2005.
27. Department of Justice, *Amerithrax*, 53–56.
28. The assays for A1 and A3 were developed at Commonwealth Biotechnologies in Virginia; those for the D morphotype were developed at the Midwest Research Institute in Florida and the Institute for Technological Research in Chicago; the E assay was developed by TIGR in Maryland.
29. Amerithrax, case #279-WF-222936-BEI-53, April 1, 2005.
30. *United States of America et al. v. Maureen Stevens et al.*, "On Certified Question From the United States Court of Appeals for the Eleventh Circuit," No. SC07–1074, August 8, 2007.
31. Ibid., 8.
32. Tania Valdemoro, "Anthrax Victim's Widow Breaks Four-Year Silence," *Palm Beach Post*, November 5, 2005.
33. Eddy Bresnitz interview, May 24, 2009, Philadelphia, Pa.
34. The FBI October 2006 Web site updated the "Amerithrax Fact Sheet": http://www.fbi .gov/about-us/history/famous-cases/anthrax-amerithrax/amerithrax-fact-sheet.

12. Living Proof

1. Douglas J. Beecher, "Forensic Application of the Microbial Culture Analysis to Identify Mail Intentionally Contaminated with *Bacillus anthracis* Spores," *Applied and Environmental Microbiology* 72/8 (2006): 5304–10, 5309.
2. Lois Ember, "Anthrax Redux," *Chemical and Engineering News* 84/40: 4.
3. Cited in the letter of Senator Charles E. Grassley to the Honorable Alberto Gonzales, Attorney General, October 23, 2006.
4. Persichini's prepared remarks were posted in October on the FBI Web site, along with a factual update on the case, http://www.fbi.gov/about-us/history/famous -cases/anthrax-amerithrax/amerithrax-fact-sheet.
5. Richard B. Schmitt and Josh Meyer, "Many Fear FBI's Anthrax Case Is Cold," *Los Angeles Times*, November 3, 2006.
6. Wen Ho Lee and Helen Zia, *My Country Versus Me: The First-Hand Account by the Los Alamos Scientist Who Was Falsely Accused of Being a Spy* (New York: Hyperion, 2003); Dan Stober and Ian Hoffman, *A Convenient Spy: Wen Ho Lee and the Politics of Nuclear Espionage* (New York: Simon & Schuster, 2002).
7. John Ashcroft, *Never Again: Securing America and Restoring Justice* (New York: Center Street, 2006), 73–88.
8. U.S. Federal law, Title 18, USC Section 2332a, "Use of Certain Weapons of Mass Destruction."
9. U.S. Department of Justice, *Amerithrax, Investigative Summary*, February 19, 2010; http://www.justice.gov/amerithrax/docs/amx-investigative-summary.pdf.
10. Ezzell spoke at a December 2010 meeting in Washington, D.C., about simple techniques to make small amounts of powdered anthrax. Megan Eckstein, "Ivins' Lawyer, Colleague Share Details FBI Left Out," *Frederick News-Post*, December 5, 2010.
11. U.S. Department of Justice, *Amerithrax*, 74.
12. FBI Amerithrax investigation, case #279A-WF-222936-BEI, interview with USAMRIID employee, Frederick, Maryland, July 18, 2007.
13. *The Amerithrax Case. Report of the Expert Behavioral Analysis Panel* (Vienna, Va.: Research Strategies Network, 2011), 46–48.

14. U.S. Department of Justice, *Amerithrax Investigative Summary*, February 19, 2010, 46–47, http://www.justice.gov/amerithrax/docs/amx-investigative-summary.pdf.
15. U.S. Department of Justice, *Amerithrax*, 31.
16. At no time were Diane Ivins or their children under suspicion in the Amerithrax case.
17. William Cohen, "American Holy War," *Washington Post*, September 12, 2001.
18. Rick Zeiss, "Bioterrorism: An Even More Devastating Threat," *Washington Post*, September 17, 2001.
19. David Brown, "Biological, Chemical Threat Is Termed Tricky, Complex," *Washington Post*, September 30, 2001.
20. Associated Press, "Microbiologist Claims Lone Anthrax Suspect Bruce Ivins Stalked Her for Decades," August 9, 2009.
21. FBI Amerithrax case #279A-WF-222936-BEI, anonymous interview, June 19, 2007.
22. FBI Amerithrax case #279A-WF-222936-BEI, interview with USAMRIID employee, Frederick, Maryland, July 23, 2007.
23. The search warrant was granted by U.S. Magistrate Judge Deborah A. Robinson, United States District Court for the District of Columbia, to Postal Inspector Thomas F. Dellafera, Case No. 07–524M01, October 31, 2007, for on or before November 9, 6 a.m. to 10 p.m.
24. Paul Kemp interview, May 27, 2010, Rockville, Md.
25. FBI Amerithrax case #279A-WF-222936-BEI, email from USAMRIID official [name redacted], Subject: Bruce Ivins, November 4, 2007.
26. *Report of the Expert Behavioral Analysis Panel*, 2011, 107–36. A chapter called "Case Narrative" summarizes the circumstantial evidence against Ivins as viewed by the panel.

13. Odd Man Out

1. John Coté, "Anthrax Victim's Widow Frustrated with Patterns of Delay," *Palm Beach Sun-Sentinel*, November 5, 2005.
2. *Maureen Stevens et al. v. Battelle Memorial Institute and BioPort Corp. et al.*, United States Court of Appeals, Eleventh Circuit, No. 05–15088, June 7, 2007, 17.
3. *The United States of America et al., Defendants-Appellants, v. Maureen Stevens, etc.* in the Supreme Court of the State of Florida, "Brief for the Appellant the United States of America," August 1, 2007, 15.
4. U.S. Department of Justice, *Amerithrax Investigative Summary*, February 19, 2010, 55–56; http://www.justice.gov/amerithrax/docs/amx-investigative-summary.pdf. The manufacturer, MeadWestvaco (formerly Westvaco), allowed the use of the same printing machine, the same plate types, and the same ink and template that had been used on February 14–15, 2001. Equivalent work and maintenance crews were on call. The 14.5-hour production cycle was continually observed and the boxes of envelopes were labeled in order of production.
5. Justin M. Palk, "Ivins Lost Lab Access in March After Anthrax Spill," *Frederick News-Post*, September 24, 2008.
6. Department of Justice, *Amerithrax*, 49.
7. Frederick Police Department, "Supplemental Report," Incident Date 7/27/2008, OCA 2008044096, August 15, 2008@1500hrs. Reporting officer: Loumis Gene Alston: ibid., August 16, 2008, at 09:10:07, statement by Ryan Forrest, Investigator.
8. FBI Amerithrax case #279A-WF-222936-USAMRIID, interview with local Red Cross chapter head, Frederick, Maryland, August 24, 2007.

9. *Daubert v. Merrell Dow Pharmaceutical, Inc.*, 509 U.S. 579 (1993). The Supreme Court unanimously decided that scientific evidence had to be both generally accepted and pertinent to the case.

10. Yudihijit Bhattacharjee, "Paul Keim on His Life with the FBI During the Anthrax Investigation," *Science* 323/5920 (2009): 1416.

11. Paul Kemp interview, May 27, 2010, Rockville, Md.

12. Department of Justice, *Amerithrax*, 70–71.

13. Ibid., 49.

14. *The Amerithrax Case. Report of the Expert Behavioral Analysis Panel* (Vienna, Va.: Research Strategies Network, 2011), 74. Gregory Saathoff, chair of the panel, had been an FBI case consultant.

15. Frederick Police Department, "Supplemental Report," Protective Order—Jean Duley, August 13, 2008@0949hrs.

16. Jean Duley, "Inside the Anthrax Killer's Mind," CNN video interview, March 5, 2010.

17. The receipts became part of Alston's police inquiry.

18. Frederick Police Department, "Supplemental Report," August 13, 2008.

19. Frederick Police Department, "Supplemental Report," interview with Diane Ivins by Detective G. Alston at her home, in presence of Rosario Garcia of the FPD Victims Services Unit, August 8, 2008@1020hrs.

20. Frederick Police Department, "Supplementary Report," August 4, 2008@1502hrs, 1–3.

21. Frederick Police Department, "Incident/Investigation Report," July 7, 2008 (OCA 2008–944096); Location: 622 Military Road, Frederick, MD, 21702. "They also advised," Pierce wrote, "that they would not be needing a case report number, a copy of this report, or any further information or assistance from us."

22. David Willman, "Apparent Suicide in Anthrax Case," *Los Angeles Times*, August 1, 2008.

23. Joel Seidman, "Reporter Miller Set to Testify at Libby Leak Trial," NBC News/MSNBC, January 30, 2007.

24. David Carr, "The Great Mashup of 2011," *New York Times*, January 3, 2011.

25. Edward G. Lake, *Analyzing the Anthrax Attacks: The First 3 Years* (Racine, Wis.: Edward G. Lake, 2005); www.anthraxinvestigation.com. Lake distinguishes between conspiracy theorists, who are anti-government, and true believers, who defend Ivins against the FBI.

26. U.S. General Accountability Office, *U.S. Postal Service: Deteriorating Postal Finances Require Aggressive Actions to Reduce Costs* (Washington, D.C.: Government Printing Office, 2009); http://www.gao.gov/products/GAO-09-332T.

27. Sean Smeland, personal communication, August 5, 2008.

28. Richard Sisk, "Experts Cast Doubt on Feds' Evidence in Anthrax Case," New York *Daily News*, August 6, 2008.

29. Richard Spertzel, "Bruce Ivins Wasn't the Anthrax Culprit," *Wall Street Journal*, August 5, 2008.

30. Dave Franz email to Dan Vergano at *USA Today*, "Q&A on Anthrax 4 August 08," August 4, 2008.

31. Ernesto Blanco interview, April 21, 2009, West Palm Beach, Fla.

32. Leroy Richmond and Susan Richmond interviews, September 21, 2009, Stafford, Va.

33. "Science Briefing on the Investigation"; www.fbi.gov/anthrax/amerithraxlinks.htm.

34. Sandia National Laboratories, "Sandia National Laboratories Makes Key Contributions to Anthrax Investigation," *Recent Accomplishments Within Homeland Security and Defense*, September 2008; https://share.sandia.gov/news/resources/releases/2008/anthrax.html.

35. FBI, "Science Briefing on the Anthrax Investigation," August 18, 2008; http://www
.fbi.gov/about-us/history/famous-cases/anthrax-amerithrax/science-briefing.
36. Ross E. Getman, "Anthrax Mystery: Evidence Points to al-Qaida," newsmax.com,
June 7, 2007.
37. Detective Loumis Alston telephone interview, June 1, 2010.

Conclusion

1. Stephen Kiehl and Josh Mitchell, "Doubts Persist on Ivins' Guilt: Scientists and
Legal Experts Skeptical," *Baltimore Sun*, August 8, 2008; Laura Fitzpatrick, "Nag-
ging Questions in the Anthrax Case," *Time*, August 13, 2008; Scott Shane and Eric
Lichtblau, "Seeking Details, Lawmakers Cite Anthrax Doubts," *New York Times*,
September 7, 2008. Each of these articles quoted associates of the Center for Biosecurity at the University of Pittsburgh.
2. Sarah Abruzzese and Eric Lipton, "Anthrax Suspect's Death Is a Dark End for a
Family Man," *New York Times*, August 2, 2008.
3. Paul Keim interview, December 8, 2009, Washington, D.C.
4. David A. Rasko, Patricia L. Worsham, Terry G. Abshire, Scott T. Stanley, et al.,
"*Bacillus anthracis* Comparative Genome Analysis in Support of the Amerithrax
Investigation," *Proceedings of the National Academy of Sciences*, 108/12 (2011): 5027–
32. Among the other authors of this summary article are Jason Bannan, Mark
Wilson, Paul Keim, Claire Fraser-Liggett, and Jacques Ravel.
5. Joseph Michael interview, February 24, 2009, Baltimore, Md.
6. Author's notes at ASM meeting, February 23, 2009, Baltimore, Md.
7. The Brokaw and *Post* letter material, for example, had been mysteriously contaminated with a common pathogen, *Bacillus subtilis*.
8. U.S. Department of Justice, *Amerithrax Investigative Summary*, February 19, 2010;
http://www.justice.gov/amerithrax/docs/amx-investigative-summary.pdf.
9. National Research Council, *Review of the Scientific Approaches Used During the
FBI's Investigation of the 2001 Anthrax Letters* (Washington, D.C.: National Academies Press, 2011), 15.
10. The history of the FBI testing at this "undisclosed overseas site," easily identifiable
as the al Qaeda laboratory near Kandahar, was first made known to the public in
the National Research Council 2011 review, 49–50.
11. Scott Shane, "Review Faults F.B.I.'s Scientific Work in Anthrax Investigation," *New
York Times*, February 15, 2011; David Dishneau, *Associated Press*, "Panel: FBI Over-
stated Science Behind Anthrax Probe," February 15, 2011.
12. From Staff Reports, "Report: Conclusion on Anthrax Origins Not Possible with
Available Scientific Evidence," February 15, 2011, FrederickNewsPost.com, http://
www.fredericknewspost.com/sections/news/display.htm?storyID=116771.
13. Dena Briscoe telephone interview, February 15, 2011.
14. *Amerithrax Case. Report of the Expert Behavioral Analysis Panel* (Vienna, Va.:
Research Strategies Network, 2011), 1–2.
15. Associated Press, "Absent NRC's EIS Review, Army Breaks Ground for Flagship
Biological Defense Lab," August 28, 2009.
16. USAMRIID, "Final Environmental Impact Statement (FEIS): Construction and
Operation of New U.S. Army Medical Research Institute of Infectious Diseases
(USAMRIID) Facilities and Decommissioning and Demolition and/or Re-use of
Existing USAAMRIID Facilities at Fort Detrick, Maryland," December 29, 2006.
USAMRIID's environmental impact submission claimed that all environmental
risks were "mostly minor and mitigable." Its two hypothesized worst-case scenar-

ios, one involving Q-fever and the other the Ebola virus, posed no hazard because the lab ventilation systems would be 1,000 feet from the base's border.

17. Ibid., app. C.

18. Ibid., app. I, 9.

19. Ibid., chap. 2, 48.

20. Associated Press, "Mikulski Seeks Safety Review of Fort Detrick Lab Expansion," April 10, 2008.

21. Department of Defense Instruction No. 5210.42, October 16, 2006.

22. Justin M. Palk, "Security at Military Biolabs to Get Tighter," *Frederick News-Post*, December 19, 2008.

23. Thomas Schelling, Foreword in Roberta Wohlstetter, *Pearl Harbor: Warning and Decision* (Stanford: Stanford University Press, 1962), vii–ix, viii.

24. "Summary of the Frist-Kennedy 'Bioterrorism Preparedness Act of 2001,'" in *Biological Threats and Terrorism*, ed. Stacey L. Knobler, Adel A. F. Mahmoud, and Leslie A. Pray (Washington, D.C.: The National Academy Press, 2002), app. D, 239–43.

25. Crystal Franco, "Billions for Biodefense: Federal Agency Biodefense Funding, FY2009–FY2010," *Biosecurity and Bioterrorism: Biodefense Strategy, Practice, and Science* 7/3 (2009): 291–309.

26. Keith Rhodes, "High-Containment Biosafety Laboratories: Preliminary Observations on the Oversight of the Proliferation of BSL-3 and BSL-4 Laboratories in the United States," testimony before the Subcommittee on Oversight and Investigations, Committee on Energy and Commerce, U.S. House of Representatives, October 4, 2007.

27. Jocelyn Kaiser, "Lawmakers Worry That Lab Expansion Poses Risks," *Science* 318/5848 (2008): 182.

28. See http://www.utmb.edu/pathology/educationtab/graduate_student/graduate_students_facilities.htm.

29. Lynn C. Klotz and Edward J. Sylvester, *Breeding Bio Insecurity: How U.S. Biodefense Is Exporting Fear, Globalizing Risk, and Making Us All Less Secure* (Chicago: University of Chicago Press, 2009).

30. Rebecca Vesely, "Anthrax Incident Spurs Concern," *Oakland Tribune*, June 12, 2004.

31. Emily Ramshaw, "CDC Suspends A&M Research on Infectious Diseases," *Dallas Morning News*, July 1, 2007. The problem was not just American. In February 2009, the pharmaceutical giant Baxter International mistakenly sent samples of the annual human flu viruses contaminated with the deadly H5N1 avian virus to an Austrian company, which then distributed the samples to labs in the Czech Republic, Slovenia, and Germany. Helen Branswell, "Baxter: Product Contained Live Bird Flu Virus," *Toronto Sun*, February 27, 2009.

32. Emma Graves Fitzsimmons, "Researcher Had Bacteria for Plague at His Death," *New York Times*, September 21, 2009.

33. National Research Council, *Continuing Assistance to the National Institute of Health on Preparation of Additional Risk Assessments for the Boston University NEIDL, Phase 2* (Washington, D.C.: National Academies Press, 2010).

34. National Research Council, *Evaluation of a Site-specific Risk Assessment for the Department of Homeland Security's Planned National Bio- and Agro-Defense Facility in Manhattan, Kansas* (Washington, D.C.: National Academies Press, 2010).

35. "Biodefense Research and Development Policy in 2009: A Citizen Perspective." Beth Willis from Frederick Citizens for Bio-lab Safety, Klare Allen and the Boston Coalition to Stop the Bio Terror Lab, Bill McKellar of Granville Non-Violent Action Team in North Carolina, Therese Folsom of the Mid-Missouri Branch of

WILPF (Women's International League for Peace and Freedom), Marylia Kelley and Robert Schwartz of Tri-Valley Cares in California, and Mike McCormick of Labwatch-Seattle, Washington, were signers of the statement, which circulated in May 2009.

36. National Research Council, *A Survey of Attitudes and Actions on Dual Use Research in the Life Sciences: A Collaborative Effort of the National Research Council and the American Association for the Advancement of Science* (Washington, D.C.: National Academies Press, 2009).

37. Matthew Meselson, "Vast Biosecurity Expenditures Require Better Oversight and Monitoring." *Nature* 457 (January 2009): 259–60.

38. National Research Council (NRC) Committee on Research Standards and Practices to Prevent the Destructive Application of Biotechnology, *Biotechnology in an Age of Terrorism: Confronting the Dual Use Dilemma* (Washington, D.C.: National Academies Press, 2003), 124. The report is commonly known as the Fink Report, after its chairman, MIT's Gerald Fink. Among the committee members were R. John Collier, David Franz, C. J. Peters, Robert Kadlec, and former ASM president Ron Atlas.

39. Jeanne Guillemin, "Seduced by the State," *Bulletin of the Atomic Scientists* 63/5 (September–October 2007): 14–16.

40. Theodore Rosebury, *Peace or Pestilence: Biological Warfare and How to Avoid It* (New York: McGraw Hill, 1949), 62.

41. David Rosner and Gerald Markowitz, *Are We Ready? Public Health Since 9/11* (Berkeley: University of California Press, 2006), 143–55.

42. Anthony Fauci, Plenary Session on Biosecurity, American Association for the Advancement of Sciences Annual Meeting, Washington, D.C., February 20, 2011.

43. Michael Chertoff, *Homeland Security: Assessing the First Five Years* (Philadelphia: University of Pennsylvania Press, 2009), 136–43, 137.

44. Helen Epstein, "Flu Warning: Beware the Drug Companies!" *The New York Review of Books*, 58/8 (2011): 57–61.

45. White House, *National Strategy for Countering Biological Threats*, November 23, 2009.

46. Ibid.

47. Philip Heymann, *Terrorism and America: A Commonsense Strategy for a Democratic Society* (Cambridge, Mass.: MIT Press, 1998), 158.

48. James Carroll, *House of War: The Pentagon and the Disastrous Rise of American Power* (Boston: Houghton Mifflin, 2006), 418–512; Andrew J. Bacevich, *Washington Rules: America's Path to Permanent War* (New York: Metropolitan Books, 2010), 222–50.

ACKNOWLEDGMENTS

No author is ever truly alone in writing a book, although at times it may seem that way. As I worked on *American Anthrax,* my third book on the difficult subject of biological weapons, I have been fortunate to have had support from two institutions, MIT's Security Studies Center in the Center for International Studies, and the Marine Biological Laboratory in Woods Hole, Massachusetts. Both offered ideal settings for thinking, research, and writing and provided excellent office and technical assistance. The Harvard-Sussex Program on Chemical and Biological Weapons has been another important source of support. I am especially grateful to Sandy Ropper, its archivist in Cambridge, who for years has kept me constantly updated on the Amerithrax case; to Valerie Thaddeus, administrative assistant at the MIT Security Studies Program, who was always ready with help and encouragement; to Sean Smeland, whose early research was invaluable, and to Vicky Cullen and Larry Fahey for sharp-eyed editorial assistance. In the years immediately after 9/11 and the anthrax attacks, when I was still teaching at Boston College, the university and its Department of Sociology gave me the means to reconfigure my role in a world urgently in need of new ways of thinking about terrorism and national security. I can also count dozens of colleagues and political actors who shared with me valuable insights about the Amerithrax case. Many of them I have cited in this book, while others requested anonymity. Among those on whom I counted as resources were Dave Franz, Paul Keim, Jacques Ravel, Ben Garrett, Jason Bannan, Jim Burans, Julian Perry Robinson, Erhard Geissler, Tom Carey, Dick Swensen, Judy Miller, Chris Farrell, Sandy Weiner, Henri Korn, Patrick Bersch, Seth Carus, Morgan Frankel, Barry Posen, Cindy Williams, Ken Oye, Phil Heymann, Graham Allison, Oliver Sacks, Don Weiss, Marci Layton, Bob Unick, Jack Potter, Tom Day, Tom Ridge, Maureen Stevens, Ernesto Blanco, Jean Malecki, Flo Freeman, Larry Bush, Jeb Bush, John Ezzell, Eddy Bresnitz, George DiFerdinando, Tanya Popovic, Ed Lake, Ross Getman, Francis Huré, Cecily Selby, Gary Borisy, Mitch Sogin, Josh Hamilton, Cathy Norton, Matt Person, Jen Walton, Janet Montgomery, Henry Kaufman, Lynne Levine, Joli Divon Saraf, Jill Gliddon, and with these, my long-term writers' group, Betsy Seifter, Miriam Weinstein, Patricia Lorsch, and Cynthia Linkas. Dena Briscoe and Terrell Worrell, along with Helen Lewis, Leroy and Susan Richmond, and others in the Brentwood community gave me a unique education in local democracy and faith in action. I thank them all for their help, and any mistakes in this account of events are mine alone. Special appreciation goes to my agent, Paul Bresnick, for his unwavering confidence and great professional advice, to Paul Golob, the editor whose vision for this book was always on target, and to Serena Jones, for shepherding the final version to completion.

Members of my family were models of loving patience. At the time of the anthrax crisis in Florida, my mother, who lived in West Palm Beach, regularly sent me local press clippings, and my brother Brian, who helped edit my last two books, also assisted with the first version of this one. My deepest debt is to my husband, Matthew Meselson, who throughout this project was, as always, my best counsel and friend.

INDEX

Page numbers in italics indicate illustrations.

About the Author

JEANNE GUILLEMIN is a Senior Advisor in the Security Studies Program at the Massachusetts Institute of Technology, in the Center for International Studies. She is the author of *Anthrax: The Investigation of a Deadly Outbreak* and *Biological Weapons: From the Invention of State-Sponsored Programs to Contemporary Bioterrorism.*